MONTAILLOU

Emmanuel Le Roy Ladurie

MONTAILLOU

The Promised Land of Error

Translated by Barbara Bray

VINTAGE BOOKS
A Division of Random House • New York

A Madeleine

Vintage Books Edition, August 1979

English translation copyright © 1978 by Scolar Press, Ltd.

All rights reserved under International and Pan-American Copyright Conventions. Published in the United States by Random House, Inc., New York, and in Canada by Random House of Canada Limited, Toronto. Originally published in France under the title *Montaillou, village occitan de 1294 à 1324* by Editions Gallimard. Copyright © 1975 by Editions Gallimard. Published in the United States in 1978 by George Braziller, Inc.

Library of Congress Cataloging in Publication Data

Le Roy Ladurie, Emmanuel.
  Montaillou: the promised land of error.
  Translation of Montaillou, village occitan de 1294 à 1324.
  Bibliography: p.
  Includes index.
  1. Montaillou, France—History.
  2. Montaillou, France—Social life and customs.
  3. Montaillou, France—Religious life and customs.
  I. Title.
DC801.M753L4713 1979   944′.88   79-11003
ISBN 0-394-72964-1

Manufactured in the United States of America

Cover photograph: William Albert Allard/The Image Bank

Contents

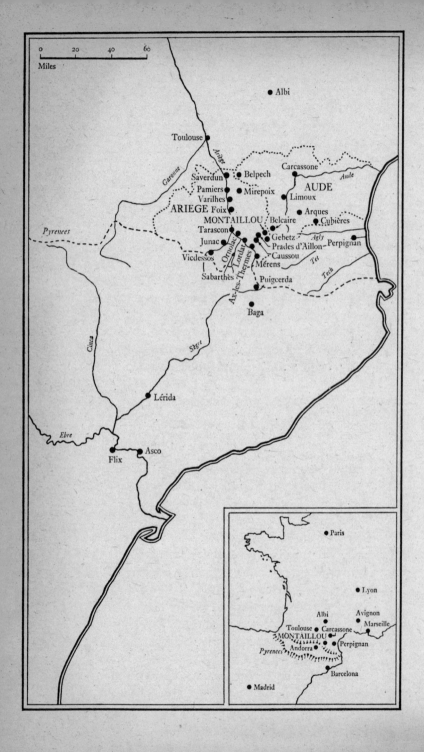

Introduction

This introduction was specially written for the English edition of *Montaillou*, which is a shorter version of the French.

Though there are extensive historical studies concerning peasant communities there is very little material available that can be considered the direct testimony of peasants themselves. It is for this reason that the Inquisition Register of Jacques Fournier, Bishop of Pamiers in Ariège in the Comté de Foix (now southern France) from 1318 to 1325, is of such exceptional interest.[1] As a zealous churchman – he was later to become Pope at Avignon under the name Benedict XII – he supervised a rigorous Inquisition in his diocese and, what is more important, saw to it that the depositions made to the Inquisition courts were meticulously recorded. In the process of revealing their position on official Catholicism, the peasants examined by Fournier's Inquisition, many from the village of Montaillou, have given an extraordinarily detailed and vivid picture of their everyday life.

Montaillou is a little village, now French, situated in the Pyrenees in the south of the present-day department of Ariège, close to the frontier between France and Spain. The department of Ariège itself corresponds to the territory of the diocese of Pamiers, and to the old medieval Comté de Foix, once an independent principality. In the thirteenth and fourteenth centuries the principality, ruled over by the important family of the Comtes de Foix, became a satellite of the powerful kingdom of France. The large province of Languedoc, adjacent to Ariège, was already a French possession.

Montaillou was the last village which actively supported the Cathar heresy, also known as Albigensianism, after the town of Albi, in which some of the heretics lived. It had been one of the chief heresies of the Middle Ages, but after it had finally been wiped out in Montaillou

---

1 Latin MS. 4030, Vatican Library. The text has been published in its entirety by Jean Duvernoy as *Le Registre d'Inquisition de Jacques Fournier, evêque de Pamiers (1318–1325)*, Toulouse, 1965, 3 volumes. This edition is not without its faults but it has the great merit of existing. In the present text, quotations from the Fournier register are set in italic type, and references in parentheses before quotations refer to the Duvernoy edition.

between 1318 and 1324 it disappeared completely from French territory. It appeared in the twelfth or thirteenth centuries in Languedoc in northern Italy, and, in slightly different forms, in the Balkans. Catharism is not to be confused with Waldensianism, another heretical sect which originated in Lyons but which hardly affected Ariège. Catharism may have been based on distant Oriental or Manichaean influences, but this is only hypothesis. However, we do know a great deal about the doctrine and rites of Catharism in Languedoc and northern Italy.

Catharism or Albigensianism was a Christian heresy: there is no doubt on this point at least. Its supporters considered and proclaimed themselves 'true Christians', 'good Christians', as distinct from the official Catholic Church which according to them had betrayed the genuine doctrine of the Apostles. At the same time, Catharism stood at some distance from traditional Christian doctrine, which was mono-theist. Catharism accepted the (Manichaean) existence of two opposite principles, if not of two deities, one of good and the other of evil. One was God, the other Satan. On the one hand was light, on the other dark. On one side was the spiritual world, which was good, and on the other the terrestrial world, which was carnal, physical, corrupt. It was this essentially spiritual insistence on purity, in relation to a world totally evil and diabolical, which gave rise retrospectively to a probably false etymology of the word Cathar, which has been said to derive from a Greek work meaning 'pure'. In fact 'Cathar' comes from a German word the meaning of which has nothing to do with purity. The dualism good/evil or God/Satan subdivided into two tendencies, according to region. On the one hand there was absolute dualism, typical of Cathar-ism in Languedoc in the twelfth century: this proclaimed the eternal opposition between the two principles, good and evil. On the other hand was the modified dualism characteristic of Italian Catharism: here God occupies a place which was more eminent and more 'eternal' than that of the Devil.

Catharism was based on a distinction between a 'pure' élite on the one hand (*perfecti, parfaits, bonshommes* or *hérétiques*), and on the other hand, the mass of simple believers (*credentes*). The *parfaits* came into their illustrious title after they had been initiated by receiving the Albigensian sacrament of baptism by book and words (not by water). In Cathar language, this sacrament was called the *consolamentum* ('consolation'). Ordinary people referred to it as 'heretication'. Once he had been hereticated a *parfait* had to remain pure, abstaining from meat and women. (Catharism, though not entirely anti-feminine, showed no great tolerance of women.) A *parfait* had the power to bless bread and to receive from ordinary believers the *melioramentum* or ritual salutation or adoration. He gave them his blessing and kiss of peace (*caretas*). Ordinary believers did not receive the *consolamentum* until just before death, when it was plain that the end was near. This arrangement allowed ordinary believers to lead a fairly agreeable life, not too strict from the moral point of view, until their end approached. But once they were hereticated, all was changed. Then they had to embark (at least in the late Catharism of the 1300s) on a state of *endura* or total and suicidal fasting. From that moment on there was no escape, physically, though they were sure to save their souls. They could touch neither women nor meat in the period until death supervened, either through natural causes or as a result of the *endura*.

Around 1200, Catharism had partly infected quite large areas of Languedoc, which at that period did not yet belong to the kingdom of France. Such a state of affairs could not be allowed to continue. In 1209 the barons of the north of France organized a crusade against the Albigensians. The armies marched southwards in answer to an appeal from the Pope. Despite the death in 1218 of Simon de Montfort, the brutal leader of the northern crusaders, the King of France gradually extended his power over the south and took advantage of the pretext offered by the heretics to annex Languedoc *de facto* in 1229, by the Treaty of Meaux. This annexation left lasting traces of resentment in what later became the south of France. These were revived in the twentieth century by the renaissance of Occitan regionalism. In 1244 Montségur, in Ariège, the last heretic fortress, was taken. The Albigensians who had long held out there were sent together to the stake in Montségur itself or in Bram.

But even after 1250 Catharism still showed signs of life. In the mountains of upper Ariège the Albigensian heresy even had a modest revival between 1300 and 1318. One of the centres of this revival was the village of Montaillou. Partly responsible for the recrudescence of heresy was the militant and energetic action of the Authié brothers, formerly notaries in Ariège who had become heroic missionaries of Albigensianism. But the Inquisition of Fournier and his colleagues, based in Carcassonne (Languedoc) and chiefly in Pamiers (Ariège), finally

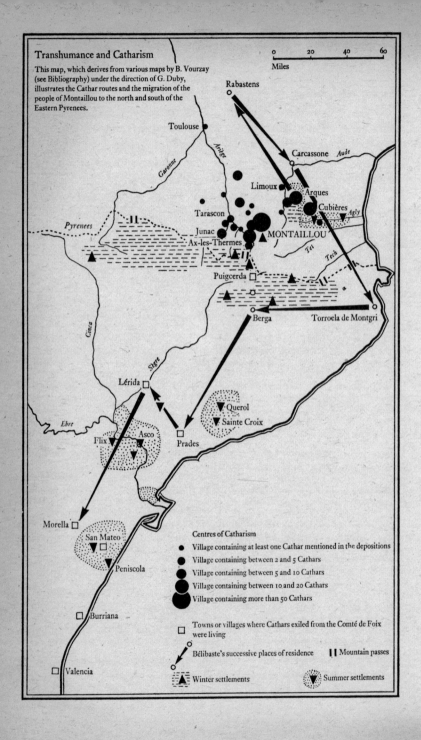

Transhumance and Catharism

This map, which derives from various maps by B. Vourzay
(see Bibliography) under the direction of G. Duby,
illustrates the Cathar routes and the migration of the
people of Montaillou to the north and south of the
Eastern Pyrenees.

0   20   40   60

Miles

Rabastens

Toulouse

Garonne

Ariège

Pyrenees

Carcassone   Aude

Limoux
Arques
Cubières
Agly
Tarascon
Junac   MONTAILLOU
Ax-les-Thermes
Tet
Tech

Puigcerda

Cinca

Berga   Torroela de Montgri

Sègre

Lérida

Querol
Sainte Croix

Ebre

Flix   Asco
Prades

Morella

San Mateo

Peniscola

Centres of Catharism

● Village containing at least one Cathar mentioned in the depositions

● Village containing between 2 and 5 Cathars

● Village containing between 5 and 10 Cathars

● Village containing between 10 and 20 Cathars

● Village containing more than 50 Cathars

□ Towns or villages where Cathars exiled from the Comté de Foix
  were living

Burriana

⟶ Bélibaste's successive places of residence   ‖ Mountain passes

Valencia

▲ Winter settlements   ▼ Summer settlements

succeeded in flushing out this last pocket of resistance, by means of a detailed inquiry followed by some burnings at the stake, many sentences of imprisonment and still more penalties in the form of yellow crosses. (Just as medieval Jews wore the yellow star, so condemned heretics were forced to wear on their backs big crosses made of yellow material sewn to their outer garments.) Catharism never recovered from this final blow in 1320. The prisoners of Montaillou were the last of the last Cathars. But it was not an absolute end. For the brave fight put up by the peasants of Ariège to preserve the remains of their heterodox beliefs after 1300 foreshadowed the great Protestant revolt two centuries later.

Jacques Fournier, the person responsible for our documentary sources, seems to have been born some time during the decade which began in 1280, at Saverdun in the north of the Comté de Foix, a region which is now part of Ariège. The precise status of his family is not known, but Fournier himself was of fairly humble origin. So conscious was he of his undistinguished lineage that when he became Pope he is said to have refused to give his niece in marriage to a brilliant aristocrat who sought her hand, saying, 'This saddle is not worthy of this horse'. But even before Jacques Fournier, there were several instances of social advancement in the family. One of his uncles, Arnaud Novel, was Abbot of the Cistercian monastery at Fontfroide. Encouraged by this model, the young Fournier also became a Cistercian monk. He went north for a while, first as a student, then as a doctor of the University of Paris. In 1311 he succeeded his uncle as Abbot of Fontfroide. In 1317, already known for his learning and severity, he was made Bishop of Pamiers, and in this new role he distinguished himself by his inquisitorial pursuit of heretics and other deviants. In his diocesan seat he kept up correct relations with the agents of the Comte de Foix and of the King of France. (Up to this point in his life, though living in Languedoc, he was pro-French.) In 1326 Pope John XXII congratulated him on his successful heretic hunt in the region of Pamiers, the congratulations being accompanied by a sheaf of indulgences. But Fournier's activities were not confined to ideological persecution. He also managed to make agricultural tithes more onerous, imposing them on cheese, beets and turnips, which hitherto had been exempt.

In 1326 Fournier was made Bishop of Mirepoix, east of Pamiers, a move that might be interpreted as a fall from favour. He had in fact made himself unpopular in his previous diocese through his obsessional, fanatical and competent pursuit of all kinds of suspects. But the see of Mirepoix contained more parishes than Pamiers, so his new appointment seems to have been a promotion rather than a disgrace. It was followed by even more dazzling advancement. In 1327 Fournier became a Cardinal. In 1334 he was elected Pope of Avignon under the name of Benedict XII. 'You have elected an ass', he is supposed to have said, with his usual self-effacement, to the College which voted him into office. But, modest or not, once he had begun to wear the tiara Fournier soon showed his not inconsiderable abilities. He reacted against nepotism. Himself a monk and an ascetic, he tried to improve the morals of the monasteries. Like many intellectuals he was unskilled in practical matters, and met with little success in foreign policy. But he was at home in the field of dogma. He corrected the theological fantasies of his predecessor, John XXII, about the Beatific Vision after death. On the subject of the Virgin, he was a maculist, opposing the theory (which later triumphed) of the immaculate conception of Mary. His various pronouncements on dogma were the crown of a long intellectual career: throughout his life he engaged in vigorous, though somewhat conformist, controversy against all kinds of thinkers whom he considered to have strayed from Roman orthodoxy; his opponents included Giacomo dei Fiori, Master Eckhart and Occam. It was Fournier who initiated the building of the Palace of the Popes in Avignon, and he who invited Simone Martini there to paint the frescoes.

But it is the Pamiers period which interests us in the life of the future Benedict XII, and particularly his activity there as organizer of a formidable Inquisition court. Outbreaks of heresy even after the fall of Montségur led Pope Boniface VIII to create, in 1295, the diocese of Pamiers, including both the north and the south of the Comté de Foix, with the object of making it easier to check religious deviance. After a comparative lull there were two new inquisitorial offensives, one in 1298–1300 and another in 1308–09. In 1308, Geoffroy d'Ablis, the Inquisitor of Carcassonne, arrested the whole population of the village of Montaillou with the exception of young children.

These drives against the heretics were the work of the Dominican court at Carcassonne, which as such had nothing to do with the new see of Pamiers or the traditional Comté de Foix. The Bishops of Pamiers, although in principle they were supposed to seek out religious unorthodoxy, for a long while preferred to lie low and not utter a word against heresy among their flock. Bishop Pelfort de Rabastens (1312–17) was so busy squabbling with his canons that he did not have time to watch over the orthodoxy of his diocese. But with Jacques Fournier, who succeeded him in 1317, things changed: the new Bishop took advantage of a decision of the Council of Vienne (1312) which stipulated that henceforward, in the courts of the Inquisition, the powers of the local Bishop were to be used in support of the Dominican official who had up till then been in sole charge of repression. So in 1318 Fournier was able to set up his own inquisitorial 'office'. He ran it in close association with Brother Gaillard de Pomiès, delegate of Jean de Beaune, who was the representative of the Inquisition of Carcassonne. Pomiès and Beaune were both Dominicans.

The new court at Pamiers was very active all the time its founder was in power locally. Even when Jacques Fournier was made Bishop of Mirepoix in 1326 the 'office' at Pamiers did not disappear. But his successors did not believe in overdoing things, and repression on the local level slumbered, leaving the people of the Comté de Foix in peace. So it is only during Fournier's episcopate that the tribunal at Pamiers gives us detailed information on peasant life in Occitania.

At the head of the 'office' was of course Jacques Fournier himself, a sort of compulsive Maigret, immune to both supplication and bribe, skilful at worming out the truth (at bringing the lambs forth, as his victims said), able in a few minutes to tell a heretic from a 'proper' Catholic – a very devil of an Inquisitor, according to the accused. He proceeded, and succeeded, essentially through the diabolical and tenacious skill of his interrogations; only rarely did he have recourse to torture. He was fanatical about detail, and present in person at almost all the sittings of his own court. He wanted to do, or at least direct, everything himself. He refused to delegate responsibility to his subordinates, scribes or notaries, as other more negligent Inquisitors often did. So the whole Pamiers Inquisition Register bears the brand of his constant intervention. This is one of the reasons why it is such an extraordinary document.

Brother Gaillard de Pomiès was his assistant (*vicaire*), relegated to second place by the strong personality and local prestige of the Bishop. Occasionally high-ranking Inquisitors from outside the diocese, like Bernard Gui, Jean de Beaune and the Norman Jean Duprat, would honour the weightier sessions of the 'office' at Pamiers with their presence. Also among the assessors was an assortment of local and regional worthies: canons, monks of all kinds, judges and jurists. At a lower level came fifteen or so notaries and scribes, there to record the proceedings but never to take part in the making of decisions. At their head was the priest-cum-scrivener Guillaume Barthe, followed by Jean Strabaud, Bataille de la Penne and a group of quill-pushers from the Comté de Foix. Sworn in last of all were the minor staff-sergeants described as 'servitors', messengers, jailers with their inevitable wives and, also among these lower depths, informers, some of them as distinguished as Arnaud Sicre.

A few details will suggest how our dossier was built up.[1] The Inquisition court at Pamiers worked for 370 days between 1318 and 1325. These 370 days included 578 interrogations. Of these, 418 were examinations of the accused and 160 examinations of witnesses. In all, these hundreds of sessions dealt with ninety-eight cases. The court set a record for hard work in 1320, with 106 days; it worked ninety-three days in 1321, fifty-five in 1323, forty-three in 1322, forty-two in 1324, and twenty-two in 1325. The court sat mostly at Pamiers, but sometimes it met elsewhere in the Comté de Foix, according to the movements of the Bishop.

The ninety-eight cases involved 114 people, most of them heretics of the Albigensian persuasion. Out of the 114, ninety-four actually appeared. Among the group 'troubled' by the court were a few nobles, a few priests and some notaries, but above all an overwhelming majority of humble folk: peasants, artisans and shopkeepers on a very small scale. Out of the 114 accused or otherwise involved, forty-eight were women. The great majority, both male and female, came from the highlands of Foix, or Sabarthès, a region worked on by the propaganda of the Authié brothers. This majority from Sabarthès was made up of ninety-two people, men and women. Our village of Montaillou alone, also in Sabarthès, supplied twenty-five of the accused and provided several of the witnesses. Three more of the accused came from the village of Prades, which adjoined Montaillou itself. In all twenty-eight people, of whom each one supplied substantial and sometimes very detailed evidence, came from the tiny region of the Pays d'Aillon (Prades and Montaillou), with which our study is concerned.

1 See J. M. Vidal (1906). Full references to sources cited only by author and date in footnotes are to be found in the Selective bibliography (pp. 357–8).

Canonical procedure against an accused person was generally set off by one or several denunciations. These were followed by a summons to appear before the court at Pamiers. The summons was conveyed to the suspect, at home or in church, by the priest of the place where he lived. If the accused did not present himself voluntarily at Pamiers, the local *bayle* (the officer of the count or of the lord of the manor) acted as the secular arm, arresting the accused and if necessary escorting him to the chief town of the diocese. The accused's appearance before the Bishop's tribunal began with an oath sworn on the Gospels. It continued in the form of an unequal dialogue. Jacques Fournier asked a series of questions, pursuing various points and details. The accused would answer at length – a deposition might easily cover ten, twenty or even more big folio pages in the Register. The accused was not necessarily kept under a state of arrest throughout the trial. Between interrogations he might be shut up in one of the Bishop's prisons in town. But he might also be let out under house arrest, bound to keep within the limits of his parish or of the diocese. When the accused was imprisoned, various pressures were brought to bear to make him confess. Apparently these pressures usually consisted not so much of torture as of excommunication or confinement either 'strict' or 'very strict' (the latter consisting of a small cell, fetters and black bread and water). In only one instance did Jacques Fournier have his victims tortured: this was in the trumped-up case which French agents made him bring against the lepers, who brought forth wild and absurd confessions about poisoning wells with powdered toads, etc. In all the other cases which provide the material of this book, the Bishop confined himself to tracking down real deviants (often minor from our point of view). The confessions are rounded out by the accuseds' descriptions of their own daily lives. They usually corroborated each other, but when they contradicted, Fournier tried to reduce the discrepancies, asking the various prisoners for more details. What drove him on was the desire (hateful though it was in this form) to know the truth. For him, it was a matter first of detecting sinful behaviour and then of saving souls. To attain these ends he showed himself 'pedantic as a schoolman' and did not hesitate to engage in lengthy discussion. He spent a fortnight of his precious time convincing the Jew Baruch of the mystery of the Trinity, a week making him accept the dual nature of Christ and no less than three weeks of commentary explaining the coming of the Messiah.

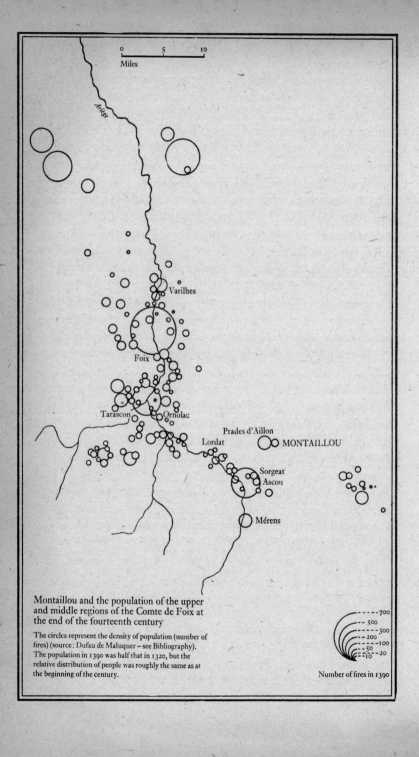

Miles

Ariège

Varilhes

Foix

Tarascon   Ornolac

                    Prades d'Aillon
        Lordat   ⬭⬭ MONTAILLOU

                    Sorgeat
                    Ascou

            Mérens

Montaillou and the population of the upper
and middle regions of the Comte de Foix at
the end of the fourteenth century

The circles represent the density of population (number of
fires) (source: Dufau de Maluquer – see Bibliography).
The population in 1390 was half that in 1320, but the
relative distribution of people was roughly the same as at
the beginning of the century.

- - - - - 700
- - - 500
- - - 300
- - 200
- - 100
- - 50
- - 20
- 10

Number of fires in 1390

When the trials were over, various penalties were inflicted: imprisonment of varying degrees of strictness, the wearing of the yellow cross,
pilgrimages and confiscation of goods. Of the five guilty who ended
their lives at the stake, four were Waldensians from Pamiers and the
other a relapsed Albigensian, Guillaume Fort, from Montaillou.

All these procedures and interrogations were written down in a
Register, two volumes of which have been lost. One of the missing
volumes contained the final sentences, but these are known to us, by
chance, through the compilation of Limborch.[1] The surviving document now in the Vatican consists of one big folio ledger, written on
parchment. This document was originally written in three stages. First,
at the actual hearing of the interrogation and deposition, a scribe quickly
wrote down a *protocol* or draft. This scribe was Guillaume Barthe, the
episcopal notary, replaced in cases of absence by one of his colleagues.
Then from these hasty notes the same Guillaume Barthe would compile
a minute, written 'in a paper ledger'. This 'was submitted to the
accused, who could have alterations made in it'. Finally, and at leisure,
several scribes copied these 'minuted' texts out again on to parchment.[2]

The surviving volume was not entirely completed in a fair copy until
after Jacques Fournier had been made Bishop of Mirepoix in 1326. This
shows how anxious he was to preserve the evidence of his work as
Inquisitor in Pamiers. When he became Benedict XII, the ledger
followed him to his residence in Avignon and from there it passed into
the Vatican Library.

1 C. Limborch (1962).
2 The final Latin text of the Fournier Register raises various problems of translation. The accused usually spoke in Occitan (or in some cases, probably very few,
in Gascon). So at some point the scribes translated the words of the accused into
Latin. This operation took place either at the first stage, when the first notes were
being taken, in a kind of 'simultaneous translation', or, at the latest, when the minute
was written (the second stage of the process). The minute was roughly the same as
the final text or third stage, which was in Latin. A spoken translation back into the
'vulgar tongue' was made when the accused had the text of the minute read out to
them so that they could have alterations made in it if they wished.

MONTAILLOU

PART ONE

The ecology of Montaillou: the house and the shepherd

Montaillou is not a large parish. At the time of the events which led to
Fournier's investigations, the local population consisted of between 200
and 250 inhabitants. At the end of the fourteenth century, after the
Black Death and the first effects, direct or indirect, of the English wars,
the hearth rolls and census books of the Comté de Foix show the same
community as consisting of no more than about one hundred souls,
divided up into twenty-three hearths or households. This was the usual
drop in population (over a half) recorded almost everywhere in southern
France after the catastrophes of the second part of the fourteenth
century. But things had not reached that pass at the time of the anti-
Cathar campaign.

The Pays d'Aillon, at the source of the river Hers, was described at
the end of last century as a fine plateau surrounded by pastures and
forests. The village of Montaillou, looking out over the plateau, was
built in tiers. At the top of the hillside to which the village itself clung in
1320 stood the château, now only an imposing ruin. Below stood the
houses, one above the other, often adjoining, but sometimes separated by
small gardens where pigs illegally disported themselves, or by court-
yards and threshing floors. The village itself was not fortified: in case of
danger the people could always take refuge higher up, behind the ram-
parts of the fortress. But the lowest houses were built sufficiently close
together for their outer edge to form a natural defence, pierced by an
entrance that was called the 'portal'. In more recent times the village has
moved away from the shadow of the château and is now situated lower
down the slope.

In the fourteenth century, as today, the curving village street led
down to the parish church, built below the village itself. Lower down
still, surrounded by the local cemetery, there is a chapel dedicated to the
Virgin Mary, though it is also linked to a traditional cult connected with
some nearby rocks. Partly at least, both church and chapel are in the
Romanesque style and date from before 1300.

At the time with which we are concerned, the immediate surroundings
of Montaillou formed a checkerboard of small, roughly rectangular
plots of land. They covered the secondary limestone of the plateau
and scrambled up with difficulty to the primary lands of the nearby

mountain. Each plot contained no more than about 20 or 30 *ares*.[1] A farmer might own several plots, scattered about the village and used as arable or pasture. The fields were cultivated with swing-ploughs drawn by oxen, cows, mules or donkeys. Ridges separated the plots, standing out clearly under the snows of winter. Wherever the ground sloped – i.e. in most cases – the plots formed the traditional Mediterranean pattern of terraces. *Versaines* were more or less permanent fields, sometimes lying fallow, and *bouzigues* were temporary fields made by burning or otherwise clearing waste land (ii.311).

In the time of Jacques Fournier, as today, Montaillou was too high and too cold for vine-growing, but it did produce cereals – oats and wheat rather than barley and rye, and only just sufficient, because of the rigours of the climate, for subsistence. Even so there were sometimes bad years. The farmers of the early fourteenth century also, in their innocence, cultivated turnips, long before English agronomists reintroduced them to the Continent in the eighteenth century. Perhaps they grew forage too – cereals that were harvested for fodder while they were still green. They certainly would have grown hemp. It was the women's job to swingle and comb it during the winter. At that altitude and at that time, it is more than likely that flax too was grown. In addition to the draught and pack animals already mentioned (oxen, cows, donkeys, mules), livestock included pigs, poultry (chickens and geese) and of course hundreds of sheep. This did not include the large flocks which the migrant shepherds used to lead every year to and from the winter pastures of Lauragais and Catalonia. Of wheeled transport there was none: there were swing-ploughs but no horse-drawn ploughs or carts. These were to be found only in the lowlands or the valley of the Ariège.

The upkeep of land for grazing was organized by the *messier*, a municipal official appointed by the lord of the manor or the inhabitants by means of procedures unknown to us. Land sometimes lay fallow once every three years, for at that altitude spring cereals could coincide with winter cereals, which were in the ground for a whole year, from September to September. But more often land lay fallow once every two years, or even, if it was poor, for several years running. There was apparently no question of dividing up the cultivated land into two or three big fields.

The division of labour was according to age and sex. The men ploughed, harvested the cereals and dug up the turnips. They also went

1 One are = 100 square metres.

hunting and fishing, for the rivers were full of trout and the forests of squirrels and pheasants. As soon as they were old enough, the children would look after their fathers' flocks. The women were in charge of water, fire, the garden, cooking and gathering kindling. They cut the cabbages, weeded the corn, tied the sheaves, mended the winnowing fan, washed the pots at the well and, each balancing a loaf of bread on her head, went harvesting with the migrant workers. Women had a hard time of it, especially when they were young.

Farming was centred on the house, part of which was divided off and used for stabling the animals: in the winter, those sheep which were not moved about with the seasons, oxen, pigs and mules were all gathered there within four walls, in close proximity to the rooms where their owners slept and cooked. Wealthier households might have a special building for the animals, a sheep-pen or stable cut off by a courtyard from the main part of the house. But I have not found any references to any farm buildings in the country outside Montaillou itself, apart from a few shepherds' huts which we shall come back to later.

North, south, east and west of the clearing in which the village stood were forests, hiding places for the *parfaits*,[1] where from time to time was heard the clash of axes and the buzz of saws. Here the villagers brought their animals and got the shingle with which they covered the roofs of their houses. Towards the south and the mountains lay the high pastures, the world of the shepherds, governed by its own laws: here ideas and men, flocks and money, moved about from hut to hut over long distances. This was in strong contrast with the timid, small-scale economy which reigned in the village itself. This economy was based on barter, loans and the exchange of gifts: there was not much money in circulation locally, and neighbours lent one another corn, grass, hay, wood, fire, mules, axes, pots, cabbages and turnips. The rich or so-called rich lent to the poor, and might give them bread on All Saints' Day. A mother would lend her daughter things, or even an animal to help with the work, when the daughter, grown up and married or left a widow, lived in a house poorer than the maternal *domus*. There is also evidence of various forms of credit among the villagers, including the pawning of objects, the transferring of debts and so on.

There was a chronic shortage of money. *My husband Arnaud Vital*

1 The *parfaits* (*parfait* = perfect) or *bonshommes* (*bonhomme* = goodman) were an élite, the most uncompromising among the Albigensian communities.

was a shoemaker in Montaillou, says Raymonde Vital (i.346). *But he had to wait until his customers had sold their poultry at Whitsuntide before they could pay him for having their husbands' shoes mended.*

Despite the presence of the shoemaker, Montaillou was under-developed as far as the crafts were concerned, compared with the low-land villages. The women span around the fire in the evening, of course, either at home or with neighbours; and even in prison when the Inquisitor sent them there. But local weaving was clearly intended only for local wearing; there was just one weaver, Raymond Maury, in Montaillou. He plied his trade (it probably called for a certain amount of humidity) in a deep, wood-lined room, a kind of half-underground cave, specially fitted up in his house. But he also reared sheep, and his children became shepherds. To find a really well-off weaver you have to leave Montaillou and go to the neighbouring village of Prades d'Aillon: this was a more populous parish and offered a more profitable market for textiles. The weaver there – Prades Tavernier, named after his own parish – made a very good living. The sale of his equipment even enabled him to finance a pious excursion into Catalonia accompanied by a noble and heretical lady (i.335, 336).

The only tailoring in Montaillou was done by *parfaits* who happened to be passing through. As good Cathars they earned their living and their salvation by patching tunics and making gloves. And when the heretics went in for sewing, the women of the parish would come to see them, ostensibly to help mend a shift, but in fact to gossip (i.373). There was one woman in Montaillou who was a kind of tavern-keeper, but Fabrisse Rives's customers did not come to her place for a drink or a chat. She went round the houses selling wine, which had been brought up from the lowlands by mule. But she was very inefficient and always finding herself without measures to dole out her wares (i.325–6). It should be remembered that there was no absolute distinction between artisan and peasant or artisan and ordinary citizen, or even between artisan and noble. In this part of the world, everybody worked with his hands, and often very skilfully too. A notary might become a tailor, a notary's son a shoemaker; a farmer's son might become first a shepherd and then a maker of carding-combs. Only the job of a pedlar, which meant carrying heavy loads, was hard on the delicate shoulders of some-one who had once been a village worthy.

We have already noted the absence of carts. There were some carts in the lower areas and near the towns, either in fact or in ghost stories, which often mentioned the tumbril of the dead. Apart from the movement of sheep, the amount of material goods moved about in the course of trade or transport was extremely small. The women fetched water, balancing it on their heads in a jar. Much carrying of goods was done by men themselves. Travellers tied their clothes in a bundle and bore them on a stick over their shoulders (i.312). Woodcutters slung their axes round their neck, together with huge bundles of sticks. Baskets and scrips were also used (i.318). Pedlars brought cumin and needles to the village and took away its 'exports' in the form of sheep- and squirrel-skins. The frontier of this economy was determined by portability rather than by the limits of cultivable land.

Asses and mules were used to import wine from Tarascon and Pamiers, together with kitchen salt, and, from Roussillon, olive oil for when guests were invited on Sundays. Tools made of iron were rare, and often lent or even rented by one family to another; they came from the nearby Vicdessos valley. There was no blacksmith in Montaillou. Nor, until modern times, was there a mill. Together with the eggs and poultry which provided the women of the village with pin-money, corn was taken to Ax-les-Thermes, to be made into flour at the mill belonging to the Comté de Foix. This was an expensive business, scarcely worthwhile. In bad years grain was imported by mule from Pamiers. In return, Montaillou and the upper valleys of the Hers and Ariège exported wood, for heating rather than construction, by mule and by water to the lowlands. The nearest fairs and markets were at Ax-les-Thermes (where, in passing, visitors also paid tribute to the prostitutes of the Bassin des Ladres). There were also corn markets and sheep fairs at Tarascon-sur-Ariège, Pamiers and Laroque d'Olmes.

Some foods were imported in small quantities, but most were produced locally. Of all the biological factors in the lives of the villagers – whether of Montaillou, the Pays d'Aillon or Sabarthès – we know most about food. Food shortages were rare in the thirteenth century. They occurred frequently in the fourteenth century, during which, surprisingly, the population of Occitania was as numerous as in the nineteenth century, when jobs and the means of subsistence were more abundantly available. The population of Montaillou itself remained within reasonable limits, but now that there were occasional shortages of corn it found itself at a disadvantage when competing with the demands of the hungry inhabitants of the lowlands. Emigration was not massive enough to bring any lasting relief to the recurrent tension. So the first food shortages for a very long time were recorded around Montaillou in 1310 and 1322. (In the north of France the great famine occurred around 1316. This difference in date is due to the different climatic conditions affecting corn. In the Paris region the danger came from heavy rain, which made the grain rot on the stalk. In the south the dangers were drought and the crop shrivelling in the sun. Moreover, agricultural disasters due to the weather occurred at different dates in north and south.)

But a food shortage was merely a bad patch. Normally, people ate fairly well. The staple vegetable food in the village was bread made from wheat, or sometimes millet. As we have seen, the grain was taken down by ass or mule to the mill in Ax-les-Thermes. Then the flour was brought back up the mountain to be sifted at home. And the bread was baked by the women at home, not in the manorial or communal oven as in the Ile-de-France. But this does not mean that every house in Montaillou had its own private oven. The possession of an oven was a sign of wealth. Those who did not have one took their dough, probably already kneaded, to the house of a more fortunate friend and neighbour. This was the case of a poor woman in the village called Brune Pourcel, a bastard, a former servant, and now a widow: Alazaïs Rives offered her cooking facilities (*cuisande*). But a comfortable farmer in Montaillou would use his oven for various purposes. When the fire was not alight, it was used for storing fish and snails.

Bread was supplemented sometimes with mutton, more often with salted and especially smoked pork. The artisans of southern Occitania living in exile in small towns in Catalonia used to buy meat twice a week. In Montaillou itself the people seem to have eaten pork quite frequently, though we cannot say exactly how often. After the pigs were killed in winter, neighbours used to help one another smoke the bacon. Someone with an ample hearth would take in quarters of pork for a poorer family. *About 14 years ago*, said Raymonde Belot in 1323 (1308 was not a very fortunate period for her),[1] *in Lent, towards vespers, I took two sides of salted pork to the house of Guillaume Benet of Montaillou, to have them*

1 iii.67: for Raymonde Belot's unprosperous marriages, see pp. 42–3. We should not be misled by the fact that she shares a name with the comparatively rich 'House of Belot'.

smoked. There I found Guillemette Benet [Guillaume's wife] *warming herself by the fire, together with another woman; I put the salted meat in the kitchen and left.*

Other proteins came from milk, which might be a gift from a relation. But the chief source of protein was cheese, made by the shepherds in the mountain pastures. Even though the diet was dull, it had a high nitrogenous content. So shortages of food, in particular bread, did not present insoluble problems in Montaillou, though they did so in the almost purely cereal country around Paris in the fourteenth and seventeenth centuries.

The soup of the region included bacon and bread, and the pot herbs of the period were cabbage and leeks. The kitchen gardens of old Montaillou, because of their altitude and lack of sophistication, were not yet familiar with the gifts of the Arabs and the Crusades, which started to be grown in Catalonia and Comtat in the fourteenth century. So artichokes, melons and peaches were unknown, or known only by hearsay. Broad beans and turnips, the latter grown in fields, were also used for the pot. Nuts, mushrooms and snails were useful supplements, most of them generously supplied by nature. Apart from game, there were trout from the mountain streams, and perhaps a little salted fish from the sea, brought up by mule. Wine was not very plentiful because of the lack of vineyards. It was drunk on great occasions, around the fire at night. In any case, at that period, as always, the people of the south were not much given to drunkenness. Sugar was extremely rare: it came originally from the Moslem world and from time to time anyone who could might send a fragment of it to the lady of his heart.

As for food taboos, they were related to the Cathar ethic, which in theory was in fashion in Montaillou. This ethic allowed people to eat fish, but forbade bacon and butcher's meat. According to the Albigensians, to eat animals was to interfere with metempsychosis, the vast circulation of souls between birds, mammals and men. But this attitude to meat was not really taken seriously by the Cathars, or so-called Cathars, of Montaillou: the ordinary 'believers' left to the tiny élite of *parfaits* the duty or privilege of refusing the flesh of two- or four-legged beasts, sheep or grouse.

We know very little about other biological aspects of the life of the average inhabitant of Montaillou: diseases like tuberculosis (with spitting of blood), epilepsy and affections of the eye are mentioned or hinted at several times. But these allusions are not enough for us to construct a frequency table, or to get an idea of the mortality rate. All we can say about the latter is simply that it was high, especially among infants, and often because of epidemics. Naturally enough, the villagers carried around with them a whole fauna of fleas and lice: people not only scratched themselves, but friends and relations from all levels in the social scale deloused one another. The thumb was called the louse-killer (*tue-poux*). The mistress deloused her lover, the servant her master, the daughter her mother. It was an opportunity for endless gossip on every possible subject – women, theology or the behaviour of the *parfaits* at the stake. There were years when fleas, flies, lice or mosquitos were particularly active, and other periods when they lay low. Then people thought less about parasites and more about the dangers of the Inquisition. We shall return later to these really 'vital' aspects of life in Montaillou.

The social and political aspects of village life are best approached by a consideration of the distribution of power. In theory the impact of external powers was decisive. They emanated from the encircling society which controlled and invested Montaillou from 'centres of direction', which rightly or wrongly tended to regard themselves as real 'centres of decision'. These centres were situated in towns, usually to the north.

In the foreground, of course, were political and feudal powers. These exercised the chief controls – in theory. In the case of Montaillou, political and feudal powers were united in one hand, the noble though somewhat distant hand of the Comte de Foix. The Comte was sovereign over the whole of the Pyrenean principality which was called the Comté de Foix and included Montaillou. Apart from his power over the principality as a whole, the Comte was also the lord (*seigneur*) of Montaillou itself (other parishes, not far away, had lords other than the Comte). The house of Foix had two on-the-spot representatives in Montaillou: the *châtelain* and the *bayle*. The *châtelain* was the Comte's military agent, appointed either for life or merely temporarily; he was there to exercise 'repression' when necessary, giving assistance to the *bayle* when the latter was pursuing some real or alleged law-breaker. The *châtelain* was also jailer in chief, in charge of the castle dungeons and of their fettered prisoners (i.406). Towards the end of the 1290s, the *châtelain* who lived in the fortress towering over Montaillou was one Bérenger de Roquefort. We know little about him except that his wife was young and pretty and that they had a steward called Raymond Roussel. Roussel probably looked after the manorial estate belonging to the castle. It could not have consisted of more than about 30 hectares of fields and meadows (excluding forest), and might well have been much smaller.[1] After Bérenger's death, he was succeeded by a *vice-châtelain*, a nondescript character, no relation to his predecessor, since the office was only a life appointment at the best. The *vice-châtelain* seems not to have had anything better to do than to put himself at the orders of the rich local peasants, when they had the ear of the Bishop of Pamiers (i.406).

The *bayle* (bailiff) was responsible for seeing that the tenants paid their rents and other manorial dues regularly. He was the inspector and receiver of taxes. In the name of the Comte he administered both high and low justice. But we must not exaggerate the significance of this division of power between a military officer and a manorial one specializing in the law. In fact, according to our records, it was the functions of the *bayle*, repressive and 'protective' as well as legal, which emerged most forcefully. The *bayles* of the villages we know through the Fournier records were responsible for arresting heretics when necessary. Together with the officials from the castle they pursued all kinds of lawbreakers through the mountains, tried to recover stolen objects, and received rents and even tithes. A shepherd who had been slandered would complain to the *bayle*. The *bayle* was not always able to settle the disputes brought before his modest 'tribunal' in the village square. Some semi-official arbiter might do the business better. *While I was living as a shepherd with Jean Baragnon of Mérens*, says Guillaume Baille, of Montaillou, *Baragnon's wife, Brune, often called me a 'heretic'. One day, in the pasture, Jean, the son of my employer Jean Baragnon, also called me a 'heretic'. I complained to the local* bayle. *Later, Pons Malet, from Ax-les-Thermes, made peace again between me and Jean Baragnon the younger.*[2]

The second power was theoretically nothing to do with that of the manor and the *bayle*. It belonged to the Dominican Inquisition in Carcassonne (ii.268). The Inquisition had its own spies, semi-official

1 One hectare = 2.47 acres.
2 ii.380. See also ii.276 (tithes etc.); iii.160 (village square).

police, and thugs. The latter, modestly known as 'servants', dealt out, or received, the occasional punch on the nose when they came to deliver summonses to the villagers of the Pays d'Aillon (ii.172). The Inquisition also possessed its notaries-cum-jailers, who directed the raids against Montaillou at the end of the summer of 1308. It had its agents in the secular clergy. For example, Jean Strabaud, who was at the same time village priest, notary of the Inquisition, and a public notary (iii.88). Also Pierre Clergue, priest at Montaillou, brother of the *bayle* and a double agent, whom I shall frequently mention again. Moreover, the Inquisition at Carcassonne had as a representative with the Bishop of Pamiers Frère Gaillard de Pomiès, a powerful and sinister character, who played his part conscientiously in all the inquiries and acts of repression ordered by Fournier.

The third power was the see of Pamiers. Theoretically ruled from above by the papacy, the diocese in its turn ruled the local 'hierarchy' at Montaillou: the priest and sometimes the *vicaire*, themselves flanked by the diocesan council. Nor was Bishop Fournier merely a skilful defender of Roman orthodoxy. He also had a care for the things of this world, and sought to make the villagers of the upper Ariège pay tithes of lambs; this was a recurrent source of rural conflict. Roger-Bernard, the old Comte de Foix, was the protector of his people and for a long while acted as an obstacle to the Bishop's attempts. But once Roger-Bernard was dead (1302), the offensive was resumed, first at the beginning of the decade starting in 1310 and then again, after 1317, in the time of Fournier's bishopric. Assisted by Pomiès, the emissary from Carcassonne, the Inquisition tribunal at Pamiers was to brood like a black cloud over Montaillou between 1320 and 1324. Carcassonne and Pamiers exercised a kind of inquisitorial condominium over the village, though not without frequent rivalry at the top.

The fourth power, distant but endowed with much greater force of dissuasion, was the kingdom of France. The Comte de Foix was in a position of *de facto* dependence on France, which subjected him to pressures of varying intensity. It was always possible for the King, in Paris, to raise an army to come to the aid of the 'true religion'. So both France and its strength were hated by many mountain folk who had never met a man of the north in flesh and blood. '*Do you think you can fight against the Church and the lord King of France?*' cried the father of the village priest to the outlaw Guillaume Maurs, formerly a peasant from Montaillou and now a shepherd (ii.171). Bélibaste, the *parfait*, went much further (ii.78–9). *There are*, he said, *four great devils ruling over the world: the lord Pope, the major devil whom I call Satan; the lord King of France is the second devil; the Bishop of Pamiers the third; and the lord Inquisitor of Carcassonne, the fourth.*

In 'normal' periods, Montaillou was a mountain-dwelling micro-society, whose people generally had little money, little prestige and little power. On the other hand it was not too difficult for them to slip between the interstices of the various external and encircling powers. But a new situation arose in the 1320s: at the time of the Fournier investigation, the four powers referred to above joined together, even though there were occasional cracks in their solidarity. It is true that private wars between feudal lords continued to be waged on the southern slopes of the Pyrenees where the Montaillou shepherds brought their flocks (iii.195). But on the northern slopes the political and ecclesiastical powers merged: the young Comte de Foix and the great ladies who dominated his court gave way to the agents of the King of France and the agents of the Inquisition,[1] whereas the former Comte had encouraged his people to refuse to pay tithes and tried to resist at all costs the encroachments of the Church and of the Kingdom of France. For their part, the Inquisition at Carcassonne and the Bishop of Pamiers went hand in hand with France in the north. France knew how to reward the clerics of Occitania for their collaboration. With the support of Paris, the papacy at Avignon was conferred on Jacques Fournier under the name of Benedict XII in 1334, and became the source of countless prelacies and sinecures for priests of southern origin.

For the peasants of Montaillou the result of this unity of action on the part of the various powers was oppression, manifest whenever the peasants challenged religion as heretics, or the tithe system as tax-payers. People who felt they were being watched used to move about at night; they would be careful what they said; both in towns and villages they were afraid of talking too much, of being caught by the jaw (*capi gula*). Men walked sword in hand and whistled softly to attract the attention of an acquaintance. A man would throw a pebble on the roof

1 During the years with which we are concerned, the agents of the King of France in Languedoc acted with extraordinary brutality towards the neighbouring Comté de Foix, virtually reducing it to the rank of a satellite. It did not recover its freedom of manoeuvre until later in the fourteenth century.

or against the shutter of a friend's house so that someone would come and open the door. The apparatus of power was not a 'police' apparatus in the modern sense of the term, but for anyone who did not keep absolutely to the straight and narrow path it was a Kafka-esque world of spies and betrayals. Even up in the mountains, the last refuge of freedom of expression, one might be trapped at any moment because of a careless word – trapped by the priest, by the *bayle*, by the *vicaire*, by a neighbour. One piece of tittle-tattle might mean prison, or having to wear stitched to one's clothes the yellow cross, symbol of ignominy imposed by the Inquisition on heretics.

But the relationship of the various powers to the peasants of Montaillou was not exclusively harsh and oppressive. Between those who dominated and those who were dominated there was an intermediary stage of intercession, occupied by influential lords and noblemen. When Bernard Clergue, *bayle* of Montaillou, was trying to have his brother the priest set free from the episcopal prison, he applied to various people who he had reason to think might be able to influence Jacques Fournier's decision. Bernard greased the palm of the temporal lord of Mirepoix. Cost: 300 livres. To Madame Constance, the lady of Mirepoix, he presented a mule. And he gave a big sum of money in silver to Loup de Foix, the bastard born of the love affair between Louve and Raymond-Roger. Other big tips went to the *prévôt* of the village of Rabat, who was the local representative of the abbey of Lagrasse, and to the Archdeacon of Pamiers, Germain de Castelnau, 'a friend of the Bishop's'. In all, said Bernard Clergue (ii.282), *I spent 14,000 sous in one year in order to have my brother set free*. This was an enormous sum even for the richest family in Montaillou. But, as it happened, the intercession did not work: Pierre Clergue remained in prison, and died there; Jacques Fournier was incorruptible. Nonetheless, an intercessionary stage did exist, providing always some possibility of reconciliation between the oppression practised by the dominating forces and the ordinary people's need for security.

The most important social divisions in Montaillou seem not to have been between a blue-blooded nobility and a rural commonalty. This is due first and foremost, quite simply, to the smallness of the group we are studying. The 'three estates' – ecclesiastics, nobles, and the common people of the towns and villages – certainly existed in upper Ariège, or

Sabarthès, as a whole.[1] But the inhabitants of Montaillou were too few for this three-fold division to exist within the parish. In the period we are dealing with, the priest was a native son of rural extraction, and he was the only local representative of the clergy. As for the substantial peasantry, they had practically no representatives of the nobility to turn up their noses at them. Only one noble family lived in Montaillou during our period, and then only from time to time. This family was the *châtelain*, Bérenger de Roquefort, and his wife, Béatrice de Planissoles. We know practically nothing about Bérenger, who died young. But his wife is well known: she belonged to the nobility both by birth and through her two marriages. Her example, like many another, reminds us that social discrimination, though by no means compulsory, operated most frequently through marriage. But in other respects Béatrice un-doubtedly formed part, even though only temporarily, of the village. (She left it later for nearby Prades d'Aillon, and then for the lowlands, a few years after the death of her first husband.) She belonged to the village through her love affairs, her friends and acquaintances, her daily social contacts and her devotions. Not only in Montaillou but in the region as a whole, rigid distinctions between nobles and non-nobles were much less apparent than in the various regions of France proper. The almost racial antagonism between noble and non-noble seen around Paris during the *jacquerie* of 1358 scarcely applied in upper Ariège: here the most important conflicts were those which ranged the Church against the peasantry and nobility together, more or less in coalition against the clergy. Many of the nobles in this little region were poor, though not proud of it as were the haughty nobles of Brittany and Burgundy at the end of the *ancien régime*. But in Foix, nobility without money conferred little prestige: *I am generally held in contempt because of my poverty*, declared the noble Arnaud de Bédeillac, of the village of that name, without any particular emotion (ii.57). Noble families like the de Luzenacs, at Luzenac, were content with a shepherd's diet: bread, sour wine, milk and cheese. Their son Pierre, to make a living, studied to be a lawyer in Toulouse, and ended up as a seedy advocate responsible for the minor business of the Inquisition.[2] Apart from the fact that some of the mountain nobility were more or less down and out, there was little distance between nobles on the one hand and lawyers on

1 On Sabarthès, see below, Chapter XVII.
2 Duvernoy (1961), p. 18 (Luzenac).

the other. The frontier between nobles and non-nobles was in general very fluid. A document of 1311, dealing with tithes in upper Ariège, speaks of '*nobles*', '*ignobles*', and 'those who pass or have passed themselves off as nobles': this third group is expressly mentioned so that they may be certain to be included in the tithe agreement of 1311 (iii.338). So was there a fully accepted group of false nobles, with fine houses and possessions, considered by other people as nobles, and perhaps even honoured as such? At the level of everyday life and the relations between men, and especially between women, but between men and women also, the relations of nobility to non-nobility were often pleasant and generally relaxed. Of course, they were tinged with a minimum of deference. But in themselves they gave rise to no problems. The nobility themselves were affected by the spirit of caste only in connection with marriage, and not always then. Stéphanie de Chateauverdun married a knight, but later on she went to Catalonia with a Cathar weaver, the brother of a goose-girl. And together they seem to have lived a life of perfect heresy and no less perfect spiritual friendship (i.223). Béatrice de Planissoles, *châtelaine* of Montaillou, married only men of blue blood, as we shall see. But she came near to granting her favours to her steward, then became mistress to a bastard and then mistress to two priests, not members of the nobility. True, during the preliminaries she invented dozens of reasons for not giving herself to the first of these clerics, but these reasons never included the fact that he was a commoner. Admittedly she shared his Cathar ideas, and heresy may make strange bedfellows. But though the second priest did not have the excuse of being a heretic, his lowly birth did not prevent him from possessing Béatrice, and even living with her as though they were married. As far as more ordinary and everyday relationships were concerned, we observe that ladies and *châtelaines*, when they met with peasant women, did not hesitate to settle down for a gossip; they might even kiss and embrace. There is no need to look at this from a modern point of view and see it as hypocritical playing to the gallery, a pretence at bridging the impassable gulf between social classes. In fact that gulf scarcely existed, at least at the level of social encounter, which was marked by an attractive absence of caste consciousness on the one hand and respect of persons on the other.

Jacques Fournier's very detailed account also shows that antagonism between nobility and non-nobility played no very important role. Of course, such enmity did exist and might even be serious. Two nobles at least – the *châtelain* of Junac (who was afraid of being denounced as a Cathar) and the squire (*damoiseau*) Raymond de Planissoles – actually murdered a neighbouring peasant apiece. In 1322, in the parish of Caussou, Guillaume de Planissoles pleaded the fact that he was a nobleman to try to get exempted from paying tallage. This led to murmurs among the common folk.

But in Montaillou itself I have not come across any conflict of this type. The antagonism that undoubtedly existed between the peasant family of the Clergues (of which one member was the manorial *bayle*) and some of the villagers, was not, and could not have been, based on the enmity between nobles and non-nobles. In general, in the period and in the area with which we are concerned, this enmity was only an occasional and probably superficial phenomenon. It was one of many equally or more important struggles which set one section of the population against real or mythical adversaries, who might be lepers, Jews, Cathars, usurers, priests, prelates, Minorites, the French, the Inquisitors, women or the rich. One could go on indefinitely. There are many explanations for the peasants' lack of belligerence against the nobility. They are connected, it seems to me, with the particular character of Occitan civilization, including its economic, social and cultural aspects. For example, there was the comparative smallness of the manorial estates generally in noble hands; there was also a certain positive social function which made the southern nobility attractive rather than repulsive. The comparatively good relations between nobles and non-nobles may be regarded, in this study, as part of our data. But the nobility played only an occasional part in the life of the inhabitants of Montaillou.

The absence of strong demarcation between groups can be explained by the relative poverty of the mountain nobility. In upper Ariège we are far from the nobles of Paris or Bordeaux, with their huge manorial estates and their vineyards worth their weight in gold. The estate of the *châtelain* of Montaillou, as far as we can tell, was scarcely bigger than the properties of the rich local peasants, and the *châtelain* himself behaved first and foremost as the factotum of the household, occupied with the work of the estate and with flirting with the mistress. He did not play the role of a great captain of agriculture, such as we find on the estates around Béziers and Beauvais. No doubt the distance from big towns also helped to defuse any conflict which might arise between the peasants and the nobles. In the Pays d'Aillon, the former were too shabby and poor, the latter too comfortably established as sturdy farmers in their homes and modest domains for there to arise the famous difference of potential which might in the long run have led to open conflict. It was in regions like Flanders, southern Beauvaisis, and the Paris area, regions far away where agriculture was most commercially active, that the clash occurred, or would occur, between a nobility made rich in the markets its estates supplied and the peasants who aspired to something more than the crumbs that fell from the table.

It would be wrong to try to explain this comparative absence of class struggle by weakness pure and simple on the part of the nobility. Poor they certainly were, but not in every respect or on every plane. In fact, since the Crusades, since the introduction of the Cathar heresy, largely due to the nobility, and also since the troubadours, the minor nobility of Occitania had played a positive role both in promoting culture and, in the case of the women, in promoting love. This latter was greatly appreciated by poets, and by lovers of all professional categories. The leading role played by the nobility in social relations and village events was accepted with a good grace by a commonalty with no major cause for complaint. The nobility of upper Ariège did not oppress the people very much, in an area which was almost without servitude. They appeared only occasionally in Montaillou, and then on occasions which might be quite pleasant. They offered models of civilization accessible to many. In short, they managed to be agreeable without costing very much.

The manorial system and the legal position of men who might be dependent on it – which could provoke social tension – are important elements of the social structure. In this connection, as has been indicated, the Fournier documents speak chiefly of the public authority and local lordship which both belonged to the Comte de Foix and his representatives on the spot, the *châtelain*, his military representative, and the *bayle*, his legal representative (in theory). But these same documents have nothing to say about manorial rights in Montaillou. In order to fill the gap we have to consult material belonging to a later period. A survey of 1672[1] shows that the King of France was then lord (*seigneur*)

1 Ariège departmental archives, J 79.

of Montaillou, as legitimate heir to the rights of the former Comtes de Foix. The lord of Montaillou dispensed, himself or through a representative (the distant successor of our *bayle*), high, medium and low justice; he collected *lods* and *ventes* (death duties and transfer tax) of 8.5 per cent on the value of the goods concerned; he also collected *pâturage* and *forestage* (common and forest rights) amounting in 1662 to between 16 and 20 *livres tournois*.[1] In return for *pâturage* and *forestage*, the inhabitants of Montaillou were more or less free to send their flocks and herds to pasture in the 250 hectares of forest and the 450 hectares of fallow land and heath. These forests, fallow lands and heaths belonged nominally to the lord, but for a consideration he handed them over for the peasants' use.[2] There was also a right of *quête* 'levied by the lord every year on every head of a family with hearth and home in Montaillou': the annual yield of this was 40 *livres* in 1672. The right of intestory (redeemed for the derisory overall sum of 5 *livres* per annum in 1672) used to allow the lord to inherit from those who died without direct or indirect heirs. Lastly there was an *albergue* (lodging tax) and a tax to be paid in oats. These two were once intended to provide shelter for the Comte or his *châtelain* and fodder for their horses: that at least was the reason, later the pretext, for extorting them. All these taxes were very ancient, and they correspond exactly to those which existed in the nearby Catalan Pyrenees during the two or three centuries around the year 1000. At some period, probably later than that covered by the Fournier Register, most of the taxes became payable in money. Thus the 200 or 300 hectares of land which the peasants of Montaillou cultivated round about

1 A *livre tournois*, i.e. a *livre* minted at Tours, equalled 20 *sous*; a *livre parisis*, i.e. a *livre* minted at Paris, equalled 25 *sous*.

2 These forests, fallow lands and heaths, which later fell into royal and communal hands, correspond, according to the Land Register of 1827 preserved in the present-day town-hall of Montaillou, to the 255 hectares of forest recorded by the Ministère des Eaux et Forêts and to the 430 hectares of 'communal' or common land. The ancient manorial estate, in fields and meadows (excluding forests, which I have counted above), corresponds to a property of 37 hectares belonging to a M. Gély, whose family, by purchase and inheritance, came into the estate in 1827. The properties of a few inhabitants of Montaillou described in 1827 as 'proprietors' (resident and usually working the land themselves), among whom were the Clergue and the Baille families, consisted of between 8 and 12 hectares each. Those of what are described as 'farmers' consisted of 2 hectares, and those of labourers one hectare or less. In 1827 the farmers formed the majority of the population of Montaillou, the labourers an important minority.

1672 as fields and meadows raised enough money to meet manorial dues without too much difficulty. But at the beginning of the fourteenth century these dues probably still weighed heavily, more heavily than in 1672 after the erosion caused by inflation.[1] But despite its probable scope, the manorial system of the 1300s did not correspond, or no longer corresponded, to a real state of servitude on the part of the people of Montaillou. They might well be annoyed at the scandals and injustices perpetrated by the family of the *bayle*, often urged on by the Inquisition. But they were not serfs, or even strictly dependents, of their temporal lord. It is possible that in the eleventh and twelfth centuries they were subjected to certain forms of strict dependence, but this was no longer the case in 1300. By the first two decades of the fourteenth century the peasant families of Montaillou owned, bequeathed and sold their land freely. (Naturally, selling was rare, for the land market in these remote parts was not very active.) Furthermore, their relations with the lord and his local agents did not prevent them enjoying great liberty of movement. This in itself implies that personal dependence on the lord of the manor was almost non-existent, even though certain manorial rights were probably the relics of former dependence. Nevertheless, the absence of dependence was accompanied by dues that were not negligible, and by respectful deference towards the distant lord and his agents on the spot. Real acts of oppression during this period did not come from the Comte, the lord of the manor, towards whom the rustics might even show a quite touching affection. The sources of oppression lay in other quarters, especially the Inquisition: and the Inquisitors would not hesitate to use the temporal lord's agent, the *bayle*, against the villagers.

Thus opposition in Montaillou and Sabarthès was directed more against the first order of the three estates, the clergy, than against the second, the nobility, whether manorial or otherwise. The countryfolk of upper Ariège were against the rich churchmen rather than the noble laymen. It is well known that in the thirteenth and fourteenth centuries the clergy of Occitania, from the Alps to the Pyrenees, behaved like a terrestrial power. But the chief area of friction concerned tithes. At the end of the summer of 1308 the Inquisition of Carcassonne arrested all

1 Unfortunately, there is insufficient documentary evidence to form an assessment of manorial dues in Montaillou between 1300 and 1320.

the inhabitants of Montaillou, male and female, over the age of twelve or thirteen. The round-up also included the shepherds, come down specially from the mountain pastures for the festivities at the end of the summer transhumance. The Inquisitor's mass arrests were a prelude to the tightening up by the Bishops of Pamiers, between 1311 and 1323, on all livestock tithes in mountain areas, which up to then had not been collected with great strictness. Jacques Fournier, whose predecessor had excommunicated those who refused to pay up, now exacted these heavy dues with the same bland but cruel perseverance as that with which he persecuted heretics. An agreement of 1311, renewed and supplemented in 1323, laid down that all the communities in the 'archpriestship of Sabarthès' – including Montaillou, Ax, Tarascon and Foix – should pay tithes in money and in kind on products arising out of livestock, plus another tithe of an eighth on grains. This exorbitant tax caused an out-cry, for at the beginning of the fourteenth century the priests began to exact it in earnest. In the end people got used to it, though they still complained: even in the eighteenth century observers were struck by the exaggerated tithes customarily paid in the Pyrenees. The grain tax of one-eighth in Sabarthès in 1311–23 amounted almost to the *champart*, a feudal harvest tax. No wonder it was challenged.

And it was challenged even in the Pays d'Aillon, which contained the subject of our survey. The weaver Prades Tavernier from Prades d'Aillon, in the course of a long march in the mountains with Guillaume Escaunier of Arques, elaborated as if it were an article of faith his hatred for tithes, mingled with other heretical propositions: *The priests and the clerks*, he cried (ii.16), *because they are wicked, extort and receive from the people the first-fruits and the tithes of products for which they have not done the smallest stroke of work*. For Prades Tavernier, tithes were just as infamous as baptism, the Eucharist, the Mass, marriage and abstaining from meat on Friday. In Montaillou itself the Clergue brothers, *bayle* and priest, took on the job of collecting tithes both for themselves and for superior powers.

As in the sixteenth century, at the time of the Reformation, heresy over tithes was sometimes hard to distinguish from heresy over religion itself. With irrefutable logic the Church applied the turn of the screw over tithes at the same time as spiritual admonition. In 1313 or 1314 the King far away in the north tried to moderate the appetite of the priests of Foix: by upsetting the people, they might endanger public order and the French presence, or whatever stood for it. But these remonstrances from Paris were scarcely audible, and could do little against the rapacity of a local Church encouraged by the economic situation. The immunity from tithes enjoyed in the mountains, even though it was only partial and relative, could not go on for ever. The boom in population, grazing, and money which took place in upper Ariège as elsewhere during the major phase of medieval growth created new possibilities of taxation, and these were eagerly watched by the clergy of the region, reinvigorated by the anti-Cathar drive. Their offensive formed part of the general clerical policy on tithes both in the Middle Ages and in modern times. The Church realized it could increase its prestige by making people pay dearly for its services.

But many people, in the Pays d'Aillon as elsewhere, saw it differently. Jokes about the wealth acquired by the clergy were always good for a laugh around the fire. The inquiries conducted by Jacques Fournier show that tithes were the favourite target of mountain malcontents as far as material grievances against the Church were concerned. Out of eighty-nine files containing every possible form of allergy to Catholic power and orthodoxy, six at least adduce non-payment of tithes as the chief or as a minor accusation. The accused express themselves very vigorously, especially on the subject of the tithe of *carnelages*, levied on sheep, which annoyed both farmers and shepherds.

This kind of grievance was felt particularly acutely against the mendicant monks settled in the towns. Despite the rule of poverty to which they were theoretically bound, they acted as accomplices of the Bishop and his policy of enforcing tithe payments. They forbade peasants excommunicated for non-payment of tithes to enter their churches (ii.317, 321).

A revealing example is the case of Guillaume Austatz, *bayle* of Ornolac in Sabarthès and typical representative of a kind of village élite infected with Catharism.[1] *My only enemies in Ornolac*, he says (i.200), *are the priest and the* vicaire. *I know no others.* Protesting to the villagers against the burning of a supporter of the Waldensian heresy he says (i.209): '*Instead of this Waldensian it's the Bishop of Pamiers himself they ought to have burned. For he exacts carnelage and makes us pay out large sums on our possessions . . . the tithes exacted by the Bishop are probably in accordance with common law, but the inhabitants of Sabarthès are right to*

1 For his curious theories on the demography of the souls of the dead see i.191.

resist them because they are against their own customs.' This diatribe is very revealing: the sheep-farmers and shepherds constituted a world apart and would not be ridden over roughshod. But their resistance was part of a long anti-clerical and anti-tithe movement in the Languedoc of the Pyrenees, the Mediterranean and the Cévennes. In the long history of heresy in Occitania from the thirteenth to the seventeenth century, the conflict over tithes is always underlying and recurrent. From Catharism to Calvinism it constitutes a common denominator more obvious than dogmatic continuity, which is often absent, or important only on a few fascinating but isolated points.

At all events, external repression on the rustics of Montaillou, the Pays d'Aillon and Sabarthès came not so much from lay society or the nobility as from the ambitions of a totalitarian Church. The resulting alienation was both spiritual and temporal.

Whether friendly or oppressive, the nobility, the lords and the Church existed mainly outside Montaillou, away from the village itself. If we exclude the case of Béatrice de Planissoles and the little-known *vice-châtelain* who replaced her dead husband as commander of the local fortress, all the inhabitants of the village, including the priest, belonged to local peasant families. Even the few artisans in the parish still had some agricultural activities and relationships. The distinction between farmers and day-labourers which gave the village its characteristic segmentation in the north of France here took on particular forms. Despite the pre-eminence of two or three families who were comparatively rich or at least less poor (the Clergues to begin with, followed by the Belots and the Benets), there were certain factors which somewhat diminished inequality. Poor young men who in the Paris basin would have stayed where they were and formed a proletariat or semi-proletariat of day-labourers, in Montaillou were, so to speak, expelled from the social structure of the village and became shepherds in the nearby mountains or in distant Catalonia.

This being so, the best way to understand Montaillou is to abandon temporarily the problems of social stratification within it and go straight to the basic cell which, multiplied a few dozen times, went to make up the village. This basic cell was none other than the peasant family, embodied in the permanence of a house and in the daily life of a group co-resident under the same roof. In local language this entity was called an *ostal*; and in the Latin of the Inquisition files it was called a *hospicium* or, more often, a *domus*. It should be noted that the words, *ostal*, *domus* and *hospicium* all and inextricably mean both family and house. The term *familia* is practically never used in the Fournier Register. It never crosses the lips of the inhabitants of Montaillou themselves, for whom the family of flesh and blood and the house of wood, stone or daub were one and the same thing.

Many passages show the crucial role – emotional, economic and lineal – played by the house-cum-family in the preoccupations of the average inhabitant of the Pays d'Aillon. One of the most illuminating on this subject is a conversation between Gauzia Clergue and Pierre Azéma of Montaillou. Gauzia, the wife of Bernard Clergue the second, proposed to confess to Bishop Fournier certain heretical facts which she had witnessed or been an accomplice to.[1] Pierre Azéma answered Gauzia, saying: *'Vain and foolish woman! If you confess all these things, you will lose all your possessions and put out the fire of your house. Your children, their hearts full of anger, will go and beg for alms . . . Let the sleeping hare lie, take another path so as not to wake him, or he will wound your hands with his feet . . . I can see an even better way to keep your house standing. For I, as long as the Lord Bishop shall live, will be of his house; and I can do much good; and I can give my daughter as wife to one of your sons. And so our house will be more successful, more comfortable. But if you confess to have meddled in heresy, you, your house and your sons will be destroyed.'* Gauzia Clergue added: *These words were exchanged without witnesses between Pierre Azéma and myself. And because of that, I gave up the idea of confessing anything.*

Everything is contained in this dialogue, positing as a supreme value the prosperity of houses, whether or not allied to each other by marriage. The essential concept of the *domus*, the domestic group of co-residents, involved various central and subordinate elements: the kitchen fire, goods and lands, children and conjugal alliances. It was a fragile reality, threatened and sometimes destroyed in each generation by epidemics, bereavements, remarriage. It could also be broken up by the Inquisitors. Nonetheless, for the average inhabitant of Montaillou the idea of the *domus* was a core reference.

The same text shows Pierre Azéma using the term *domus* in a derived and somewhat distorted sense, that of relationships (*parentela*). When Azéma speaks of being of the Bishop's house, he does not mean that a mere peasant such as he lives in the Bishop's palace in Pamiers; he merely claims to be a sort of distant relative of Jacques Fournier.

Nothing shows more clearly the importance of the *domus* as a unifying concept in social, family and cultural life than the key role it played in the construction or reconstruction of Catharism in upper Ariège and in Montaillou itself.

One day, says Mengarde Buscailh of Prades d'Aillon, the next village

1 iii.366, 367. This Bernard Clergue was the son of Arnaud Clergue, and not to be confused with the Bernard Clergue who was the son of Pons Clergue and *bàyle* of Montaillou.

to Montaillou (i.499), *I met my brother-in-law, Guillaume Buscailh, on the way to my parish church.*

'*Where are you going?*' *asked Guillaume.*

'*I am going to church.*'

'*What an excellent ecclesiastic you are!*' *answered Guillaume.* '*You would do just as well to pray to God in your own house as in the church.*'

I answered that the Church was a more suitable place to pray to God than one's own house.

Then he simply said to me: '*You are not of the faith.*'

Thus for Guillaume Buscailh, so zealous a supporter of Cathar ideas that he one day tried to make his sister-in-law stop feeding her baby and let it die in *endura* (i.499), the Albigensian faith was something which existed and was practised at home, unlike the Roman faith, properly celebrated in the parish church. This was a generally held idea. One peasant told Jacques Fournier that when heresy entered into a *domus* it was like leprosy and entrenched itself there for four generations or for ever (ii.100). Aude Fauré of Merviel, a neurotic, lost faith in the Eucharist and confided her doubts to her neighbour and relative Ermengarde Garaudy. The latter, horrified, warned her against the evil consequences her scepticism might have for the house and village she lived in. '*Traitress!*' said Ermengarde (ii.87). '*This village and this ostal have always been pure from all evil and heresy. Beware lest you bring evil upon us from another place, lest you make our own place accursed.*' Conversely, the violence of the Inquisition was regarded by its victims as an act of aggression against the heretical *domus*, and only secondly as an attack on the liberty or life of the individual. When the priest of Montaillou was arrested after being denounced by two spies (ii.281), Bernard Clergue exclaimed: *These two traitors have brought misfortune upon our house and upon my brother the priest.*

People might be converted to heresy house by house, rather than individual by individual. Pierre Authié, the Cathar missionary, preferred the group method. To the assembled family of Raymond Pierre he said (ii.406): '*It is God's wish that I come into your house to save the souls of those who dwell in it.*' Pierre Maury of Montaillou quotes the case of a *domus* at Arques which was converted 'like one man'. He says (iii.143): *I believe that Gaillarde, sister of Guillaume Escaunier and wife of Michel Leth, and Esclarmonde, Guillaume's other sister, who might well have been twelve years old, were believers [credentes] in the heretics. And*

in my opinion the same was true of Arnaud, Guillaume's brother. All these
people were converted at once, the whole household at a blow, together with
Gaillarde, the mother of Guillaume Escaunier and Marquise, her sister. In
Montaillou itself the missionary work of people like Authié was based
on a network of certain houses. Béatrice de Planissoles relates: *When I*
lived in Montaillou and Prades d'Aillon the rumour among the believers in
heresy had it that the heretics frequented the houses of the brothers Raymond
and Bernard Belot, who at that time lived together; also the house of
Alazaïs Rives, sister of Prades Tavernier the heretic. Also the house of
Guillaume Benet, brother of Arnaud Benet of Ax. All the people of these
various houses came from Montaillou.[1] Béatrice was shrewd enough to see
one of the secrets of heresy's success in her village: dangerous ideas
crept like fleas from one *domus* or domestic group to another. Once
heresy was implanted, the *domus* acted as a kind of conservatory, a
barricade limiting compromising contacts with houses which were not
heretical. The secrecy of the new faith was preserved to the utmost
when whispered beneath the door of the *domus* (ii.10) or, preferably,
when shut up in the damp fug of the *ostal*'s four walls. In Montaillou
itself, Alazaïs Azéma spoke heresy only in her own house, with her son
Raymond (i.319). But she also did so with the members of the house of
Belot (the three brothers – Raymond, Bernard and Guillaume – and
their mother, Guillemette) as well as with the members of the house of
Benet (Guillaume, his son Raymond, and Guillemette, Guillaume's
wife) related by marriage to the house of Belot. (Note how, in the list
given by Alazaïs Azéma, the men, whether young or old, regularly take
precedence over the women, even when the women are old.) Similarly,
Raymonde Lizier, later to become Raymonde Belot by another marriage,
and end in prison for heresy, *entertained a great familiarity with*
Guillemette Belot and with Raymond, Bernard and Arnaud Belot; she
frequented their house and spoke much in secret with them.[2] Both in
Montaillou and in the other villages one could go on indefinitely giving

1 i.233, and iii.161. Heresy was introduced to Montaillou by the Authiés in 1300, in
the house of Guillaume Benet (or rather re-introduced, for heresy had already been
present to a modest degree during the last decade of the thirteenth century, according to Béatrice de Planissoles's evidence about Raymond Roussel, I, 219). The fact
that Guillaume Benet was the brother of Arnaud Benet of Ax, himself the father-in-
law of Guillaume Authié, clearly made contacts easier between town and village.
2 ii.223. Arnaud was Raymonde Lizier's future husband.

examples underlining the special social links between houses belonging to the heretical movement.

This communicating yet exclusive network acted as a logistic support to Cathar clandestinity. But the role of the network derived from prior social links between the *domus*; it made use of these social links, it did not create them. Certain other *domus*, just because they were not Cathar, served as a structured social outlet for people who were good though perhaps vacillating Catholics. Jean Pellissier, a shepherd in the village, declared that he was not a heretic, at least in his youth (iii.75): *I used to visit four houses in Montaillou, and not one of them was heretical.*

In Montaillou the usual collective organization, the assembly of heads of families, was perhaps not entirely absent, but, if it functioned at all, seems to have enjoyed a somewhat ghostly existence. It was probably paralysed by the internal division of the village into religious factions and antagonistic cliques. As for the confraternities, societies of penitents, and other usual ingredients of Occitan social life, they were absent, if not from the period in general, at least from the mountain communities with which we are concerned. This being so, I see Montaillou first and foremost as an archipelago of *domus*, each one positive or negative in terms of the currents of heterodox beliefs.

The peasants and shepherds of Montaillou were conscious of this situation. The farmer Guillaume Belot and the brothers Pierre and Guillaume Maury, both shepherds, out one day for a walk together, made an informal census of the village, dividing it up into houses of believers and houses of unbelievers – the belief in question being, of course, heresy. Among the houses which the two Guillaumes expressly described as 'believing' were the house of Maurs, the house of Guilhabert, the house of Benet, and those of Bernard Rives, Raymond Rives, Maury, Ferrier, Bayle, Marty, Fauré and Belot.[1] The eleven 'believing' houses often corresponded to nuclear families each formed of two parents and their children. One of the eleven heretical *domus*, however, departs from this model, consisting of an aged mother (Guillemette 'Belote') and her four grown-up sons, all still bachelors at that period. The eleven 'believing' houses, according to this list, consisted of thirty-six heretics in all; but this total must be regarded as incomplete since for many of the couples listed Belot and the Maury brothers mention

1 iii.161. The list is incomplete: Maury and Belot do not mention the important house of Clergue.

only the names of the husband and wife and not those of the children, the latter probably being considered a negligible quantity.

The rest of the enumeration shows that the *domus* was not always coextensive with the opinions of its members. Maury and the two Belots mention a certain number of maverick heretics in Montaillou not attached to a *domus* (which would then, ipso facto, be considered as 'believing'). The 'houseless' heretics (iii.162) were nine in number, and included two married couples (the Vitals and the Forts), who probably lived in houses belonging to other people; two married women (whose opinions perhaps differed from those of their husbands); an illegitimate daughter; and two men, members of families but mentioned separately.

Other houses in Montaillou which were not regarded as 'believing' adopted a collective attitude of benevolent neutrality towards Catharism. One of these was the *domus* of the Liziers (iii.162, 490). Maury and the Belot brothers said there was nothing to fear from the Lizier *domus* since the murder of Arnaud Lizier, an anti-Cathar. After his death, the house of Lizier came into the sphere of influence of the Clergues, and even into the personal harem of the priest, since Pierre Clergue took Grazide Lizier as his mistress.

In Montaillou, Catholicism also went by houses. Jean Pellissier, farm servant and shepherd, said there were five houses in the village which were not heretical. These were the house of Pellissier itself, probably 'non-nuclear' because it included five brothers of whom some at least were grown up; the house of Na Carminagua, Madame Carminagua, mother of the Azéma brothers (the brothers sometimes showed something more than reserve towards heresy); the house of Julien Pellissier; the house of Pierre Ferrier, which according to Maury and Belot afterwards went over to Albigensian sympathies; and finally the house of a woman called Na Longua, mother of Gauzia Clergue, herself related by marriage to the Clergues, but not a heretic as they were.

So among the houses listed there were in all eleven heretical *domus*, five Catholic *domus*, some houses which changed sides (for example, the Clergues) and a few mixed, neutral or divided houses, sometimes containing people with 'split' hearts, volatile and treacherous (ii.223). The list is incomplete, since in the decade beginning 1300 Montaillou probably contained over 200 inhabitants, in other words at least about forty houses. But out of these forty houses the majority at one time or another showed some weakness in favour of heresy. In all, according to

Guillaume Mathei and Pons Rives, two well-informed witnesses, there were in Montaillou only two houses *untouched by heresy* (i.292). As for Guillaume Authié, the Cathar missionary who enthused about Montaillou, about Clergue the priest and about the house of the Clergues (*No*, he said, *I have nothing to fear from Clergue the priest nor from the house of the Clergues. If only all the priests in the world could be like the priest in Montaillou*), he confirms what Mathei and Rives say about the two anti-Cathar houses: *In Montaillou there are only two men whom we have to be careful about*.[1] (Rives and Mathei speak of two anti-Cathar houses, i.e. one anti-Cathar individual for each house.)

All the evidence we have emphasizes the mystical, religious and central significance of the *domus* for the people of Montaillou. Conversely, *as one measly pig contaminates the whole sty*, an individual infected with dogmatic deviation soon spread the disease to all his *domus*. Though there were exceptions, a person's belief was generally that of his house. It took the great waves of repression after 1308 to break up the network of Cathar *domus* in Montaillou, and to turn the village into a tragic rat-race where everyone worked to encompass his neighbour's ruin, thus, mistakenly, hoping to avert his own.

Whatever the dénouement, it is certain that for the people of Montaillou the house (*ostal*) occupied a strategic position as regards worldly possessions. Here is Jacques Authié addressing the shepherds of Arques and Montaillou and adapting for their benefit the Cathar myth of the Fall (iii.130; ii.25): '*Satan entered into the Kingdom of the Father, and told the Spirits of that Kingdom that he, the Devil, owned a much better Paradise . . . "Spirits, I will bring you into my world", said Satan, "and I shall give you oxen, cows, riches and a wife for company, and you will have your own ostals, and you will have children . . . and you will rejoice more for a child, when you have one, than for all the rest which you enjoy here in Paradise."* ' In the hierarchy of essential possessions, then, the *ostal* comes after the cow and the wife, but before the child.

From the ethnographic point of view the juridical-magical significance of the *ostal* of Ariège, just like the *casa* of Andorra, was greater than the sum of the perishable individuals who went to make up the household. The Pyrenean house was a moral entity and its goods were indivisible. It possessed a certain number of rights, rights which were expressed in

i.279. One of these is Pierre Azéma and the other is not named.

ownership of land and in rights of usage in the forests and common pastures of the mountains, the *solanes* or *soulanes* of the parish. The *ostal* or *casa* 'continued the personal existence of its dead master'; it was regarded as 'true mistress of all goods which go to make up the heritage'. All the more so because in the village of Montaillou the peasants, well-to-do or otherwise, all owned some possessions. They might even be said to be de facto proprietors of the fields and meadows which, if one excludes forests and commons, made up the major part of the cultivated land.

In Montaillou the house had its 'star', its 'luck', *in which the dead still had a share* (i.313–14). Star and luck were protected by keeping in the house bits of fingernail and hair belonging to the deceased head of the family. Hair and nails, which went on growing after death, were regarded as bearers of especially intense vital energy. Through this ritual the house 'was imbued with certain magic qualities belonging to the deceased', and could subsequently convey those qualities to other people belonging to the same line. *On the death of Pons Clergue, father of the priest at Montaillou,* said Alazaïs Azéma (i.313–14), *Mengarde Clergue, his wife, asked me and Brune Pourcel to cut some locks of hair from around the forehead of the corpse, together with fragments from all his finger- and toe-nails; and this so that the house of the dead man might remain fortunate; so the door of the house of the Clergues, in which the dead body lay, was closed; we cut his hair and nails; and we gave them to Guillemette, the servant of the house, who in turn gave them to Mengarde Clergue. This 'abscission' of hair and nails was performed after water had been sprinkled on the dead man's face (for in Montaillou we do not wash the whole of the corpse).*

   The person behind these practices was a peasant woman of Montaillou, Brune Vital. *'Madame,'* she had said to Mengarde, Pons's widow (i.313–14), *'I have heard that if you take locks of hair and bits of finger- and toe-nail from a corpse, it does not carry away with it the star or good fortune of the house.'* Fabrisse Rives, another woman of Montaillou, gave further details (i.328). *When Pons Clergue, the priest's father, died, many people from the Pays d'Aillon came to the house of the priest, his son. The body was placed in the 'house within the house', called the* foganha [kitchen]; *it was not yet wrapped in a shroud; the priest then sent everyone out of the house with the exception of Alazaïs Azéma and Brune Pourcel, the bastard daughter of Prades Tavernier ; these women remained alone with the dead man and the priest ; the women and the priest took the locks of hair and bits of finger- and toe-nail from the corpse . . . Later there was a rumour that the priest had done the same with the corpse of his mother.* Thus the heirs, to prevent the dead person carrying away with him the good fortune of the *domus,* sent away the many visitors come to express their condolences, shut the door and barricaded themselves in the kitchen, the 'house within the house'. They did not wash the body for fear of rinsing away some precious qualities attached to the skin and the accumulated dirt. These precautions may be compared with those Pierre Bourdieu mentions in connection with Kabylie in Algeria: there too every possible precaution is taken to prevent the dead person, while being washed and buried, from taking away with him the *baraka* of the house.[1]

One day, to the south of the hill where the local château stood, Alazaïs Fauré of Montaillou, carrying an empty sack on her head, met Bernard Benet of the same village (i.404). Bernard proposed to denounce to the Inquisitor at Carcassonne the 'heretication' before his death of the late Guillaume Guilhabert, Alazaïs's brother. Alazaïs was horrified. She said at once that she was ready to do anything to protect her brother's memory; when that was retrospectively threatened, so was his *domus. I told Bernard Benet,* said Alazaïs, *that I would give him half a dozen sheep, or a dozen sheep, or whatever else he wanted, to avoid this affliction which would bring down harm and malediction on my dead brother and on his* domus.

The use of bits of the human body to preserve simultaneously the continuity of the family and that of the house relates to other, similar magic rites belonging to Occitan folklore. Béatrice de Planissoles kept the first menstrual blood of her daughter to use as a love potion to bewitch some future son-in-law. She preserved the umbilical cords of her grandsons as talismans to help her win her lawsuit. These two examples again involve the family line and the family prosperity. Until quite recent times the girls of Languedoc used to put a drop of their blood or a nail-paring into a cake or a potion in order to make a boy fall in love with them.

The fragments taken from the body of the chief of a family in Mont-

1 P. Bourdieu, *Esquisse d'une theorie de la pratique* (Towards a theory of practice), Geneva, 1972.

aillou were linked to the *domus* in which they were preserved by a relationship analogous to that between the relics of a saint and the shrine which contains them. Theories on the indestructibility of a king's body and the continuity of the royal house are equally relevant. A few fragments were enough to maintain the physical permanence of the family line and the sacred fire of the *domus*. Both conceptions, royal and peasant, noble and common, must have germinated at some period unknown to us, in the same magical subsoil.

Pierre Clergue the priest, according to Fabrisse Rives, preserved locks of hair and nail-parings not only of his father but also, afterwards, of his mother. He even went so far as to have her buried beneath the altar of the Virgin in Montaillou parish church.

The preoccupation with the *domus* was not 'patrilocal' or 'matrilocal', but ambivalent. True, the citizens of Montaillou and other places speak with emotion about the paternal *ostal* or *domus*: *It would be better*, said Clergue the priest, thinking expressly of the house of his own father (i.255), *for a brother to marry his sister rather than to receive a wife who was a stranger, and similarly, for a sister to marry her brother, rather than to leave the paternal house taking with her a large amount of money as a dowry in order to marry a husband who was a stranger: under such a system, the paternal house is practically destroyed.* The paternal house was also the house where a daughter of Montaillou, married elsewhere and then falling incurably ill, came back to die: *Esclarmonde, daughter of Bernard Clergue (the son of Arnaud and Gauzia Clergue), was married to a man in Comus* [near Montaillou]; *she fell mortally ill; she was brought back to the house of her father, where she remained bedridden for two years before she died. When she was on the point of death, the other Bernard Clergue – brother of the priest – brought into the house the heretic who hereticated Esclarmonde.* The paternal house might also be the infected cell suspected of having transmitted heresy to a daughter who had left to marry elsewhere. Jacques Fournier asked one informer (ii.92), *'Does the witness know whether the paternal* ostal *of the woman Fauré, at Lafage, was ever in the past dishonoured by heresy?'* The maternal *ostal*, very important in the Basque region, could also play an important part in the mountains of Ariège. It was in order to get back the maternal *ostal*, confiscated by the Foix authorities because of the heretical acts of his mother, who was burned for them, that Arnaud Sicre embarked on his career as an informer (ii.21). When it existed as such, the maternal *ostal* created matriarchal structures: the son who inherited it and lived in it tended to take his mother's name, attached to the house itself, rather than that of his father. And the son-in-law who came to live with his wife in her home often took his wife's name instead of the other way round.

Whether it derived from the mother or, as happened more often, from the father, the house in Montaillou, like every self-respecting Pyrenean *domus*, had a head: *cap de casa* in the Andorran region, *dominus domus* in the Latin of the scribes concerned with upper Ariège. The *dominus domus* had jurisdiction over his wife and children; also, in certain circumstances, over his mother. Alazaïs Azéma shows this clearly (i.308): *My son Raymond once used to carry victuals to the* parfaits *in a scrip or a basket; and he never asked my permission to do so, for he was the master of my house*.

Alazaïs Azéma did not feel badly done by in this; she too was a friend of the *parfaits*. But it often happened that the head of the house, peasant or noble, tyrannized over his mother. Stéphanie de Chateauverdun threw herself at the feet of her old friend the heretic Raymond Pierre, a stock-breeder, and said (ii.417–18): '*I am ruined, I have sold my possessions and enslaved my dependents, I live humbly and miserably in my son's house; and I dare not move.*'

Oppression on the part of the head of a *domus* might affect both his wife and an elderly father. Pons Rives of Montaillou ruled his *ostal* with a rod of iron (i.339–41). He drove his wife, Fabrisse, out of the house, saying the devil had sent her to him: ever since she had been there it had been impossible to invite the *parfaits*! As for Bernard Rives, Pons's old father, he did not carry much weight now that the house he lived in was ruled over by his son. One day his daughter Guillemette, wife of the other Pierre Clergue (not the priest), came to borrow a mule to go and fetch corn from Tarascon. But Bernard Rives could only say: '*I dare do nothing without my son's approval. Come back tomorrow, and he will lend you the mule.*' Alazaïs Rives, wife of Bernard and mother of Pons, was equally terrorized by her son, and slipped away.

When the head of a house had a sufficiently powerful, attractive or diabolical personality, submission to him might turn into a personality cult. When Bernard Clergue, in prison, learned of the death of his brother the priest, who even before the death of old Pons Clergue had become the real head of the fraternal house, he collapsed in front of four witnesses, lamenting (ii.285). *'Dead is my god. Dead is my ruler. The traitors Pierre Azéma and Pierre de Gaillac have killed my god.'*

It should be noticed, despite the undeniable predominance of the male sex, that when a woman in Montaillou was mistress of an *ostal* of some importance she had the right to the title of 'Madame' (*domina*). Alazaïs Azéma, a simple peasant, was called 'Madame' by a woman selling cheese. True, the woman hoped to help sales by doing so. Mengarde Clergue, wife of a rich peasant and leading citizen, was also addressed as 'Madame' by the lesser women of her village (i.312–14).

As the mortal ruler of an entity if possible immortal, each head of a family was invested with the right of designating his own successor, at the expense of other descendants or rightful claimants. This seems to have something to do with the Occitan and Roman traditions of the supplementary portion (*preciput*). The power exercised in this respect by heads of houses in Ariège was in contrast to the egalitarian traditions of Normandy and Anjou, where equitable division of an inheritance between all the brothers – and in the case of Anjou, even between all the brothers and sisters – was ferociously insisted upon. But in upper Ariège it is probable that the will of the father usually prevailed: *There lived in Tarascon two brothers called d'Aniaux or de Niaux, and one of them was a friend of the heretics. He had two sons, and one of these sons was a sympathizer with heresy. His father left him a large part of his possessions and gave him in marriage to the daughter of Bertrand Mercier, because her mother was a heretic* (ii.427). The customs of Ariège and Andorra were based on the testamentary freedom of the head of the family: it was the best way of preserving the *domus* against parcelling up into small divisions. But there remained the vexatious problem of the other children, who would not succeed the head of the family. When they left the family house they merely took with them a dowry or 'legitimate portion'. The dowry was eminently personal; it was detached from the original *domus* of the young woman when she got married, but did not disappear into the undivided mass of the couple's possessions. If the husband died first, the dowry remained the property of the widow, and not of the husband's or the wife's heirs. As Béatrice de Planissoles said after her first widowhood (i.233), *Pierre Clergue the priest sent me a messenger with a document relating to my first marriage, containing the assignation of my dowry. I had once deposited this document with the priest. I did not care a jot whether he gave it back to me or not, because I had already left the heirs of my first husband!* No doubt she meant she had left them with her dowry under her arm.

Dowries presented a major problem in a rather poor society. The prevailing degree of economic stagnation turned every daughter's marriage into a tragedy for the *domus*, which was threatened with a loss of substance. The problem caused Pierre Clergue sleepless nights, so attached was he to the indivisibility of the *ostal*. His preoccupation even drove him to the justification of incest: '*Look*,' said the priest to his mistress in a moment of affectionate abandon and ideological ferment (i.225), '*we are four brothers (I am a priest, and do not want a wife). If my brothers Guillaume and Bernard had married our sisters Esclarmonde and Guillemette, our house would not have been ruined because of the capital [averium] carried away by those sisters as dowry; our ostal would have remained intact, and with just one wife brought into our house for our brother Bernard, we would have had enough wives, and our ostal would have been richer than it is today.*'

Incidentally, this apology for incest also explains the (non-chaste) celibacy of churchmen, and the concubinage frequent in Montaillou. The argument derives from the fear inspired in every aware and organized *domus* by the thought of losing its 'detachable adjuncts', among which were the dowries taken away by the daughters. Also involved was the *fratrisia*, fraternal portion, due to each son who, because he was not the eldest or for some other reason, did not become head of the household. He was thus disinherited except for the *fratrisia* accorded to him by way of compensation by the *domus* or the head of the *domus*: '*I lost my fraternal portion* [fratrisia] *in Montaillou, and was afraid* [because of the Inquisition] *to return to the village to claim it*', said Pierre Maury, in Catalonia, in a conversation with Arnaud Sicre (ii.30).

All the evidence, then, suggests that the primacy of the *domus* was highly characteristic of Occitan and mountain liberty. It is significant that in the thirteenth century, when some traces of serfdom still survived in Languedoc, the settlers at Mas d'Azil, and probably those in many other country farms, became free automatically once they had built their own house.

Central though it was in the culture of upper Ariège, the *domus* was more notable for its material and emotional investments than for its market value: a village house was worth 40 *livres tournois*, i.e. only twice the price of a complete Bible, twice the wages of a team of hired assassins, and almost twenty times less than the amount of money Bernard Clergues spent to free his brother the priest from the clutches of the Inquisition. The dowries and fraternal portions detached from it, small as they were, and despite the compensation represented by dowries brought into the family, always threatened to impoverish the *domus*, if not ruin it altogether. Moreover, the forces of repression, which well understood local ethnographical structures, used to destroy the houses of heretics, burning them or razing them to the ground. It only needed a woman with a long tongue to look through a crack in the door and see Pierre Authié converting a sick person to heresy, and lo and behold the paternal or maternal *domus* at Prades d'Aillon was demolished by the Inquisition (i.278). This being the case, the law of silence was observed as far as possible. Raymond Roques and old Guillemette 'Belote' were united in their advice to women who were too talkative (i.310): *If you don't want the walls of your house knocked down, keep your mouth shut*. If the house of a convicted heretic was not reduced to ashes, at the best it would be confiscated by the Foix authorities, now obedient to the Inquisition's every whim.

Despite its notional durability the Montaillou house was in reality a flimsy and fragile construction. The central and essential part of the *domus* was the kitchen (*foganha*), its rafters covered with hams hung out of reach of the cat. It was here that the neighbours came, like Alazaïs Azéma, a simple body despite her title of 'Madame', to borrow a light for the fire, the precious fire which was covered up at night for fear an accident might reduce the *ostal* to ashes (i.307, 317). The fire was watched over by the housewife (*focaria*), the 'woman at the hearth', as the priests' concubines were called in the diocese of Palhars.[1] But the man of the house did not leave the women in sole charge of the fire: it was his job to break sticks for kindling (*frangere teza*). The hearth was surrounded by cooking utensils – earthenware pots, pans, cauldrons, jugs and basins, the latter sometimes decorated. There were never enough utensils, particularly of metal, but what was needed could, in the traditional Montaillou way, be borrowed from the neighbours. Near

1 i.253. Apparently the fire did not burn in a chimney but in a hearth in the middle of the room. Was there a hole in the roof?

the hearth stood, by way of dining furniture, a table and benches, the latter also used for sitting round the fire in the evening. Sometimes, but not always, the use of this furniture corresponded to a fairly rigorous segregation by sex and by age, such as still existed until quite recently in lower Languedoc and in Corsica. The shepherd Jean Maury, son of a Montaillou peasant, tells of an evening meal in his father's *foganha*, a somewhat more distinguished meal than usual because the *parfait* Philippe d'Alayrac was a guest (ii.471): *It was winter. Montaillou was covered with a thick layer of snow. My father, Raymond Maury, my brother Guillaume, the heretic Philippe d'Alayrac, and Guillaume Belot* [invited as a neighbour] *dined at the table. I and my other brothers, my mother and my sisters, ate sitting round the fire.* The kitchen, as our documents expressly say, was the house within the house, the *domus* within the *ostal*, where people ate, died, were converted to heresy and told each other the secrets of the Faith and the gossip of the village (i.268–9). *In those days*, says Raymonde Arsen, a servant in the house of the Belots (i.372), *Bernard Clergue (the* bayle, *brother of the priest) used to come to the house of Raymond Belot and talk to his mother-in-law Guillemette Belot in the house called the kitchen* ['in domo vocata la foganha'] *and they used to send me away for a while (so that I should not hear their conversation).*

So the most intimate part of the house, the *foganha*, fitted inside the larger house, or *ostal*, like one of a set of Russian dolls.

Sometimes people slept in the kitchen. But more often they slept, in several beds, in rooms surrounding the kitchen or on the first floor (*solier*). Was a Montaillou house usually a roomy one, up there in the spaciousness of the mountains? It seems to have been slightly larger, anyhow, than its counterpart in Burgundy, which archaeological evidence has shown to be so small.

Excavations would very likely soon reveal the layout of medieval houses in Montaillou, vestiges of which can still be discerned at the foot of the château. Until these are undertaken we must rely on documentary evidence throwing light on the way the rooms were arranged. In Prades d'Aillon, a village analogous to Montaillou because it was so close and shared the same way of life, Raymonde Michel describes the house of her father Pierre: *In the cellar of our house there were two beds, one where my mother and father slept and the other for any heretic passing through. The cellar was next to the kitchen and had a door leading into it. No one slept on the floor above the cellar. My brothers and I slept in a room on the other side of the kitchen, so that the kitchen was between the children's room and the cellar where our parents slept. The cellar had an outside door opening on to the threshing floor.*[1]

It was in a cellar (*sotulum*) of this kind, containing both beds and barrels, that Béatrice de Planissoles, then living with her second husband, Othon de Lagleize, made love for the last time with Clergue, the priest of Montaillou, who had come to her house under an assumed name. The servant, Sybille Teisseire, Béatrice's fellow countrywoman from Montaillou and her accomplice, kept watch at the door of the cellar while Béatrice, between the casks, *mingled her body with that of the priest.*

Many passages confirm the existence of a cellar beside the kitchen, and also of bedrooms which could be locked and contained beds and benches. Each room was intended for one or two people, who might sleep together or in separate beds. In the house of the Maurys, simple peasants who were weavers and shepherds, the elder brother Guillaume Maury had a room of his own; similarly old Guillemette 'Belote', the widowed mother, in the house of the Belot sons. Clergue the priest had a room of his own in the big family house, which was large enough to have an antechamber on the first floor as well. The bedrooms had windows, without glass but with wooden shutters. At night, anyone wanting to attract the attention of the people inside would throw a pebble at the shutters. More important people, and intellectuals such as notaries and doctors – there was neither the one nor the other in Montaillou – also had an office (*scriptorium*) in their houses, and it was there that they slept.

In general, the fact of having a *solier* (the first floor above the kitchen, communicating with the ground floor by means of a ladder) was an external sign of wealth. To build a *solier*, as did the shoemaker Arnaud Vital, showed that you were going up in the social scale, or at least that you thought you were. As far as we know, only the Clergues, the Vitals (though they weren't all that rich) and the Belots had a house with a *solier*. The *foganha*, heart of the *domus*, was built of stone. The *solier*, and the offices on the ground floor, were lightly built of wood and daub.

But kitchen, *solier*, bedrooms and cellar were not all. The farmers of Montaillou set aside part of the house for the animals. *Eighteen years*

1 i.401. The richer houses, such as that belonging to the Clergue family, and perhaps the Belots also, had one or two bedrooms on the first floor.

ago, said Alazaïs Azéma (i.311), *when I had just brought my pigs out of my house, I met Raymond Belot leaning on his stick in the square in front of the château. He said to me: 'Come into my house.'*

I answered: 'No – I have left my door open.'

This passage suggests that people and pigs lived together in the same house; they may even have used the same door. Similarly, Pons Rives, son of Bernard Rives, kept his mule and his ass in his house. Guillemette Benet shut up her oxen in her house when they had been brought home from ploughing in the evening. Guillaume Bélibaste thought of bringing up a lamb *in domo sua.* Every morning Jean Pellissier, a small shepherd from Montaillou, brought his sheep out of the house. When they were ill, men used to sleep with the animals, perhaps because of the warmth they gave out. *Guillaume Belot,* says Bernard Benet (i.401), *brought Guillaume Authié the heretic to the place where my father, Guillaume Benet, lay ill; it was in the part of the house where the cattle slept.*

The house had various offices, including an adjacent yard or poultry yard, where people could sit among the chickens and take the sun. The yard was generally decorated by a dung-heap, on which an inquisitive servant might climb to spy on what her employers and the *parfaits* were saying to each other in the *solier.* Beyond the yard was the threshing-floor. The biggest farms, like that of the Martys at Junac, and some others, possessed both yard and garden, a stable for oxen (*boal*), a dove-cote, a pigsty near the garden, and barns (*bordes*) for straw on the other side of the yard or near a spring; also a sheep-pen (*cortal*), either adjacent to or at some distance from the *domus.* But these big farms were hardly typical of Montaillou. On the street side there was often, just as today, a bench or table set in the open air beside the door, for people to sit and warm themselves in the sun or chat with their neighbours. The problem of how to shut up the house was not always satisfactorily resolved: when there was only a ground floor, which was often the case, you could lift the edge of the shingle roof with your head and look in to see what was going on in the kitchen (ii.366). (The roof-cum-balcony was flat, or almost, and so could be used for keeping sheaves of corn or as a platform for the women to shout to each other: in the Catalan Pyrenees it did not become a sloping roof until the sixteenth century.) To enter the house one sometimes had only to move aside a plank or a slat. The walls were so thin that everything could be heard from one room to the next, including heretical conversations between a lady and her lover (i.227). When two houses were adjacent a hole might be made to enable people to pass from one to the other. *Guillemette Benet must know a good deal about heretics*, alleged Raymond Testanière (i.463), *because in the days when the people of Montaillou were rounded up by the Inquisition of Carcassonne there was a hole between the house of Bernard Rives (where the heretics had their chapel) and the house of Guillaume Benet. By means of this hole the said heretics passed from one house to the other*. Montaillou was a veritable ant-hill. Another direct passage had been made, enabling the *parfaits* to slip unseen from the house of Bernard Rives, mentioned above, to that of Raymond Belot.

Over and above these not always impressive material appearances, what interests us chiefly here is the *ostal*'s content of people, of souls. The population of the *domus* often and in various ways went beyond the strict framework of the family of the parental couple and their children. First of all, there were the servants. Jean Pellissier, a shepherd from Montaillou, lived away from the village with various people at various times in order to learn or establish himself in his trade. Then he came home again, but instead of living in the house where he was born he dwelt for three years as a shepherd in the house of Bernard and Guillemette Maurs, a married couple. We do not know what wages he was paid. In the same *domus* lived Jean's brother Bernard, not a shepherd but a ploughboy (*labarator vel arator*). There were also Bernard Maurs's two children and his mother, Guillemette Maurs the elder, now a widow (iii.161). So this was not a strictly nuclear family: it consisted of a couple, two children, a grandmother and two servants. The structural mixture did not end there. Next to Bernard Maurs's house was that of his brother Pierre Maurs, another house with Cathar sympathies living in a state of open warfare with Pierre Clergue. (It was Pierre's wife, Mengarde Maurs, who was to have her tongue cut out for speaking ill of the priest.) The two Maurs houses, at once fraternal and neighbourly, formed a unit of friendship and sociability: *A the time when I lived with Bernard Maurs*, said the servant and shepherd Jean Pellissier (iii.76), *I often used to visit the house of Pierre Maurs*.

In addition to the husband and wife, the children, the other descendants, forebears or collaterals and the male domestics, the house might be extended to include one or more female servants. Some of these were simply illegitimate children, such as were employed regularly in the Clergue *domus*. Thus the illegitimate Brune Pourcel was the daughter of Prades Tavernier, a heretic weaver who became a *parfait* and did not hesitate, from time to time, to let his daughter worship him, according to the Cathar rite. After her service in the Clergue household, from which she brought away several spicy details for the Inquisition, Brune Pourcel married and was left a widow. She then lived in her own very indigent *ostal*, where she spent her time begging, cadging or borrowing hay, wood, turnips or a sieve to bolt the flour. Brune Pourcel was riddled with superstition: when she worked for the Clergues she took hair and nail-parings from the corpses of her employers; she was afraid of owls and other night birds, devils flying over the roof to carry away the soul of Na Roqua ('Madame' Roques), recently dead. But it is only fair to add that many other inhabitants of the village shared Brune's beliefs.

Another servant who was an illegitimate child was Mengarde, the natural daughter of Bernard Clergue. She lived with her father, and was in charge of making bread and washing the shirts of the *parfaits* in the brook – they were made of finer linen than that worn by the simple peasants of Montaillou (i.416–17). She later married a farmer.

The servant maids (not illegitimate) who worked in the house of the Belots are better known to us than those of the Clergue *domus*: a good example is Raymonde Arsen, sentenced in 1324 to wear a double yellow cross because of her connections with the heretics. Young Raymonde came from a poor but not destitute *ostal* in Prades d'Aillon and was the sister of Arnaud Vital, a cobbler in Montaillou who was also parish guardian of the harvests (*messier*). In her early youth, around 1306, she went to work as a servant in town, in the house of Bonet de la Coste in Pamiers (i.379ff.). Here she met one day Raymond Belot of Montaillou, her first cousin (i.458); he had come to market to buy a load of grain. Raymond suggested to Raymonde that she should come and work in his house as a servant. The Belot house, which was considered very wealthy (i.389), included Raymond himself, his brother Guillaume, his sister Raymonde, and another brother, Bernard, who was about to be married to Guillemette, née Benet, the daughter of Guillaume Benet, whose house stood a few yards away from that of the Belots. Once again the links of neighbourhood, marriage, cousinship and domestic service mutually reinforced one another. Also in the Belots' house lived Raymond's mother, Guillemette, a widow. So in all the house contained a married couple, their children, the husband's grown-up brothers and sister, all unmarried, his old widowed mother and a servant girl. There were also several others, of whom we shall speak later.[1]

Raymonde Arsen explained to Jacques Fournier why the Belots took her on as a servant (i.370): '*Raymond and his brothers wanted to give their sister Raymonde in marriage to Bernard Clergue, the priest's brother.*' To ally the Belot brothers to the Clergue brothers by means of a sister was to weld together two of the most influential groups of brothers in Montaillou. It also supplemented the Belot-Benet axis already mentioned, and turned it into a triple alliance of the Benets, Belots and Clergues. To the old links of friendship were joined the even stronger bonds of marriage. Mengarde Clergue, Bernard's mother, and Guillemette Belot, Raymonde's mother, were old friends long before their children got married (i.393). Once again, as in the case of the Belots and the Benets, marriage sprang out of neighbourhood: the Belot house was only across the street from the Clergue house (i.372, 392). But despite these favourable beginnings, the triple alliance (which was also a quadruple alliance – with heresy – since the Benets were allied to the Authiés) did not stand up well to the attacks of the Inquisition.[2] It tells us something, however, about the local attitude to marriage.

So the Belots took on a servant, Raymonde Arsen, to make up for the departure of a sister, Raymonde Belot. The functions of the sister before she left must have closely resembled those of a maid of all work. The taking on of Raymonde Arsen occurred at a special point in the family cycle (the departure of a sister), just as the Maur family's engagement of a ploughman and a shepherd (Jean Pellissier) took place at a time when the children of the young farming couple, who lived with the husband's mother, were still too young to work in the fields.

So the proposal made by Raymond Belot to Raymonde Arsen in

---

1 The evidence on the structure of 'more than nuclear' families concerns chiefly old widowed mothers living with their sons; but there were some cases of 'matrilocal' affiliation where a mother-in-law lived with her son-in-law (i.260 and *passim*).

2 We may recall that it was through the *domus* of Guillaume Benet that heresy was re-introduced into Montaillou around 1300, by the Authiés, back from Lombardy (i.471). The Authiés and the Benets were closely linked by a marriage between the two families (i.233).

Bonet de la Coste's house in Pamiers that day stood at the intersection of several strategies: strategies of family, marriage and business. Raymonde Arsen gave an evasive reply (i.370): '*I cannot accept your offer for the moment, for I have made a contract with my master Bonet up to the next Feast of St John the Baptist* [24 June] *and now it is only Easter . . . I will see, at the Feast of St John, whether or not I shall come to your house.*'

This little dialogue illustrates the modernity of the contractual bond in upper Ariège: serfdom was non-existent or at the most insignificant, and feudal dependence did not weigh very heavily. At the end of June, Raymonde Arsen made up her mind; she gave notice to her master, Bonet, and went to fetch her natural daughter, Alazaïs, whom she had put out to nurse at Saint-Victor. Then, with her bundle over her shoulder and her baby in her arms, she went up into the mountains which overlooked Pamiers from the south. When she reached Prades, near Montaillou, she entrusted her daughter to another nurse, also named Alazaïs, who took the child to the village of Aston (now in Ariège). Raymonde Arsen herself then went down again into the present department of Aude, to help get in the harvest in the Arques valley.[1] After that she went back to Prades d'Aillon, which, being higher up, gathered the harvest later. So during one short summer Raymonde Arsen lived as an itinerant child-mother, harvester and outsider; she only left this wandering existence to settle as a servant in the house *of Raymond Belot and his brothers*,[2] which Raymond Belot had just left, as arranged, before the harvest, to marry Bernard Clergue.

In the Belot family, where she remained for a year (the traditional length for a contract of employment), Raymonde Arsen was relegated outside the house in the strict sense of the term. Her bed, which she got ready every evening, was set amongst the straw in the little barn on the far side of the courtyard. Her daily work consisted chiefly in looking after the bread in the family oven and in washing the clothes. True, Guillemette 'Belote', the old mother, undertook part of these tasks: with her own hands she made the fine bread for the visiting *parfaits*, as

1 i.370–71: Arques and Montaillou–Prades complemented each other in seasonal harvest work and transhumance; also in the exchange of Cathar ideas.
2 The house was also referred to (i.458) as *the house of Bernard Belot and his brothers*. The headship of the family was thus spread over or divided between the two brothers.

in the case of Guillaume Authié, a faithful frequenter of the Belot house who made long stays in the *solier*, clad in dim blue and dark green (i.458). Guillaume Authié's presence was the occasion for a veritable family group. The gathering took place on the occasion of the marriage between Bernard Belot and Guillemette Benet (i.371) which, as we have seen, crystallized a whole network of previous relationships: Guillaume Benet, father of the bride and neighbour of the Belots, was also, and had been for a long time, godfather of Guillaume Belot, brother of the bridegroom (i.389). Guillaume Authié descended from his perch in the *solier* and came down into the kitchen where all the rest of the party were met. The brothers Belot were sitting on a bench. The women of the *domus* sat apart on another, lower bench. Raymonde Arsen sat a little way off by the fire, holding the baby belonging to the young Alazaïs, Raymond Belot's other sister, married and living elsewhere but come for the wedding (i.370–71). Raymonde Arsen later left the Belots' house and married Prades den Arsen, taking his family name, the one by which we know her. She settled in Prades d'Aillon in her husband's house, thus completing the circle and returning to her original village (i.370–77). Note the fact that her having had an illegitimate baby was no obstacle when it came to finding a husband.

After Raymonde Arsen had left, there remained another 'female domestic' in the Belot house, who also served as a concubine. Raymonde Testanière, otherwise known as Vuissane, of Montaillou, remained for three years (1304–1307) in the Belot house (i.455–70). She was mistress to Bernard Belot, her employer, and had at least two children by him, one of them named Bernard also. Apparently this subsidiary liaison, made official by co-residence, did not shock anybody, either in the *domus* or in the village. (Bernard Belot, Vuissane's lover, was a very enterprising fellow in general: he tried to rape the wife of his fellow-citizen Guillaume Authié of Montaillou, for which attempt he was imprisoned (i.411) and only released on payment of a 20-*livres* fine, paid to the officers of the Comte de Foix.[1] This incident caused an understandable, if not lasting, cooling off in the relationship between Bernard Belot and Guillaume Authié.)

Vuissane Testanière certainly did not have much luck with Bernard Belot, her lover, landlord and employer. She gave him children, and

1 Twenty *livres* was equivalent to the value of 40 sheep, or half a house. This Guillaume Authié should not be confused with Guillaume Authié the *parfait*.

literally worked herself to death for the family in the hope that its head
would marry her. But Bernard would only marry a heretic from Montaillou whom he could trust, such as the daughter of the Benets. And
Vuissane, unfortunately for her, had no Cathar tendencies in those days.
Also, it need hardly be added, the Testanières were much less well off
than the Belots.

As well as domestics of both sexes, a house in Montaillou, especially
if it was rich, might also contain a lodger, usually unmarried. The house
of the Belots, which was large and full of people, at one time sheltered
Arnaud Vital, a cobbler in the village, brother of the servant girl
Raymonde Arsen. Arnaud was a heretic and used to guide the *parfaits*
through the mountains, wearing a blue overtunic for the purpose. In
exchange for rent or some domestic duties, he had a bedroom in the
Belots' house, or perhaps just a bed which he might have had to share
with someone else. His workshop was in another house in the parish.
Like many cobblers, he was a village Don Juan. He was the lover of
Alazaïs Fauré, who loved him and whom he instructed in the heretic
faith. She then undertook to convert her father and brother. One day in
the Belots' house, where he was a lodger and she a servant, Arnaud
played the 'hen trick' on Vuissane Testanière. He gave her a hen to kill –
a deed which from the point of view of the Cathars, who believed in
metempsychosis, was a crime. Vuissane tried to kill the fowl, but could
not bring herself to do it. Having thus established his power, Arnaud
tried to rape Vuissane there and then in the Belots' house. She easily
stopped him, objecting that this would be incest (i.457–8). '*Are you not
ashamed? You forget that I am mistress to your first cousin (and landlord)
Bernard Belot, and that I have children by him.*' Arnaud nevertheless
continued to live under the same roof, and even married another servant
of the *domus*, also named Raymonde. It was an unhappy marriage.
Arnaud, in the tradition of certain husbands in the Pyrenees, was
strangely silent with his young wife, but would stay away whole nights
visiting new mistresses, such as Raymonde Rives and Alazaïs Gavela.[1]
But at least this marriage marked the end of Arnaud's residence as
lodger or tenant with the Belots. Two months after they were married,
the Vital couple left the Belots' house and set up in their own *domus*,

---

1 This Raymonde, when Arnaud Vital died and left her a widow, married Bernard
Guilhou. She became delouser to Mengarde Clergue and her son Pierre, and even,
temporarily, the latter's mistress (ii.223–5).

which prospered. One of the unwritten rules of the Montaillou *ostal* was that it might harbour all kinds of adults but, in the long term, it generally contained only one married couple.[1]

With this one restriction, the Belots' *ostal* was Liberty Hall. Maid-servants, lodgers and *parfaits* rubbed shoulders with the family; some fornicated or even committed rape; others converted as many people as they could to heresy. It was a rich and complex *domus*. Like other important *domus* in Montaillou, including that of the Maury family, it was noted for its sense of hospitality, which implied duties on both sides. To utter threats under the roof of someone who had received you in his house was considered boorish: '*You dare to threaten me in my own* domus!' cried Guillemette Maury, addressing her young cousin, Jean Maury from Montaillou, who though he was her guest had quarrelled with her and threatened to have her locked up (ii.484–5). Guillemette tried to revenge herself for this impoliteness by poisoning her cousin with salts of mercury – an attempt which failed.

Montaillou contained some truncated nuclear families (widows living alone, or with one child), some nuclear couples with children, some couples with several children and one parent (a widowed grandfather, or, more often, grandmother) and some groups of brothers, sometimes together with an elderly mother, sometimes with both parents, in which only one of the brothers would be married (the other brothers and sisters, even if they were grown up, would remain unmarried all the time the group continued to live together). The purely nuclear family was per-haps the most common, but it did not have a local monopoly.

Family structure, in fact, varied chronologically. The same family was successively extended, then nuclear, then extended, and so on. Let us take an imaginary family called Vidal, which resembles as closely as possible the families Clergue, Belot, Benet, Rives and others in Mon-taillou which are known to us. To begin with the family is nuclear, con-sisting of the Vidal couple and their children. At the death of the father we have a truncated nucleus, which soon becomes a phratry, the posi-tion of the brothers gaining in importance as the surviving parent, Guillemette, withdraws to the position of respected widow-matriarch living half apart in a room specially assigned to her. She still keeps an

1 This general but not absolute rule derives from the chronological structure of the family cycle.

eye on the household, but one of her grown-up sons succeeds to the position of head (*chef d'ostal*).

Then the family becomes again more or less extended: one of the brothers, Bernard, marries, and the new couple live for a while with the other brothers and the elderly mother. Subsequently the *domus* becomes nuclear once more: old Guillemette dies and all the brothers except Bernard leave the family house. They either try to build their own *ostal* elsewhere or they enter into another household, probably through marriage. Or again, they might become shepherds – or prisoners of the Inquisition. Bernard Vidal, his wife and their children remain alone as a simple and complete nucleus.

The taking on and dismissal of servants coincides with turning-points in the family cycle, such as the moment when the children become old enough to work, or the time when a daughter leaves home to get married. In some very rare cases we have a fully extended family, a multi-generational group including both mother and father and a younger couple who are their successors. In Montaillou only the Rives family corresponds to this arrangement, and even here a quarrel broke up this group when the daughter-in-law was turned out because of temperamental incompatibility.

Another version of the fully extended family was the multi-fraternal group. This included two brothers, or a brother and sister, with their respective spouses. They lived in a group of four, together with their children (there is no instance of this arrangement in Montaillou itself, though I have come across several true *frérèches* – sibling groups – in other localities in upper Ariège at the period with which we are concerned).

Although these forms of family extension were conceptually possible, they were not very frequent in Montaillou. Elderly adults, especially the men, died too soon to form a 'quadriga' with a younger couple. And neither custom nor the somewhat restricted scope of agriculture encouraged *frérèches*. They did become more common later, during the fifteenth century in the southerly estates enlarged through depopulation, and, at the beginning of the Renaissance, in the big share-cropping areas of Tuscany and the Bourbonnais.

Finally, the *domus* cannot be understood without its genealogical links, which connected it with other related, living *domus* through consanguinity (*parentela*). These bonds also linked the *domus* with the past, under the auspices of the lineage (*genus*) of the family, which was the *domus* looked at against the background of the past four generations at the most.

Some authors have seen lineage as one of the most important values of ancient societies. This is certainly true in the case of the nobility. But, as regards Montaillou, the sense of lineal continuity was a local and rural one, not of primary importance. It was subordinate to the value embodied in the *domus* itself, in its restricted sense of a family and domestic group of living people residing under the same roof. In Montaillou, and in upper Ariège in general, the sense of *genus* was quite vivid, but no more than that: the peasants spoke of someone belonging to a race of priests, a race of liars, a race of heretics, a race of curmudgeons, or a race of lepers. (*Genus* is here translated by the word 'race', though it would be more correct and scientific to talk of '*lines* of priests' etc.) The inhabitants of the Comté de Foix regarded leprosy as an example of genetic or lineal continuity extending over four generations, though in fact, with leprosy, the continuity was only pseudo-genetic, arising as it did through infection. Even the humblest were aware of lineal continuity. The shepherd Pierre Maury of Montaillou implied that a lineage was either all good or all bad, all Cathar or all spy; but Raymond Issaura of Larnat, a leading citizen and a *parfait*, answered philosophically, referring to the *genus* of the Baille-Sicres, which had produced an outstanding spy, that: *In every lineage there are some decent people and some bad people.*

In general, the *genus* (or, as our villagers sometimes saw it, the *domus*, taken in the long-term sense of lineal continuity) was the bearer of the family name, transmitted in the paternal, sometimes the maternal, line.

More present or influential than the *genus*-lineage aspect was consanguinity, made up of cousins and relations of all kinds living in other *domus* in the same village or other localities near or far. When the shepherd Pierre Maury of Montaillou successfully kidnapped his sister Guillemette (with her consent) from her bullying husband he soon began to wonder anxiously (iii.149–53), *What should we do if some of the husband's relations followed us to get Guillemette back again?*

The *domus* was thus at the centre of a whole network of links of varying importance: they included alliance through marriage, family relationship, friendship arising out of common hatreds and sometimes embodied in invitations to be godmother or godfather to children. Last but not least the network included relationships of neighbourhood.

Neighbourhood could work for the destruction of a neighbour, against whom all the others might unite: *Four of my neighbours, including a woman and a priest, plotted against me to make me lose my possessions and to denounce me to the Inquisition as a heretic*, said Arnaud de Savignan, a plasterer from Tarascon (iii.432). But family solidarity, often inseparably linked with neighbourhood structures, seems to have been very important. When Pierre Casal accused the Cathar missionaries Pierre and Guillaume Authié of having stolen a cow, and threatened to denounce them, the whole clan of Belots and Benets, connected with one another and with the Authiés by marriage, were up in arms and threatened with death any man or woman who denounced the missionaries. *'Take care!'* said Guillaume Benet to Alazaïs Azéma of Montaillou (i.318). *'If you denounce them, you are dead!'* Raymond Belot was even more blunt. *'One of these days,'* he told Alazaïs (ii.64), *'they'll find you with your head separated from your body.'*

A typical example of family solidarity was the vendetta of Guillaume Maurs. He was the son of a *domus* in Montaillou which the Clergue family determined to destroy. Guillaume Maurs, his father and his brother were all arrested by the Inquisition in August 1308, together with the rest of the population of the village. The mass arrest was the result of denunciations in which Clergue the priest, changing course and renouncing his former Cathar friendships, was implicated. Guillaume was subsequently let out of prison, though two other members of his family remained there. One day, near Montaillou, he came face to face with the priest, and seized the occasion to reproach him vehemently for his conduct (ii.171). Pierre Clergue, who knew all about family solidarity, replied with equal vehemence: *'I will see that you all rot in Carcassonne prison – all the Maurs, you, your father, your brother, all that belong to your domus.'*

He more than kept his word: it was because of him, acting through his brother the *bayle*, that Mengarde Maurs, Guillaume's mother, had her tongue cut out for 'false witness'. He and other members of the Clergue family hunted Guillaume Maurs up hill and down dale in an attempt to get him arrested (ii.176, 178). He conducted a veritable vendetta against the whole Maurs *ostal*, a vendetta more 'domiciliary' than the true

Corsican vendetta, later, which was more a matter of general blood relationship.

The exchange between Pierre Clergue and Guillaume Maurs ended symmetrically with Maurs threatening reprisals. '*I will be revenged,*' he cried, '*so beware of me and of all my supporters!*' They went their separate ways, Guillaume to search for aid among his brothers and friends and the allies of his friends.

In 1309 Guillaume Maurs took refuge in Ax-les-Thermes. His brother, Raymond Maurs, and Jean Benet, from another *domus* victimized by the Clergue family although linked to them by marriage, joined him there. The three of them all swore on bread and on wine to be revenged; they would kill the priest, pooling their meagre resources in order to do so (ii.171). This was a genuine pact of brotherhood, with its oath on bread and on wine and its pooling of possessions. Between 1309 and 1317 the conspirators made several attempts to murder Pierre Clergue, either themselves or through hired assassins. Guillaume Maurs, the outlawed shepherd, was so eager for revenge that when he went to confession the priests refused to give him communion because of the hatred he nourished in his heart against Pierre Clergue (ii.173). Even if he had forgotten it, his friends and fellow shepherds would have reminded him. One day when Guillaume was quarrelling with Pierre Maury, the latter reminded him (ii.178), '*Fight against the priest of Montaillou and not against us. He will give you plenty to think about.*' Only the waning enthusiasm of one of the conspirators (Pierre Maurs) and the lack of suitable opportunity caused the final murder attempt against Pierre Clergue to fail. It was not for want of trying: Guillaume Maurs had hired two Catalan assassins and brought them specially from Gerona, promising them 500 *sous*, all included, if they succeeded (ii.190).

The Maurs vendetta was an extreme example. But family solidarity played a part even in the most prosaic cases. Two examples will suffice. A relation by marriage interceded with the Foix officials and activated networks of friends in support of one of his relatives who had been accused of rape (i.280). When Pierre Maury wanted to buy a hundred sheep which he did not wish to pay for straight away, he offered his own brother Jean as security and guarantee (ii.185).

But although the *domus*, in certain circumstances assisted by its relations, could assemble all its forces against a person, a cause, or another *domus*, it could also be subject to internal conflict and tension.

This was especially serious when mother and son, or mother and daughter, were separated by the barrier of heresy. Arnaud Baille-Sicre, for example, railed against the memory of his mother, Sybille, since it was because of her heresy that the maternal *ostal* had been confiscated by the Inquisition. As for Emersende, Guillemette Maury's heretical sister, she took part in a conspiracy against her daughter Jeanne Befayt, a good Catholic, a plot by which the mother's faithful friends were to kill the daughter by pushing her off the bridge of the Mala Molher (ii.64, 65).

These two cases of disintegration of the *domus* were the result of family disintegration caused by the exodus of the heretics to Catalonia. In upper Ariège, before the great departure to the south, Jeanne Befayt had practised Catharism with her mother and father, like an obedient daughter. In Montaillou, the Inquisition might somehow succeed in ranging one *domus* against another even though they were connected by a series of marriages: Jacques Fournier managed to set the Clergue family against the Benets. But blood relationship held out better than marriage relationship; the authorities in Carcassonne and Pamiers could not turn brother against brother. The break-up of the Montaillou *domus* was only a hypothesis; Pierre Clergue played with the idea only to amuse himself and for the edification of Béatrice de Planissoles during one of their fireside chats (i.225). '*When the world began brothers knew their sisters carnally, but when many brothers had one or two pretty sisters, each brother wanted to have her or them. Hence many murders. That is why*', concluded the Rousseau of Montaillou, '*the sexual act between brother and sister had to be forbidden.*' But Pierre Clergue could sleep soundly: the Montaillou *domus* might be threatened with destruction by the activities of Bishop Fournier, but there was no possibility of its being broken up from within.

The *domus* of Montaillou belonged to different social and economic strata. Some houses were comparatively well off or even rich (the Benets, the Belots, the Clergues) and some were poor, or thought to be poor (the Maurys, the Bailles, the Testanières, the Pellissiers and some of the Martys). The poor families probably formed a large minority in the village. In the absence of land registers it is hard to arrive at any statistics, but various texts suggest that there was a difference of fifty to one between the most opulent (non-noble) *ostal* in the parish – that of the Clergue brothers – and the possessions of a poor man. The well-to-do might own eight to ten hectares of land and meadows per *domus*. Poor people might own one or two hectares, or less. Such differences did not prevent social intercommunication, but they did sometimes turn it rather sour, even when there was no real class struggle.

Local differences in wealth expressed themselves in a number of ways. There was the amount of liquid money a man possessed: little, very little or none. But above all it was a matter of ownership of land; and of ownership of sheep. The man who owned a few dozen sheep was fairly well off. But at a lower level almost every family, except the poorest widows, owned at least a few ewes, which lent security to the household and a certain minimum dignity to the *domus*. Other decisive criteria were the presence of oxen in the stable, and of at least one mule or ass for ploughing and for transporting goods; whether there were living-in servants; whether the children were apprenticed as shepherds or domestics; whether the house had a first floor; whether there was an ample supply of kitchen utensils; and whether there were stocks of hay, grain and tools. Illegitimate children and children who were not heirs all tended to sink to the status of servant or shepherd, and were likely to find themselves ultimately, at the end of a process of downward social mobility, at the head of a poor *domus*. The criteria of wealth and poverty were more complex and more general than the later contrast between farmers and day-labourers in the north of France, who were separated by the possession or otherwise of horses for ploughing. There are two simple reasons for this geographical difference: in Montaillou there was no large-scale tenant farming as such and arable farming was not more important than sheep-raising. Moreover, such ploughing as took place was not done by horses but by oxen, mules and asses, typical of farming on a more modest scale.

At the top of this social and economic stratification and at the centre of the pattern of *domus* there sat, like a spider in the midst of its toils, the ruling *ostal* of the Clergue family. Demographically speaking, the Clergue houses dominated the village. According to the figures, admittedly incomplete, which can be derived from the Fournier records, there were at least twenty-two people bearing the name of Clergue in Montaillou. A long way behind came the Maurs (thirteen), the Martys (eleven), the Bailles, Belots, Benets, Azémas (ten), the Pellissiers (eight), the Rives and the Argelliers (seven), the Authiés and the Forts (six), and the Bars and the Vitals (four). But, of course, these figures mean nothing in themselves. What contributed to the predominance of a *domus* was wealth, influence and connections of patronage and 'friendship'. The *domus* of the Clergues had all these.

It would be instructive to visit this *domus*, but until excavations are undertaken at Montaillou we must be content with a glance through the eyes of Fabrisse Rives, wine-seller in the village. One day, finding herself short of measures for doling out the wine, she decided to borrow one from her neighbours the Clergues. At the entrance to their *ostal* she first met three elderly local matrons sunning themselves by the door. They were Mengarde Clergue, the priest's mother, and her two friends Guillemette Belot and Na Roqua (i.327), all solid pillars of Catharism. Fabrisse entered and went up to the anteroom (*aula*) on the first floor, situated above a little half-underground shed (*sotulum*). In the anteroom Fabrisse passed Pierre Clergue and in his room she saw not only the famous wine-measure on the table, but also the *parfait* Guillaume Authié, who was, not very assiduously, hiding there.

With its anteroom, first floor, portico (iii.58) and individual bedrooms, the Clergue house was one of the largest in the village. It had plenty of land. The *bayle* Bernard Clergue, the priest's brother and a co-resident member of the domus (i.327), cultivated not only his own agricultural land but also that which the Comte de Foix confiscated from the heretic peasants of Montaillou and which *ipso facto* came under the control of the *bayle*, who farmed it for his own profit. Bernard passionately loved the Pays d'Aillon, the estate he managed for the Comte. It was 'his' land, and later, when a prisoner of the Inquisition, he still looked at it wistfully from a distance as he warmed himself in the sun on the Tour des Allemands in Pamiers (i.279). For his part, Clergue the priest kept an eye on the land of all his relations: it was he who acted as proxy for his niece when Bernard Malet of Prades, her husband, bought some land which used to belong to Raymond Malet, son-in-law of Raymond Pierre (iii.77). The Clergue *domus* certainly possessed herds of pigs and sheep. Bernard Clergue protected his garden against the damage done by his own pigs, and when he was in prison he *gave three fleeces of wool to Garnot, sergeant of the prison; after that, the sergeant did all that Bernard wanted in the prison; and Honors, the sergeant's wife, gave Bernard the key to the rooms of the prisoners* (iii.289, 274). Lastly, the Clergues had either money or credit: in order to set his beloved brother Pierre free, the *bayle* did not hesitate to spend 14,000 *sous* in bribes to various important people.

But money was not everything. In the case of the Clergue family, peasants though they were, wealth was accompanied by a certain degree of power, and also by useful connections. Bernard Clergue knew people who were influential at the court of the Comte de Foix, and he made no bones about greasing their palms (ii.282). The family exercised a three-fold power: at the court of Foix; in the regional Church; and in the village and surrounding district. The influence of Clergue the priest was known to be far-reaching: *He has great power at the Court of the Comte de Foix and in the Church*, said Guillaume Maurs (ii.171–2). *One of these days, he can have us taken and destroy us; that is why I left the kingdom of France and went to Puigcerda.* Even beyond the frontiers of the Comté de Foix, a satellite of the kingdom of France, the power of the Clergues gave them influence as far as Carcassonne, where the Inquisition made use of them and sometimes listened to their opinions. *'If you go and confess to the Inquisitor in Carcassonne the misdeeds which I have suggested to you,'* said Bernard Clergue to Bernard Benet, though the misdeeds were imaginary ones (i.404), *'I will pay the expenses of your journey, and get the Inquisitor to annul the sentence which condemned you to wear the yellow crosses.'* Regional influence was backed by local authority: Pierre Clergue, at the height of his power, was nicknamed the 'Little Bishop' of the Pays d'Aillon (iii.182). *The Clergues are very rich and exercise great power in the Pays d'Aillon*, said Pierre Maury (iii.193). As a matter of fact, the priest was for a long while a respected intermediary between Carcassonne and Montaillou, and used his connections in the first to protect his clients in the second. He was thus able to consolidate his power in both.

About 12 years ago or thereabouts, said Guillemette Benet in 1321 (i.476), *Arnaud Clergue, bastard of Guillaume Clergue, the priest's brother, came to see me in my house on behalf of the priest. He said to me : 'Tomorrow the priest will come to your house to tell you that you are summoned to Carcassonne, where the Inquisitor will inform you of your sentence of imprisonment. The priest says you must find an excuse not to go to Carcassonne; so tomorrow go to bed and pretend you are ill ; say you fell off the ladder in your house ; pretend you have broken bones everywhere. Otherwise it's prison for you.'*

And so next day when the priest came with the witnesses, I was in bed and said to him : 'I fell off my ladder. I have broken bones everywhere!' And that is how he found me an excuse!

This consideration on the part of Pierre Clergue did not prevent Guillemette Benet from being sentenced, much later, to life imprisonment, fetters, and bread and water (i.534). But at the time it meant that Guillemette, connected by marriage with the Belots, who themselves were connected by marriage with the Clergues, enjoyed twelve more years of freedom. So occasionally, for the benefit of some family among his parishioners, the priest did do some violence to the law of the Inquisition which he represented in the village. Was not this the best way for him to be their protector, and at the same time to protect his own power? The shepherd Pierre Maury, for a long while an outlaw pursued by all the forces of justice, was categorical on the subject (ii.187), though it is true that Maury might have blackmailed Clergue because of their former common connections with the Cathars: *If the priest of Montaillou had wanted to catch me he would have done so a long time ago! One day when he came to collect the tithes in my father's house he saw me and talked to me, but he did not have me arrested.*

Formerly implicated in Catharism, the Clergues thus belong to those *domus* which had 'fat mules' (ii.58) and fat fortunes, and managed for years to get the better of the odds, both on their own account and on that of their friends. But it was a dangerous game, and in the end they lost.

The local power of the house of Clergue implied a complex and ambivalent relationship with the local peasants. For one thing, the Clergue house regarded itself as superior to the *domus* of the rustics, and in the end it broke with them.

When I was ill at Varilhes, said Béatrice de Planissoles (i.239), *the priest came to see me and said: 'I have the men of Montaillou just where I want them, thanks to the Inquisition.'*

Then I answered: '*How is it that you persecute the good Christians* [i.e. the heretics] *whereas before you used to be very fond of them?*'

'*I have not changed,*' answered the priest. '*I still am very fond of the good Christians. But I want to be revenged on the peasants of Montaillou, who have done me harm, and I will avenge myself in every possible way. After that, I shall know how to settle up with God.*'

The word peasant or rustic was regarded as an insult in Montaillou, and yet the village was inhabited by farmers and shepherds. An inhabitant of the Pays d'Aillon who was dying insulted the priest who brought him the Eucharist by calling him *a vile, stinking, rustic* (i.231). When, in talking to Béatrice, the priest called his fellow-citizens in Montaillou peasants or rustics, he meant at once to belittle them and to differentiate them from his own family. But in vain. The *domus* of the Clergues was linked by flesh and blood to the other *domus* in the parish. The Clergues were closely connected by marriage or cousinship, or both at once, to the Benets, the Belots, the Rives, the Martys, the Liziers and the Forts. Nor must we forget the many temporary unions indulged in by the very active male members of the Clergue family, among whom, in this field as in all the others, Pierre the priest led the field. It happened to all the women of Montaillou, from the poorest to the *châtelaine*: they all loved, deloused and admired the Clergues. These bonds of blood, marriage or concubinage provided the Clergue family with indispensable support or complicity both in the time of their splendour and in the time of their decline. But these connections did not exclude, later, violent hatreds or conflicts with certain *domus*, such as that of the Benets, even though they were indirectly connected with the Clergues through a chain of marriages.

There was also the essential complicity in heresy. Before his final betrayals, based on revenge and not on ideological conversion, Pierre Clergue was a stalwart supporter of Cathar ideas, which he shared with members of other influential houses. *Ah, if only all the priests in the world were like the priest of Montaillou*, sighed Guillaume Authiè in 1301 (i.279), adding that one could have complete confidence in every member of the Clergue *domus*. In fact, in their stormy youth Pierre and Bernard Clergue both gave undoubted proof of loyalty to the heretics. The evidence of Guillaume Maurs on this point is categorical (ii.173).

Guillaume Maury told me this: one night in Montaillou, while they [the Inquisition] *were burning Arnaud Fort's house, the priest got two heretics out of the house of the Belots and arranged for them to escape into the maquis* [barta], *called A la Cot.* On another occasion, according to Alazaïs Fauré, Pierre Clergue kept watch at a place called la Paredeta to prevent anything untoward happening while Prades Tavernier, disguised as a peddler of leather and wool, 'consoled' a dying inhabitant of Montaillou (i.415–16). Alazaïs Azéma denounced Bernard Clergue's former involvement (i.317). *This Bernard collected corn for tithes, placed a certain amount of it on the low roof of Raymond Belot's house, and told Raymond Belot to give it to the heretics.*

Wealth, family connections, heresy and power: these were the four bases on which rested the influence of the Clergues in Montaillou. Their local power was institutional. Pierre Clergue was the village priest, though his performance of those duties was somewhat limited by his constant extra-curricular activities. Mistresses took up part of the time and care which Pierre should have devoted to the edification of his flock. Nevertheless, Pierre, superficially speaking, was quite a conscientious priest, hearing confession, saying mass on Sunday and feast-days (even in a state of mortal sin), attending diocesan meetings, collecting tithes. Finally, he was one of the few people in the village who was more or less educated, one of the rare owners of books. Did he not have in his possession the Cathar calendar, part folklore and part liturgy, lent to him by the Authié brothers (i.315)? He sometimes acted as notary, taking charge of important documents, such as the one relating to the dowry of his friend Béatrice. He was also official representative of the Carcassonne Inquisition, and used this position to protect as well as to oppress. Local opinion of him was far from being entirely negative. After many years, Béatrice remembered him as a *good and competent man, and regarded as such in the region* (i.253).

In Montaillou the two chief members of the Clergue family – Pierre and Bernard – managed to get hold of both the spiritual and temporal swords. Pierre was the priest, Bernard the *bayle*. Bernard, as *bayle*, worked in collaboration with his brother Pierre (each of them collected tithes on different occasions). Bernard acted as magistrate, and as collector of dues for the Comte, since the Comte de Foix, repository of political power, was also lord of the village. While Pierre was de facto bailiff of the Inquisition, Bernard was Justice of the Peace and police commissioner for the Comte. He arrested accused persons and, when necessary, seized their livestock. Needless to say, the Clergue brothers – Pierre, Bernard and Raymond – also found many occasions to combine forces and make use of the feudal and, in particular, the manorial authority for their own ends. Raymond Clergue took the *vice-châtelain* of Montaillou, Jacques Alsen, with him to pursue Guillaume Maurs, once a personal and now a family enemy, through the Pedorres Pass in the Pyrenees at Puymorens (ii.176). The two men failed in this mission. At Pedorres, the only prey they encountered was the outlawed shepherd Pierre Maury, whom they kindly allowed to escape, after having 'borrowed' some provisions from him. Similarly, at the time of the great round-up by the Inquisition in August 1308, Pierre Clergue helped to lock up in the château of Montaillou all his parishioners aged over twelve or thirteen, some of whom he had released later, according to a selective process of liberation (iii.82). In his parish Pierre was 'the castle's man', a position he used for his own astute personal ends until, by a kind of poetic justice, the *châtelaine* (or rather ex-*châtelaine*) became 'Pierre's woman' during the brief duration of their illicit relationship.

The Clergues and their rivals in the village took it in turns to make use, at a peasant level, of the local offices of *seigneur*, *bayle* and *châtelain*, seeking to control them for their own purposes. When, after 1320, the star of the Clergues began to wane, their enemies (among them Pierre Azéma of Montaillou, cousin of Bishop Fournier; Raymond Triahl, *vicaire* of Montaillou and Prades; and Bernard Marty, consul of Montaillou) in their turn manipulated the secular arm of the local *châtellenie* against the Clergues and their friends or clients (i.406).[1] Thus we see Pierre Azéma, a simple peasant, ordering the lieutenant of the Comte de Foix's *châtelain* to throw Bernard Benet, a temporary and involuntary accomplice of the Clergues, into the dungeons of the château.

The lieutenant was obsequious. Pierre Azéma airily gave his orders, and did not ask his permission to have Benet's livestock seized and put *into the Count's hands* (i.395–6).

These details illustrate better than any theoretical charter certain

1 This is the only time the Fournier Register mentions a consul in Montaillou. At a later date there were consuls in the village, in theory appointed as a result of a free election by the municipal assembly of heads of families, but they played only a subordinate role.

aspects of the 'class struggle' or rather 'group struggle' in Montaillou. For the various rural cliques involved, including the Clergue *domus*, the problem was not so much a struggle against oppression on the part of the *seigneurie* and *châtellenie* as such, as to annex (sometimes taking it in turns) the local powers of the *seigneurie*, *baylie* and *châtellenie* in order to crush the rival clan. The power of the authorities was, therefore, felt less as a consequence of oppression on their part than through their role as institutions which competing interests sought to influence.

Having described the Clergue house and placed it in the *domus* system in Montaillou, we must now say a few words about its members. First of all there is a problem of title and leadership. After the death of the patriarch Pons, Alazaïs Azéma calls the Clergue *domus the house of the sons of Pons Clergue* (i.315). Fabrisse Rives, the wine-seller, speaks of *the house of the priest and his brothers* (i.327). Alazaïs Fauré, sister of Guilhabert the heretic, calls it *the house of Bernard Clergue* (i.413). Raymonde Arsen, the Belots' servant, is one of our best sources of information, and she uses indiscriminately the two expressions, *the house of Bernard Clergue and his brothers* and *the people of the priest's house*. Theoretically, then, Pierre and Bernard were equal as leaders of the Clergue *domus*. But one was rather more equal than the other. When Pierre Clergue died, his brother Bernard, who loved him and eagerly recognized his superiority, called him *my God*, *my governor*, *my* capdelador (ii.87).

The strong cohesion which existed between the members of the Clergue house does not mean that they were always united in thought or in mutual confidence. The partriarch Pons Clergue himself, an old diehard Cathar, finally grew alarmed at the depravity and spying of his son Pierre. Pierre, the priest, had suggested to Raymond Maury that he should bring back to Montaillou his son Pierre Maury, who had long been outlawed for heretical activity and other 'crimes'. When he heard about it, old Pons flew into a rage and warned Raymond Maury (ii.285, 289). '*Do not trust the words of that treacherous priest. Simply say to Pierre Maury, if you are in the Pass of the Seven Brothers* [near Montaillou], *flee to the Marmara Pass; if you are at the Marmara Pass, flee to the Pass of Puymorens, where the Pamiers diocese ends; and do not stay there, but flee even further!*' Did Pierre Clergue know about this broadside? If he did, he showed no malice. He went on regarding his father's corpse as the receptacle of the fortune of the *domus* since, as we have seen, he had hair and nail-parings taken from it in order to preserve the family's good fortune. Pierre always felt a warm attachment, at once Cathar and Catholic, to his mother, Mengarde. When the village gossips, Alazaïs Azéma, Guillemette 'Belote' and Alazaïs Rives, coming back from Mengarde's funeral, said that she had brought forth a *bad litter of pups* and that all her sons were bad men, Pierre paid no attention. '*My mother*', he told Béatrice (i.229), '*was a good woman. Her soul is in Heaven. For she did much good to the "good Christians" and sent parcels of food to the heretics of Montaillou shut up in prison, as for example old Na Roqua and her son Raymond Roques.*' This devotion to the Cathar memory of his mother did not prevent him from hedging his bets and having Mengarde buried near to the altar of the Virgin in Notre Dame de Carnesses, the pilgrim chapel in Montaillou (iii.182). *It is a shameful thing for that woman to be buried there*, said Pierre Maury, referring, sympathetically, to Mengarde's heretical past. Emersende Marty, another Montaillou heretic, went on paradoxically (ii.182), *If the Bishop of Pamiers knew about the past of the priest's worthy mother, he would have her corpse exhumed and thrown out of the church where she is buried.* Pierre Clergue was a good son and a bad priest. He was naturally proud of having had Mengarde buried near the altar of the Virgin, but at the same time he told Béatrice (i.230): '*Mary is not the mother of God; she is the vessel of flesh in which Jesus Christ was "shadowed forth".*'

Pierre was so faithful to the memory of his mother that he took as confidante, regular delouser and occasional mistress Raymonde Guilhou, who, while Mengarde was alive, deloused her and let herself be converted by Mengarde to Catharism.

While the Clergue brothers were on good terms with their mother and father, despite the occasional tiff, were they united among themselves? There are occasional signs of superficial tension. When Bernard Clergue wanted to give corn to the heretics, he kept out of sight of his brothers, or at least some of the four (i.375). But this was merely an episode, and could not jeopardize the fundamental unity of the *domus*, maintained by its men and by several faithful relations, among whom was Bernard Gary of Laroque d'Olmes. This consistently devoted nephew was able to help the Clergues in the difficult circumstances that accompanied their downfall (i.396).

This downfall came after a long period of power. At the beginning, around 1300, Pierre and Bernard Clergue were solidly installed in their offices of priest and *bayle*. They were the local correspondents of the Authié brothers, and with the other two Clergue brothers, who remained rather in the background, they were the local protectors of a village cankered with heresy. Pierre and Bernard, both more or less heretics themselves but with good connections with the Catholic Church in the lowlands, played one side off against another in a masterly manner. Bernard collected the tithes of the Church of Rome, and handed over part of them to the Cathars: the left hand did not know what the right hand was doing. Pierre, established both in the parish church and in the *domus* of the heretics, was assured of a strong social position in the village through his liaison with the ex-*châtelaine*. His intellectual prestige was guaranteed by his learned contacts with the Authiés, and by the presence of a student to whom he was supposed to give lessons (i.243, 279). This young man, Jean, had Catharist sympathies, and Clergue used him to deliver love letters, and even practically to hold the candle during his rendezvous with Béatrice de Planissoles.

But in the long run the family's position of secure domination could not last. The Carcassonne Inquisition had its eye on Montaillou, and the house of Clergues had to make up its mind to break with heresy or perish with it. Pierre and Bernard betrayed the Albigensian ideas in which perhaps they now only half believed: in such cases people are always renegades in the opinion of their former sect, while for themselves it is a case of the scales having fallen from their eyes. It is possible that Pierre Clergue had already contracted the execrable habit of informing as early as 1300. At the time of his mother's death, before the end of his affair with Béatrice, the sharp-tongued Cathar women of Montaillou were already accusing their priest of *destroying the whole country*. At any rate, in the course of the first decade of the fourteenth century the peasants and heretical community of Montaillou realized they had been nourishing a viper in their bosom. A new Clergue was revealed: the scribes of Pamiers paint a striking portrait, warts and all, of a sophisticated man puffed up with pride, lust and vengefulness, and with the truculence typical of his region.

We have two versions of Pierre Clergue's great betrayal: that of the priest himself, which we shall examine later, and that of the people he betrayed, who were also his relations by marriage, some of them for a long while his friends. They included the Maurys, the Benets, the Belots and even the Maurs. The survivors of these proud mountain houses, thrown down by repression, unanimously accused the priest and all his *domus* of having changed coats and become out-and-out instruments of the Inquisitors (i.405). One day Guillaume Belot told Raymonde Arsen straight out, in the course of one of their encounters at La Calm (i.375): '*The people of the priest's house and the priest himself cause many inhabitants of Montaillou to be summoned by the Lord Inquisitor of Carcassonne. It is high time the people of the priest's house were thrust as deep into prison* [as ex-heretics] *as the other inhabitants of Montaillou.*' And it is true that Clergue, the former Cathar who remained half an Albigensian in his heart, did not spare his parishioners: the Maurs family, enemy of the Clergues, were through the good offices of the priest either sent to rot in prison or outlawed in Catalonia (ii.171). Pons Clergue tried to excuse his son's behaviour by alleging the unavoidable necessities imposed by collaboration with France (ii.171). Pierre Clergue acted, in fact, like a typical collaborator. Disowned by some of his own people, he thought, rightly or wrongly, he could cut his losses by putting his friends and clients out of the reach, direct or indirect, of the colonizing power and the Carcassonne Inquisition.

It is against this background that the tragedy of August 1308 took place, when Clergue looked on as an accomplice while the henchmen of the Inquisition locked up his flock (i.373, n. 158). All the inhabitants of Montaillou, male and female, over the age of about twelve or thirteen, were arrested. This measure may have been based on the confessions of Gaillarde Authié, wife of Guillaume Authié the heretic, who was questioned by the Inquisition during Lent 1308. More decisive were the denunciations of Pierre Authié's nephews: *These nephews, who were called de Rodès, came from Tarascon. One of them was a Dominican in Pamiers.* The round-up itself was dramatic in the extreme. The dread Poloniac directed the agents of the Carcassonne Inquisition and had no difficulty in arresting all the inhabitants of Montaillou over the required age, for they were all gathered together for a feast of the Virgin, a popular occasion in which the Saint Mary and the God of the Cathars were both honoured simultaneously. With the end of the summer pasturing most of the local shepherds had come down from the mountains to Montaillou. Fortunately for him, Pierre Maury had remained up in the Quériu Pass; a man transporting flour informed him that the village was now under lock and key (iii.162–3). A few Montaillou women managed to escape, carrying loaves of bread on their heads and pretending that they were agricultural migrants from elsewhere.

The lucky ones and the fugitives went and settled in Spain on the Catalan or Saracen borders. The village became temporarily a republic of children and sheep. The adults and adolescents of Montaillou, at first shut up in the château, were later taken to the prison in Carcassonne. Some were burnt at the stake. Others were for a long time kept, men and women separately, in common cells in the prison, where they were allowed to receive parcels of food (*victualia*) from their families.

The rest of the prisoners were released fairly quickly, and the Inquisition allowed them to go back to Montaillou, where they lived henceforward under the at once protective and dangerous rule of the Clergue clan. The village, or what remained of it, found itself willy-nilly grouped around its priest, growing old in debauchery and denunciation. The mangled village was a parish of yellow crosses, the badges which former heretics had to wear. Pierre Clergue took advantage of these circumstances to settle some old accounts with his enemies, the Maurs, who had been victims of the round-up. Mengarde Maurs then insinuated that the priest's own past was not free of heresy: we know what happened to her.

Pierre Clergue's image of himself was obviously slightly less damning than the image of him formed by his victims. He did not see himself as a renegade, but rather as one charged with carrying out a vendetta, an executor of justice in his own cause. In the same year, 1308, or thereabouts, when Béatrice, twice a widow, was seriously ill at Varilhes (i.234, 239), Pierre, travelling to attend a diocesan council, came to visit his ex-mistress for the last time. She was still a very dear friend. He sat on the bed, inquired after her health and the state of her heart, took her hand and stroked her arm. Béatrice told him of the fears which haunted her about the heretical conversations they had had together in the past. She said she had never dared to confess them to a priest. Then, more boldly, she asked Pierre why he was persecuting his former friends, the heretics. He replied in substance, as we have seen, that he was still well disposed towards the good Christians – the heretics – and that he only wanted to revenge himself on the peasants of Montaillou who had done him harm.

To demonstrate the persistence of his Cathar faith, undamaged by his denunciations in Carcassonne, Pierre repeated one of the theories he used to propound to her when they were still lovers (i.226, 234, 239). '*God alone*', he said, '*can absolve sins, and you have no need of confession.*'

Eight years before, when he was still a Cathar without being as yet too much of a spy, he had gone into more detail: '*The only valid confession is the confession people make to God; He knows the sin before it is committed; and He can absolve it.*' A comparison of the two statements shows that in 1308 Clergue was more than ever a double agent. But he had remained a heretic at heart.

Pierre wished also to remain leader and patron of his network of clients in the village and the region. In this respect, despite inconsistencies inevitable in such hard times, his behaviour before and after 1308 was of a piece. For nothing or for a consideration, according to circumstances, Pierre would act as protector to certain local people against the authorities in Carcassonne. One day when he was sunning himself at the door of his church, Fabrisse Rives came and announced, or denounced, the recent heretication, on her death-bed, of Alazaïs Benet (i.324). Pierre was furious. '*Be quiet, be quiet.*' he said to Fabrisse. '*You do not know what you are saying. There are no heretics in these parts, and if there were, they would soon be routed out.*'

According to Fabrisse, she was taken aback and went and confessed to a Minorite friar, who in his turn pretended to be astonished and not to understand. '*What has your priest been doing then?*' he asked Fabrisse.

The Minorite friars then approached Pierre Clergue and told him, '*Your whole district is full of heretics.*'

'*I don't know of any,*' replied the priest with a perfectly straight face, at the very moment when a *parfait* known as the White Wolf was actually strutting about in Montaillou.

And there the matter rested. The Carcassonne Inquisition was manipulated by Pierre Clergue, and as he denounced to them only the personal enemies of his own clan they were left in ignorance about Fabrisse Rives, and the idea of summoning her never entered their heads.

After the round-up of 1308 it became difficult for Pierre Clergue to go on playing the part of protector or saviour to those of his friends, clients or friends of friends who were involved in heretical activities. But he did not give up his protective functions altogether. As we have seen, Pierre Clergue and the men of his *domus* on two occasions allowed the outlawed Pierre Maury to escape; they even lent him money (ii.178, 186–7). In 1320 just before his downfall, Clergue, in return for 100 silver *tournois*, had Guillaume Mondon of Ax relieved of his yellow crosses.

But the Inquisition devoured its own children, even and especially when they were double-faced like Clergue. In 1320 Jacques Fournier struck his final blow. This time even those former heretics of Montaillou who were disguised as defenders of the Church were ferreted out. The Clergue gang met the same fate as those whom they had previously denounced. In their last extremity, two cliques tore each other apart and divided up Montaillou between them. The Azéma-Guilhabert clan (represented by Alazaïs Fauré, née Guilhabert) tried to destroy the Clergue clan. Alazaïs accused Esclarmonde, wife of Raymond Clergue, of having been present at the heretication of Guillaume Guilhabert. The Clergues reacted vigorously. Pierre the priest, thrown in prison at last by Jacques Fournier, tried to use his surviving influence with the Inquisition at Carcassonne. Through his relatives still in the village, he tried to force Bernard Benet to bear false witness against the Guilhabert-Azémas. '*Bear false witness or you will be burned. Bear false witness, or you will be taken, bound hand and foot, to Carcassonne,*' the Clergues told Bernard Benet, while Azéma brought pressure to bear on him from the other direction. But the efforts of the priest's family were in vain; it was the turn of the Clergue brothers to rot and die in prison. But at least Pierre Clergue, for reasons unknown to us, kept silent to the end. This man who knew too much died without speaking – or without any declaration he may have made to the Bishop being taken down by the scribes. Rightly or wrongly, one would like to think he did not squeal, unlike so many other unfortunate victims of the Inquisition.

This account of the activities of the Clergue clan brings us to some more general reflections on the nature and exercise of power in Montaillou. Reference to feudalism and the manorial system is to some extent relevant because of the network of obligations which enveloped the microcosm of the village and its inhabitants. However, in Montaillou the level at which power was effectively exercised and transmitted downwards was below the level of feudal and manorial structures. True, official relationships were hierarchical, such as those which linked the *bayle*, as representative of the Comte, to the Comte's humble dependants, and those which existed between the priest as such and his parishioners. But these links would have been of little importance if they had not been subtended by relations of friendship, family and patronage, these being sometimes accompanied by links of vendetta and enmity. The Clergue *domus* was the meeting-point of all these inter-connections. The Clergues, though they were not noble and had no manorial rights, combined the functions of *bayle* and priest, and simul-taneously filled the roles of friend, lover, patron, fellow-sponsor and influential relation towards a large number of the inhabitants of the village; they also played the part of oppressor and enemy towards an-other section. Over a long period Bernard Clergue and, above all, Pierre his brother ruled Montaillou through the *domus* allied to them through blood or marriage. But when Montaillou began to be persecuted, power weakened as much as it corrupted. The Clergue clan's local enemies, long held under, ended by having the Clergues' blood. But during his great period the priest established in his parish, and through-out the entire Pays d'Aillon and Sabarthès, a veritable mafia of friends, relations, fellow-sponsors and mistresses (Béatrice de Planissoles was both his mistress and his fellow-sponsor). Bribed, the priest would have an erstwhile heretic exempted from wearing the yellow cross. Or he might say to a woman, either you sleep with me or I'll see that you are denounced to the Inquisition in Carcassonne (i.279, iii.391).

The Clergues, themselves mediators between village society and the society which surrounded it, in turn had need of mediators and pro-tectors higher up than themselves and with access to the supreme powers of the region, subsumed in the court of Foix, the bishopric and the Inquisition. But only a few of these higher intermediaries are known to us: most though not all of them were local nobles, or priests, or manorial magistrates or *prévôts*. It was this chain of protection which Bernard Clergue tried – in vain – to bring into play by bribery when his brother the priest was imprisoned (ii.282). Pierre Maury was acquitted by similar means (see below, Chapters IV and V). Thus all over Occitania, mafias of priests, *bayles*, minor local noblemen, rich peasants and friends of friends, tried, sometimes successfully, to counter the Inquisition and the oppression of France and the Church.

But they only partly succeeded: between the system of friendship and marriage and patronage which reigned in the village of Montaillou and the system based on political authority and ecclesiastical oppression which emanated from the surrounding society, relations were extremely tense. For one thing, there was a great divergence between Cathar and peasant values on the one hand and Catholic and urban values on the other. For another, the geographical proximity of Carcassonne and Pamiers to Montaillou and Sabarthès greatly increased the danger of a conflagration. Montaillou, which was far from being one solid block without any cracks in it, had to use all its resources of secrecy and invention to parry the thrusts aimed at it from without. And finally the system, or rather the junction of two systems, broke down.

Most of the *domus* we have examined so far belonged to the traditional world of settled farmers. But the village also contained woodcutters, who might work part of the time as farmers or even shepherds. This group was very little infected by heresy and so, since they did not interest the Inquisition, we do not know much about them.

But we do know a good deal about the shepherds. They were comparatively numerous in Montaillou. There were about ten specifically referred to as such, belonging to at least eight families in the village. They included Guillaume Pellissier, Guillaume Belot, Guillaume Guilhabert, Jean Marty, Pierre and Guillaume Baille, Pierre and Jean Maury, Guillaume Maurs and one of the Benets. Among the occupations not strictly 'agricultural', the profession of shepherd is most frequently mentioned in Montaillou.

The word 'shepherd' itself is ambiguous. In the villages of the upper Ariège, villages such as Montaillou and Ornolac, everyone was in a sense a shepherd because everyone was more or less engaged in raising sheep. The *bayle* of Ornolac, Guillaume Austatz, speaking to the men of the community gathered together under the elm tree in the square, said (i.208-9), '*Instead of burning heretics they ought to burn Bishop Fournier himself, because he demands that we pay carnelages, or tithes in lambs.*' With these sacrilegious words Guillaume Austatz made himself the spokesman of a community of farmer-stockbreeders, holders of the land and of the *domus* but also owners of flocks. These men often acted as their own shepherds, with the aid of their children.

But we have already been able to form some impression of the lives of these people. Here we are chiefly concerned with the iterant shepherds who moved about the country.[1] They formed a rural nomad semi-proletariat, without hearth or home but with their own traditions, their own pride and their own special conceptions of mountain liberty and fate. They contributed, both temporarily and permanently, to the great

---

1 Because of the exodus of young men, many of whom left the village to become long-term bachelor shepherds, it is possible that the remaining residents of Montaillou were mostly women. The preponderance of widows, due to the fact that men died earlier, could only have accentuated this trend.

wave of Pyrenean emigration which gradually flowed towards the low-lands, especially towards Spain.

The shepherds functioned within the framework of existing authority. As they travelled about from village to village they formed part of the network of *domus* which were often friendly to them. Pierre Maury, a shepherd of Montaillou, travelled through Catalonia and what is now the department of Aude; but he still maintained relationships with, and could count on protection from, the Clergue clan (ii.176). On the other hand, the lives of the mountain shepherds were made more difficult by private wars between local lords on the Spanish side of the mountains, always ready to tear one another to pieces as in the heyday of feudalism. This would scarcely have mattered if the shepherds had not had to foot the bill. But if one of these private wars broke out between Guillaume d'Entensa, lord of Casteldans, and another lord about whom we know nothing except that he was called Nartès or En Artès, the Maury brothers were obliged to withdraw their flocks from the Casteldans lands (ii.479; iii.195).

Many of these wandering shepherds came from Montaillou, and some of them we know. A few were suspected of crime, or were merely un-stable characters who had taken to the road, the *draille* (transhumance), or even the maquis, as the result of some brawl or tiff. Jean Maury, who was involved in a fight with some other shepherds, explained quite simply how this incident confirmed his inveterate wanderlust (ii.476). *I was involved in a brawl with some shepherds from Razès, in which I was injured. A certain Vézian, who was then living with Raymond Lizier of Montaillou, took my part in the quarrel. I went and lodged a complaint about my injuries with Bernard Clergue, who was then* bayle *of Montaillou acting for the lord Comte de Foix; I also complained to the* châtelain *of Montaillou. He did not want to compensate me for the injury I had received at the hands of the shepherds from Razès. Because of this wrong, I left Montaillou and went to Puigcerda where I hired myself out as a shepherd to the lady Brunissende de Cervello; I remained with Brunissende and her sheep for four years and two and a half months.* Similarly, Guillaume Bélibaste took to the road after a set-to that went too far. He was the guilty party and killed another shepherd in the fight. So he had to leave his prosperous farm and the fraternal *domus* at Cubières. He became first a shepherd, then a *parfait*. It was not until later that he settled down as prophet to a little Albigensian colony in Catalonia, where he exchanged the occupation of shepherd for that of a maker of baskets or carding combs.

In a slightly different style, Bernard Benet was another victim of downward mobility.[1] He came from a worthy and prosperous family of farmer-stockbreeders in Montaillou. But his people were ruined by the Inquisition, and their lands confiscated and handed over to the Comte de Foix, who administered them through Bernard Clergue, the *bayle*. The most obvious result of this operation was to add to the Clergue *domus* at the expense of the Benet *domus*, though these were once indirectly connected. Bernard Benet himself was ejected into the proletariat of the shepherds. His material and moral situation was not strong. At the time when the Inquisitors of Pamiers were interested in him, his livelihood depended entirely on his flock, and in Montaillou itself he was caught between two fires: the Clergue clan which wanted to make him bear false witness to the Carcassonne Inquisition, and the Azéma clan, enemy to the Clergues, who wanted to make him retract his deposition. Bernard Clergue, following the instructions of his brother the priest, promised Bernard Benet to give him back one of his confiscated meadows in return for his cooperation. Pierre Azéma, using the stick rather than the carrot, tried to influence Bernard Benet in the opposite direction by confiscating his precious sheep, his last remaining wealth. Finally Bernard Benet was arrested. He managed to escape from Mas-Saint-Antonin, where he was under house arrest (i.408). But after a detour in Cerdagne he was taken again at Ax-les-Thermes: Pierre Roussel of Ax and his wife Alissende had given him away. This Alissende was none other than the sister of Gaillarde Benet, wife of Pierre Benet, himself the brother of Bernard. So Bernard was given away by his sister-in-law's sister. It was not very nice, but there was an explanation: at different times Alissende and Gaillarde had both been mistress to Pierre Clergue the priest. Betraying their legitimate connections with the house of Benet in order to perform the behests of the Clergues, they had first been lovers and later spies. Thus did Pierre Clergue's harem contribute to the prosperity of his *domus*. As for Bernard Benet, this young man of good social position who might have looked forward to a future as a farmer-proprietor ended up a mere

1 The Fournier Register is particularly valuable in that it is largely concerned with downward social mobility, whereas most documents of the *ancien régime* treat chiefly of upward mobility.

shepherd, at the mercy of the various village clans. In these circumstances he was lucky to emerge unscathed from the heavy hands of the Inquisitors (i.395, 405–06, 408).

Another déclassé shepherd who fell even lower than Bernard Benet was Guillaume Maurs. He too came from a respectable *domus* of farmers in Montaillou who had been ruined by the Inquisition, backed up as usual by the good offices of the house of Clergue. Guillaume Maurs's father and brothers were arrested. His mother, Mengarde, who had spoken out imprudently about the heretical youth of the Clergues, had her tongue cut out, through the judicial powers invested in the *bayle*, Bernard Clergue. Guillaume Maurs himself managed to escape prison and torture. He fled over one mountain pass after another from the Comté de Foix to Catalonia and back again, nourishing revenge in his heart rather than heresy in his soul. (His absence of Cathar zeal is illustrated by a surly remark to the *parfait*, Guillaume Bélibaste (ii.187). '*I would rather eat tripe than be one of your company.*' There was nothing surprising in this: the wandering Guillaume Maurs wanted to kill the Clergues, who had ruined his *domus*, but fundamentally he cared little about the fate of Albigensianism, though it was for this that the Inquisition had imprisoned his family.) The unwilling shepherd ceaselessly ruminated on the faded splendours of his family's past; they were modest enough, but distance lent enchantment. His life of seasonal migration took him to various cheese-producing shepherd communities in the mountain, but finally he was captured at Puigcerda, and from there the representative of the King of Majorca had him transferred to the prisons of Bishop Fournier.

The shepherds Bélibaste, Maurs and Benet are instances of people who came down in the world, examples of more than individual or purely local interest. In this connection see the long, fascinating and miserable biography of the shepherd Bernard Marty of Junac (iii.253–95). Born of a rich family of blacksmiths ruined by the Inquisition and its henchmen, Bernard Marty was reduced to keeping other people's sheep, tossed hither and thither, unemployed as often as not.

Some, however, were shepherds not through misfortune but by vocation. As younger sons, or members of poor families, they made no bones about settling down in the lower stratum of rural society. They were comparatively well-adjusted to their fate and in some cases might even be happy and proud to be shepherds. One who is well known to us is Jean Pellissier; more familiar still is Pierre Maury.

Jean Pellissier, son of Bernard Pellissier of Montaillou, became a professional keeper of flocks when he reached the age of twelve or so. (It was usually from the age of twelve that young peasants used to be made responsible for looking after the sheep: this has been an age-old feature of rural education.) For these modest beginnings young Pellissier's parents apprenticed him in Tournon, a long way from home, where his first employer was a woman called Thomassia, probably a widow.

Even at the start young Pellissier was not outstanding for intelligence, and he made a poor showing beside his colleague, Pierre Maury, who was very bright. Pellissier did not know the surname of his first employer, and could not say exactly how old he was when Thomassia first engaged him. He was just as vague when asked to say how long he worked for her. *I stayed with Thomassia five or six years.*

When he was about eighteen Jean Pellissier, now established as a shepherd, went home and lived there for an indefinite period, together with his mother, Alazaïs, and his brothers Raymond, Guillaume, Bernard and Pierre. As well as his own *domus*, he used to frequent four neighbouring or related houses. *I never met in these houses any stranger or heretic*, he declared.

But while his circle of acquaintances was limited, his wanderlust was boundless. He left home again and was taken on as a shepherd in Niort by Guillaume Castellan, for two years; after that he went for a year to Mompret to work for Raymond Jean (iii.75ff.). These periods of service were short: it appears that in rural Occitania employers and employees could quickly come to agreements concerning work and as quickly terminate them. There is no element of feudal bondage in the relations between them.

After Mompret, Jean Pellissier set out again for Montaillou: it was becoming a habit. There he took employment as a shepherd in the house of Bernard Maurs (iii.75, 76). The Maurs were in a sense related to him, and it was one of their womenfolk's propaganda which momentarily converted him to Cathar ideas. The social or family distance between a farmer and his hired shepherd was often small.

But to the horror of the shepherd, the thunderbolts of the Inquisition fell on the house of Maurs. As Jean Pellissier related (iii.76), *My employer Bernard Maurs and his mother Guillemette[1] were at that time imprisoned for heresy. Pierre Maurs, his brother and neighbour, and the other Pierre Maurs (his son) were thrown for a while into the prison at Carcassonne. The other sons of Pierre Maurs the elder – Bernard and Guillaume – were also imprisoned in Carcassonne for heresy. Another Pierre Maurs, son of Bernard Maurs, fled from Montaillou [in 1308] after the raid by the Inquisition on the local heretics, and he settled in Catalonia. He returned to Montaillou two years ago [in 1321] in order to marry one of the daughters of Guillaume Authié of Montaillou (now imprisoned for heresy in Carcassonne). This Pierre Maurs, before setting out again quite recently for Catalonia, lived in the village until the beginning of this winter, and I carefully avoided talking to him.* These arrests and acts of oppression (which included the cutting out of Mengarde Maurs's tongue) demolished the Maurs family, making prisoners or exiles of some and reducing others to social ruin or despair. Pellissier's evidence is an eloquent witness to the ever more painful and silent tragedy in which existence in Montaillou was shrouded between 1305 and 1320. All around him Jean Pellissier saw the blows of the Inquisition decimating his employers' relations. So in accordance with his natural vocation as a shepherd, he decided to take off. He went to Prades d'Aillon, a village a league away from Montaillou and almost as badly infected with heresy. *After leaving the employment of Bernard Maurs, I was taken on in the village of Prades d'Aillon by Bernard Malet and his sons Bernard, Raymond and André. About two months after I was hired by Bernard Malet senior, he was summoned to appear before the Inquisition at Carcassonne, which then imprisoned him. Bernard later died in prison* (iii.76). Jean Pellissier consoled himself as best he could for this new catastrophe, telling Jacques Fournier that at any rate, *None of the aforesaid three sons of Bernard Malet senior was ever troubled by the police on the subject of heresy.*

But this was poor compensation. Leaving Montaillou only for Prades d'Aillon, Jean Pellissier never really emerged from the family and Cathar-inclined network of the Maurs, the Clergues and the Malets. This network, despite terrible internal dissension, connected village to village in a web of complicity: Bernard Malet junior of Prades, son of

---

1 Not to be confused with Bernard's wife, of the same name.

Bernard Malet senior (the imprisoned employer of Jean Pellissier), had married one of the nieces of Pierre Clergue the priest, who set himself up as the young couple's protector (iii.77). In the Pays d'Aillon all roads, even those of the shepherds' migration in search of employment, sooner or later led to Clergue the priest.

Finally, after many years of wandering, Jean Pellissier came back for good to Montaillou, his native village. He was absorbed into the life of his community, where he had his own family house. We glimpse him from time to time, unwell and lying in the sun at his own front door (iii.79, 104 – his health was in general not strong).

But most of the time he was out and about, whether in the spring before the sowing of the meadows, or in summer after the hay harvest (iii.84). He was now quite well off and had sheep of his own. But – and this indicates the limits of his modest success – it was on other people's grass that he looked after his own sheep. A typical scene shows him in the meadows and demonstrates that his eyes were sharp even if his chronological sense was dim. He begins with the usual vagueness about time (iii.84): *Was it the year* [1308] *when all the men in Montaillou were picked up by the Carcassonne Inquisition, or was it the year before? I can't remember very well. Was it during the summer, after the hay had been cut, or in the spring, before the meadows were sown? I can't remember that very well either. I was with my own sheep at Combe del Gazel, in the meadow belonging to Guillaume Fort and his brothers.* [Guillaume Fort was burnt in 1321 for having lapsed into heresy.] *I myself was on the left of the meadow by the path which leads to the mountain pastures of Montaillou. To the right of the said path was Pierre Baille, son of Raymond Baille of Montaillou. Pierre Baille was grazing sheep in the meadow belonging to Bernard Marty (known as 'Goat'). There also was Jean Marty of Montaillou; he was grazing his sheep in the meadow belonging to him, and adjacent to that of Raymond Marty. It might have been noon when there appeared upon the said path, coming from Montaillou, Arnaud Vital of Montaillou, wearing a blue surcoat over his tunic and with an axe hanging round his neck and balancing a big faggot of beechwood which he was carrying round his neck also. With him were two men, each dressed in a brown hooded mantle over a blue or green garment; and they too carried axes over their shoulders. Arnaud and his companions approached through the field belonging to the Belots. Once there they saw me and my associates, Pierre Baille and Jean Marty. Arnaud came up to Pierre Baille, greeted*

*him and was in turn greeted by him . . . And since at that time Arnaud was
assistant bailiff of Montaillou, he reprimanded Pierre Baille and Jean
Marty for letting their sheep stray over the sown fields. As a joke, Jean said
to Arnaud: 'Do those two woodcutters come from Lavelanet?'*

The scene reveals the small world of the Montaillou shepherds in the
fourteenth century, distinguishing between their respective meadows
devoted to hay and pasture, divided between the sown *infield* of the
parish and the distant *outfield* of the mountain pastures. A social
stratification emerges between the shepherds who grazed their own
sheep (and other people's) on other people's meadows and the shepherds
who were also farmers and owners, who kept their sheep on the family
meadow which was their own property. But these more or less subtle
differences did not prevent the formation of teams or informal co-
operatives between associated shepherds (*socii*) from various different
layers in the stratification. In addition to these little groupings, our text
shows the communal services involving the village as a whole. Grazing
was regulated by the sowing of the meadow for hay; the meadows when
sown were guarded by a communal crop-watcher, or assistant bailiff,
who worked half-time, and also mended shoes and ran after the girls.
The chronology of the village universe was uncertain, and divided by the
catastrophies of the Inquisition or the work involved in pasturing or the
hay harvest: Jean Pellissier's vague temporal bearings were derived from
the round-up of 1308, the sowing of the grass and the hay-cutting. His
field of vision also gives us a momentary glimpse of the little-known
world of the woodcutters. But from this point on, it is all sham. For the
two woodcutters are not real foresters but *parfaits*! As they pass briefly
through our text they are about to take to the maquis after a brief time in
hiding in the house of the Belots. One of them is Prades Tavernier, often
met with along the paths of the Pays d'Aillon. The other is Guillaume
Authié, the famous and valiant notary of Ax-les-Thermes, directly
linked with Montaillou by marriage and family ties. His wife, Gaillarde,
was the daughter of Arnaud Benet, himself a member of the Benet clan
of Montaillou.

The career of the shepherd Jean Pellissier was thus bound up over
and over again with the various families of his own village. On the other
hand that of Pierre Maury, also a shepherd, was completely at the mercy
of long journeys, adventure, passing love affairs and above all friendship.
The story of his life is worth going into, for it closely reflects the great

cycle of transhumance on which the Pyrenean economy was based in those days.[1]

Pierre Maury

Pierre Maury, born around 1282 or 1283, was the son of Raymond Maury, a weaver of Montaillou, and of his wife Alazaïs. The Maurys' was a traditional *domus*, like a number of others in the village. Raymond and Alazaïs had six sons – Guillaume, Pierre, Jean, Arnaud, Raymond and Bernard. There were also at least two daughters – Guillemette, who made an unsatisfactory marriage to Bertrand Piquier, a carpenter of Laroque d'Olmes, and Raymonde, who married Guillaume Marty of Montaillou. Both daughters married at the age of eighteen, or even earlier.

The documents concerning Montaillou, like others, exhibit both male and adult chauvinism, omitting to mention the existence of some daughters, the presence of young babies or the death of children who perished very early. So the eight births which we do know about in the Maury family must be considered a minimum. Despite Raymond Maury's theoretically non-agricultural occupation of weaver, his family's way of life was mixed, based on stock-raising, farming and handicraft. By the time he reached the age of eighteen, Pierre Maury was still only a young Montaillou shepherd. Guillaume Maury, his brother, was a woodcutter: *Twenty-three years ago*, said Pierre Maury in the deposition he made in 1324, *I kept the sheep of Arnaud Fauré of Montaillou, and of Raymond Maulen, of Arques, on the land belonging to Montaillou. Guillaume Maury, my brother, and Guillaume Belot of Montaillou, who are now dead, used to go to the wood at Ausa to cut laths.*[2] It was at this period that Pierre Maury had his first contacts with heresy. They came from his brother Guillaume and from the Belot clan, always

1 Transhumance was concerned with large flocks of at least several hundred head of sheep. This was what distinguished stock-raising as practised by the Pyrenean farmers of Ax and elsewhere, who employed the migrant shepherds of Montaillou, from minor stock production based on small flocks, as in Montaillou and other regions where traditional mixed farming was practised.

2 iii.120. When they were young the Maury boys already had a professional bent towards the shepherd's life. But poverty and the confiscation by the Inquisition of their parents' possessions inclined some of them, especially Jean, even more towards a pastoral existence (i.444).

a decisive factor in spreading Catharism in the village. The contacts took the form of a kind of sermon – half evangelical and half Kantian before its time – delivered to Pierre by the two woodcutters. *Guillaume Belot and Guillaume Maury*, Pierre's deposition went on, *came up to me and said: 'The good Christians have come into this land; they follow the path of Saint Peter, Saint Paul and the other Apostles; they follow the Lord; they do not lie; they do not do to others what they would not have others do to them.'*

In those days Pierre Maury was still a young man, devoted to the worship of the saints. *I had just shorn my sheep, and had given a fleece to Saint Anthony and another to the Virgin Mary of Montaillou. I still had a little wool left to make myself some clothes. Then my brother and Guillaume Belot said to me: 'The good people* [the heretics] *are not well clad. Give them some of your wool. They can use it to make clothes. You will thus be doing them a great charity, greater than what you did when you gave to Saint Anthony, for many give to Saint Anthony and few give to the goodmen. Yet the goodmen pray to God for their benefactors ... and with effect! For they walk in justice and truth.'*

Thrilled at the idea that the holy men would pray for him, young Maury finally let himself be persuaded. *They spoke to me to such effect that I gave them the value of a fleece to take to the heretics.*

Shortly after these first relations with heresy, towards 1300 or 1301, Pierre Maury, aged eighteen, fled from the paternal roof (iii.110). It was not that he was on bad terms with his parents, but already a whiff of brimstone surrounded the Maury *domus*, which the Inquisition suspected of being heretical. It was better to be off. So the following winter Pierre Maury went down to what is now the department of Aude, where he intended to winter sheep in the warm lands of the Val d'Arques, between Razès and Fenouillèdes (iii.121).[1] In Arques, Pierre Maury became the hired shepherd of his first cousin Raymond Maulen (kinship and economic ties linked once again). Soon after that, when he was about twenty, Pierre Maury fell in love (iii.110, 121). *The following winter I grazed my flock in the Val d'Arques. I lived in the house of my first cousin, Raymond Maulen, of Arques. I fell passionately in love with a girl in the village, Bernadette den Esquinath. And for two years no one spoke to me of*

1 The migration of the shepherds between the Aude lowlands and the mountains of Ariège helps to explain the way Catharism was to be found scattered about the highlands and lowlands of this part of Occitania.

heresy, because they could see that I was passionately in love with this girl.
It seems that pretty Bernadette was not unkind to Pierre Maury. One
day, talking to him in his sheepfold, Raymond Pierre, who was soon to
become Pierre's new employer, rebuked him angrily over this affair,
going so far as to call Bernadette a whore. '*You, Pierre,*' said Raymond
(iii.121), '*You, Pierre, who used to be so fond of the goodmen, you no longer
care about them. And instead you are converted to whoredom. You are
looking for a wife. Well, we'll give you one. One who will have good understanding of the faith* [the heretical faith]. *And if you have a wife like that,
it will be better for you than to have one who does not share our beliefs. For
if you have a wife who has our faith, you can receive the goodmen in your
house. You can help them. You can even talk with your wife in safety about
such things as the understanding of good, and so on.* Such prospects might
be highly attractive. To have subjects of conversation with one's wife
when they were so often lacking in some of the strangely silent households of old Occitania – it was tempting, at least.

So no more was heard of Bernadette den Esquinath, with whom
Pierre Maury had been so passionately in love. Another Bernadette,
Bernadette Pierre, made her entrance. Pierre Maury now became her
father's hired shepherd. Pierre himself, by means of his meagre savings
and small speculations, had amassed enough money to buy some land in
Arques. Bernard Bélibaste, another stock-breeder in the region, who
appointed himself negotiator of the marriage, could describe the match
in glowing terms. '*If you really want to find a wife who has understanding
of good,*' said Bernard (iii.121), '*I know a little girl who will be just right
later on. She is so rich that with what her father will give you and with
what you have already at Arques, where you have bought land, you will be
well enough off not to have to work with your hands any more . . . For
Raymond Pierre, who will thus become your future father-in-law, will adopt
you as a son; and he will give you to wife his daughter Bernadette Pierre,
who must now be about six years old; and you will live in the* domus *of
Raymond Pierre, who has understanding of good.*'

Bernard Bélibaste's harangue is interesting in that it incidentally
underlines the fundamental values of these Occitan sheepfarmers: the
close connection between the *domus* and heresy; the importance of the
domus itself, with its possible extension into other institutions such as
the adoption of the future son-in-law, co-residence, the giving of
dowries; and the practice by which the father, taking a son-in-law as an

adopted son in order to ensure the continuation of his line and *domus*, enters into a genuine treaty by which his daughter, still very young, will be handed over with a dowry as soon as she is nubile to the young co-resident adult whom the father has designated as his heir. The motives behind this diplomacy are quite simple: Raymond Pierre had three daughters – Bernadette, Jacotte and Marquise – but no sons. So he was obliged to find a man who would agree to come and live with him and be a 'son-in-law'.

But even faced with this dazzling future, Pierre Maury did not lose his head. '*How do you know in advance, Bernard,*' he said (iii.122), '*that Bernadette, when she is nubile, will have the understanding of good?*' (iii.122). This was by no means a stupid question. The Fournier Register shows us certain planned marriages where a Cathar believer joyfully wed a girl he thought to be a heretic, hoping she would entertain him for the whole of his married life with agreeable Albigensian fireside chats. And then the unfortunate fellow, shamefully deceived by his father-in-law, found himself married to a Catholic shrew, with whom, because of the dangers of the Inquisition, he had to live shut up in the silence of the grave for nearly a quarter of a century (iii.322).

But Bernard Bélibaste had an answer for everything. '*Raymond Pierre,*' he answered (iii.122), '*will nurture his daughter Bernadette so well that with the help of God she will have the understanding of good. And if by chance she has it not when she becomes nubile, then, Pierre, all you will have to do is leave Raymond Pierre's house, taking your own property with you. All you will have to do is simply leave the girl, for it would be absolutely bad for you, Pierre, to take to wife someone who had not the understanding of good.*' (This passage shows that in the Pyrenees and their foothills in the fourteenth century, as in the Cévennes of the sixteenth and seventeenth centuries, a young man intended as a future son-in-law and already co-resident in the house brought his own property into the family, and took it away with him if the projected marriage was broken off.)

Pierre Maury, tempted by these plans, decided to get to know the goodmen. They were at the centre of the matrimonial plot by means of which Raymond Maulen and Raymond Pierre, who were as thick as thieves, wanted to draw Pierre into the camp of *the understanding of good* (iii.110). So Pierre Maury asked Raymond Pierre – and also Bernard Bélibaste, who as we shall soon see had important connections with heresy – the crucial question (iii.122). '*What sort of men are these good-men I hear so much about?*'

Their answer was enlightening. '*They are men like the others! Their flesh, their bones, their shape, their faces are all exactly like those of other men! But they are the only ones to walk in the ways of justice and truth which the Apostles followed. They do not lie. They do not take what belongs to others. Even if they found gold or silver lying in their path, they would not "lift" it unless someone made them a present of it. Salvation is better achieved in the faith of these men called heretics than in any other faith.*'

A fortnight after this conversation Pierre Maury was to have his first, and decisive, interview with a *parfait*. This is the first recorded contact in that long 'quest for the goodman' which was to make up this shepherd's life. It was 1302, and Pierre was about twenty.

The first interview took place at a big dinner given by Raymond Pierre (iii.122). Raymond was, as has been indicated, a substantial farmer and stock-breeder in Arques. His flocks moved seasonally between the Val d'Arques and the mountain pastures of Aillon, his house had a *solier* (ii.17, 404) and at this period he had at least two permanent employees (perhaps because he had no grown-up sons). One of the two servants was a shepherd (at that time Pierre Maury himself) and the other was a muleteer. This second post was filled first by one Arnaud from the area of Sault, who was suddenly dismissed because he was not a Cathar; and then by Pierre Catalan of Coustaussa, who was *a believer in the heretics* (iii.135).

The dinner at Raymond Pierre's naturally took place in the kitchen: with certain exceptions, the distinction between kitchen and dining-room did not exist among the rich peasants of Occitania in those days. Present at the dinner were the master himself, Raymond Pierre of Val d'Arques, also called Raymond Pierre of Sabarthès because of his original place of residence (iii.100, 121). Also present were his wife, Sybille, and her mother, whose co-residence with her son-in-law made it a moderately extended family (iii.122). The two women had prepared a meal. Other more or less local stock-breeders, often from the Pays d'Aillon or the Ax-les-Thermes area, both linked by transhumance with the Val d'Arques, had come as guests or neighbours. Among the guests that day were Raymond Maulen, cousin and first employer of Pierre Maury, and Bernard Vital, who lived in the Val d'Arques but was from Montaillou, where he was cousin of Arnaud Vital, cobbler and crop-watcher, girl-chaser and notorious Cathar. Other guests were Guillaume Escaunier – stock-breeder of Ax-les-Thermes, in Arques on business connected with transhumance – and Marquise Escaunier, Guillaume's sister. The Escauniers, brother and sister, were friends of the Authiés; it was at Marquise's house that Guillaume, that same day, had come across Pierre Authié calmly frying himself some little fish (ii.12, 13).

There was no difficulty about Pierre Maury himself being invited. In fact, his position as servant-cum-shepherd meant that he didn't even need to be asked, since he was a full member of the household like all farm servants at the time. This position was so assured that he did not hesitate, when the occasion arose, to insult his master's wife, thus merely echoing his master. '*Bad mother, devil!*', he was sometimes to call Sybille Pierre (ii.415).

So at this dinner in the kitchen of a *domus* in the Aude there were, in addition to Pierre Maury, members of four major heretical peasant families of the Val d'Arques and the Pays d'Aillon: the Vitals, the Maulens, the Pierres and the Escauniers. In the next room, *the room beside the kitchen*, Pierre Authié, the 'lord' of the heretics, and two men, also heretics, from Limoux, were eating fish; every so often they sent some dainty tit-bits to Raymond Pierre in his *foganha*. In the course of the evening Pierre Maury fell victim to the prevailing atmosphere. Up till then he had been fond of the Catholic preaching of the Minorite friars, of which he had heard a good sample in the church at Arques a few days before (iii.123), but now, overcome by the festive warmth, he began to feel his Roman faith vacillating. And so he was made into a *believer in the heretics* by Pierre Authié, who addressed him with the familiar 'tu' while Maury himself continued to say 'vous' to the Cathar missionary. The evening ended with joyful carousings, in the course of which the company celebrated the admission of a new member.

Pierre Maury was never to see Pierre Authié again. But every week he came down from the local pastures where he kept his own and his employer's sheep, and went to stock up with bread at the house of Raymond Pierre in Arques, where he would often meet some heretic or other. One day when he was in the kitchen, where his employer's mother-in-law was preparing bacon and eggs for him, he learned that in the next room, prudently locked, was Prades Tavernier, the ubiquitous heretical ex-weaver from the Pays d'Aillon. Tavernier for his part was enjoying a Cathar repast of bread, fish and wine. When he learned of the shepherd's arrival, Tavernier sent for him, stood up in his honour, sat down again and gave him a piece of bread which he had blessed. Pierre Maury was delighted: his collection of bits of bread blessed by various different *parfaits* soon became famous throughout the Pyrenees.[1] After that, said Maury, *I took my leave and went back to my sheep, bearing my stock of bread, the blessed and the unblessed.*

A week later Pierre Maury came down again for a fresh supply of bread (the shepherds were great bread eaters). In his employer's house he met Guillaume Bélibaste, a rich farmer from Cubières and the father of Guillaume Bélibaste junior, the *parfait* or pseudo-*parfait* for whom Maury was later to entertain so ardent and constant an affection (iii.194). Guillaume Bélibaste the elder and Pierre Maury the shepherd then left Raymond Pierre's house and went to that of Raymond Maulen. There they found Prades Tavernier, who that week was hiding with Maulen, behind the barrels in the cellar. The various conversations concerning this encounter, in the course of which Guillaume Bélibaste addressed his *melioramentum* to Prades Tavernier, provide a lively description of the arrangements and customs practised in the *domus* of Raymond Maulen, who it will be remembered was Pierre Maury's first employer after he left Montaillou (iii.128–9 and see p. 78).[2]

Pierre Maury's decisive though unique interview with Pierre Authié, the heretical notary soon afterwards burned, was followed by another important encounter, this time with Jacques Authié, Pierre Authié's son. By now it was May and the flowers had long been in bloom. One day when Maury was with his sheep in the pastures at Arques, Raymond Pierre sent a poor child to fetch him. Pierre Maury went down once more to Raymond Pierre's *domus*, where he found two well-known heretics warming themselves by the fire: they were Jacques Authié and Pierre Montanié of Coustaussa. Sitting with them were Raymond Pierre, his wife and his mother-in-law.

After a while Pierre Maury, Jacques Authié and Pierre Montanié left

1 ii.75. Pierre Maury kept some crumbs of this collection for twenty-two years! The mother of Guillaume Austatz of Ornolac had a similar collection of crusts which had been blessed; she kept them in a hole in her house (i.204).

2 The *melioramentum* ('amelioration') was a simple rite required of Cathar sympathizers, which consisted in kneeling down as a *parfait* went by and asking him his blessing and absolution.

the house and set out in the dark for the village of Rieux-en-Val. Authié, a local dignitary, rode on a mule; his two companions walked. It was the ever-obliging Raymond Pierre who had lent and equipped the mule for the preacher. And Jacques Authié continued to preach throughout the journey from up there on his mule, while Pierre Maury acted as audience and foil, and Pierre Montanié played the non-speaking crowd. This was a typical sample of Cathar preaching, specially designed by the Albigensian militants for use with the shepherds. We shall return later to the Cathar myths which were propagated in this manner.

When they got to the end of their long journey Master Jacques Authié stopped preaching and Pierre Maury, overwhelmed by his eloquence, seemed converted once and for all to the dogmas of Albigensianism. Converted, that is, as far as this naive but wily shepherd could be converted: all his life he kept two strings to his bow, one Cathar and one Roman. When he had left Jacques Authié and gone back to Raymond Pierre's house in Arques, Pierre Maury met three men from Limoux who had come there to see Authié. But the three men had arrived too late and missed him, so they were staying overnight with Raymond Pierre, who offered them compensation for their disappointment in the form of an early breakfast of fried bacon and eggs. After that they went back to Limoux. *As for me*, concluded Pierre Maury philosophically (iii.135), *I went back to my sheep.*

In the course of this same memorable summer, Pierre Maury took his sheep to a place called La Rabassole in Arques (iii.135), together with seven other shepherds, who included the brother and father-in-law of his former employer Raymond Maulen, two members of the Garaudy family from the neighbourhood of Arques, and three other shepherds also from Arques, but who as far as we know were not related to the other families represented in the group or to one another. The group of shepherds, taken together, formed a *cabane*, or hut, at the same time a temporary home and a sort of cooperative. *I was the hut leader or* cabanier, said Pierre Maury. *I was in charge of the cheese-making . . . I gave cooked meat, cheese, milk, and bread to passing believers in heresy.*[1] There is nothing surprising about the leading role played by Pierre Maury, whose professional virtues were generally recognized.[2] We shall

1 'Believers' who were not *parfaits* were allowed to eat meat.
2 ii.387: *Guillaume Maurs admired Pierre Maury very much, and wanted him to rule over the other shepherds.*

return in more detail to the *cabane*, a fundamental institution which was to the world of the shepherds what the *domus* was to the world of the sedentary. For the moment, let us simply note that it was during this phase in Pierre's life that he renewed his connection with the Bélibaste clan. Raymond Bélibaste, a believer in the heretics, and Amélien de Perles, a *parfait*, came up to the hut during the cheese-making and Pierre Maury gave them cooked meats and dairy produce. The *parfait*, a vegetarian of course, refused the meat, but both men took Pierre Maury aside behind the hut and asked him for a present. Pierre gave Amélien de Perles a silver *tournois* and, as he had hoped, Amélien said (iii.136), '*I will pray for you.*'

At the end of that year Pierre Maury, accompanied by his cousin Raymond Marty, brother or perhaps half-brother of Raymond Maulen, wintered his sheep in other pastures, though still in the Val d'Arques. One Sunday Pierre and Raymond, still faithful to Catholic routine despite their heterodoxy, attended Mass in Arques. When they came out of church they went to Raymond Maulen's house. Here, in the cellar (*cellier*), they found the heretic Prades Tavernier, once again solemnly hiding behind a barrel. Maury greeted the *parfait* and then went up to the *solier* to get some bread. (In this house, a typical dwelling for someone who combined stock-raising with wine-growing, the kitchen was on the first floor, above the cellar, which was next to the sheep-fold; this was quite a different layout from that of the *domus* in the Pays d'Aillon, with their kitchen on the ground floor.) In the *solier* the shepherd found a number of people sitting around the fire having a meal. Among them was a short fellow with blue-green eyes. This brown-clad stranger was a villager from Coustaussa or Cassagnes. He was acting as guide to Prades Tavernier. Beside the guide sat Raymond Maulen, the master of the house, flanked by his mother-in-law Bérengère and his wife Eglantine. So there were five people altogether sitting around the fire. Having got his bread, Pierre Maury went down again to the cellar, to Marty and Tavernier (iii.136–7). The three swiftly put up a table, a plank set on trestles, for their meal. For Maury and Marty it was bacon or meat supplied by the Maulen household, and for the vegetarian Prades Tavernier it was lentils, oil, wine and nuts. Courtesies passed between the table in the cellar and the table in the *solier*. At one point Maury was sent up to the first floor with a piece of bread or biscuit blessed for the purpose by the heretic Tavernier. In return, Raymond Maulen brought a piece of bacon to his three guests eating in the cellar. But he had not reckoned with the dietary orthodoxy of Prades Tavernier. '*Take away this horrid wild meat*,' said Prades to Pierre, marking his authority by the use of 'tu'. The incident was enough to set Prades off preaching. Having no books or manuscripts to read to the rustics, who in any case were illiterate, the *parfaits* were in the habit, as we have seen, of preaching to them in all kinds of circumstances – walking, on horseback, on muleback or while they were having their meals. Now, in the cellar, the preacher treated his audience to a few variations on the theme of abstinence from meat, quoting sayings which he attributed to Christ in person. '*My children*,' said Christ, according to Prades (iii.137), '*do not eat any kind of meat, neither that of men nor that of animals, but only that of fish from water, for that is the only flesh which is not corrupt.*' There followed a thinly disguised appeal to his audience's purse, an appeal which, at least as far as Pierre Maury was concerned, did not fall on deaf ears. Then Prades, well away, recounted a myth about metempsychosis.

After all this speechifying, Pierre Maury said goodbye to Prades and withdrew. He was never to see him again. But a little while later, to thank him for his edifying sermon, the shepherd, through his brother Guillaume Maury, sent the *parfait* a *gros tournois*, a silver penny and four silver farthings. With these Prades Tavernier was able to buy himself a pair of shoes. One wonders whether up till then he had gone barefoot.

The following Easter Raymond Pierre charged Pierre Maury with a confidential mission: the shepherd was to go to Guillaume Bélibaste the elder, a rich farmer at Cubières, and bring back some money which the old man was either giving back or perhaps lending to Pierre's master.

The elder Bélibaste was a paterfamilias well provided with farm premises and possessing very good connections. He had a *domus* in Cubières in which he co-resided in an extended family with his three sons and the wives and children of two of them. One of the wives was called Estelle. The Bélibaste family also had a barn for straw built independently of the main house and a sheep-fold out in the country.

The evening Pierre Maury spent at the Bélibastes' house followed the model frequent in his social activities, and fell into two different parts. Those at supper included Pierre Maury, Guillaume Bélibaste, his three sons and his two daughters-in-law. (The Bélibastes seem to have been a very united family: they were welded together by co-residence and the fact that they cooked their meals together, by working in common on the family land and by heresy, which was common to both the men and the women.) It seems the children of the two married couples had gone to bed by supper time. The guest of honour was Pierre Girard, proxy of the Archbishop of Narbonne. Girard was sufficiently distinguished for his presence to lend the occasion a certain lustre, but in Occitania in those days social distances were sufficiently small for the presence of such a guest not to be unusual in the house of a rich farmer like Guillaume Bélibaste. Despite his official position, which in theory ranged him on the side of the established Church, Girard was perhaps vaguely sympathetic, either in ideas or in friendship, to the Cathars. Or maybe he was merely tolerant. Anyhow, he knew how to shut his eyes to what people would prefer him not to see. During the meal he took no notice of the comings and goings of suspicious characters whose head-quarters were in the neighbouring barn. The indulgent attitude of Pierre Girard was to stand Pierre Maury in good stead some time later when he was tried in Fenouillèdes on a charge of complicity in heresy. The meal, despite the master's wealth and the prestige of one of the guests, was of antique sobriety and consisted of meat, milk and cheese – a meal fit for the shepherds of Virgil. When supper was over Pierre Girard went to bed. As for Pierre Maury, he, together with several members of the Bélibaste clan, crept out to the nearby barn to greet, on Raymond Pierre's instructions, *all our friends*, i.e. the heretics who were Guillaume Bélibaste's guests that night among the straw. Then the shepherd too went to bed. Next day he set out again for Arques.

A few months later, in August, the middle of the summer, Pierre Maury was keeping Raymond Pierre's sheep at a place called Pars Sors, near Arques. Helping him were some typical representatives of his old group from Aude and Sabarthès: Jean Maulen, brother or perhaps step-brother of his former employer Raymond Maulen, and the two Guillaume Martys, father and son, from Montaillou. One evening at the time when people have fallen into their first sleep, two men came to see Pierre Maury among his pastures. They were Raymond Bélibaste, son of Guillaume Bélibaste the elder, and Philippe d'Alayrac, the *parfait*, originally from Coustaussa. They had come from Limoux (iii.140–42). As we have seen, Pierre Maury had known Raymond Bélibaste for a long time. He offered the two men a typical meal of meat, goat's milk, cheese, bread and wine. Raymond ate it (iii.141). But Philippe d'Alayrac as a perfect *parfait* refused the meat, and would only drink the wine out of his own cup, being allergic to receptacles soiled by contact with the mouths of those who had eaten meat. After the meal the shepherd, at the request of his guests, led them through the darkness up steep and dangerous paths over the fifteen or so kilometres to the Bélibastes' sheep-fold (*courral*) at Cubières, some distance from their family house. On the way Philippe stumbled and slipped so much on the rough paths that he lost any inclination for preaching. Every time he fell he exclaimed: '*Holy Spirit, help me!*'

After these various incidents and visits given or received, Pierre Maury soon broke with Arques and its inhabitants. Jacques Authié was taken by the Inquisition in 1305. At that the heretics of Arques, who included many local families, took fright, and at great expense went to the Pope to confess and abjure their heterodoxy. Either because he did not want to spend all his possessions on the journey or for some other reason, Pierre Maury did not accompany these pilgrims. He merely did them the favour of looking after their sheep during their absence. Once they were back, he decided to make off. He was afraid his kindnesses towards the Authiés, unredeemed by papal absolution, might cost him dearly. So he took his stocks of wheat and the cloth he had had made from his own wool by a weaver called Catala and set off. At Christmas 1305 he was in Montaillou, celebrating the feast with his brothers and father in the family house. But even his native soil was uncomfortable. He was suspect, and his fellow-villagers steered clear of him. So he went and hired himself out to one Barthélemy Borrel. Borrel was the brother-in-law of yet another native of Montaillou, Arnaud Baille senior (iii.148), and his maid, Mondinette, was also from Montaillou.

Hardly had Pierre Maury been hired than he had to move again. Barthélemy Borrel's affairs had led him to take an interest in trans-humance beyond the Pyrenees, and his sheep were at that time in the pastures of Tortosa in Catalonia. So there Pierre Maury was sent by his new employer. For the first time in his life he went over the line where the snows divide, and crossed the mountains to the south. Hence-forward the Pyrenees would no longer be an obstacle, and for the rest of his life he would shuttle backwards and forwards between Spain, the kingdom of France and the Comté de Foix.

On this first journey of the series, Maury was accompanied by a fellow-shepherd, also from Ariège, Guillaume Cortilh of Mérens. The two men never had occasion to speak of heresy. Without unnecessary chat, they merely melted into the flood of migrants, shepherds, un-employed and misfits which the Languedoc dialect called *gavaches* and which the ebb and flow of 'human transhumance' drove towards Iberia (ii.35, 291). By Whitsun of 1306 Pierre, now with seven-league boots, was back in the Sabarthès area, preparing to graze Barthélemy Borrel's sheep during the summer on the 'French', or rather the Foix, side of the Pyrenees; he had wintered them in Catalonia. In accordance with a frequent ritual, Pierre extended his contract with Barthélemy for a year. Borrel was an easy employer: there was no question of heretical con-versations with him and his sons. This was a change from the fascinating but dangerous life Maury had led when he was employed by Raymond Pierre.

The Fournier Register gives some details about Maury's life during the time he worked for Barthélemy. Apparently, in the large Borrel household Pierre Maury acted not only as shepherd but also as man of all work. He chopped wood, helped to entertain and flirted, though he didn't go any further, with the maidservant from Montaillou. This was Mondinette (Raymonde), daughter of Bernard Isarn. A briefly described scene shows Pierre Maury taking Mondinette out one evening to the tavern. After which the maidservant walked along behind him in the street singing at the top of her voice. However, Pierre, though he could be a ladykiller on occasion, was in a chaste mood that evening. Mon-dinette and he did not end the night together. He slept with Bernard

Baille, the son of Sybille Baille of Ax-les-Thermes. As we know, local custom and the scarcity of beds often obliged men, quite respectably, to sleep together (iii.157).

Pierre often visited Sybille Baille's house at that time. She was a stock-raiser of Ax, separated from her husband, who was a notary, and she had entrusted one of her ewes to Maury's care. The Baille *domus* was a large *ostal* with a kitchen on the first floor. The many bedrooms were full of people, and the beds overflowed with guests, friends, servants, sons of the household and passing *parfaits*. It was such a fine house, in fact, that Arnaud, Sybille's son, acted as informer to the Inquisition in order to get it back after it had been confiscated by the authorities on the grounds of his mother's Catharism. She was to end her days at the stake.

But there were other things in Pierre's life besides work and visits to the Borrels and the Bailles. As always, he could prove an excellent guide and even, as will appear, a first-class dupe. So he used to lead goodmen along the difficult path from Ax-les-Thermes to Montaillou, a path so steep that even the most talkative of *parfaits* had no inclination to preach on the way. But the shepherd and the goodmen used to stop for a pleasant, if not always very liturgical, snack on the journey: galantine of trout, meat, bread, wine and cheese. They had a Cathar good time, while the tentacles of the Inquisition had not yet extended to an altitude of 1,300 metres. When they got to Montaillou Pierre would go and see his father, his old mother and his five brothers, who welcomed him with open arms. He would sleep at home, then set off again next morning, after having kissed goodbye, as he lay in bed, the goodman he had escorted the day before. Then back to Ax-les-Thermes and his employer Barthélemy, who had had to keep his own sheep in the absence of the shepherd he paid to do so. The harsh words that ensued precipitated the break between employer and employee which took place after the big fair at Laroque d'Olmes in June.

Laroque d'Olmes, below Montaillou, was a small market town which produced cloth. At the local fair, which in the fourteenth century was held on 16 June, local cloth was sold, together with wood, fish, sheep, pottery and blankets from Couserans (iii.148ff., 153). Fairs were a convenient meeting place for the heretics, and the *parfaits* often resorted to them (iii.153). One year Pierre Maury himself went down to the fair at

Laroque on 16 and 17 June to buy some sheep. He stayed the night with his brother-in-law Bertrand Piquier, husband of his sister Guillemette Maury and a carpenter (*fustier*) at Laroque d'Olmes. It was not a very peaceful night. Bernard seized the occasion of his brother-in-law's visit to beat up his wife. Guillemette, aged eighteen, who didn't get on at all well with her husband, had already, quite recently, run away from him briefly (iii.148). Accustomed though he was to the ways of Mediterranean husbands, Pierre Maury was upset by Bertrand Piquier's behaviour. Next morning, wandering about like a lost soul and worrying what was to become of Guillemette, he met two old acquaintances at the fair, the *parfait* Philippe D'Alayrac and the heretic Bernard Bélibaste. He went for a long walk with them beside the river and told them his family troubles. The verdict of the two Cathars was categorical: Pierre must kidnap his sister and save her from ill-treatment by one who was not only a cruel husband but also an incurable Catholic. '*But*', added Philippe D'Alayrac, '*What is to be avoided at all costs is that Guillemette, once she is freed from the tyranny of her marriage, should become a whore at everyone's beck and call.*' So the three accomplices, Pierre, Philippe and Bernard, agreed that Guillemette should be placed in the service of some pious heretic. No sooner said than done. Pierre finished off his business at the fair, and after a lightning visit to Montaillou, perhaps to ask advice in his *domus*, came back to Laroque and kidnapped his sister. He escorted her to Rabastens and there entrusted her to the Bélibaste brothers, who were already fugitives for heresy and had become his great friends. Then, immediately, *I returned to my sheep ... for the cheese-making season was approaching*. Pierre was very fond of Guillemette, but he was never to see her again. Soon afterwards she was taken prisoner by the Inquisition.

When he got back to his employer's house after the fair, Pierre found that he had been replaced: his absenteeism had angered Barthélemy Borrel, who thereupon found a successor. It did not matter. Pierre was a competent shepherd and had no difficulty finding another job. He hired himself out to Pierre André, a sheep farmer in Fenouillèdes (iii.159), and then to a relative of his, Guillaume André. Working for Guillaume, Pierre Maury was one of a group of eight or ten shepherds (the farmers took on more staff during the summer), among whom were his employer's two sons and other groups of brothers from the Foix and

Cerdagne region. Pierre spent three peaceful years with Guillaume André, migrating backwards and forwards with the seasons – Aude in the winter, upper Ariège in the summer. Ideologically speaking, it was a long fallow period for Maury. They were three quiet, rather tedious years, without any of the Albigensian militancy which had made him an activist, with already a whiff of the stake in Montaillou, Arques and sometimes even Ax-les-Thermes (iii.159–60).

The Inquisition, or at least the established Church, continued to keep an eye on him. One day towards the end of his time with Guillaume André, Pierre Girard, the proxy of the Archbishop of Narbonne, summoned him to the main square at Saint-Paul-de-Fenouillèdes, and accused him of having met with two heretics, one of them a certain Bélibaste. (We do not know at whose instigation Girard sent for Maury.) There was some piquancy about this accusation: Pierre Girard had been the guest of honour at the very dinner where Pierre Maury had first met Bélibaste. Pierre Girard was as much an accomplice as an accuser, so he did not press his advantage. And Pierre Maury, fortunately for him, had friends even in the court. The lord of Saint-Paul, Othon de Corbolh, was very fond of him. As for the local *bayle*, he was a fellow-sponsor (*compère*) of Maury's. In these circumstances the shepherd had no difficulty in providing himself with a cast-iron alibi. He told the magistrates, in substance: *At the time when I was supposed to be seeing Bélibaste, I was in fact leagues away: I was digging the vineyards of the André family.*[1] The court, with its uneasy conscience, swallowed this blatant lie whole. Pierre Maury was set free. The incident was a good example of how the networks of patronage, friendship, complicity and compaternity could often paralyse the repressive force of the Inquisition in Occitania.

In 1308 Pierre Maury went up again to upper Ariège, passing through Ax-les-Thermes. In this large village, near the Bassin des Ladres, he had a fascinating discussion on fate with his brother Guillaume Maury and Guillaume Belot of Montaillou (see below, Chapter VII). Then he went to the pass at Quié, and with five other shepherds looked after the Andrés' sheep. Bernard Fort, who brought flour up to this little group,

[1] iii.160. The shepherds and migrant workers, including goodmen, who looked after the sheep, sometimes left the flocks for a few weeks for the lucrative seasonal work of digging vineyards (iii.165).

was the first to inform Maury about the great round-up, effective for once, which had just been carried out in Montaillou by the Carcassonne Inquisition. Pierre could secretly congratulate himself. Once again fate had been on his side. Though he knew that some day or other his turn would come he didn't lose any sleep over it.

Again he had a few 'apolitical' or rather 'a-heretical' years. At the beginning of 1309 he once again showed the indomitable independence typical of the shepherd's trade: he gave Guillaume André notice and hired himself out to Pierre Constant of Rasiguières (in the present department of Pyrénées-Orientales). He spent the summer in the mountain pastures of Mérens, south of Ax-les-Thermes, with five other shepherds, two from Fenouillèdes and two others at least from Mérens itself. One of them, named or nicknamed Guillot, was the illegitimate son of the priest at Mérens. Guillot specialized in keeping goats, and looked after the flock belonging to Madame Ferriola (Na Ferriola) of Mérens (iii.163).

At Michaelmas 1309 Pierre Maury again felt an urge to be free and gave notice to Pierre Constant: it was as if the man were dismissing the master rather than the other way round. He then hired himself out to the Cerdan Raymond Boursier of Puigcerda. This job lasted two years, from 1310 to 1311. Here the team of shepherds included Raymond Boursier himself, Pierre Maury, his brother Arnaud, and another from Cerdagne, Albert de Bena. Arnaud Maury apart, there was no question of talking heresy with any of these people.

At the end of two years, perhaps late in 1311, the Maury brothers left this group: Arnaud went back to Montaillou and Pierre headed due south towards Catalonia, which was to become his second home. At Baga, near Barcelona, he hired himself out as a shepherd to the Catalan, Barthélemy Companho. Here the team included eight shepherds, six Catalans and two Ariègeois.

During the first year, 1311 or 1312, there was no heretic on the horizon. But the next year, 1312 or 1313, in the friendly house of a Moslem shepherd called Moferret, Pierre, through the good offices of a Catalan, made contact with a peddler of cumin and needles who was none other than the Cathar Raymond de Toulouse (iii.164). The following Lent (1313?), Pierre was presented to the little Albigensian colony at San Mateo and Morella, in the Tarragona region. This consisted of a small group of heretics from Montaillou and elsewhere who had gathered around Guillaume Bélibaste the younger. He had gratified them by becoming a minor prophet, whom they and he himself identified with Christ or the Holy Ghost. But he was recognized only by himself and the 'happy few'. For financial or other reasons, Guillaume Bélibaste occasionally helped the team of shepherds led by Maury. So did the Maurs, who were also shepherds who had fled from Montaillou. All these connections were renewed in 1315.

It was during the winter of 1315–16 that Pierre Maury made his first contact beyond the Pyrenees with other members of his family who were part of the Catalan diaspora from Montaillou. A woman from Tortosa selling flour told him that one of his female relations was trying to get in touch with him. The good shepherd was a man devoted to family and *domus*, and the idea of resuming a link with someone of his own blood was irresistible. At Orta, a village near Tortosa, Pierre Maury met his fellow-countrywoman, Guillemette Maury, a capable woman with on the whole a good heart, but somewhat cunning. A short while after their reunion she did not hesitate to reward her good cousin by cheating him in business.

On the Sunday when Pierre went to see her, Guillemette Maury, whose husband, Bernard Marty of Montaillou, had died quite recently, was still living in Orta, but soon afterwards she moved with her two sons, Jean and Arnaud, to San Mateo, a village which had the inestimable advantage of being nearer to Morella, where Bélibaste lived. Moreover, *People say that San Mateo is more lucrative than Orta.*[1] It was easier to make one's way there, which suited Guillemette and her family of rough, hard-working mountain folk. And the exiled Guillemette, whom Pierre, who never bore a grudge, continued to visit frequently right up to the end, 'made good' in San Mateo, where she bought the house known as 'the house of the Cerdans' in the Rue des Laboureurs, in a quarter reserved for farmers. The house had a courtyard and several rooms. Guillemette's prosperity also derived from the fact that she had three people in the family who could work on the land. She

1 iii.169. For the material success of some people from Ariège who emigrated to Catalonia, especially skilled artisans like shoemakers, smiths, etc., who had no difficulty in making a living there, see iii.171. But widows, when they had no grown-up children to support them, often fell into poverty as they grew older.

became a small farmer, with a vineyard, a she-ass and a flock of sheep. In her own house she set up a workshop for combing wool. And to balance her budget she and her children hired themselves out as seasonal workers during the wine and other harvests. She was very hospitable and always had visitors or friends in the house – Pierre Maury, or one of God's poor or a Basque priest wandering about with his concubine (iii.166, 188 and *passim*). She was typical of many emigrants from Ariège, whether Cathar or not. For these people emigration, which did not involve any homesickness for their native mountains, meant emancipation and rapid adaptation to urban and Spanish freedom. It gave women a more important role and allowed young people a freer choice in marriage than they had enjoyed before, up in their lofty, strict community in Sabarthès.

The relationship between Pierre and Guillemette Maury was poisoned for a while by a sordid business over a lease of livestock. Before departing on his professional migrations Pierre leased his own sheep out to Guillemette. The contract, which seems to have been purely oral, covered five years and provided for profits and losses to be shared equally (iii.169). The obligations were equitably though unilaterally divided: Pierre supplied the sheep and Guillemette was responsible for the running expenses. It was a sensible arrangement so long as Guillemette did not cheat Pierre, but unfortunately this condition was not fulfilled. Guillemette took advantage of her partner's absence to deprive him of the income he should have had from the hides and fleeces of 150 sheep which died. She claimed that the hides and wool were used only for her own household purposes and to clothe her children and friends and herself (iii.184). On his return one day from Cerdagne, Pierre, taken unawares by this bad news, pressed Guillemette for an explanation, and she was forced to admit that she had given part of the spoils from the 150 sheep as a present to the goodman Bélibaste. Pierre was so furious that one day, taking leave of Bélibaste, he called him *minudier* (miser), and omitted to give him the ritual salutation (iii.169, 172, 173 and *passim*). The shepherds' lives were full of such incidents, when unscrupulous heretics like Bélibaste would use their position as *parfaits* to change a debt into a gift which they regarded as only their due. One day Pierre Maury and Guillaume Bélibaste bought six sheep which they were to own in joint possession (iii.167). Pierre paid his own share and advanced the money for Bélibaste's share; in addition he lent him the princely sum of five *sous*. But then Bélibaste suddenly decided to withdraw his three sheep. '*What does it matter to you?*' he said to Pierre. '*You did not lend me the money – you gave it to me for the love of God.*' Maury was goodness itself, but he was no fool, despite his naivety. This was too much for him, and for several days he gave his friend the cold shoulder.

A brief summary will be sufficient to cover the subsequent rather repetitive period in Pierre Maury's career. At Easter 1315 or 1316 he hired himself out as a shepherd to Arnaud Fauré of Puigcerda for five or six weeks. This gave him an opportunity to move northwards again to the Roussillon and Catalan border, where he took his new master's sheep, perhaps together with his own, to Cerdagne.

Back in his beloved Pyrenees, Pierre temporarily left Arnaud Fauré, for whom he had performed various tasks in connection with the seasonal movement of livestock, and took service again with his former employer, the lady Brunissende de Cervello. This Catalan lady was an important stock-breeder associated with Raymond Boursier of Puigcerda, another of the shepherd's old acquaintances. Pierre had spent two years as Boursier's shepherd in Cerdagne some years earlier. Now that he was well known to be competent in his profession, Pierre could choose his masters from among the network of employers available as he moved about between southern and northern Catalonia, Cerdagne and upper Ariège. That summer Pierre took Brunissende's sheep up into the mountains of Ariège. In addition to himself and his brother Jean, his team consisted of the usual Pyrenean quartet, three Cerdans and one Andorran, plus another from the region of Teruel in Aragon. At the end of the summer Pierre, having completed his work for Brunissende, decided to spend the winter in southern Catalonia again, summoned there by his long-standing affection for Bélibaste. So he took employment again with Arnaud Fauré, whom he had left the previous spring, and undertook to bring Arnaud's sheep down to the winter pastures of the Plana de Cenia, not far from Tarragona. This brought him close to Morella and San Mateo, the permanent homes of Bélibaste's little colony (iii.172). During the next few years Pierre Maury, absorbed in his more or less friendly dealings with the Bélibaste clan, led a slightly more stable life. But in the summer of 1319 he set out for the north again, and we see him once more on the Puymaurens Pass (L'Hospitalet) with his old team of Montaillou shepherds, which included the Maurs brothers, another shepherd from Prades d'Aillon and a Cerdan (iii.181). In conversation around the camp fire that summer the shepherds often talked about Bishop Jacques Fournier: he had a reputation for being able to make suspects *bring forth their lambs* – in other words, confess the truth. The shepherds also spoke of Pierre Clergue, the priest: *He is now known as the little bishop of Sabarthès, because of the power he wields; he is said to be bringing about the destruction of the country, through his complicity with the Inquisition.* Little did the shepherds realize that many of them, together with Pierre Clergue himself, would soon end up in the clutches of the real Bishop.

On the Feast of Saint John that year, Pierre once more succumbed to his old and profitable habit of changing jobs. He gave notice to his then employer, the Cerdan Raymond of Barri, and took service again with Brunissende de Cervello, whom we now meet at Pierre's every turn (iii.181). For the remaining months of that summer Pierre went with his flock to La Cavalerie and Fontaine-argent, some way from L'Hospitalet. His group of shepherds, which included his brother Jean Maury, consisted of men from Cerdagne, Catalonia, Andorra and from Montségur and Montaillou in Ariège.

There were no heretics on the scene that summer, but nevertheless Pierre preferred not to leave his Pyrenean fastness for the lower regions of Sabarthès, which might be dangerous. Even the mountain regions of Sabarthès might prove unhealthy. In the summer of 1319–20 Pierre hesitated no longer, but set out southwards on the winter migration to the Tarragona area, near Carol and the monastery of Sainte-Croix (iii.181, 182). Thenceforward his fate merged with that of the friends of Bélibaste; and, as we shall see, his arrest followed soon after theirs.

It was during a visit to Guillaume Bélibaste, probably in about 1319, around Easter, that Pierre Maury was faced with a definite prospect of marriage (iii.185). After some circumlocution about Pierre's over-long absences and the moral impossibility for Christ, if he were really present in the Eucharist, to pass through the unmentionable parts of the human body, Bélibaste turned to the crucial question of getting Pierre married. His argument began with some friendly criticism. '*Pierre, you have gone back to your whoring. For two years, in the pastures, you have kept a mistress.*'[1] Bélibaste went on to say it was time Pierre settled down and that he, Bélibaste, would undertake to find him a wife who would have the understanding of good, i.e. be a heretic. '*She will look after your possessions. Moreover, you may have children who will help you and look after you in your old age. In any case it would be more respectable for you to have one woman than to frequent any number of girls, who tear out your heart and liver, root and branch.*'

'*I do not want a wife,*' answered Pierre. '*I can't afford to support one. I don't want to settle down because I would not be safe*' (he means he is afraid of the Inquisition).

So Bélibaste's first offensive was a failure. Guillemette Maury, who understood her compatriot very well, soon diagnosed the cause of this failure as Pierre's *itchy feet* (iii.186–7). The other Pierre Maury, her brother, told the shepherd: '*Pierre, you are homesick. You are absolutely determined to go back to your wretched, dangerous native land, and one of these days you will be caught.*'

But Pierre Maury remained unmoved by all their arguments. '*And in fact,*' he said (iii.187), '*I went back to Brunissende's sheep!*'

His return followed the usual pattern: winter in the Pyrenees, summer in Catalonia, with shepherds from Catalonia, Cerdagne, Ariège and Aragon. The following year, loyal to his own ideological migrations, Pierre was back again with the Bélibaste colony. One November night he shared a bed with Guillaume Bélibaste at Morella (iii.188). Next morning the two men set out on foot for San Mateo, stopping on the way at Dame Gargaille's inn. After their meal they resumed their journey, and Bélibaste stopped beating about the bush and spoke again,

---

1 iii.185. Unfortunately we know no more about this mysterious mistress. True, there is some hint that she was none other than the lady Brunissende de Cervello. But I am rather sceptical about this. Although noblewomen tended to be easy-going about their lovers' social position, the difference here was a very great one, and it is hard to imagine Pierre Maury, despite his comparative wealth and despite his savoir-faire, bridging the gap so completely. However, here is the snatch of conversation in which the suggestion occurs: Bélibaste, after rebuking Pierre for having kept a mistress for two years in the pastures, goes on to say (iii.186), '*Pierre, do you intend to go back and live with the lady Brunissende de Cervello?*'

'*Yes,*' answered Pierre.

'*Then,*' replied Bélibaste, '*since you will not abstain from women, I will find you a good one.*'

after a lapse of over a year, about marriage. But this time he had a definite name to suggest. '*You cannot always be gadding about from one woman to another,*' said Bélibaste. '*It is my opinion that you should accept a wife, one with the understanding of good, and that you should remain with her. And she will look after you in your old age. And she might bear you sons and daughters. She will give you pleasure, And she would help you in your infirmities. And you would help her in hers. And you would have no need to be circumspect with her*' (meaning, as he would have to be with mistresses).

But these prospects apparently did not tempt Pierre, who answered with his usual excuse about being too poor to afford a wife. '*I do not want a wife,*' he said. '*I have enough to do, providing for myself.*'

'*I have a wife for you,*' said Bélibaste. '*Raymonde, the woman who lives with me. She will just do for you.*'

'*But perhaps her husband, Piquier, is still alive,*' said Pierre.

'*No,*' was the reply, '*I do not think he is any longer of this world. And anyhow, dead or alive, he is not likely to bother you much here. Meanwhile, Raymonde and you can do what you have to do, if you manage to agree.*'

Pierre's position began to alter slightly. '*Raymonde is not a suitable wife for me,*' he said. Raymonde was in fact the daughter of an iron-master or wealthy blacksmith, and her social position was higher than that of a Montaillou shepherd. '*But talk to Raymonde about it if you like,*' said Pierre. '*I see no objection. But there is no question of my approaching her about it.*'

The two men then arrived at Guillemette Maury's house in San Mateo. As usual the house was full of people, including besides the hospitable hostess her invalid son, Arnaud Maury, her brother, a woman who had been taken on to card the wool and a poor man whom Guille-mette had invited in for a meal *for the love of God* (iii.188–9).

First they had a snack, and then they had dinner. Pierre took up the question of marriage again with Bélibaste. '*If you think it is a good idea for me to marry Raymonde,*' he said, '*speak to her about it. And if she agrees, then I agree. And tomorrow, while you are about it, you might have a word too with my uncle Pierre Maury.*'

After dinner Guillemette, not knowing the battle was almost won, returned to the attack. '*Lord,*' she said, '*what a trouble our Pierre is to us. We cannot keep him. And when he leaves us we do not know if we shall ever see him again, since he goes to places where our enemies are and where, if he were recognized, he would be taken prisoner; and then the rest of us would be destroyed.*'[1]

After a night at San Mateo during which, for want of space, the two Pierre Maurys, Guillaume Bélibaste and Arnaud Maury were all obliged to sleep in the same bed, Bélibaste and Pierre Maury the shepherd set out next morning on the way back to Morella. They stopped once again at Dame Gargaille's inn, where Pierre finally capitulated. '*Since you are so anxious for me to marry Raymonde, I will do as you wish.*'

That evening they arrived at Morella and Bélibaste asked Raymonde Piquier: '*Do you agree to be Pierre Maury's wife?*'

'*Yes, I do,*' she said.

At this, Bélibaste began to laugh, for reasons we shall shortly understand. Or perhaps his laughter was just a way of signifying that the couple were now united in marriage. After this ceremony the three supped, without formality, on conger eel and bread blessed by Bélibaste. And according to the brief and simple account given by Pierre Maury himself to the Inquisition, *Raymonde and I slept carnally together* that night (iii.190).

The marriage which had taken so long to bring about was very swiftly broken up. The next morning Bélibaste, usually of a cheerful disposition, seemed depressed. He even went so far as to undertake a fast for three days and three nights. At the end of this penance he took Pierre Maury aside and suggested point-blank that the marriage should be dissolved. Pierre could not refuse his friend anything. And perhaps he smelt a rat. At any rate he agreed to this strange request, Bélibaste had a word with Raymonde, and Pierre found himself a bachelor again after having been a married man for less than a week. Shortly afterwards he went back to his sheep, and Raymonde gave birth to a child.

Whose child? Pierre's? Or Guillaume's? It is difficult to say, but the baby was probably Guillaume's. For a long time he had been living with Raymonde in Morella, though he told anyone who cared to hear that he never touched a woman's naked flesh. It is true that he sometimes slept in the same bed as Raymonde quite openly, when they were travelling or

1 iii.189. Guillemette was of the opinion that if Pierre Maury was taken prisoner by the Inquisition he would speak. Because of their horror of lying this was a common practice, if not of ordinary 'believers', at least of the *pʋ faits* imprisoned by the Roman Church.

putting up at an inn. But Bélibaste always gave out among his disciples that this was just to hoax the Catholics and make them believe that he was a married man and not a *parfait*. Moreover, he said, whenever he did sleep with his housekeeper he always took care not to remove his underclothes. But in fact Raymonde had long been his concubine, and it took someone as naive as Pierre Maury not to see it. More probably he was blinded by his generosity and brotherly friendship towards Guillaume, a friendship as ardent and warm as that between Bernard Clergue and his brother Pierre, the priest. When his brother Jean Maury reproached him for his ridiculous 'marriage', Pierre explained: '*I could not do otherwise, because I was so fond of Guillaume Bélibaste.*'[1] Pierre Maury was so affectionate he would swallow anything.

But those around him did not have such strong reasons for keeping silent. Emersende Marty (of Montaillou) and Blanche Marty (of Junac), Raymonde Piquier's sister, both of them refugees in Spain, disapproved of the whole business and soon afterwards bluntly told Pierre so. '*I do not think much of the way lord Bélibaste has behaved to you,*' said Emersende (iii.198). '*He married you to Raymonde; then separated you from one another; and then created such a disturbance in his house after the marriage that he forced you to leave right in the middle of a hard winter. So much so that you nearly died of cold in a mountain pass.*'

Blanche Marty enlightened Pierre about the woman who had been his wife for three days (iii.198). '*Guillaume Bélibaste and Raymonde and I all used to live together once in the village of Prades.*[2] *One day I went un-expectedly into the room where Guillaume and Raymonde slept and found them in bed, Guillaume with his knees bent as if he was just about to know Raymonde carnally or had just done so. When Guillaume, thus caught in the act, noticed me, he cried: "You bastard, you have just interrupted an act of Holy Church!"*'

Blanche went on: '*Either I ought not to have believed my eyes, or*

---

1 iii.194. But the holy man only thought of exploiting the good shepherd's friendship and his financial generosity towards him. After his 'brief encounter' with Raymonde, a well-meaning compatriot from Montaillou told Pierre outright (iii.195): '*Guillaume Bélibaste and Raymonde do not want you to stay on with them at Morella. Guillaume would never have a minute's peace for thinking you might be trying to sleep with Raymonde. All that interests Raymonde and Bélibaste as far as you are concerned is to get your money out of you; they want neither to see you nor to have you with them.*'
2 iii.198. Prades near Tarragona, not Prades in the Pays d'Aillon.

Guillaume really was doing you know what with Raymonde.' The thing was plain: Guillaume had made his mistress pregnant, and to save his honour as a *parfait* had married her for a few days to the shepherd so that he would be thought the father of the child.

But the shepherd of Montaillou was a generous friend, and decided to overlook it. He remained devoted to Bélibaste, who continued to sponge on him. Pierre even took part in the long march of Bélibaste and his friends to the north, the result of the activities of Arnaud Sicre, the informer, who had insinuated himself into Bélibaste's colony in order to bring about its destruction. Shortly after Guillaume was captured, Pierre, after a few further wanderings of little interest, was himself taken captive by the Inquisitor. In 1324 he was sent to prison and thereafter disappears from the records.

CHAPTER VI

The life of the shepherds in the Pyrenees

The lives of Pierre and Jean Maury, Pellissier, Benet, Maurs and a few others, as they are revealed by the Fournier Register, together with many minor facts about the shepherd's life scattered throughout the documents, provide a useful basis for an ethnography of the sheep-raising regions of the Pyrenees in the first quarter of the fourteenth century.

Considering first its economic aspect, the shepherds and shepherdesses were men and women of business, of *borias*,[1] and sometimes tough. *Boria* is *boria*, as Pierre Maury learnt to his cost from his dealings with Guillemette Maury over wool, lambs and sheepskins. Trade in the mountain pastures was to a certain extent carried out in money, but not to the point of excluding barter and pledges in kind when there was a temporary lack of cash. *Pierre Maury had no money, so he pledged thirty sheep, all he had, to Raymond Barry as part of the price he would normally have paid to buy a hundred sheep from him* (iii.186). This practice seems to have been quite widespread. Alazaïs Fauré of Montaillou offered half a dozen *or even a dozen* sheep to Bernard Benet of the same parish if he would agree to conceal from the Inquisitors the fact that her brother Guillaume Guilhabert had been hereticated (i.404). More generally, whether it was a question of bribing a gaoler or winning the goodwill of the goodmen, a gift of wool would always help. But the widespread use of barter did not preclude a monetary economy as well, probably more active in the sheep-producing mountains than in the cereal-producing lowlands. Money intervened between the sale of wool and the purchase of lambs. *Pierre Maury asked Guillemette for the money she had got from the sale of the wool produced by the flock he had left in her charge the year before.* She answered (iii.172), '*I bought some lambs with that money.*'

Guillemette was not always to be believed, but it was true that wool, with its high purchasing power, could realize considerable sums to be metamorphosed into sheep in the course of the economic cycle. *The heretic Arnaud Marty of Junac had great need of money: so he sold twenty sheep for ten* livres *tournois, and the wool of these sheep for six* livres tournois. So the wool alone was worth over a third of the total price of a flock (six *livres* out of sixteen). It was not surprising if the shepherds

1 *Boria* meant both barn and business: ii.184.

sometimes had the feeling that they had got rich, or at least comparatively rich, rich enough for their eyes to be bigger than their purses. It was because he suddenly decided to buy a hundred sheep for a thousand Barcelona *sous* that Pierre Maury sank to his neck in debt (iii.177; ii.186).

Fortunately, we are relatively well informed concerning the territorial organization of this pastoral economy. Migratory sheep-raising had to cope sometimes with the rights of the big village communities, sometimes with the rights of nobles who had managed to assert their authority over part of the mountain pastures in Spain or the Pyrenees. This duality of powers already existed in the period we are dealing with. For example, when Pierre Maury was in the Flix Pass in the region of Tarragona, he grazed his sheep in an extensive pasture cultivated and ruled over by the Bishop of Lérida (iii.170). Twelve of the Bishop's agents, enraged at this trespass, came up specially from Bisbal de Falset in order to confiscate Pierre's sheep. Pierre only extricated himself from this tight corner by cooking an enormous pie which was shared between the Bishop's henchmen and the shepherd's friends from Cerdagne, Catalonia and Ariège. Manorial authority could operate at two levels: that of the land, and that of the flocks themselves, often the property of nobles, ecclesiastics or Knights Hospitallers. Among the great sheep-owners with whom the shepherds from Ariège had dealings as employees or competitors were Brunissende de Cervello (ii.185 and *passim*), and the Hospital of Saint John of Jerusalem in the region of San Mateo (iii.179).

As well as all these gentry, the urban and peasant communities also had a right of inspection, concerned more with the land over which the flocks passed than with the sheep themselves. Guillaume Maurs relates that *Pierre Maury for two summers grazed his sheep in the Pal Pass in the territory of Baga and, another summer, in the Cadi Pass, in the territory of Josa.*[1] The reference to territorial limits seems to suggest that the Catalan communities of Baga and Josa exercised jurisdiction over the migrant flocks which made use of their common pastures. The outer limits of these pastures were the limits of the commune's actual territory. The inner limits were marked by the plantations and market gardens bordering the parish, where sheep were forbidden to graze. *Jeanne Befayt* [of Montaillou], *who lived in Beceite, helped Pierre and Arnaud Maurs to lead their flock out of the village, taking care that the*

1 ii.183. These were mountain areas near Barcelona and Gerona.

flock should not invade the gardens and vineyards of the said village (ii.390). Another frontier was that which separated the pastures, whether communal or otherwise, from the crops. The great problem for the parishioners charged with crop-watching was to prevent flocks from trampling the standing harvest (ii.505). There was always this danger, because near habitation, cornfields and vineyards there were, at least in some places, areas where wild animals had become scarce, so that the shepherds might risk leaving their sheep unattended and go off to enjoy themselves. *Guillaume Bélibaste and Pierre Maury, as they grazed their sheep, could go where they pleased, because in the meadows where they were there was no fear of wolves; the only danger was of 'trampling': so at night the shepherds could send their flocks to graze in the pastures and go where they pleased until daybreak* (ii.182).

Sometimes some of the nearest or most fertile meadows had become the private property of local sheep-farmers. Some were still common land (often under the 'eminent proprietorship' of a nobleman). We can only conjecture how the pastures were allocated to the migrant shepherds. Sometimes it was done by drawing lots, as in the case of the Montaillou shepherds who brought their own or other people's sheep to graze on the territory belonging to Arques, in the Aude region (iii.140). In other places, on the Catalan side of the mountains, the conditions imposed on the Ariège shepherds were more drastic. The migration of flocks was more or less forbidden, and in order to have the right to graze sheep on the common land a man had to marry a local girl and become a resident. *While Jean Maury was living in Casteldans,[1] the local* bayles *ordered him either to get married on the spot or to get out, so that his sheep should not eat up their pastures. And Jean Maury could not find a woman in Casteldans who would agree to be his wife. So he went ... to Juncosa[2] and lodged in the house of Esperte Cervel and Mathena, her daughter. With the help of the priest of Juncosa, he arranged to marry Mathena, who had taken his fancy.*

Though village communities kept jealous watch over the territory where sheep could graze, they seem to have played only a small part in the way the flocks were organized. The nineteenth century was the heyday, in upper Ariège, of the *ramados*, communal and intercommunal flocks. In

1 ii.487. Casteldans is in the region of Lérida.
2 Juncosa is in the region of Tarragona.

the fourteenth century there was nothing comparable. In this area, and among the migrant shepherds who came from it, flocks belonged either to a single person or, at the most, to associations of individuals (groupings which in modern times have been called *orrys*). So the communal spirit, far from being a survival from pre-history, must have developed in upper Ariège between the fourteenth and eighteenth centuries, parallel with the growing role of the village community as a force within the state and as a fiscal and political unit.

In Montaillou, the Pays d'Aillon or Sabarthès there was no communal organization of flocks in the period 1300–25. However, not far from this area there was communal herding of cattle, which remained very important right up to the nineteenth century (as in the big communal and inter-communal dairy farms (*bacados*) of around 1850 in the region of Tarascon and Montségur). But apart from a few oxen used for ploughing, there were hardly any cattle in Montaillou in 1320, and the problem of a communal *bacado* did not arise. But slightly to the south, in the village of Ascou, which was to remain one of the outstanding centres for collectivist dairy-farming right up to the twentieth century, there is every reason to believe that this tradition goes back to the fourteenth or even the thirteenth century. Raymond Sicre of Ascou relates (ii.362): *One Sunday in the month of May [1322], I was leading a heifer of mine to the mountain called Gavarsel near Ascou ; and when I saw that it was beginning to snow I sent my heifer to join the herd of common cows of the village of Ascou, and I went back to the village.*

The role, then, played by the village community in the shepherd's life was real but limited. For them the essential social unit, independent of the village, was the *cabane*. We have already seen how in his youth, at La Rabassole near Arques, Pierre Maury had been in charge of a *cabane* (*chef de cabane*) during the summer, where he had to see to the making of cheese and was responsible for a team of eight shepherds.[1] The Fournier records contain other passages about this system of *cabanes*, which the shepherds from Montaillou regularly adopted. Guillaume Baille (iii.519) alludes to a shepherds' *cabane* in the Pyrenean pass of

1 iii.135. In the region of Montaillou and Prades, where there were no isolated farms, the *cabanes* acted in a sense as scattered though temporary dwellings. See ii.172 for the few '*cabanes* for animals' in Prades d'Aillon, belonging to a couple of local farmers.

Riucaut, between Andorra and L'Hospitalet (this may be the present Envalira, near the Mérens Pass). *That summer two shepherds from Cerdagne, together with Guillaume Maurs of Montaillou, lived in a* cabane *in the Riucaut Pass. Arnaud Maurs, brother of Guillaume Maurs, was the* cabanier [*chef de cabane*] *and made the cheese* (ii.381).

After the summer *cabane* in the Pyrenean mountain pastures came the winter *cabane* in Catalonia. *The following winter*, said Guillaume Maurs (ii.186), *I went with my brother and our flocks to winter in the plain of Peniscola . . . and we already had so many sheep that we could form our own* cabane. It should be noted that the winter or Lent *cabane* had a certain minimum of comfort. There was a kitchen area, and a corner for hanging clothes (ii.181) and for sleeping. The shepherds entertained their friends there. It was in this *cabane* at Peniscola that Pierre Maury and his cousin Arnaud visited the Maurs brothers. The four men discussed, with some satisfaction, Jacques Fournier's recent capture of the priest Pierre Clergues. The *cabanes* were where dairy products were made, where the various shepherds' comings and goings intersected and where news was exchanged from their native village far away (ii.477). The Maurs brothers had spent the previous season in upper Ariège and Aragon. As for Pierre Maury, his travels in the past two years had included Aragon, Cerdagne, the Comté de Foix and south Catalonia. And yet what did they talk about in the *cabanes*, these men who could not be accused of parochialism or even provincialism? They had each of them been all over several different provinces, but now they chatted quite simply about the village, about home, about Montaillou, out of sight but not out of mind.

Another *cabane* briefly sheltered the shepherd Guillaume Gargaleth, perhaps a Saracen, and his partner Guillaume Bélibaste, who had been hired for a fortnight by the farmer Pierre Capdeville (iii.165, 166). This cabin was in the spring and summer pastures of Mount Vézian, near Flix in Catalonia. *Gargaleth and Bélibaste grazed the sheep during that fortnight, until Easter ; they stayed alone in the* cabane, *and had their own hearth, away from everyone else.* Not far away were some of the temporary sheepfolds (*cortals*) for migrant shepherds. Around these the men erected fencing and, under the guidance of Pierre Maury, who was appointed chef, Catholic, Cathar and Saracen shepherds cooked and shared garlic-flavoured pies, mingling together as brothers regardless of their different opinions (iii.165).

So the *cabane* was to the migrant shepherd of Montaillou what the *domus* was to his family back at home in the old country. It was an institution: *cabanes*, designated as such, with all their weight of human relationships, are recorded from Ariège and Cerdagne in the Pyrenees to the Catalan and Moorish areas of Spain. The *cabane* area stretches a long way south, as far as southern Andalusia, which long remained under Saracen domination. Under the Andalusian system of the *cabañera*, the shepherds were paid a small salary in money supplemented by a fixed contractual amount of food. So both *cabane* and *cabañera* are well-defined institutions: they belong to that community of culture, at once Moorish, Andalusian, Catalan and Occitan, in which both the local and the migrant civilization of the people of Montaillou were involved at so many levels.

In contrast to the *cabane*, the corral (*cortal*) was simply a space with the minimum of roofing and a floor of earth or trodden dung, enclosed with branches or stones as a defence against wolves, bears and lynxes. One end of the enclosure consisted of a narrow entrance which would let in only one sheep at a time. In the fourteenth as in the nineteenth century, the essential element in the *cortal* was the fence. Pierre Maury, who in the *cortal* as in the *domus* was a generous host to seasonal migrants and heretics (iii.165, 199 and *passim*), did not for all that forget his fences. *At the beginning of Lent, Pierre Bélibaste, the heretic Raymond of Toulouse, and the believer in the heretics Raymond Issaura de Larnat, came to my cortal in the pastures at Fleys. I was making bread. I told one of the shepherds, a Saracen who was working with me, to give the heretics something to eat . . . As for the heretics themselves, I told all three of them to make some fences, and this they did all day long in the* cortal *. . . I myself went out with my sheep . . . In the evening, in the* cortal, *we ate a dish of garlic, bread and wine. One of the heretics blessed the bread secretly in the heretical manner. (We spent the night in the* cortal). *Next day I made two big pies, one for the above-mentioned heretics, and another for myself and my friends in the team of shepherds. The heretics then set out for Lérida, where they knew Bernard Cervel, a smith from Tarascon who was of their faith; they planned to hire themselves out to dig the vines in the region of Lérida.* This passage clearly illustrates the functions of the *cortal*, both complement to and substitute for the *cabane*. A passing labour force (in this instance polarized by heretical friendships) built the indispensable fence against wild animals, before going down again to the lowlands to engage in other seasonal work. The *cortal* acted not only as a sheep-run but also as kitchen and bakery for the various workers who passed through. It was a cultural cross-roads for the lower classes, which in this case were heterodox and consisted of Cathars and even Moslems. The way in which work was organized in the *cabane* and the *cortal* in Pierre Maury's time seems not to have been very different from what it was five hundred years later. Each *cabane* sheltered a team of from six to ten shepherds who lived there either seasonally or temporarily, to be replaced by another team, equal in number but of totally different geographical origin and identity. There were also smaller *cabanes*, of two or three shepherds.

Agricultural inspectors of the nineteenth century found from two hundred to three hundred sheep to each *cabane*, and this was about the same as in the Middle Ages. Sometimes there were only between a hundred and a hundred and fifty. The two or three hundred sheep to each *cabane* would be provided by several shepherds joined together. Often each one would bring his own sheep and almost always he would bring those of his employer. Pierre Maury, for example, might bring thirty to fifty of his own sheep among the much larger flock entrusted to him as chief shepherd, *cabanier*, *fromager* or *majoral*. He was, as we shall see in greater detail later, at one and the same time a partner, an employee and foreman over his friends, the other employees.

The rhythms of the daily or, rather, monthly life of these shepherds during winter and summer pasturing were dictated by lambing and milking. The lambs were born at Christmas, as in the story of the crib in Bethlehem, already popular in the iconography of the fourteenth and fifteenth centuries. At the beginning of May the lambs were weaned, and from May onwards the milking began. Associations were formed between shepherds, or between shepherds and employers. In June the shepherds went up to the *cabanes*. The chief shepherd (*majoral*) armed with ladles and wooden bowls, supervised the making of cheese, to be sold in the shops in Ax-les-Thermes to all the neighbouring villagers, including those from Montaillou.

The *cabane* of Spain or the Pyrenees contrasted with the *domus* of Sabarthès or Montaillou in that it was entirely masculine, only disturbed from time to time by a brief visit from some courtesan or mistress come to disport herself with a shepherd richer or more attractive than the others. In the *domus*, despite a certain division of labour which assigned outdoor matters to the men and indoor matters to the women, masculine and feminine roles did interact and overlap. But in the *cabane* everything was strictly adult and masculine.[1] In fifteenth-century paintings of the Adoration of the Shepherds, the presence of a Virgin and child in the sheep-fold in the pastures is an unexpected element, surprising and wonderful. But although the *cabane* was a society of men, brought together through cooperation and not ties of blood, it was nonetheless a repository of the most ancient traditions, lunary and mental, of one of the oldest occupations in the world. These were shortly afterwards to find public expression in the shepherds' calendars. The summer mountain *cabanes* played a similar role for Cathar as for cultural survivals, guarding them as long as possible from the persecuting forces of the lowlands, through oral transmission from old shepherd to young shepherd. Perhaps it is a vestige of this transmission that is referred to by La Roche-Flavin in the only known text alluding to a possible Cathar survival after the beginning of the Renaissance. 'A saintly bishop,' says La Roche-Flavin, 'going to Rome to be made a cardinal, met near the mountains of Albi an old peasant of the fields, and as he spoke to him about the news of the country the old man said that there were a multitude of poor people, wearing only sackcloth and ashes, living on roots in the wastes of those mountains like brute beasts, and these were called Albigensians, and the continual war that had been waged against them for fifty or sixty years, and the murder of more than fifty thousand men, had only served as seed to make them grow and increase, and there was no means of wooing them from their error, except the preaching of some excellent person.'[2]

So far we have been dealing with long-term tendencies, transhistorical trends, during which, from the fourteenth to the nineteenth century, the *cabane* remained unmoved, a living institution. Underlying these struc-

1 As noted elsewhere, the occupation of shepherd in this region was essentially masculine: there was no Joan of Arc or 'little shepherdess' in upper Ariège. However, it did sometimes happen that a women, especially a widow, took her sheep to the pastures. See the cases of Guillemette 'Benete' and Raymonde Belot (iii.70), though the text is ambiguous.

2 La Roche-Flavin, *Treize livres des Parlements de France*, pp. 10–20, quoted by Louis de Santi and Auguste Vidal, *Deux livres de raison* (record books or registers) (1517–1550), special volume of *Archives Historiques de l'Albigeois*, fasc. 4, Paris and Toulouse, 1896.

tures are the great movements of migration. A concrete picture of the details of migrant life during the decade beginning 1310 is provided by Guillaume Baille, a shepherd of Montaillou (ii.381, 382). *That year we lived in a summer* cabane *with the Maurs brothers and two Cerdans, at Riucaut.* In September, at Michaelmas, the Maurs and the two Cerdans, now joined by Pierre Maury, went south with their sheep, a long stretch of some thirty leagues right across Catalonia. *We went to spend the winter with our sheep in the pastures at Peniscola, and in the plain of San Mateo, among the first territories of the kingdom of Valencia.* Pierre Maury went as far as Tortosa, *where he recruited two more shepherds,* two Occitans. One of them, Raymond Baralher, was from Aude; the other was from Mérens in upper Ariège. Once the team was complete and settled down with the sheep, the winter timetable followed the traditional pattern. *Up to Christmas, the whole team remained mostly together. We had our two meals together,* prandium [at the beginning or in the middle of the day] *and* cena [dinner, in the evening]. *After each meal we split up, both day and night, to graze our sheep.* The sheep were divided up into several different flocks or sub-flocks. The division into sub-flocks was a regular feature of pastoral life, then as now. Guillaume Maurs declared (ii.188), *Raymond, of Gébetz, and Guillaume Bélibaste (then Pierre Maury's partners in guarding the same flock) could easily have talked to one another, even on heretical subjects, in the pastures at Tortosa, because the sheep they were each in charge of grazed close together.*

Things became more complicated for Guillaume Baille's team at the end of December. At Christmas, when the lambs were born, a happening which witnesses explicitly associate with the Nativity, the division of tasks and of space, hitherto only begun, grew more marked. *I, Guillaume Baille, went on looking after the sheep 'properly speaking'* [i.e. gelded]. *Not far away, Pierre Maury looked after the group of lambs and* marranes – *in other words, the lambs of the present and of the previous year. Maury and I were thus separated at work both day and night; but we had our midday meal* [prandium] *and dinner* [cena] *together, in company with Raymond Baralher, who brought our provisions. As for the other members of the team, Guillaume Maurs, Jacques d'Antelo, Guillaume de Via and Arnaud Moyshard, they were settled some distance away in the village of Calig. There they had taken charge, from the beginning, of the ewes, first with lamb, and then suckling.* The division of labour did not always coincide with relationships between friends. *In those days Pierre Maury showed greater familiarity to Guillaume Maurs and Raymond Baralher than to his other work-fellows* (ii.382). 'External' social relationships linked the team to the people of the nearby Spanish towns and villages, such as Calig and San Mateo, which were full of emigrants from Narbonne and Cerdagne (ii.188, 382). They used to go to these places, on foot or by donkey, to fetch provisions. In the tavern, where people would bring their own food at Christmas, they met shepherds working in the same region but for different farmers. These meetings provided opportunities for seeing passing heretics. *That winter*, says Pierre Maury (iii.171), *I came back to spend the winter in the pastures at Camposines, in the territory of Asco* [in the Tarragona area]. *And there, around Christmas, I met two friends: Raymond, who was staying with Pierre Marie* [probably a sheep-farmer from Ariège], *and Pierre, who was staying with Narteleu, of Villefranche-de-Conflent* [Roussillon]; *we had all three gone into a tavern in Camposines and suddenly I saw Raymond de Toulouse, the heretic, come up to me with his bale of peddler's goods. I went out to meet him and talk to him, while my two friends cooked the meat and eggs they had brought with them.*

For the summer work, generally done in or around the Pyrenees, we have fewer details than for the winter. But Pierre Maury throws some light on the chronology of the summer hirings (iii.163). *After having given notice to Guillaume André, my former employer, I hired myself out as a shepherd to Pierre Constant of Rasiguières in the Fenouillèdes. I stayed with him from Easter until Michaelmas in September of the same year, and I spent the summer on the passes of Mérens and the Lauze* [in upper Ariège]. *I had with me . . . five shepherds. That summer I did not see any heretics or any believers in the heretics. And then, around Michaelmas, I gave notice to Pierre Constant, and hired myself as a shepherd to Raymond Boursier of Puigcerda, with whom I remained for two years.*

We have scattered information about various episodes in the summer pasturing, in particular about the shearing, which was done in May, just after the arrival of the flocks in the mountain pasture (*alpage*). As Guillaume Maurs says (ii.185), *We set out again from San Mateo towards the mountains and the pass of Riucaut. When we got to the pass, near the Mérens Pass, we sheared our sheep.* Shearing-time, followed by the sale of the wool, was the time for settling urgent debts. It also provided an opportunity for the social intercourse which the shepherds loved, between the people of Montaillou itself and with those from elsewhere. *I was with Pierre Maury my brother at the Lalata Pass* [in Cerdagne], says Jean Maury (ii.505). *We were shearing our sheep. Pierre Maurs came to see us there on a mule that he owned. We all ate together – I, my brother Pierre Maury, the three brothers Pierre, Guillaume and Arnaud Maurs, their cousin Pierre Maurs and Guillaume Baille* [all of Montaillou]. *The shearers also ate with us, but I have forgotten their names. We had both mutton and pork. And then Pierre Maurs loaded Arnaud Maurs's wool on to his mule to take it to Puigcerda.* But this social activity could also be the occasion for 'evil communications' with mountain heresy. In 1320, Arnaud Cogul of Lordat said (i.380): *Sixteen years ago or thereabouts – I don't exactly remember how far back – I went up to Prades d'Aillon to shear my sheep, which were being looked after for me by Pierre Jean of Prades. I spent the night there, and during the night I was seriously and painfully ill. Next day I got up and found myself in the courtyard of Pierre Jean's house, because I meant to leave, and Gaillarde, Pierre Jean's wife, said to me: 'Do you want to speak to the goodmen?'*

And I replied: 'You go to blazes, you and your goodmen!' I knew very well that the goodmen in question were heretics, and that old Gaillarde was thinking of having me hereticated by them if I were to die of my illness!

Shearing in May was followed in June and July by the cheese-making up in the *cabane*. Round about the feast of Saint John, Pierre Maury said to his sister Guillemette, whom he had just rescued from the clutches of her Catholic husband (iii.155), '*It is time for me to leave you, for I am worried about my master's sheep; and above all it will soon be time for making cheese.*' In the case of both summer and winter pasturing, there is a great contrast between the internal social inter-course among the groups of shepherds, which was necessarily inter-regional, and the external social intercourse which the wandering shepherd sought as often as he could in the villages of the exodus, where he met friends from home and mixed with the diaspora, Cathar or other-wise, from Montaillou. *I brought my sheep back*, said Pierre Maury (iii.168), *from the winter pasture* [in Catalonia] *to the summer pasture* [in the Pyrenees]; *the shepherds in my group, apart from the Maurs brothers from Montaillou and Charles Rouch from Prades d'Aillon, were all from Cerdagne . . . ; when we stopped over in the village of Juncosa, in the diocese of Lérida, I met Emersende, the wife of Pierre Marty of Montaillou, Guillemette Maury, the wife of Bernard Marty, Bernard Marty, her husband, Arnaud their son, all of Montaillou, all believers in the heretics except for Bernard Marty.* Whenever they could, and wherever they were, the shepherds and emigrants from Montaillou got together and recreated, though on a different scale, their native village.

The world of the shepherds, involved on the one hand in the ecology and chronology of transhumance, was on the other hand part of the network of wage-earning and association, though it was never, as such, involved in the concatenations of feudal dependence, still less in those of serfdom. The shepherd from Ariège or Cerdagne in the fourteenth century was as free as the mountain air he breathed, at least as far as feudalism was concerned.

We may disregard the future shepherd's earliest days, when he was training for what was to become his life's work: *When the heretics came to my house*, said Jean Maury (ii.470), later one of Montaillou's best professional shepherds, *I was not at home; I was out, keeping my father's sheep. I might have been about twelve or thereabouts*. But the adult shepherd was an employee, a wage-earner. In stock-rearing regions he occupied a place parallel to that of the skilled labourer in grain-producing regions; but he had greater opportunities for getting rich and developing his potentialities, though set against these advantages was the risk of accident, not negligible in that mountain country. Instability was the hallmark of a shepherd's life, as of the lives of all rural workers in Occitania: 'Every year', says Olivier de Serres in his book on agriculture, 'change your farm hands, make a clean sweep. Those that come after will put all the more heart into their work.'[1] The people we are concerned with did not feel this instability as some kind of oppression or alienation. On the contrary, the migrant shepherd changed his master more often than his shirt! Pierre Maury was quite typical in finding it equally usual to be dismissed by one employer, to give in his notice (*dimittere*) to another, and to hire himself out (*se conducere*) to a third. The fact that the sheep farmer who employed him was called master (*dominus*), just like a feudal lord, added no extra element to the contractual link between the sheep-owner and the shepherd. As we have seen, the hiring of shepherds might be seasonal, based on the pattern of migration: Pierre Maury relates how, finding himself in the Tarragona area of Catalonia at Easter (iii.172), *I hired myself out as a shepherd to Arnaud Fauré of Puigcerda, and remained with him some six or seven weeks, or almost; I took his sheep to Puigcerda* [the summer pastures in

1 *Théâtre d'agriculture*, Paris, 1600, Vol. I, Ch. VI.

the Pyrenees]. *When I got there I hired myself out as a shepherd to the lady Brunissende de Cervello and to Raymond Boursier of Puigcerda; and during the summer I remained in the Quériu Pass on the land belonging to Mérens* [in Ariège]. *And then, when the summer was over, after the end of my summer pasturing in the service of the lady Brunissende and Boursier, I hired myself out again to Arnaud Fauré of Puigcerda! And I came down again with his sheep to pass the winter on the plain of Cénia* [south Catalonia]. Thus Arnaud Fauré was Pierre Maury's employer for two successive winter pasturings, or more precisely migrations between winter and summer pasturings; while Brunissende de Cervello was his employer for the summer pasturing itself.

Some passages speak of shepherds being hired specifically for a year, after a probationary period arranged through some third party, a friend or relation or fellow-citizen of employer and shepherd. Pierre Maury says (iii.148), *Arnaud Baille the elder, of Montaillou, son-in-law of Barthélemy Borrel of Ax-les-Thermes, said to me: 'If you want to hire yourself as a shepherd to my father-in-law, I will see to it that he gives you a good wage.'*

I agreed to this suggestion. My new employer sent me to winter his sheep at Tortosa [Catalonia]. *When I returned to Sabarthès* [for the summer pasturing], *the said Barthélemy gave me a shepherd's contract by the year.*

Instability of employment was more marked in the case of those who specialized in the seasonal migration, like the Maurs and the Maurys, than in that of comparatively sedentary and stationary shepherds, with more or less fixed employers, like for example Jean Pellissier.

The relationship between employer and shepherd was generally close and easy. The employer might be a relative of his employee, or a relative of one of his friends or fellow-citizens. In any case, the employee had no hesitation in speaking his mind to his employer's wife. He often actually lived in the same place as his master, either in the master's house, on Sundays and feasts and days when he had come down from the mountains, or in the pastures themselves, where the master would often spend several weeks or months together with his employees. *I hired myself out to Pierre Constant of Rasiguières*, says Pierre Maury (iii.163), *and I stayed with him from Easter until Michaelmas in September, keeping his sheep on the summer pasture in the Mérens Pass.* On other occasions, Maury tells how he stayed with his master Barthélemy Borrel of Ax (iii.155, 156) or with Brunissende de Cervello, whose sheep he was pasturing.[1]

The shepherd was a wage-earner. Part of his 'salary' or 'pay' was in kind, or in food. When Pierre Maury was staying in Arques, he regularly left his flock to go to his employer's house for bread: *One morning I went down from the pastures to Raymond Pierre's house, for my stock of bread* (iii.127). But when they were in the Tarragona area, where their employer was too far away, it was Pierre Maury himself who acted as baker, cooking the bread in the oven of the *cabane* or the *cortal*: *These people came to see me in the* cortal *where I was at that time, in the pastures at Fleys. I was making bread* (iii.165).

The other part of the wages was in money, a very small sum which might be paid monthly: *When Pierre Maury and Guillaume Bélibaste were in the service of Pierre Castel of Baga* [in the diocese of Urgel], says Guillaume Maurs (ii.176, 181), *Pierre Maury collected the month's wages which Guillaume was supposed to receive from Pierre Castel; and with this sum he bought peas and leeks for the said Guillaume.*

In addition to wages, the contract between employer and shepherd often provided for the sharing of the natural increase of the flock, the cheese and sometimes the wool. The frontier between wage-earning pure and simple and a lease of livestock was often vague.

An employee was a factotum, entrusted with every kind of task. He could be postman as well as baker. In a world where people could not read or write and where there was no official post, the shepherd in his seven-league boots might act as go-between, carrying verbal messages for his employer about some business affair, or perhaps some matter Cathar and ultra-secret.[2] *Pierre Maury*, said Guillaume Maurs, *remained as shepherd and as messenger with Barthélemy Borrel of Ax for a year; and he went with Borrel's sheep to Tortosa. Afterwards he brought them back to the Comté de Foix. During the time he dwelt thus with Borrel he carried various different messages to various different places, but he never told me what he was charged to convey, nor to whom.*

At some periods of his life the shepherd who had hitherto been an employee might become, temporarily or permanently, an independent

---

1 iii.186. ii.183 is more ambiguous.
2 ii.175. The shepherds' world was itself a vast information network: the shepherds and the mountain folk in general were linked by signals and shrill cries which carried over large distances from one hill to another (i.403).

sheep-farmer. This was what happened with Pierre Maury, when he happened to find himself in good shape financially, a state which usually did not last long. Guillaume Maurs again (ii.183): *My brother Arnaud and I were then shepherds to Raymond Barry of Puigcerda; and we had wintered with his sheep on the plain of Peniscola. That winter Pierre Maury stayed with us on the said plain, but he was independent, without a master, because he had bought a hundred sheep from Raymond Barry; while I and my brother were shepherds to Raymond Barry, Pierre Maury, though he lived with us, lived at his own expense.*

Finally, the shepherd might remain an employee and never become an independent sheep-farmer, even temporarily. But he might, just the same, become an employer by, so to speak, taking a sub-lease on some lesser shepherd. In the only known example of this, the 'employee-cum-employer' was in fact a collective, a team of shepherds all from Montaillou and strongly bound together by family ties. *I hired myself out as a shepherd*, says Pierre Maury (iii.166), *to Pierre Castel of Baga. I stayed two years with him, wintering in the pastures at Tortosa. Also shepherds with me were Guillaume Maurs and Pierre Maurs (Pierre Maurs is the first cousin of Guillaume, and the son of Raymond Maurs of Montaillou). The first year, around Lent, Guillaume Bélibaste came to see us in the pastures; he stayed with us for three months, because we had taken him on as a shepherd.* Other hirings or sub-hirings were purely seasonal; additional workers might be taken on for shearing towards the end of spring.

As well as vertical links between employers and workers, such as still exist today in agriculture and stock-raising, there were also horizontal links, forms of association between colleagues, or with employers of other shepherds, owners of other sheep. Guillaume Baille (iii.390) recounted how *he and his companions, Guillaume, Pierre and Arnaud Maurs went to winter in the pastures at Calig* [near Tarragona]. *We did not have many sheep: because of this, we joined together with a group of shepherds and sheep which belonged to Pierre Vila of Puigcerda; this group contained four shepherds and one muleteer, all from Cerdagne.* On another occasion Pierre Maury, the Maurs brothers and the employer of them all (who at that time was none other than the Catalan, Pierre Castel of Baga), entered into association with some Cerdans. *The following summer*, says Pierre Maury (iii.167), *we took our sheep to the pass of Pal* [in the present-day department of Pyréneés-Orientales] *and we entered into*

*association with the shepherds and sheep of Arnaud Fauré (of Puigcerda);
all his team of shepherds came from Cerdagne.*

Sometimes, for a few seasons, when favoured by good fortune and well
rewarded for his labours, Pierre Maury managed to be his own boss. He
would then use various techniques: fraternal mutual aid, the hiring of
paid shepherds or association with another employer – of whom he
himself became, in fact, the employee. These combinations usually
occurred when the situation in the mountains grew difficult as the result
of some private war between feudal lords. *That summer*, says Pierre
Maury (iii.195), *I went to the Isavena Pass* [in the Pyrenees] *near
Vénasque. I stayed there during the summer pasture with my brother Jean;
Jean and I then took on Bernard of Baiuls to help us guard our sheep . . .
afterwards, at Michaelmas, we came down from the pass and went to
Lérida ; we had to avoid the Casteldans territory because of the war there,
between Nartès and Guillaume den Tensa. So we joined our sheep with those
of Macharon and Guillaume Maurier, two sheep-farmers of Uldecona* [in
the Tarragona region]. *With the sheep of these two farmers, we went and
wintered in the pastures of San Mateo, I, my brother and two shepherds,
one from Cerdagne and the other from Vénasque.* These various types of
association broke up almost as easily as they were made: *Pierre Maury*,
says Guillaume Maurs (ii.182), *decided to separate his own sheep from
those of his then employer, Pierre Castel. . . . So he went off with his animals
and claimed, when he came back, that he had sold them to a merchant in
San Mateo.*

As well as wage-earning and what might be called 'simple association',
there was also a whole class of contracts covering 'sheep share-cropping'.
Among the people from Montaillou, whether they stayed in the village
or emigrated, this kind of lease of livestock took the form of the *parsaria*.
The contract between Pierre Maury and the sheep-farmer Guillemette
Maury, the relation and fellow-countrywoman whom he met again near
Tarragona, was a variation of this arrangement (iii.169). Despite the
somewhat acrimonious disputes between the two partners, this association lasted some time. Shortly afterwards, Guillemette invested twenty
additional sheep in the association, as well as her money. Pierre Maury
notes (iii.181), *The next morning I received twenty sheep from Guillemette
and I returned with them to the pastures at Calig.*

The *parsaria* also existed in Montaillou itself. In about 1303 Guillemette Benet, whose husband Guillaume Benet was a kind of labourer-

cum-farmer – he owned oxen for ploughing which had to be shut up in the evening after work (i.478) – entrusted her sheep by means of a *parsaria* arrangement to the people of the great house of Belot, who seem to have specialized in sheep-rearing. *About eighteen years ago, or thereabouts*, said Guillemette Benet in 1321 (i.477), *my husband and I held some sheep in* parsaria *with the house of Belot. It was evening, sunset, during the summer pasturing. I was taking some bread to the Belots' house so that they could send it to Guillaume Belot as well as to Raymond Benet, my son, who were guarding the 'partiary' sheep.* Thus, by means of a contract which was probably merely verbal, without benefit of notary, the Benets supplied the Belots with part of their livestock and part of their labour, together with home-made bread for the shepherds.

We must now go beyond these descriptions of economic and professional links and try to decipher, through the appealing personality of Pierre Maury, the social position and mental outlook of a migrant shepherd of Montaillou in the early decades of the fourteenth century.

In the first analysis, Pierre Maury and those like him seem to be at the bottom of the relevant social scale. Their situation is similar to, but not the exact counterpart of, that of the skilled labourers in the north of France during the last years of the *ancien régime*. Their life was full of discomfort and even danger. '*You were forced to leave Bélibaste's house during a hard winter; you came to a mountain pass where you almost died of cold*', said Emersende Marty to Pierre Maury one day, reminding him both of the holy man's ill-treatment and the hardships inherent in Pierre's own profession (iii.198). Bélibaste himself had called his friend's attention to these (ii.177). '*Pierre, your life is made up of disagreeable nights and disagreeable days.*' The daily round of a shepherd like Pierre Maury, especially in winter, was almost as hard and sometimes as dangerous as the life of a woodcutter like Bernard Befayt, victim of an accident at work (ii.190). *Bernard Befayt* [husband of Jeanne Marty of Montaillou] *died in the forest of Benifaxa* [in Spain]. *He was digging up the stump and roots of a tree, when the roots and the rocks above it collapsed on him. He was killed outright.*

Despite passing phases of prosperity, Pierre Maury regarded himself as a poor man, and for that reason unable to found a family. More often than not he went to bed wifeless, on the same couch as two or three other men. The following is one example of many (iii.202). *That night we slept, I, the heretic Bélibaste and Arnaud Sicre, all three in the same bed.*

For Pierre Maury, poverty was not only a frequent fact and a cheerfully accepted companion, but also an ideal and a system of values. Of course, this ideal was one transmitted in various ways by the neo-evangelical culture spread through Occitania by the diverse advocates of voluntary poverty, including the Franciscans. But in Pierre, and in many another Cathar shepherd of Montaillou, this ideal found a receptive audience. As far as one could be in the fourteenth century, Pierre Maury was a democrat through and through. He had only hatred and contempt for ornament and the pleasures of the table, at least when those pleasures emanated from the Church. Though he could be caustic enough on occasion, he was more indulgent towards the gluttonous or well-to-do when they were not clerics. He was hostile to the Minorites, whom he accused of feasting, against all the rules, after a funeral. All these roisterings and gormandizings, he said, were harmful to the dead person's soul, and prevented it from reaching Paradise (ii.30). He uses the same terminology as Saint Matthew, referring to the camel which cannot pass through the eye of a needle. This is evidence of a certain degree of evangelical culture, which had reached him through the good-men or through the preaching monks to whom he listened despite his gibes. If Pierre loved the *parfaits* it was because, among other reasons, they put into practice an ideal of industrious poverty denied by the mendicant friars, although they had once ardently preached it.

As to the laity, Pierre denounced those he called *the riders of fat mules* (ii.58). These were people with false consciences, who pretended to forget their heretical past. After they had half retracted, their powerful connections saved them from prison: *I know many people in Sabarthès who ride fat mules, no one bothers them; they are sacrosanct and yet they have dabbled in heresy.* Pierre contrasted this earthly injustice with the ideal of a democratic Cathar paradise, *where great and small live together* and rub shoulders freely (ii.179).

This egalitarian ideal is a hundred miles away from the rapacity of people like Pierre Clergue or Arnaud Sicre, men who wanted to promote or to recover their *domus* at any price. Pierre Maury laughed at such greed: he had no house, he lived anywhere, detached from the goods of this world. His outlook as a wandering shepherd was very different from that of the village stay-at-homes, wealthy or otherwise, who remained muffled up in their *domus* and on their lands at Montaillou until the Inquisition came to flush them out.

We can guess one of the reasons for the shepherds' attitude to poverty, acquired through experience and accepted quite simply. This reason lay in the fact that they were nomads. The shepherds might well, from time to time, have a mule and a muleteer to go back and forth with wool and food, and to carry some luggage during the migrations. But basically the shepherds carried their fortunes on their own backs. Their physical strength and endurance were such that the burden might sometimes be quite heavy: Pierre Maury forded a fairly wide river carrying Arnaud Sicre and Bélibaste on his shoulders, one after the other. So he could take a considerable amount of baggage with him from the Pyrenees to Catalonia. But there were limits to what one individual could manage. A bundle of clothes and an axe did not leave much room for other impedimenta (ii.337).

For a shepherd to accumulate wealth like the permanent residents of Montaillou, he would need his own *domus*. But this he did not have. During the summer pasturing and especially during the winter, the shepherds usually slept in other people's houses: with their employer, with a friend, with a fellow-sponsor or, perhaps, with some house-owner, who made them pay rent as occasional tenants who spent most of their time in the pastures. At worst, they might take refuge in a *maison du berger*, a shepherd's hut on wheels, but I have not come across this kind of mobile dwelling among the Pyrenean shepherds of the fourteenth century – there were no roads suitable for carts and wheeled traffic in those mountains. Even in the following centuries the *maison du berger* was more common in northern France than in Occitania.

The migrant shepherd of Montaillou, with no *domus* of his own except during brief visits to elderly parents at home, developed a very different notion of wealth from that of his sedentary contemporaries. The shepherd might be comparatively well off in terms of flocks and even money, but he was necessarily poor in terms of objects, clothes, crockery, furniture, stores of grain and so on.

This was probably one explanation, though not the only one, of the extreme detachment as regards the goods of this world which Pierre Maury manifested when confronted with the problems of wealth. He liked it well enough to enjoy it when he had the chance; but he was never attached to it. One day in Spain the shoemaker Arnaud Sicre, the as yet undetected informer, complained to the emigrant colony from Montaillou that he had been impoverished because of his mother's heresy: she had been burned by the Inquisition, after her property and *domus* had been seized. Pierre Maury immediately replied (ii.30): '*Don't you worry about your poverty. . . . There is no disease easier to cure! Just take my case. Three times I have been ruined, and yet now I am richer than I have ever been. The first time it was in the valley of Arques, when Raymond Maulen and many others went to the Pope to repent* [of their Catharism]; *and I had perhaps the equivalent of 2,000 sous, and I lost everything.*

Afterwards I lost my share of the fraternal inheritance [fratrisia] that I had at Montaillou; for I did not dare [for fear of the Inquisition] *to go and collect it. Later I hired myself out as a shepherd to people in Ax and Puigcerda. With them, I earned 300 sous; I entrusted the money to one of my friends in Urgel; and afterwards he refused to give it back to me. And yet now I am rich, because our custom, thus ordered by God, is as follows: if we have but one farthing, we must share it with our poor brothers.* At various times Pierre had owned a hundred sheep and some asses (ii.57), and once as much as 300 sous. On another occasion he had as much as 2,000 sous. Quite a tidy sum, but much less than the amount owned by a big local landowner like Bernard Clergue, who could spend 14,000 sous to get his brother out of the clutches of the Inquisition (iii.282–3). Anyhow, when Pierre Maury, our goatskin philosopher, said he was 'rich', he was aware that this was very relative. A really rich man was not a wage-earner like himself but a farmer and landowner with enough wealth to be able to use others to work for him (iii.122). Moreover, Pierre knew very well (he said so to Bélibaste on various occasions) that despite his assertions of wealth he was too poor – financially, materially and because he had no house of his own – to maintain a wife properly, with any children she might give him. He remained faithful to the teachings of his master Jacques Authié, in the valley of Arques (iii.130–31): *'With the riches Satan shall give you will never be satisfied, however much you possess. He who has will always want more. And you will have neither pause nor end, for this world is not the realm of stability; and all that is of Satan is only passing and doomed to destruction.'* These stinging words applied very well to people like Pierre Clergue and Arnaud Sicre, obsessed with domestic cares and frustrations; but measured by this yardstick Pierre Maury was sure to find grace, so liberated was he by his shepherd's outlook from the ordinary laws of village lumpishness.

And yet, if we set aside material objects, undesirable because too difficult to transport, Pierre Maury was rich, at least in terms of the satisfactions which came his way. His life was interesting, full, exciting. His flocks browsed in pastures not exhausted by over-grazing. He used his own wool. From the social and economic point of view he was, like all his colleagues, almost completely outside the scope of feudal oppression. From time to time he might have to pay some toll or due to a feudal lord, for grazing or for going through a pass. But on the whole the

'relations of production' in which he was involved were by nature contractual and mobile, salarial or cooperative. Though there is no need to
talk of modernity (we must not forget that this pastoral world derived
from the early Neolithic age, and its basic principles were laid down well
before the fourteenth century), it is plain that Pierre Maury and his like
lived outside the purely subsistence economy on which the residents of
old Montaillou continued more or less to thrive. Maury, because of the
final destination of his flocks, was part of the market economy of the
transhumance. Needless to say, this does not mean that he was subject
to the pitiless timetable of capitalist organization, far removed from the
easy norms of the century before the Black Death. Everyone who has
studied the daily life of the people of Montaillou, whether locals or
emigrants, has been struck by the relaxed rhythm of their work, whether
they were shepherds, farmers or artisans. Like the rest of them, Pierre
Maury had his leisure moments. When necessary he got his friends to
look after his sheep for him while he went down to the neighbouring
town, to take, or to collect, money (iii.166). Or he might absent himself
for purely personal reasons, without any problems of time-keeping or
supervision, to go and visit friends, mistresses (unless they came up
directly to see him in his *cabane*) or fellow-sponsors, friends acquired at
baptisms recently or long ago. There was nothing parochial or even
provincial about Pierre Maury. Like the Maurs and all the other shepherds from Cerdagne and Ariège, he stood at the intersection of a whole
news network stretching from one mountain pass to another, thanks to
which they were in touch with everything that was going on in Catalonia, the Pyrenees and their own native region. And Pierre made
frequent visits home, despite the dangers of the Inquisition.[1]

Pierre Maury, a wage-earner, not alienated, informed, informal, and
sociable, enjoyed parties and entertainment, and even just a good meal
among friends. There was nothing outstanding about his ordinary
meals, but he had plenty of solid, nourishing food – meat, goat's liver,
pork, mutton, eggs, fish, cheese and milk – in people's houses, in
taverns and in the open air, with brothers, relatives, friends, comrades,
enemies or bravos who had been sent to confiscate his flock and whom
he had got round by making a big pie which they all devoured together.[2]
Pierre Maury was one of the chief stalwarts of the room serving as salon,

1 iii.186, 187 and *passim*.
2 ii.158, 184; iii.139, 140, 141, 148, 151.

dining-room and kitchen in the house of Guillemette Maury, the small farmer in exile from Montaillou who had re-settled with her family in San Mateo, in the street reserved for agricultural workers. People crowded there at midday or in the evening for meals distinguished by the number of guests and the liveliness of the conversation, if not always by the quality of the food. *At Eastertime, in the house of Guillemette Maury in San Mateo*, said Guillaume Maurs (ii.183–4), *I have seen Pierre Maury, Guillemette Maury herself, her sons Jean and Arnaud and her own brother, also called Pierre Maury, and Arnaud Sicre of Ax* [the informer] *and many others, almost a dozen or fifteen. And they all ate their midday meal together there. And they ate fish. But I don't like fish. And anyway it wasn't the right time of year for it. So I was surprised. And I sent one of Guillemette's sons to buy a goat's liver. And I ate that; and I gave some of it to the other guests who sat at table with us that day.* Even in times of famine or shortage (e.g. 1310), Pierre Maury managed to find enough flour to feed not only himself but also the other shepherds in his team and his friend Bélibaste: they had a quarter of a quintal of flour per week per person.[1] At holiday times, as far as his modest means allowed, and with the help of his friend and enemy Arnaud Sicre, he used to subsidize the festivities of Guillaume Bélibaste and Raymonde, Bélibaste's concubine. Arnaud Sicre (ii.69) tells how *Pierre Maury and I agreed to pay the Christmas expenses fifty-fifty: I was to pay for myself and for Bélibaste; Pierre Maury for himself and for Raymonde.*

Pierre Maury owned no real estate nor many permanent possessions, but he had plenty of friends. These friendships were based in the first instance on family relationships. Maury no longer had a house which belonged to him personally, but the paternal *domus* and links of relationship and lineage still represented for him cardinal values and sources of loyalty. This loyalty extended to ideology. Pierre Maury said to Guillaume Maurs (ii.174): 'Three times the house of my father and mother was destroyed for heresy; and I myself cannot cure myself of heresy, for I must hold the faith my father held.' This short passage, together with others, shows that in Montaillou heresy was not a subject of conflict between fathers and sons or ancients and moderns.

If Pierre was a good son, he was even more a good brother. As we shall see, his highly developed sense of friendship was merely the expression of a fraternity not based on ties of blood. The possibilities

1 ii.176. One quintal equals approximately one hundredweight.

of fraternal attachment are evident in the kind of system which prevailed in Montaillou, with its strong stress on lineage. Pierre demonstrated this very early, when he kidnapped his sister, with her consent, to save her from a brutal husband.[1] As for Pierre's affection for his brother Jean, also a shepherd and a fellow-worker, this never failed, despite passing tiffs, like the one which occurred one summer in the Isavena Pass (iii.195). In the course of this argument, Jean called his brother a heretic. Pierre relates how he answered: '*You're not so far removed from heresy yourself!*'

But the quarrel was nothing serious. Pierre later showed how attached he was to his brother. One day when Jean was ill and delirious, he threatened to have all the heretics taken prisoner: he had never been a complete believer. Guillemette Maury, who was nursing him, said in alarm (iii.206), '*We must kill him; otherwise, if he gets better, he will send us all to prison and the stake.*'

Pierre at once replied: '*If you have my brother killed, I will eat you alive with my teeth, if I can be revenged no other way.*' Guillemette soon changed the subject.

The love of brother for brother could be metamorphosed into profound friendship towards someone who presented no links of blood and who was known as a 'friend in the flesh' (*ami charnel*). As Pierre Maury said (ii.182), *I love Guillaume* [Bélibaste] *more than any of my brothers; although I have four brothers in the flesh. For those who are of the faith practise concord in everything. So they are more one another's brothers than those born of the same father and mother in the flesh: such brothers are always quarrelling with one another! And I shall never let Guillaume down: for all that we possess we pool, half and half.*

Either Pierre Maury deluded himself or he deliberately turned a blind eye to Bélibaste's feelings towards him. The fifty-fifty arrangement was strictly one way. But this unrequited friendship was not only the result of individual magnanimity. It belonged to a general background of Occitan culture and artificial relationships in which total brotherhood between friends unlinked by blood, who shared everything equally without hesitation, was institutionalized in the ritual forms of fraternity (*affrèrement*), recorded from the beginning of the fourteenth century.

Another form of artificial relationship which affected the Pyrenean

1 iii.148, 151, 154, 155. See above, Chapter IV.

shepherds of the early 1300s was that which linked man to man, man to
woman or woman to woman in the relationship of fellow-sponsor
(*compère* and *commère*). The institution of baptism gave godfathers, god-
mothers and the parents of the infant baptized a common responsibility
in the education and future of the infant. The pure friendship between
Pierre Maury and those he loved and was beloved by was often not
simply an affection in itself, as it would be nowadays. It was frequently
based on a precise relationship of compaternity. In an interesting passage, Bélibaste actually reproaches Pierre Maury for having interested
motives in this connection. '*You make yourself many* compères *and*
commères *because you take part in so many baptisms; you spend all
you have in this kind of festivity; and yet these baptisms and com-
paternities are good for nothing except to establish friendships between
people.*'[1]

Pierre replied: '*I earn my money and fortune myself; and I mean to
spend them as I like; I will not give it up either for you or for anyone else,
because in that way I acquire many people's friendship.*' An additional
philosophy underlies this attitude: '*If I try to acquire so many friends in
this way, it is because I think I should do good to everyone; if someone is
good* [i.e. a heretic] *I shall be rewarded; if someone is bad, at least he will
try to return the good he receives at my hands.*'

It was to an unnamed *compère* that Maury entrusted his money when,
fearing the Inquisitors, he sold all his sheep (ii.175). As this and other
incidents show, a fellow-sponsor would sometimes act as trustee, though
not always a worthy one. *At one time*, said Pierre (ii.30), *I had earned 300
sous working as a shepherd for employers in Ax-les-Thermes and Puigcerda.
I entrusted the said sum to a fellow-sponsor of mine who lived in the region
of Urgel. He never gave me the money back.* Not only money but also an
individual might be deposited with a fellow-sponsor – a woman, for
example, some relation through blood or marriage, whose virtue or
safety the depositor hoped thus to preserve. A *compère* might also be
used as a landlord, especially if he had a large house. The great thing
was to choose the right person in the first place. *That winter*, says Pierre
(iii.194–5), *my brother Jean Maury and I wintered at Casteldans. We both
stayed in the house of the notary, Bérenger de Sagria, who was none other
than Jean's* compère ... *Later I took Blanche Marty to Casteldans; and
installed her in Bérenger's house.* (Blanche Marty was the sister of

1 iii.185. See also iii.209.

Raymonde Piquier, Bélibaste's concubine and for a brief period Pierre Maury's wife.) Lastly, as we have already seen, the testimony of a fellow-sponsor might provide a useful alibi.

His life as a migrant provided Pierre Maury with many opportunities to be invited to baptisms and acquire fellow-sponsors as friends. He might have several fellow-sponsors in one parish, and this, especially in winter, would often be an excuse for absenteeism, especially when Bélibaste was living in the neighbourhood. Under the pretext of going to see his fellow-sponsors, Pierre could visit his friend. *Pierre Maury and I and seven other shepherds*, says Guillaume Maurs (ii.177), *were wintering with Pierre Castel's sheep in the pastures at Tortosa. And just before Lent, Pierre Maury took leave of me and the sheep, saying: 'I want to go and see one of my fellow-sponsors called Eyssalda in the village of Flix* [near Tarragona]. *I have many other fellow-sponsors in the same village, including one called Pierre Ioyer.'*

And indeed, Pierre Maury was away three weeks or thereabouts, staying in Flix. When he came back to our pastures in Tortosa he brought with him the heretic Guillaume Bélibaste, whom he got Pierre Castel to take on for a month as a shepherd.

In addition to all these other relationships, Pierre Maury and his colleagues often established associations in which it is difficult to separate the practical element from the emotional one. When he was in Fenouillèdes, spending the summer in the Pyrenean pass of Orlu, Pierre Maury, together with his team of shepherds, took service with Pierre André, a farmer from Planèzes (iii.159–60). The team of shepherds included Pierre André's two sons, Bernard and Guillot. Moreover, the team, apparently quite independently and without expressly consulting their employer, associated themselves with another team of shepherds employed by Master Roquefeuil, a farmer from Saint-Paul-de-Fenouillèdes. For at least two summers and one winter all the André team and all the Roquefeuil team were associates (*socii*) among themselves, without their association involving their employers as such. Such informal workers' associations could lead to the exchange of medieval-type vows of loyalty. Here again, it is hard to distinguish between emotional impulse and the pressures of work. Bélibaste tells Pierre Maury of three migrant shepherds from north of the Pyrenees (iii.168): *'On the way from Servière to Montblanch, I passed three people, Raymond Maurs* [of Montaillou], *Bernard Laufre* [of Tignac], *and Raymond*

Batailler [of Gébetz]; *they had sworn loyalty to each other and were going to Montblanch to earn their living.*'

These forms of social relationship were typical of the mountains of Ariège, but reinforced by the needs of exile and migration. They are to be found not only among the shepherds but also among the women – widows, or those separated from their husbands – whom the exodus had carried to Catalonia: *Blanche Marty* [from a family of wealthy blacksmiths in Junac] *had associated herself,* says Pierre Maury (iii.197), *with old Esperte Cervel* [from Montaillou, widow of a blacksmith from Tarascon]. *They lived together, with Mathena, Esperte's daughter, in a house near the bridge in Lérida.* Both in Montaillou and in Sabarthès, association could lead to some form of vendetta. The men of the Maurs family had long been members of associations concluded for better or worse, i.e. either to earn a living together or to avenge themselves as a family group. Reference has already been made (see p. 51) to the way three men from Montaillou, two of them shepherds belonging to the Maurs family, entered into association, sworn *on bread and on wine,* the object of which was to murder the priest.

Filial, fraternal, compaternal and associative friendships combined with ordinary friendships and complicity, heretical or anti-heretical, to form each individual's and each *domus*'s circle of friends. '*Say hallo to all our friends,*' says Raymond Pierre to Pierre Maury when the latter goes off to visit a house sympathetic to the Cathars (iii.129). '*Be off with you; because of you, misfortune could come upon all our friends,*' says Guillaume Belot to Pierre Maury in Montaillou itself, speaking for Arnaud Fauré, Pierre Maury's uncle (ii.174). At this, Pierre Maury bursts into tears. He realizes that through fear of the Inquisition the Belots and the Faurés, his relatives and fellow-citizens, no longer number him among their friends. They now refuse him the sacred gift of hospitality. They implore him to be on his way, if necessary throwing him a crust of bread to buy his departure. Even when its laws were broken, friendship among the shepherds of Aude and Montaillou in the old days, as among the Corsicans and the Andalusians still, remained a relationship of the utmost importance, much stronger than in the individualistic societies of the modern industrial world.

In general, the shepherds remained unmarried and without children, for rightly or wrongly they regarded themselves as too poor to take a wife. The exceptions to this rule were sufficiently rare to be mentioned explicitly: *I was a shepherd with Guillaume Ratfre, of Ax, who had taken a wife in Caudiès*, says Pierre Maury one day with some astonishment.[1] But on the whole professional shepherds did not marry, and external recruiting was necessary if their profession was not to atrophy or disappear.

The shepherds' attitude towards the rest of the world was easy-going, often friendly. One of them might, like Guillaume Maurs, pitilessly seek revenge against the Clergues, but that was because they had persecuted his family and destroyed them. The cross-section of shepherds in the Fournier Register, quite a large one, does not contain any characters as despicable as one finds without difficulty in the amoral world of non-shepherds (for example, Pierre Clergue, or Arnaud Sicre, or Bélibaste, a shepherd in emergencies but sedentary by vocation).

Among this society of shepherds, more attractive as a whole than the stable group of *domus*-dwellers, Pierre Maury is the easy-going hero par excellence, the embodiment of cheerful openness towards the world and other people. When he greets anyone, even someone he scarcely knows and whom he has good reason to mistrust, he welcomes him with a ringing shepherd's laugh. Arnaud Sicre, the secret informer, is greeted like the rest. *When I went into Guillemette Maury's house*, he says (ii.28), *Pierre Maury, who was sitting on a bench, stood up and showed me a smiling face, and we greeted one another in the usual manner.*

Pierre Maury saw his relationship with Sicre and the other members of Bélibaste's colony as one of cheerful conviviality: speaking of the meeting shortly to take place in Guillemette Maury's house, he said (ii.30), *We shall all talk together and enjoy ourselves, because we ought to enjoy ourselves among friends.*

Pierre could also inspire enjoyment, though his friends' feelings were often contradictory. '*When we saw you again*,' said Guillaume Bélibaste to Pierre one day, after his return from summer pasture in the mountains (iii.183), '*we felt both joy and fear. Joy, because it was a long time since we had seen you. Fear, because I was afraid lest the Inquisition had captured you up there: if they had, they would have made you confess everything and come back among us a spy in order to bring about my capture.*'

1 iii.159. See also the case of Jean Maury, who got married in a Catalan village in order to acquire the right to use the pasture. In his case, the only one of its kind recorded, marriage was a step on the way to sedentarization.

Bélibaste was wrong about the informer's identity, but not about the procedure. The man who was to bring about his capture exactly as he had foreseen was not Pierre Maury but Arnaud Sicre. Pierre Maury only smiled, up in the pastures, when Guillaume Maurs talked of how the Inquisition would treat him one day (ii.181). '*You will be revealed, denounced and captured, like Bélibaste,*' said Guillaume. '*And they will crush your nails.*'

After listening to me speak like that, continued Guillaume, *Pierre Maury began to smile.*

Guillaume Maurs was met with the same smile when he criticized Pierre one day for his heterodox connections. '*Pierre,*' said Guillaume (ii.185), '*you are always collecting for the wrong causes, and you visit many bad men; there are no wicked devils in the world that you don't know.*' *At these words, Pierre smiled and said nothing.*

We see the same smile in Béatrice de Planissoles. During the frequent domestic quarrels between the ageing Béatrice and her young lover, Barthélemy Aurilhac, the latter threatened to denounce her to the Inquisition. *And I said to Béatrice*, says Barthélemy, *that if I found myself in the diocese of Pamiers or somewhere where there was an Inquisitor, I would have her taken . . . and then she smiled and said :* '*The priests who belong to the sect of the good Christians*[the heretics] *are better than you are.*'

Psychological details on the subject are fragmentary and scattered, but if we want to know how the people of Montaillou saw the meaning of their lives, and what their awareness was of their own identity, answers are supplied by Pierre Maury himself.

An early discussion on the subject took place near Ax-les-Thermes. Pierre Maury had been living in Fenouillèdes, but had come to Ax to convoy a mule from Roussillon laden with salt. Near the local baths at Ax-les-Thermes, reserved partly for lepers, he met two other people from Montaillou, Guillaume Belot and Guillaume Maury, his own brother. The three men went for a walk together and talked about philosophy. Their conversation was tinged with anxiety. Rumour had it that there was to be a big round-up of heretics, thought to be plentiful in Montaillou and Sabarthès. The two citizens of Montaillou, who were experts on the subject, asked Pierre Maury (iii.161), '*How is it that you dare to live in Fenouillèdes when you are being sought for heresy?*'

Pierre replied: '*I might as well go on living in Fenouillèdes and*

Sabarthès; for no one can take away my fate [fatum]. And I must bear my fate, whether it be here or there.'

Fate: the word was often to be met with in Pierre Maury's conversation, at table, in the pastures or when he had been drinking with his friends.

This idea of ineluctable fate pursued Maury in all his subsequent travels, even as far as Spain. He referred to it when Bélibaste wanted to find him a wife and bitterly reproached him for his wandering life. '*You go away from us, Pierre,*' said Bélibaste (iii.183). '*Your regular returns to the Comté de Foix for the summer pasturing may make you fall into the hands of the Inquisition; remember that once you are out of our presence some accident might bring about your destruction, without any possibility of your being hereticated, received or consoled on the eve of your death.*'

Pierre replied, '*I cannot live otherwise than the way I was brought up. If I lived all the time in Morella* [a traditional place of winter pasturing in Spain], *I should die during the summer. I must follow my fate. If I am allowed to be hereticated on the eve of my death, I shall be. Otherwise, I shall follow my destined path.*'

On another occasion, when Guillaume Maurs criticized him for his life as a hunted heretic, Pierre Maury said (ii.184), '*I cannot do otherwise. That is how I have lived up till now. And that is how I shall go on living.*'

From where could Maury have got this idea of fate? From his friends the Cathars? Yes and no. They certainly had a firm belief in necessity.[1] But they also contradicted themselves. Bélibaste, always somewhat ambiguous, occasionally referred to the old subject of free will (ii.183): '*A man may well help himself*', said Bélibaste, '*to obtain some end which may be either good or bad.*'

If we set the Albigensian influence aside, we may easily compare Pierre Maury's idea of fate with similar notions popular among the various cultures of the western Mediterranean. The people of the Maghreb and the Moslems of Africa and Spain also had a sense of fate, and Pierre Maury's many contacts with Saracen shepherds could only have reinforced his thoughts on the question.[2] Even if we do not seek quite so far, medieval Christianity (influenced in this by the pre-Islamic North African, Augustine) possessed a very comprehensive theory of Grace, which in its crudest versions might also be regarded as

1 See below, Chapter XVIII.
2 Pierre Maury's first mention of the idea of fate comes after his first visit to Spain.

destiny. Finally, we may recall that Pierre Maury was a mountain shepherd, and that it was just these 'great shepherds of the high mountains'
who, before the Renaissance, gave in their calendars the most complete
version of the relationships uniting macrocosm and microcosm. Astro-
logy, through the twelve signs of the zodiac, ruled the twelve months of
the agricultural year and the twelve periods – seventy-two years in all –
into which the life of a man was divided. We should also note that Pierre
Maury's sense of destiny had no connection with absurd superstition.
One day Guillaume Bélibaste was anxious because he had seen a magpie
cross his path three times. (He might well have been anxious – for him
the stake was not far off.) Pierre laughed at him (iii.210): *'Guillaume,
take no notice of signs of birds and other auguries of that kind. Only old
women bother about such things.'*

Pierre Maury's sense of fate was thus not vulgarly magical but loftily
philosophical. In him as in others it is simply a very old peasant idea
quite natural in societies where there is no growth and, where people
literally have no choice. We have seen how Clergue the priest preserved
the hair and nail-parings of his father in order to protect the star or good
fortune (*eufortunium*) of his family house. The same term, fortune, is
found, reversed, in Guillaume Maurs's reproaches to Pierre Maury on
the subject of his evil communications (ii.184): *'Pierre, you meddle in bad
business [borias]; and you will all endure misfortune [infortunium] as a
result; and one day the Devil will carry everything off.'* Pierre answers by
referring to his own fate as a homeless migrant: he can do nothing about
it, he cannot do otherwise, for thus he has lived so far, and thus he will
live in the future. But we should note a nuance between Pierre Clergue's
idea of fate and that of Pierre Maury. For Pierre Clergue, a man of the
domus, astral fortune is above all connected with the common fate of his
line and his household. But Pierre Maury's motto is 'without hearth or
home'; for him, fate and fortune are primarily individual entities,
affecting the life of one person rather than the future of an *ostal*.

Pierre Maury's awareness of *fatum* also reflects a deep sense of occupational continuity. To fulfil one's destiny is to keep one's place and not
depart from one's condition or profession. And one's profession is seen
as a source of interest, a fount of vital energy, not a cause of unhappiness
and alienation. Guillaume Maurs, Pierre Maury and Guillaume Bélibaste had a very revealing discussion one day on this subject as they
were all guarding their sheep in the pastures at Tortosa. *'Pierre,'* said

Bélibaste to Maury (ii.177), '*stop leading that dog's life of yours; sell all your sheep, and we shall spend the money you get from them. I for my part will make combs. And then both of us can manage to live.*'

Pierre immediately replied: '*No, I do not want to sell my sheep. A shepherd I have been. A shepherd I shall remain as long as I live.*'

Fate, which underlies this phrase as it does so many others, is thus seen as the shepherd's vocation; and mountain liberty is the happy counterpart of the migrant's destiny, even if he has to sleep under the trees, to freeze almost to death in winter and be soaked to the skin by autumn showers (i.178; ii.15). This fate is inseparable from the young shepherd's upbringing, seen in terms of the daily bread received from his parents. One day at Beceite, near Teruel, Emersende Befayt of Montaillou attacked Pierre Maury on the subject of his journeys to the mountains of Ariège. She told him how anxious it made all his friends, the 'believers' as well as the *parfaits*. Pierre answered (iii.182): '*I cannot do otherwise, for I cannot lead a life different from that for which I was brought up.*' (The word he used was translated as *nutritus*, which implies the notions both of nourishment and of education.) Behind the common-place idea that a man is the product of his education lies the more complex notion of a physical link with the bread which built the body, and, through the bread, with the land which produced the grain and to which the man will one day return. *The soul of man is bread*, as a materialistic peasant of upper Ariège remarked; his heretical words were to attract the attention of Jacques Fournier. *What one has kneaded, that one must bake*, said one of Pierre Maury's friends, thus trying to justify Emersende Befayt's continuing to live with her daughter Jeanne, despite the fact that the latter kept attacking her (iii.174). Guillaume Fort of Montaillou recalled that, in spite of all the doctrines about resurrection, that which comes from the earth must go back to the earth. *After death*, he said (i.447), *the human body dissolves and is transformed into earth.* Thus man's destiny, though directed from afar by the stars, still remains, for the thinkers of Montaillou, strongly carnal and terrestrial. The physical link between a man's destiny and his native soul is referred to in a conversation when Emersende Marty affectionately reproaches Pierre Maury for his constant voyages home (iii.183). '*My son, you should not go back there. Why not stay here with us? You have no son or daughter or anyone to look after except yourself. You could live here without too much effort. But if you are captured there, you are lost.*'

Pierre replied: '*No, I could not live here* [in Catalonia] *permanently ; and anyhow, no one can take away my fate.*'

Maury and his peers, great voyagers, had neither wife, nor children nor household. Despite their comparative wealth in terms of money and flocks,[1] they could not accumulate much in the way of objects, limited as they were by considerations of mobility which prevented them from acquiring all the possessions with which those who were sedentary systematically surrounded themselves. So Maury chose instead to desire few objects, and to transfer his wants to other kinds of wealth, which for him took the place of family: temporary unions with mistresses in the pastures or the taverns; a full network of human relationships based on both artificial and natural fraternity, on compaternity, on pure friend-ship or friendship through association. He liked this life-style, based on fate freely accepted – but is this not the very definition of Grace? His destiny was a destination. For him, sheep meant liberty. And he would not trade that liberty for the plate of gritty lentils often held out to him by friends, employers or parasites, offering to marry him, to help him settle down, to have him adopted into a rich family. But he saw his destiny as travelling over hill and dale, with friends everywhere and temporary sweethearts. Material wealth would have been literally a burden to him. Maury had few possessions, but he was not destitute. And when he lost those few possessions he lost them with a smile, for he knew that by working he could easily get them back again. Well shod for his long journeys in a pair of good shoes of Spanish leather – the only luxury he allowed himself (i.20) – detached from the goods of this world, careless of the almost inevitable certainty of being arrested at some time by the Inquisition, leading a life that was both passionate and passionately interesting, Pierre Maury was a happy shepherd.

1 Bélibaste, who was kept by Pierre Maury, even said on occasion – for interested reasons, it is true – that Maury was 'rich' (ii.42).

PART TWO

An archaeology of Montaillou: from body language to myth

On the level of the simplest emotions, I have already talked about smiles and laughter in connection with Pierre Maury. So here I shall dwell on tears. We have no statistics on the subject, but it may be that the people of Montaillou wept slightly more easily than we do, both in happiness and in sorrow. People cried, of course, at the prospect or reality of misfortune, or for the death of someone dear to them, in particular for the death of a child, even when it was very young. Both men and women grew pale, trembled and wept when afraid that they were about to be betrayed to the Inquisition (ii.227, 279; iii.357). Among the shepherds, we see men bursting into tears at a breach of friendship or solidarity, especially when accompanied by threats fore-shadowing arrest by the Inquisitors. Such was the case of Pierre Maury when turned away by his uncle Arnaud Fauré and fellow-citizen Guillaume Belot (ii.174).

Guillaume Bélibaste, more vulnerable than one might imagine, reacts in the same way despite all his experience – murder, mistresses, migra-tion – when Jean Maury, Pierre's brother, refuses to genuflect to him and threatens to have him taken by the Inquisition (ii.483): '*If you ask me to make you one more genuflection, I will see that you are captured.*' *At these words*, continued Jean, *the heretic left me, weeping.*

Conversely a woman from Ariège wept with joy when she met a shep-herd from her own part of the world who gave her news of those she loved: *I met Blanche Marty at Prades*, says Pierre Maury, *in the village square. I greeted her and gave her greetings from her sister Raymonde and from 'lord' Bélibaste. When she heard these words, Blanche was very happy, and wept with joy; and she embraced me.*[1]

The joys of revenge were accompanied by the lifting of both arms up to heaven, a gesture of thanksgiving with different connotations from those it has today. Guillaume Maurs (ii.189): *As I was passing through Beceite with my flock, I met in the street Emersende Befayt, who asked me for news of Montaillou. I told her that Pierre Clergue the priest had been arrested for heresy. When she heard that, Emersende lifted up her hands to*

1 iii.194. Blanche Marty, who had taken refuge in Spain, was from Junac, in present-day Ariège. The village of Prades was not the one near Montaillou, but another of the same name near Tarragona.

heaven, saying 'Deo gratias'. Similarly (ii.281), *When he heard that the two men had been captured, Bernard Clergue stretched up his hands towards heaven, fell on his knees, and said: 'I am delighted that those two are now behind bars.'*

The Montaillou documents show in passing that certain gestures of politeness still used today are very ancient and to a certain extent of peasant origin. People like the inhabitants of Montaillou used to raise their hoods and stand up, even more automatically than people do today, to greet a friend or acquaintance, an inferior or superior. The whole Belot family, gathered round the fire for a wedding, stood up to show the respect due to Guillaume Authié, who had just come down the ladder from the *solier.* Pierre Maury, chief *cabanier,* stood to salute passing heretics, and offered them bread and milk. Conversely, Prades Tavernier, a *parfait* of some reputation, stood to salute Pierre Maury, a simple shepherd, and then sat down again.[1] This 'surrection' was also taken for granted between equals: Pierre Maury got up from the bench with a broad smile to welcome the shoemaker Arnaud Sicre (ii.28). It is possible that men also stood to greet a woman but not at all certain, especially when one thinks of the strong masculine bent of Montaillou society. The only passages which mention such a reaction describe a *parfait* standing up in order to get away from a woman for fear of impurity; or again, two goodmen drawing back hastily so as not to touch the breasts of a peasant woman.[2]

The people of Montaillou were not in the habit of shaking hands as we do by way of greeting. After a separation, they would simply take one another by the hand. Pierre Maury: *When I was going through the mountains with my sheep on the way to the summer pastures, I met near La Palma the heretic Raymond de Toulouse, accompanied by a woman. In accordance with the heretical custom of praying while travelling, he was praying behind a stone. He saw me and called me. I immediately went over to him; and I recognized him in the customary way, taking him by the hand.*[3] Pierre Maury stresses that this taking by the hand is common

1 i.371, 337; iii.101, 135, 127. See i.129 and iii.294 for raising the hood. It was only in front of the bishop or the high officials of the Inquisition that greeting, out of both fear and politeness, tended to take the form of falling to one's knees. On taking leave, people said *Adieu* (iii.284).

2 i.337. See also i.311, and iii.91.

3 iii.170. La Palma is near Tarragona.

practice, as distinct from the heretical customs concerning prayer and other salutations. As well as taking one another by the hand in 'recognition', women would go about arm in arm, giving a squeeze to warn one another of the dangers lurking in the words of some third person.[1]

In Montaillou, people did not shave, or even wash, often. They did not go bathing or swimming. On the other hand, there was a good deal of delousing, which was an ingredient of friendship, whether heretical or purely social. Pierre Clergue had himself deloused by his mistresses, including Béatrice de Planissoles and Raymonde Guilhou; the operation might take place in bed, or by the fire, at the window or on a shoemaker's bench, the priest taking the opportunity to air his ideas about both Catharism and love. Raymonde Guilhou also deloused the priest's mother, wife of old Pons Clergue, in full view of everybody in the doorway of the *ostal*, retailing the latest gossip as she did so. The Clergues, as leading citizens, had no difficulty in finding women to relieve them of their insect life. Bernard Clergue had recourse to the services of old Guillemette 'Belote' who, as she looked for nits, advised Bernard to give corn to the *parfaits*. As he was in love with Guillemette's daughter Raymonde, he of course hastened to comply (ii.276). The operation might take place on the flat roofs of the houses, which stood close together either side by side or facing one another. Vuissane Testanière (i.462–3): *At the time when the heretics dominated Montaillou, Guillemette 'Benete' and Alazaïs Rives were being deloused in the sun by their daughters Alazaïs Benet and Raymonde Rives. All four of them were on the roof of their houses. I was passing by and heard them talking. Guillemette 'Benete' was saying to Alazaïs, 'How can people manage to bear the pain when they are burning at the stake?'*

To which Alazaïs replied, 'Ignorant creature! God takes the pain upon himself, of course.'

Note that delousing was always carried out by a woman, though not necessarily someone of low degree: Béatrice de Planissoles, who was noble, did not hesitate to delouse her beloved Pierre Clergue.

Delousing appears to imply relations of kinship or alliance, even if it was illegitimate: the mistress delouses the lover, as well as the lover's

1 i.191. There are many examples of nudging, putting the finger on the lips for silence, etc.

mother; the future mother-in-law delouses her prospective son-in-law; the daughter delouses the mother.[1]

If delousing was common, ablutions were so summary as to be almost non-existent. Crossing water was very dangerous, and people did not bathe or swim. They might linger near the baths at Ax-les-Thermes, but that was only to sell sheep or visit the prostitutes. The springs themselves, which were of the simplest description, were mainly reserved for lepers and people with ringworm.

The *parfaits* or pseudo-*parfaits* considered the 'toilet' as such as a technique for restoring their ritual purity (ii.31; i.325). *When Guillaume Bélibaste has touched meat with his hands, he washes them three times before eating or drinking.* The problem, for Bélibaste, was not so much the cleanness of his hands themselves, as the cleanness of his face, especially the mouth, the organ used both for giving blessings and for introducing polluted nourishment into the body.[2] Here is a mental attitude which helps to explain the remarkable external dirtiness of the people of Montaillou. It was not so much the outside as the inside of the body which had to be kept clean. Was this so absurd? As late as the eighteenth century, many people considered that to emit an odour of unwashed body was a sign of personal virility, at least in men.

In Montaillou the toilet, when it existed, took no notice of the anal or genital areas, but was restricted to those parts of the body which blessed, handled or swallowed food – i.e. the hands, face and mouth. *To give water to someone's hands* was a sign of politeness and friendship. What applied to the living applied to the dead. Alazaïs Azéma: *In Montaillou we do not wash a dead person's body, but simply sprinkle water over the face.*[3] After this a piece of cloth was put over the dead person's face, perhaps also to guard against impurity.

---

1 Delousing, and the fact that the people of Montaillou, like most of their contemporaries, slept several to a bed, drank out of the same cup and ate from the same bowl, etc., indicates a 'culture of promiscuity' which has its own peculiar rituals of politeness. For example, drinking from the same cup raises the burning question of precedence: who is to drink first? (see ii.24, a typical passage on Bélibaste and his crew).

2 See also i.67, 417; iii.151.

3 See i.314 for ablutions performed on the face of a corpse. (This was an old local tradition: in the first half of the thirteenth century, a woman heretic about to go to the stake washed her face and removed her make-up (ii.220–21) *so as not to go painted before God.*

Only the *parfaits* used a piece of fine linen to dry their faces. The ordinary people of Montaillou had, at the best, a coarse cloth (i.416–17).

The people of Montaillou, and of the Ariège or Aude region in general, used to undress to go to bed. One day, Jeanne Befayt threatened Bélibaste as he got out of bed (iii.175), hoping that *the fire of the stake would burn through his ribs*. Bélibaste fled through the fields, *without shoes, for two leagues; he left some of his clothes in the bed where he had spent the night*. So he must have taken the trouble to undress before he went to bed. However, when he was travelling and obliged to share his concubine's bed at an inn, Bélibaste slept with all his clothes on, thus avoiding touching Raymonde's bare flesh and helping to deceive his followers about his irregular union. But ordinary peasants or artisans had none of these reasons for hypocritical scruples. They must often have slept naked. Arnaud Sicre tells how one night, at San Mateo, he shared a bed with Bélibaste. The informer notes that Bélibaste took off his shirt but not his underpants, an observation that suggests that Arnaud himself was less prudish and had taken off all his clothes (ii.31, 33).

So the inhabitants of Montaillou took off their linen at night. They even changed it sometimes!

At considerable intervals, Pierre Maury had a change of shirt brought to him in the pastures by his brother Arnaud. The fact struck him as sufficiently remarkable to be included in his deposition (ii.34, 181). But we cannot say how often people changed, or washed, their clothes. Raymonde Arsen, a servant maid with the Belots, used to wash the clothes of the *parfaits*, and perhaps also those of her employers.[1]

The shepherds Pierre Maury and Guillaume Maurs, despite their heretical sympathies, regularly made the sign of the cross over their food before eating. (Even today many French peasants 'cross' a loaf with the point of their knife before cutting it.) But not everybody did this: Bernard Clergue, the *bayle*, a man strongly marked by heresy, refused. So did Guillaume Bélibaste, who saw himself as a *parfait*. But so common was the gesture of blessing food among the simple peasants and shepherds that Bélibaste, as a good Cathar, made a circular gesture over

1 i.376. Clothes were certainly considered precious. Jean Maury walked for several days over mountainous country to bring Bélibaste (who thus seems to have dressed in reach-me-downs) the patched-up garments of a dead friend (iii.172).

the bread he was about to eat instead of the traditional sign of the cross (ii.181, 283).

People also crossed themselves before going to bed. And only an out-and-out heretic like Bernard Clergue would refuse this simple gesture (ii.283).

In order to mock some apocalyptic prophecy heard on the bridge at Tarascon, Arnaud de Savignan, a stonemason and bold thinker, gave a flick of the wrist such as we still make today (i.161): *He turned his hand over in derision.* This was one of the reasons he was convicted for heresy.

An obscene gesture, which has come down through the ages, consisted in striking one hand against the other, or one hand against a fist, to symbolize the sexual act. Raymond Segui, a villager of Tignac in the upper valley of the Ariège, relates (ii.120): *'Do you know how God was made?', I asked Raymond de l'Aire, of Tignac.*

'God was made fucking and shitting,' answered Raymond de l'Aire, and as he said these words he struck one hand against another.

'Those are wicked words,' I replied. 'You ought to be killed for saying such things.'

Underlying body language and gestures is emotion – and the Register has plenty to say about love.

For the shepherds, life was celibate apart from temporary unions; only occasionally they might have a woman, sometimes regarded as a whore, either in the pastures or the town. But in the village of Montaillou itself, relations between couples were naturally complex, including every possible variety of marriage and concubinage. There were grand passions, ordinary marriages with or without love, and liaisons both temporary and habitual, venal and affectionate. It was only in the town that boys of good family, who had left the country to attend 'the schools', might get mixed up in the few homosexual networks that then existed. These were urban rather than rural, clerical rather than lay. In this connection, Jacques Fournier's Register expands into a real psychological biography. The example comes not from Montaillou itself but from the diocesan town of Pamiers.

Arnaud de Verniolles of Pamiers, a sub-deacon and outlawed Franciscan, was initiated in childhood into 'homophilia' by a fellow-student and future priest (iii.39, 49). *I was then between ten and twelve years old. It was about twenty years ago. My father had sent me to learn grammar with Master Pons de Massabucu, a schoolteacher who later became a Dominican friar. I shared a bedroom with Master Pons and his other pupils, Pierre de l'Isle (of Montaigu), Bernard Balessa (of Pamiers), and Arnaud Auriol, the son of Pierre Auriol, the knight. Arnaud was from La Bastide-Serou; he had already started to shave, and now he is a priest. My brother Bernard de Verniolles was also there, and other pupils whose names I have forgotten.*

In the bedroom shared by master and pupils, I slept for a good six weeks in the same bed as Arnaud Auriol. . . . On the fourth or fifth night we spent together, when Arnaud thought that I was fast asleep, he began to embrace me and put himself between my thighs . . . and to move about there as if I was a woman. And he went on sinning thus every night. I was still no more than a child, and I did not like it. But I was so ashamed I did not dare tell anyone of this sin.

Later, Master Pons de Massabucu's school moved and Arnaud de Verniolles had other sleeping companions, including his teacher. To save bedding, Master Pons slept with two of his pupils. No one now made any attempt on young Verniolles's virtue. But the harm was done. A latent tendency was awakened, and Arnaud de Verniolles was doomed to become a homosexual.

This tendency was finally confirmed in the city of Toulouse, where Arnaud de Verniolles continued his studies for a while. The confirmation was due to a series of accidents which Arnaud probably tended to exaggerate and misinterpret (iii.31): *At the time when they were burning the lepers, I was living in Toulouse; one day I 'did it' with a prostitute. And after I had perpetrated this sin my face began to swell. I was terrified and thought I had caught leprosy; I thereupon swore that in future I would never sleep with a woman again; in order to keep this oath, I began to abuse little boys.*

We do not know what caused Arnaud's face to swell. Perhaps it was an allergy, or an insect bite. Infection is not ruled out altogether. One thing is certain; Arnaud had not caught leprosy. But in a period of popular hysteria against the lepers, fear of the disease was mixed up with sexual dread.

After these two traumatic experiences Arnaud turned away from women. He was an active, though not yet notorious, pederast, and experienced considerable success. His conquests included adolescents of between sixteen and eighteen; for example (iii.49), Guillaume Ros, son of Pierre Ros of Ribouisse in what is now the department of Aude, and Guillaume Bernard of Gaudiès in the present department of Ariège. Both Guillaume Ros and Guillaume Bernard came from the country but were living in the city. Sometimes Arnaud would unceremoniously 'lay' his young men on a dungheap. On other occasions, more elaborate, he would take them to a little cabin in the country, among the vineyards. According to Guillaume Ros (iii.19): *Arnaud threatened me with a knife, twisted my arm, dragged me by force despite my struggles, threw me down, and made love to me, kissing me and ejecting his sperm between my legs.* But Arnaud himself denied that there had been any violence on this occasion. He said (iii.43): *Both parties were consenting.* Arnaud naturally performed his acts of sodomy in various positions: as if with a woman, or from behind, and so on (iii.31). Sometimes, before proceeding to the main point, the lovers would dress in tunics and wrestle and dance. Sometimes they undressed altogether (iii.40, 41, 42, 44 and *passim*). Afterwards Arnaud and his friend of the moment would swear on the four Gospels, or on a calendar (iii.40), or on the refectory Bible of a monastery, never to reveal to anybody what had passed between them. Arnaud used to give his young men little presents – a knife, for example. All this served to fill his leisure time, especially in the holidays. Among the young men concerned, and the monks and mendicant friars who made up Arnaud's social circle, these activities were accompanied by marked masturbatory tendencies (iii.43 and *passim*). According to him, Arnaud did not realize how criminal the act of sodomy was in the eyes of the Church of Rome (iii.42, 49). *I told Guillaume Ros, in perfectly good faith, that the sin of sodomy and those of fornication and deliberate masturbation were, in point of gravity, just the same. I even thought, in the simplicity of my heart, that sodomy and ordinary fornication were indeed mortal sins, but much less serious than the deflowering of virgins, adultery or incest.* The social groups among whom sodomy was practised, according to the Pamiers record, made up a fairly distinguished circle which though urban had some connections with the country. One individual lived entirely in the country. But he was not a mere bumpkin. He belonged to one of those slightly superior groups from which homosexuals tended to come in those days. He was a squire who lived in the region of Mirepoix. He was the first to seduce Guillaume Ros as a child (iii.41).

Generally speaking, the schoolboys courted by Arnaud and his like were of country birth, but their families were sufficiently well off and enlightened to send them to study in town. In short, they came from the rural bourgeoisie or country gentry.

One, however, came directly from the people, though he was not a peasant. He was a shoemaker's apprentice aged eighteen and came from Mirepoix. He was doing his apprenticeship with Bernard de Toulouse, a shoemaker in Pamiers. He claimed to know some pretty women (iii.45), and did not carry his homosexual experiment with Arnaud very far. It took place on a dungheap (there was one in nearly every courtyard in Pamiers, as in Montaillou).

Fournier's Register is categorical on one point: whatever the origins of the young person concerned, sodomy meant the city. Arnaud claimed (iii.32) that *in Pamiers there are over a thousand people infected with sodomy*. Perhaps he was exaggerating the number. As we have seen, homosexuals were recruited more among students than among apprentices. They were also found at quite an early age among the secular clergy. Arnaud frequently mentions a certain canon who, when drunk, had his feet massaged by his footman or by a book peddlar who lodged in his house. The canon soon began to kiss and embrace his masseur, and perhaps went even further (iii.41, 44).

The Minorites, to whose order Arnaud de Verniolles himself belonged, were also accused of straying from the straight and narrow path of heterosexuality (iii.31, 32). *A certain Minorite of Toulouse, son or nephew of Master Raymond de Gaudiès, left the order because, according to the monk's own accusations, its members indulged in the sin of sodomy.*

Arnaud de Verniolles conformed to the urban, clerical, comparatively élitist model, non-peasant and non-domestic, of homosexuality in Ariège and Toulouse. He was sophisticated, in the worldly sense, and his culture was literary and far beyond the almost purely oral culture of Montaillou. There it was extremely rare to own a book, or even just to be loaned one. But for Arnaud de Verniolles it was quite a common thing to buy or borrow books, and to lend them to his friends. Among the works he handled – and sometimes he would lose his temper and throw one at some young man's head – were Bibles, Gospels and a calendar. Also, for this was the beginning of the Renaissance, an Ovid, a work by one who knew, in theory and in practice, all the arts of love. Arnaud visited the city of Toulouse, and travelled as far as Rome (iii.33). In Pamiers he met the Waldensian Raymond de la Côte. In short, he was cultivated, and had connections and experience of the world.

But he is not to be regarded as a symbol of social success. Although of noble origin, he was in fact a misfit and a failure. He never rose higher than the rank of sub-deacon (iii.35) though he must have aspired to become a full member of the priesthood. So he resorted to what was a common practice in the 1320s, and pretended to be a priest. On various occasions he heard young men's confessions; he celebrated, with much emotion, his 'first Mass', though it was by definition valueless. On every level – as a secret sodomite and as a pseudo-priest – he played a double game. His relations with the Catholic Church were also ambiguous. On the one hand he longed to be a priest, with a real right to say Mass and give absolutions, but on the other hand he had apostasized and left the Minorite order. As for dispensing sacraments, he was himself in a state of mortal sin since for years he did not confess or receive communion.

In the end it was his illegal exercise of the priesthood which brought about Arnaud's downfall, for it was on these grounds that he was first denounced to the Bishop (iii.14). One thing led to another, and Jacques Fournier finally detected, behind the crime of performing Mass illegally, the crime of homosexuality. On its own, this second 'misdemeanour' might never have been discovered, since, if it was not too flagrant, it was regarded with a certain degree of tolerance by Pamiers society. In both Pamiers and Toulouse, other sodomites less imprudent or luckier than Arnaud carried on undisturbed. Despite the comparative tolerance he had met with, Arnaud seems not to have regarded his own homo-sexuality as a form of real love, consciously expressed and organized. Although he was a reader of Ovid, his evidence never mentions the words *amare* (to love), *adamare* (to love passionately), *diligere* (to be fond of) or *placere* (to please). Arnaud might have experienced such feelings towards some of his friends. But he never dreamed of mentioning them in words during his questioning by the bishop. Was it for fear of seeming out-rageous, and shocking the Inquisitor? Very unlikely. Jacques Fournier had heard plenty in his time. It is more likely that on such feelings Arnaud maintained a silence which amounted to a cultural 'expression gap'. Pamiers was not pagan Greece, and to talk of love in connection with sodomy, even if such love had been 'objectively' real, would have been meaningless.

So Arnaud's evidence presents homosexuality not as an expression of real feeling but as a cure for lust. After between a week and a fortnight of chastity, Arnaud claimed he could not help throwing himself into some man's arms; except, of course, in the unusual case when a woman was available. To the boys he was courting Arnaud de Verniolles described love between men as an amusement, a kind of game, or even a form of instruction: *I will show you what the canon used to do* (meaning the canon that liked to have his feet massaged).

So despite his culture, his sensibility and his ambitions, Arnaud did not really live his passions or his impulses to the full. In him Languedoc homosexuality found neither its troubadour nor its philosopher.

So much for the town. In the Occitan village, the range of cultural behaviour was less varied, and rural homosexuality was not a problem.[1] It did not occur, or was not supposed to occur, except between some noble squires and a handful of rich schoolboys, exported towards the temptation of the nearby city, Pamiers or Toulouse. In the country, the real question was relationships with women, the only sexual object usually tolerated by rural culture. But although women in rural Occitania were oppressed, they were not reduced to total slavery, and they got their own back in the intimacy of the *domus* and the power that belonged to age.

When they were young, the women of Montaillou or Ariège in general went in danger of rape, perhaps in even greater danger than elsewhere and in other ages. Guillaume Agulhan of Laroque d'Olmes, living in Ax-les-Thermes, raped a woman and was locked up (i.280). Fortunately, Raymond Vayssière was allied by marriage to the Agulhan family, and he interceded with the Authiés, who at this time had influence with the Foix authorities. The latter immediately set Agulhan free, despite the lord of Mirepoix, in whose jurisdiction he normally belonged. This is not the only rape referred to in the Fournier records. We have already seen how, in Montaillou itself, Bernard Belot tried to rape Raymonde, wife of Guillaume Authié (local namesake of the *parfait*). Bernard Belot got off without too much difficulty, apart from a row with the victim's husband and a 20 *livres* fine paid to the Foix officials (i.411). This was a considerable sum, equal to half the price of a village house. Béatrice de

---

1 There are no references to bestiality traceable in the Fournier Register, usually so detailed about different forms of 'deviance'; but this proves nothing one way or the other. There might also have been some latent homosexuality between Pierre Maury and Bélibaste, but the evidence of the Register does not deal with the unconscious.

Planissoles herself, though she was the *châtelaine*, was raped like any country girl by the bastard Pathau Clergue, cousin of the priest.

Rape was not very severely punished. Sometimes the 'victims' were more or less consenting. But at Montaillou, it did not occur between cousins; at least, one did not rape a first cousin's concubine. This prohibition combined the power of lineage with that of alliance, even though the relationship was not a legal one. Raymonde Testanière (i.458): *One evening the shoemaker Arnaud Vital tried to rape me, disregarding the fact that I had children by Bernard Belot, who was his first cousin. So I stopped Arnaud from getting his way, although he kept on saying that I would not be committing any sin if I slept with him.* This attempted rape against a cousin's mistress was an attack on the principles which forbade incest within the dense network of kinship complicated by concubinage. It was such a psychological shock to Raymonde Testanière that she renounced her Cathar beliefs (i.469): *I believed in the errors of the heretics until Arnaud Vital* [himself a Cathar] *tried to rape me. But then, because of this incest, I stopped believing in these errors.*

To avoid the extremity of rape, a man might have recourse to prostitutes. But of course there were not many prostitutes in a village like Montaillou; in fact, they were non-existent as such. But the towns, where the peasants went occasionally to visit the fairs (i.370) or on ordinary business, provided opportunities. '*I committed fornication with public prostitutes, I stole fruit, hay and grass from the meadows*', confessed one penitent to the pseudo-priest, Arnaud de Verniolles. Another penitent said much the same: '*I fornicated with public prostitutes, I made dishonourable suggestions to married women, and even virgins! I was sometimes drunk. I told lies. I stole fruit.*' Only the third of the three whose confessions Arnaud de Verniolles relates (iii.35, 36, 38) does not accuse himself of having visited paid women: '*I stole fruit and other crops. I swore.*'

It was quite common to visit prostitutes, and by no means always met with strong moral objections. Pierre Vidal, who lived in Ax-les-Thermes, was of peasant origin, born in the village of Pradières in the present department of Ariège. His views on the subject were very lax. *Yesterday,* he said, *I was going from Tarascon to Ax-les-Thermes with two mules laden with corn. I met a priest I knew and we went along together. As we were going down the slope after the village of Lassur, the conversation turned to prostitutes.*

'If you found a prostitute,' said the priest, *'and agreed with her on a price, and then slept with her, do you think you would be committing a mortal sin?...'*

Finally I answered: *'No, I don't think so.'*

From various similar discussions between Pierre Vidal and other witnesses, it emerges that Vidal believed the sexual act to be innocent when performed with a prostitute, or even with any other woman (iii.296; ii.246), on two conditions: first, it had to be a monetary transaction (the man paying, of course); secondly, the act in question had to 'please' both parties.

Pierre Vidal was of lowly, peasant origin. He was a muleteer who transported grain, and his various interlocutors – priests and schoolmasters – always addressed him immediately with the familiar 'tu', whether they knew him or not. So, in the dialogues between him and them, the official teaching of the Church is expressed by a group of relatively educated and comfortably-off men, whereas the muleteer's beliefs, asserting the innocence of the sexual act when it is venal and mutually agreeable, derive directly from an ancient source of popular peasant wisdom.

In Montaillou itself, Vidal's views are corroborated by the innocent answers given by little Grazide Lizier, born of a bastard branch of the Clergue family. When asked about her happy past liaison with the priest, she said (i.302–03): *In those days it pleased me, and it pleased the priest, that he should know me carnally, and be known by me; and so I did not think I was sinning, and neither did he. But now, with him, it does not please me any more. And so now, if he knew me carnally, I should think it a sin!*

We are still a long way from the rigours of the Counter Reformation. In the remote countryside a certain innocence still survived. Many people were of the opinion that pleasure in itself was without sin, and if it was agreeable to the couples concerned it was not disagreeable to God either. As for the idea that to pay for one's pleasure was to be without sin, it was long to remain widespread in this region. Detailed records of the Inquisition have revealed this attitude unaltered among many Spanish peasants in modern times. Ethnology has familiarized us with the idea that women are objects of exchange, like words or signs. Was it not even more 'natural' to think, like Pierre Vidal, that the sexual act was also a kind of trade, payable in love and pleasure, money and kind? Anyhow,

Jacques Fournier was not too severe on the muleteer's theories, and he was sentenced to only a year in prison and the wearing of single yellow crosses.

What really mattered in village sexuality were affairs, liaisons, concubinage and, last but not least, marriage. We shall begin with the amorous activities of a single *domus*, that of the Clergue family and its satellites. The illegitimate births in the Clergue family are a first, though indirect, clue. The two Guillaume Clergues, brother and son respectively of the patriarch Pons Clergue, were each father of a bastard. The more notorious of these natural sons was Raymond Clergue, known as Pathau, the son of Pons's brother. We have already seen that Pathau raped Béatrice de Planissoles. By the following year, Béatrice was a widow and bore no grudge against Pathau for his presumed violence. She became his mistress and was publicly kept by him. She broke with him when she joined up with the priest, Pierre Clergue. Disappointed but not discouraged, Pathau Clergue fell back on Béatrice's servant, and took Sybille Teisseire as his concubine. In Montaillou, Sybille had literally been Béatrice's maid of all work (i.227, 239 and *passim*).

Bernard Clergue, *bayle* of Montaillou, had love affairs which are better known to us. In his youth he fathered a natural daughter, Mengarde (i.392), who served as messenger to the heretics, bringing them provisions from the Clergue *domus* to the Belot *domus*. Later she married the peasant Bernard Aymeric of Prades.

But Bernard Clergue was a creature full of romantic affection and passion. He burned with an ardent friendship for his brother Pierre. He loved (*adamat*)[1] the girl who was to be his wife, Raymonde Belot, the daughter of Guillemette. And as this was Montaillou, his feeling immediately crystallized around the girl's whole *domus*. Bernard Clergue relates (ii.269), with charming naivety: *I was then already* bayle *of Montaillou; and because of the love I bore for Raymonde, my wife, I loved all that belonged to the* ostal *of my mother-in-law Belot; nothing in the world could have induced me to do anything which might displease my mother-in-law or cause harm to her ostal. I would have preferred to suffer myself or in my possessions rather than witness any prejudice against my mother-in-law's ostal.*

But as a seducer Bernard Clergue is a pallid figure compared with his

1 ii.269, 273, 275. His wife returned his love with great affection (ii.466).

brother Pierre. The priest of Montaillou was the womanizer par excellence of the Clergue family. Bernard was a romantic. Pierre was a swashbuckler. Cathar, spy and rake – he was everywhere. As we have seen, his influence was very great at the time when the Albigensian heresy was spreading in Montaillou: *All the houses in Montaillou, except two or three, were infected with heresy*, says Raymond Vayssière (i.292), *because the priest Pierre Clergue read the book of the heretics to the people.* But Pierre's influence was not limited to proselytizing. He scattered his desires among his flock as impartially as he gave his benediction, and in return won the favours of many of his female parishioners. He was helped by the general tolerance with which concubinage among ecclesiastics was regarded in the Pyrenees. At an altitude of 1,300 metres the rules of priestly celibacy ceased to apply. An energetic lover and incorrigible Don Juan, he presents the spectacle, rare in records of rural history, of the typical village seducer of ancient times. No question of this great carnivore restricting himself to one woman.[1] If he had done so, the fact that he was a cleric would have meant that she became his official concubine. He coveted all women, whether they belonged to his flock or not, whether they belonged to his parish or neighbouring parishes. He said so straight out to Raymonde Guilhou, wife of the shoemaker Arnaud Vital, one day when she was delousing him on the bench in Arnaud's workshop. He took the opportunity of ogling the girls as they went along the village street. Hunting was his vocation.[2] He adored his mother and burned with incestuous passions, sometimes carried into practice, for his sisters and sisters-in-law. He was the narcissistic lover of his own *domus*, just as his brother Bernard was of his wife's *domus*. Unsuited to marriage, he transferred his desires on to many fragile conquests. As far as one knows, Pierre was only once unsuccessful in love. And this was merely an attempt at seduction by means of a female go-between who refused to cooperate. *I had a niece called Raymonde*, says Alazaïs Fauré. *She was the daughter of Jean Clement, of Gébetz.*[3] *Raymonde had married Pierre Fauré of Montaillou, who could not manage to sleep with her. That at least was what my niece told*

1 'Great' is used in the figurative sense: on Pierre Clergue's smallness of stature, see ii.389.
2 On his claim to polygyny, see i.491 and ii.225.
3 Gébetz was a locality which no longer exists, near Camurac and not far from Montaillou; it was in the present department of Aude.

me, and it was what was commonly said. Because of this, my niece no longer wished to stay with her husband. She lived with me. One day I was going to the château of Montaillou, and by chance I met the priest; he made me sit down beside him, and said: 'What can I do, if you don't say a word in my favour to your niece Raymonde, and if you don't arrange for me to possess her? And afterwards, once I have possessed her, her husband will succeed in knowing her carnally.'

And I, went on Alazaïs Fauré, *told Pierre that I would do nothing in the matter: 'You arrange things for yourself with my niece, if she agrees,' I said to him. 'But aren't you already satisfied with having possessed two women in my family, myself and my sister Raymonde? Do you need our niece as well!...'*[1]

Whereupon, concluded Alazaïs, *my niece, beset by the dishonourable importunities of the priest, left Montaillou and went back to her father's house at Gébetz.*

Was the irrepressible Pierre arrogating to himself some *jus primae noctis*, which he exercised when the opportunity arose? It is not impossible; he was to deflower and then marry off to a village bumpkin one of his nieces, Grazide.

The Fournier Register tells us of some dozen authenticated mistresses of Pierre Clergue;[2] but the list is certainly incomplete. Three of them were from Ax-les-Thermes, and the nine others lived permanently or temporarily in Montaillou. They were Alazaïs Fauré and her sister Raymonde (nées Guilhabert), Béatrice de Planissoles, Grazide Lizier, Alazaïs Azéma, Gaillarde Benet, Alissende Roussel (otherwise known as Pradola, sister of Gaillarde Benet), Mengarde Buscailh, Na Maragda, Jacotte den Tort, Raymonde Guilhou and Esclarmonde Clergue, who was none other than Pierre's own sister-in-law (wife of his brother Raymond, Pons Clergue's legitimate son).[3] Should we call it incest? Yes, according to the ancient definitions. No, according to our modern concepts. In any case, Pierre professed very advanced, even though hesitant, theories (i.225–6, 491) on the subject of incest with one's sister. And he had few qualms about knowing his sister-in-law carnally.

1 i.148. The priest addresses Alazaïs Fauré as 'tu', while she addresses him as 'vous'. This is a sign of difference in social status, but it should not be exaggerated and may also be interpreted as due to differentiation between the sexes.

2 i.216–50; i.279, 302–06, 329 and *passim*.

3 For an excellent passage on the priest's 'affair' with Mengarde Buscailh, see i.491.

Whatever irresistible personal charm he may have possessed, his position as priest, invested with power and prestige, helps to explain his easy successes with his female parishioners. As for the dames of Ax-les-Thermes, he used to meet them at the baths and then take them secretly to a room in the hospital there. To overcome their last attempts at resistance he had only to invoke the threat of the Inquisition (i.279).

So power and wealth were among the primary reasons for his successes with the women. As Pierre Maury said one day to another Montaillou shepherd, the priests formed a sort of equestrian class, who finally bestrode anyone they fancied. *The priests*, said Maury (ii.386), *sleep with women. They ride horses, mules and she-mules. They are up to no good.*

Conversely the priest's good fortune in love became a source of power. Pierre Clergue knew that there were friendly beds available to welcome him all over the Pays d'Aillon and Sabarthès, and knowing this he did not shrink from using his mistresses to denounce his enemies to the Inquisition of Carcassonne.[1]

As he grew older, Pierre acquired the repulsive habit of making his influence with the Inquisition serve his conquests. But he was not always so unattractive. Béatrice de Planissoles knew him when he was young, and remembered him as *good, competent and regarded as such throughout the region.* Even now that they were separated, she still looked on him as a friend. In short, for many years after the end of their affair she was still under his spell. It had not completely evaporated when she met Barthélemy Amilhac, *vicaire* of Dalou. But compared with the powerful personality of Pierre Clergue, this new fancy man cut a very poor figure.

Of course, not all the priests of Sabarthès or the Pays d'Aillon were such skilful or energetic lovers as their colleague Clergue. He would declare, *I love you more than any woman in the world* (i.224, 491), and proceed forthwith to action. But although he did not bore his conquests with preliminaries, he did not force anyone.

The power did not exclude gentleness: among the 'rough' peasants, the priest stood out as someone sympathetic to women. Although he could behave very badly in other contexts, he seems as a lover to have been gentle, kind, comparatively cultivated, sensitive, affectionate and ardent in pleasure and love. *You priests desire women more than other men*

1 See above, Chapter III; i.408.

do, said Béatrice de Planissoles,[1] both delighted and shocked by the behaviour of her two successive ecclesiastical lovers. And she had reason to know what she was talking about.

La Planissoles was not the only one who looked back kindly on an adventure with the priest. Another of his mistresses recalls with pleasure how, when he deflowered her among the straw in the family barn, he did not offer her any violence. This was in contrast to certain rustics who would have made no bones about raping her (i.302).

Clergue had several reasons for being a seducer: from his point of view, womanizing was also remaining faithful to the ideology of the *domus*. One day he said to Béatrice, '*I am a priest, I do not want a wife*' (implying that he wanted all women). Pierre thus dissociated himself from his brothers, who had impoverished the paternal house by marrying outsiders and not leaving one of their number to marry their sister and so keep her dowry in the family.

Some of Pierre Clergue's love affairs are better known than others. About 1313 or 1314 he was Gaillarde Benet's lover; he also had her sister, Alissende Roussel. There had been no great difficulty in seducing Gaillarde, a poor girl whose family had been ruined by the Inquisition. Her husband Pierre Benet and her brother-in-law Bernard Benet were formerly farmers working their own land, but they were subsequently forced to become migrant shepherds (i.297, 395–6). Did Pierre Clergue take advantage of Pierre Benet's being away, perhaps in the mountain pastures, to seduce his wife? Not necessarily. The priest was usually sufficiently bold and influential not to have to bother with such precautions in the case of a poor fellow like Benet. The affair with Gaillarde produced a striking conversation between Pierre Clergue and Fabrisse Rives. Fabrisse, referring to village gossip on the subject, said to Pierre (i.329): '*You are committing an enormous sin by sleeping with a married woman.*'

'*Not at all,*' answered the priest. '*One woman's just like another. The sin is the same, whether she is married or not. Which is as much as to say that there is no sin about it at all.*' But here Pierre's views on love were cut short because Fabrisse's pot began to boil over and she had to hurry into the kitchen. However, we know enough to be able to interpret with certainty what Pierre said. Starting from the Cathar proposition that 'any sexual act, even between married persons, is wrong', he applied it to suit

1 i.255. See also, on Pierre Clergue's non-violence as a lover, i.302 and ii.26.

himself. Because everything was forbidden, one act was no worse than another.

Fabrisse had no particular reason for affecting outraged virtue. Shortly before this conversation she had delivered over to the priest the virginity of her own daughter, Grazide Rives; or at least had allowed him to know her carnally in her own *domus*. It had happened in about 1313, at the time of the cereal harvest. Fabrisse, not very well off, was a sort of illegitimate cousin of the Clergue family.[1] She was more or less under the thumb of her legitimate relations, belonging to the dominant house. On the day in question she was out reaping corn – hers or some-one else's. Pierre took advantage of her absence to practise on Grazide, who was left at home, his theories on incest (not a very close case as it happened – the cousinship between them derived from the fact that Grazide was the granddaughter, in the illegitimate line, of Guillaume Clergue, himself the brother of the priest's father), but blood will out. Grazide gave a frank account of her adventure (i.302–04). *Seven years ago or thereabouts, in summer, the priest Pierre Clergue came to my mother's house while she was out harvesting, and was very pressing:* 'Allow me,' *he said,* 'to know you carnally.'

And I said: 'All right.'

At that time, I was a virgin. I think I was fourteen or fifteen years old. He deflowered me in the barn [borde] *in which we kept the straw. But it wasn't a rape at all. After that, he continued to know me carnally until the following January. It always took place in my mother's* ostal; *she knew about it, and was consenting. It happened chiefly during the day.*

After that, in January, the priest gave me as wife to my late husband, Pierre Lizier; and after he had thus given me to this man, the priest continued to know me carnally, frequently, during the remaining four years of my husband's life. And my husband knew about it, and was consenting. Sometimes he would ask me: 'Has the priest done it with you?'

And I would answer: 'Yes.'

And my husband would say: 'As far as the priest is concerned, all right! But don't you go having other men.'

But the priest never permitted himself to know me carnally when my husband was at home. We only did it when he was out.

Later on in her deposition, Grazide pronounced judgment on herself

1 Fabrisse, married to Rives and the mother of Grazide, was the bastard daughter of Guillaume Clergue, the brother of Pierre Clergue's father (i.302).

and her lover. She employs the same tone as the *Bréviaire d'amour* and the *Flamenca*: 'A lady who sleeps with a true lover is purified of all sins . . . the joy of love makes the act innocent, for it proceeds from a pure heart.'[1] She went further: *With Pierre Clergue, I liked it. And so it could not displease God. It was not a sin.*[2] Grazide had not read the poets, but like them she derived her intuitions from the common fund of Occitan culture as felt and experienced by couples who took pleasure together, both in Languedoc and the Pyrenees. True, Pierre's young sweetheart added a stratum of Cathar culture to this element of southern innocence which came to her from her village education. This was the special contribution of her lover. For Grazide, while convinced that there was no sin in her affair with Clergue, also believed, in general, that all sexual union, even within marriage, was displeasing to God. Nor was she certain of the existence of Hell, or of the fact of the Resurrection of the flesh.

Pierre Clergue, having enjoyed Grazide's maidenhood, married her off to the perhaps elderly Pierre Lizier, who left her a widow at the age of twenty. Lizier offered no objection to his wife's affair with the priest; it was not a good thing to resist the Clergue clan. Grazide herself believed this. When Jacques Fournier reproached her for not having denounced Pierre Clergue's heresy earlier, she answered (i.329): *'If I had denounced them, the priest and his brothers would have killed me or ill-treated me.'* Fabrisse, Grazide's mother, said (i.305): *I did not want to admit that I knew the faults of the priest and his brothers, for I was afraid that if I did I would be ill-used by them.*

But the day came nevertheless, before 1320, when Grazide and Pierre wearied of being lovers. Then, Grazide told Jacques Fournier, since she no longer felt desire, any carnal act with the priest would be consummated coldly and would ipso facto become a sin. It was pleasure alone which guaranteed the innocence of a liaison.

Pierre Clergue's most important love affair was with Béatrice de Planissoles, who came from the lesser nobility of Ariège and who lived all her life in the country and in the mountains. She was the wife of the

1 *Breviaire d'amour*, quoted by R. Nelli (1963), p. 65; and *Flamenca*, R. Nelli (1963), p. 173.
2 i.303. The same idea is to be found in the poets of the late Middle Ages and the early Renaissance.

châtelain of Montaillou. At that time Pierre Clergue was the young and spirited priest of Montaillou, his native village. Philippe de Planissoles, Béatrice's father, had some urban and suburban connections (Planissoles is in the commune of Foix, in the locality of La Bargilière). Philippe bore the title of *chevalier*, and was witness to the confirmation of the charter of Tarascon-sur-Ariège in 1266 (i.244, note 96). But his roots were in the country villages of upper Ariège: he was lord of Caussou, and married his daughter to Bérenger de Roquefort, *châtelain* of Montaillou. Philippe was friendly towards Catharism and sought out by the Inquisition, which condemned him to wear the yellow cross. Later his daughter tried in vain to hide this fact from Jacques Fournier. In her childhood and youth, Béatrice does not seem to have been keen on reading – there are even various indications that she was illiterate. (On the other hand her daughters were given some slight education at Dalou, where the *vicaire* (i.252), who taught the few schoolchildren in the parish, had his pupils' mothers making eyes at him.) So Béatrice had not read the heretical books; but, apart from her father, she had had contact from youth with Albigensian sympathizers. In about 1290, in Celles, a village south-east of Foix in middle Ariège, she heard a mason called Odin say certain things which savoured of heresy. They made her laugh, and she told them to the people around her. It was a mistake, for the priests and the village gossips passed them on to Jacques Fournier. What Odin and others of his kind had said was that *If the Eucharist was really Christ's body, he would not let himself be eaten by the priests. And if Christ's body was as big as Mount Margail, near Dalou, the priests would have eaten it in a pie long since.*[1] This was only a small extract from a whole body of anti-Eucharistic folklore general throughout the Pyrenees. Peasants made fun of the sacrament by brandishing slices of turnip. People on their deathbed insulted the priest who brought them the Host, calling him a stinking, fetid lout. Witches profaned the body of Christ.[2]

Among the young Béatrice's heretical connections were members of the Authié family, later to become Cathar missionaries. Guillaume Authié mingled with the dancers at Béatrice's wedding to Bérenger de Roquefort. Pierre Authié had acted as notary in the sale of a piece of property belonging to Roquefort, on which Béatrice held a mortgage as

1 i.215–16. Dalou was a village between Foix and Pamiers on the right bank of the Ariège.
2 See below, Chapters XVIII and XIX; ii.305.

part of her dowry. What with her father's yellow cross, the blasphemy of the mason, and her relations with the Authiés, young Béatrice smacked of heresy from her earliest years. And yet she was devoted to the Virgin. She was later to be an ardent penitent before a Minorite friar who felt like hearing confession, and always regarded herself, in her soul and conscience, as belonging more or less to the Catholic line.

After her marriage to Bérenger de Roquefort she was left a widow, then married again, then was left a widow again. Her second marriage was to Othon de Lagleize, who did not make old bones in her company. These successive widowhoods were commonplace in *ancien régime* demography. Later they are to be found all over the parish registers. There is not much to be said about Béatrice's two husbands, except that both belonged to the lesser Ariège gentry, and that neither of them aroused in Béatrice more than a certain indifference, perhaps tinged with affection. But if she did not love her husbands, Béatrice was very much afraid of them. She hid her escapades from them, though these adventures were minor enough during their lifetimes. She was afraid that if they found her out they would kill either her or her lover (i.219, 234).

All this was quite usual. The troubadours, excellent witnesses of the love-life of Languedoc, said much on the subject of the unhappily married wife. The husband was a 'jealous wretch' a miserly cuckold, 'scratching someone else's arse', as Marcabru said.[1] The wife, if possible, 'escaped another way'. The Languedoc poets considered it bad taste for a wife to love her husband, and according to them the wife was always afraid lest the husband beat or imprison her. The lengthy testimony of the Pamiers Inquisition confirms that this was no mere literary theme. Occitan marriage in the period before 1340 was not, despite some examples to the contrary, the best place to look for emotional fulfilment. From this point of view Béatrice is not untypical.

Within her two marriages, Béatrice's affection went to her children rather than her husband. And she was rewarded. For when she was threatened with arrest by Bishop Fournier her four daughters – Condors, Esclarmonde, Philippa and Ava, who adored the mother who had always cared for them intelligently and with love – shed torrents of sincere tears.[2]

1 Macrabru in R. Nelli (1963), p. 109.
2 i.257. See also Chapter XX below for the magic philtres which Béatrice prepared for her daughters and their children.

In the 1290s, Béatrice, a young and pretty bride, had one initial inconclusive affair while her first husband was still alive. Bérenger de Roquefort, as stupid as all husbands (in those days), noticed nothing. A young peasant of the Pays d'Aillon, later to appear in the records grown older, married, and working his own plot, was the somewhat pitiful hero of this abortive idyll.

In the château of Montaillou, Raymond Roussel ran the household of the Sire de Roquefort and his wife, Béatrice. This meant, in Occitania, that Raymond was not only steward of the domestic affairs of this modest household but also in charge of its farming activities, sowing the grain, directing the farm workers and taking the ploughshares to the forge to be sharpened or strengthened.

What I have said earlier about the lesser mountain nobility applies exactly to Béatrice's relationship with the villagers in general and with her steward in particular. When she became a widow, she went to live in a very ordinary house in Montaillou. So the social distance which set her apart was not very great. She would sit and warm herself by the fire with the village women, exchanging the latest Cathar gossip. The peasant Alazaïs Azéma might easily direct a few unceremonious shafts the ex-*châtelaine*'s way: '*You have large eyebrows, you are haughty; I will not tell you what my son does.*' But this was a mere figure of speech, for a moment afterwards Alazaïs, who like all the ladies only wanted to be persuaded, did not hesitate to tell Béatrice her secrets: '*Yes, it is true, my son Raymond Azéma goes and takes food to the goodmen.*'[1]

Madame de Roquefort lost no time in starting up a more or less amorous friendship with her steward, Raymond Roussel. Roussel, who had Cathar tendencies, invited her to flee with him to Lombardy, then a favourite refuge for heretics. Many *parfaits* from Languedoc, persecuted in their own country, used to go there for a spell of peace and quiet. But Béatrice answered: '*I am still young. If I go away with you, Raymond, tongues will start to wag. People will say that we have left the country to satisfy our lust.*'[2] But the idea of this journey did appeal to the *châtelaine*, and she thought of a compromise solution. She was willing to go with Raymond, but only if accompanied by a couple of duennas to

1 i.237. See also i.233. On the network of Béatrice's feminine friendships, see below Chapter XVI.
2 i.221. The wife of a notary in Ax really did run away to Lombardy at about this time, for reasons which were perhaps sentimental as well as heretical (i.290).

protect her reputation. Raymond agreed and even put Béatrice in touch with two women who offered to go with her to Lombardy (i.222). Both women had connections with the Clergue *domus*: Alazaïs Gonela was the mistress of Guillaume Clergue, the priest's brother, and Algaia de Martra was the sister of old Mengarde, Pierre Clergue's mother. The offer made by the two duennas came to nothing, but it is worth noting since it represents the first appearance of the Clergue clan in Béatrice's life.

Raymond Roussel, like Pierre Clergue later, was a peasant with a glib tongue. He mixed chat about going away with a few rather broad remarks about metempsychosis. He explained to Béatrice, who was pregnant (i.220), '*how the future soul of a child yet to be born could enter into the foetus in a woman's womb through any part of her body.*'

On which Béatrice ingeniously asked: '*If this is the case, why don't babies speak when they are born, since they inherit old souls?*'

'*Because God does not wish it!*' replied Raymond Roussel, never at a loss for an answer.

So far all is in the best tradition of the troubadours, those connoisseurs of regional ethnography. The young and lovely lady of Montaillou has a 'lover' from a social level lower than her own. Raymond, in fact, was not merely non-noble but also a villager. Thus Béatrice, though she never thought to theorize on the subject, contributed to the democratization by love which was one of the Languedoc poets' essential themes. Towards a lover 'patient, complimentary and discreet', offering both respect and temptation, Béatrice played the role of muse and inspiration, and in her turn was educated by him. Heresy gave Raymond a marvellous opportunity to flirt and show off. All would have been well, and even the husband would have had nothing to take exception to, if Raymond had remained the Lenten lover, 'the lover of emerald and sard' that Marcabru desired for every woman truly courted. (According to the *Bréviaire d'amour*, the emerald symbolized the repression of sexual instinct and the sard was the symbol of chaste humility.)[1] Unfortunately for himself, Raymond Roussel wanted to sleep with his beloved, another essential theme of Occitan lyrics. As Bernard de Ventador wrote, 'I should like to find her alone, asleep or pretending to be asleep, so that I could steal the sweet kiss for which I am too unworthy to ask'.[2]

1 See R. Nelli (1963), p. 154.
2 See M. Lazar (1964), p. 219.

Béatrice tells the story (i.222). *One evening Raymond and I had dined together. Afterwards he secretly went into my bedroom and hid under the bed. Meanwhile I had set the house in order. I went to bed. Everyone in the house was asleep and so was I. Then Raymond came out from under the bed and got into it, in his shirt! He made as if to sleep with me carnally. And I cried out: 'What is happening?'*

Upon which Raymond said: 'Be quiet.'

To which I replied: 'You peasant! Keep quiet, indeed!'

And I started to cry out and call my servants who slept near me in other beds in my room. And I said to them: 'There's a man in my bed.'

At that, Raymond emerged from my bed and left the room ... A little while afterwards he left our service and went back to his own ostal *in Prades.*

Exit Raymond Roussel. Enter Pathau.

Pathau was a bastard. But he was a cousin of Pierre Clergue's and so, although he was not noble, he came from a leading village family. Pathau did not beat about the bush, but raped Béatrice while Bérenger de Roquefort was still alive. However, it does not seem to have been too traumatic an experience, for when Bérenger died and Béatrice was free and, as a widow, a step lower down the social scale, she became Pathau's concubine. *Pathau then kept me publicly as his mistress*, she told Bishop Fournier when he was later inquiring into her private life.

The real love affair of Béatrice's first widowhood, however, was not with Pathau but with his cousin the priest. The liaison began in the confessional and ended in the church, where one dark night Pierre Clergue, in his perversity, made up his mistress's bed.

At the beginning Béatrice was only one female penitent among others. For a long while she had been friendly with the Clergue family and spent long evenings with them around the fire (i.235–7). But one day when she went to confess to the parish priest, Pierre did not give her time to admit her sins, but declared: '*I prefer you to any other woman in the world*,' and embraced her fervently. She made off – thoughtful, surprised, but not angry.

This was only a beginning, for Clergue took his time enjoying this gratifying conquest. There was no question of real passionate love in the matter, only desire and mutual affection. Béatrice's and Pierre's feelings were translated by the verb *diligere* (to be fond of), whereas the passion between Béatrice and Barthélemy Amilhac, later, was rendered by Fournier's scribes in terms of the Latin words *adamare* and *adamari*, both connoting passionate love.

After a courtship of normal length, lasting from Lent to the beginning of July, Béatrice at last succumbed to the priest's charm and eloquence. During the octave of Saint Peter and Saint Paul in a late thirteenth-century summer, 'the fine rich summer which gives birth to dalliance',[1] Béatrice gave herself to Pierre. She was a very obliging sweetheart, and even committed sacrilege to please him. She slept with him during Christmas night, and, as we have seen, she slept with him in the parish church. Despite her natural reserve, Béatrice belonged in the direct line of the boldest lady-loves in Languedoc literature and Languedoc life.[2]

The affair between Pierre and Béatrice was, as far as we know, agreeable for both of them. For two years they met, presumably in secret, two or three nights a week; and in one night they would make love *twice or more*.[3] In bed, by the fire or by the window, Béatrice used to delouse Pierre, an act which combined rudimentary hygiene with affection ritualized in the customary manner. Pierre talked to Béatrice about family sociology, Albigensian theology and contraception.

But after two years Béatrice broke off the affair. Intellectually, she was hemmed in on all sides by the Cathar priest's powerful dialectic. But she was torn between the heretical mountains on the one hand, the home of her loves and her friends, and, on the other, the lowlands now reclaimed by Catholicism. She yielded to the seduction of the plains and the prospect of a second marriage; she was also influenced by the preachings of the Minorites and the insistence of her sister Gentile, a zealous Catholic. In a way, Béatrice still considered Pierre a good man; but from the point of view of a pious young woman who as a girl had dedicated coloured candles to the Virgin, he was the Devil (i.223). Because of him she might end up being burned at the stake, not to mention the flames of hell. So she decided to leave him and go down into the plain and marry the noble Othon de Lagleize, despite the protests of her friends in the Pays d'Aillon, who all, with Pierre at their head, came in a body and begged her not to do so (i.231, 254): '*We have lost you ; you are going down among the wolves and the dogs.*'

But Béatrice refused to listen, and went to live in Crampagna, Dalou

---

1 Marcabru, quoted by R. Nelli (1963), p. 115, n. 21.
2 R. Nelli (1963), p. 195.
3 i.226, 244. The affair took place around 1299–1301 (Béatrice left Montaillou shortly after 1300: ii.291). In 1305 (i.232), Béatrice was still married to her second husband, whom she had married shortly after 1300 (*ibid.*)

and Varilhes, all about fifteen to twenty kilometres north of and lower down than the Pays d'Aillon, where her new husband, Othon de Lagleize (i.e. Othon of the Church), lived at different times. In these circumstances the relations between Béatrice and Pierre Clergue became intermittent; but they remained fond of one another. One last time Pierre, pretending to be a priest from Limoux, came to see his former mistress in the house at Dalou, and there 'their bodies mingled' in the cellar, with a maid keeping watch at the door (i.239). But after that their relationship was purely spiritual. There was one more visit, chaste and brief, after Béatrice was widowed for the second time. Pierre asked after his former mistress's heart, and later sent her a last present of an engraved glass and some sugar (*zacara*) from the land of the Saracens. These little attentions show that the priest was not unfeeling; but once the affair with Béatrice was over, Pierre departed more and more from the romantic model. Whether it was as a cure for melancholy or to satisfy the growing lust of an ageing priest, at any rate he became more fickle than ever, making love 'fit to break his breeches'[1] with the women of Ax-les-Thermes and Montaillou, winning them over partly by his presumed charm but more still by his power and by his threats.

Béatrice looked back on her two years with Clergue with nostalgia and regret. Her second marriage brought her no more emotional satisfaction than the first. But she was not disappointed, for all she had expected was to attain a position in life.[2] She was a faithful wife to Othon de Lagleize, apart from the single lapse in the cellar (i.239). Othon died soon afterwards, so Béatrice was free again, for the grand passion.

Béatrice's second lover was also a priest. He was the young *vicaire* of a parish, but later on Bernard Clergue, in prison, addressed him with respect and called him 'my lord priest'. But Barthélemy Aurilhac was only a pale imitation of Pierre Clergue. He knew how to be a rake, but he was not a Cathar, and only became an informer when forced to do so. (It must be admitted he did not feel any remorse).

It was in the village of Dalou that Béatrice, now widowed for the second time, got to know Barthélemy. She had sent Ava and Philippa, her daughters, to his school. Already getting on in years (*I was past the*

---

1 *A s'en rompre les braies*: Raimbaut d'Orange and Guillaume d'Aquitaine, quoted by M. Lazar (1964), pp. 129 and 143.
2 Béatrice had two daughters known to us from her second marriage, born 1303–04 and 1305–06.

change of life), Béatrice fell passionately in love with the young priest; her feeling was translated by the verb *adamare*. She threw herself at him. As Barthélemy Amilhac himself said later (i.252): *It was she who made the first advances; one day, when I had just finished teaching my pupils, among them Ava and Philippa, Béatrice said to me: 'Come to my house this evening.'*

I did. When I was in her house, I found that she was there alone. I asked: 'What do you want of me?'

And she said: 'I love you: I want to sleep with you.'

And I answered: 'All right.'

Straight away I made love with her in the antechamber of the ostal, *and subsequently I possessed her often. But never at night. Always in the daytime. We used to wait until the girls and the servant were out of the house. And then we used to commit the carnal sin.*

Their passion was mutual. *Beatrix Bartholomeum nimis adamabat . . . et ipse dictam Beatricem adamabat* (i.249, 256). It is true that the young *vicaire* was of weak character, even a coward, unworthy of his mistress. In the end he left her, partly because she was old, but mostly because he was afraid his involvement with her would get him accused of heresy. What she loved in him was his gentleness and his desire – priests were known to be much more lustful than mere laymen. One day, in a moment of truth, Béatrice said to Barthélemy (i.255): *'You priests and priors and abbots and bishops and archbishops and cardinals, you are the worst! You commit the sin of the flesh more, and you desire women more than other men do.'* Barthélemy's philosophical comment was: *That was how Béatrice used to try to justify herself for committing the sin of the flesh with me.*

Béatrice loved the young man so much that she accused him of having bewitched her (i.249): *I have never committed the sin of sorcery*, she said one day. *But I think the priest Barthélemy did cast a spell on me, for I loved him too passionately; and yet when I met him I was already past the menopause.*

The affair, begun with so much zest, continued equally colourfully. After she became the *vicaire*'s sweetheart Béatrice was continually annoyed by village gossip, spread by the parish slanderers (*lauzengiers*), the chief village priest at their head. She was also subjected to vexation by her brothers, who in typical Occitan style set themselves up as custodians of their sister's virtue. She was afraid they might hurt her, and thought of going with her lover to Palhars, a remote diocese in the Pyrenees between Aragon and Comminges-Couserans, where priests, in accordance with an old pre-Gregorian and Nicolaitan tradition, were still allowed at this period to live with their housekeepers, concubines or *focarias*. Permission to do so was granted by the bishop in return for a financial consideration. So Béatrice, taking with her her clothes and thirty *livres tournois*, decided to go to Palhars. She went first to Vicdessos, where she was joined by Barthélemy, and from there they both went on to Palhars, where a priest-cum-notary 'married' them, but without giving them his blessing. There they lived for a year in the same *domus* without causing the slightest scandal. They lived meagrely on the thirty *livres tournois* which had served as the ex-*châtelaine*'s dowry. Gradually Barthélemy got to know about his mistress's Cathar past. He was afraid. There were quarrels. He called her *a wicked old woman, a heretic*. They parted.

When they met again later it was just before they were both put in prison. Barthélemy had been earning his living by hiring himself out as vicar or priest in charge in the country or the mountains. Béatrice had already been roughly handled by the Inquisition, and she asked her former sweetheart to help her. Once again, as before with the priest Clergue in the cellar at Dalou, Béatrice made love with the young vicar in a vineyard while her faithful maid kept watch: this time the servant's name was Alazaïs. The rest of Béatrice and Barthélemy's story belongs to Bishop Fournier. He put them both in prison. Then, a year later, on the same day, 4 July 1322, he set them both free. She had to wear the double yellow cross. He did not (i.553).

Béatrice and her friends the Clergues are not the only ones who can tell us something about village sexuality. Apart from the extravagances of one of the leading *domus*, morals in Montaillou and in Foix as a whole were certainly comparatively free: comparatively, because they were merely slightly more relaxed around 1320 than they were to be during the rigours of the Counter Reformation, in the seventeenth and eighteenth centuries. Setting aside the adventures of the priest, the records show us five or six illicit couples at the least in Montaillou around 1300–20. The list is not exhaustive. If we compare this figure with the fifty or so couples at the most, licit or otherwise, which the parish must have contained during the first two decades of the fourteenth century, we arrive at a minimum of 10 per cent of couples 'living in sin'. Around 1700 Monseigneur Colbert, the Jansenist bishop of Montpellier whose episcopal visitations I studied fifteen years ago, would have been shocked by such a high proportion. And from a rigorist point of view the most outrageous thing was that in or around 1310 such liaisons were brazenly advertised; a man would 'publicly keep' or 'publicly maintain' a concubine (i.238). At the beginning of the eighteenth century, people carefully hid such things to avoid the wrath of the priest and the gossip of the devout. But in Montaillou at the beginning of the fourteenth century it was the priest himself who set the bad example. We have already seen how in the pastures as well as in the town the shepherds did not hesitate to entertain a mistress when the occasion offered. If anyone came across a couple openly living together, the reaction was much the same as it would be today. Were they legally married or not? That then was the question Guillaume Escaunier of Ax-les-Thermes asked himself, without trace of shock, on a visit to Limoux (ii.12): *In the house of Martin François at Limoux we found a woman who must have been his wife, unless she was his concubine; because she was permanently kept and maintained by him in the house.* None of Escaunier's interlocutors seems to have been unduly worried about the uncertain legal status of Martin François's companion.

Although people did have some sense of carnal sin in the Comté de Foix at that time, it was less developed than later. We have already seen that for Arnaud de Verniolles sodomy was no worse a sin than mere fornication. But for Grazide Lizier of Montaillou and for Pierre Vidal of Ax-les-Thermes mere fornication was not a sin provided both parties took pleasure in it and, in the case of Pierre Vidal, provided the man paid a fair price. Permissiveness in Montaillou at the beginning of the fourteenth century was a modest minority affair, but it was an undoubted fact, both in theory and in practice. Béatrice de Planissoles, a widow for the second time, and the bastard Pathau Clergue lived together publicly in Montaillou without arousing anyone's anger. At the most there was some ill-natured gossip. Gauzia Marty, later to become the wife of the other Bernard Clergue (the *bayle*'s namesake), was for a while the concubine of Raymond Ros of Montaillou, *whose bones will be burned as a heretic after his death* (i.459). Raymonde Testanière, known as Vuissane, was Bernard Belot's mistress; she had children by him, one of them also called Bernard. She worked hard in the house of her lover and employer (i.456): *I thought that Bernard Belot would take me for his wife; and because of that I worked hard and did all I could in his house.* But she was disappointed. Arnaud Vital did not hesitate to explain why: '*Even if you had been as rich as any woman in the Comté de Foix, Bernard would not have taken you for his wife because you are not of his faith, so there could be no question of his trusting you.*'

This passage shows one of the reasons why concubinage was so frequent in Montaillou. Marriage was a difficult business because it might involve feelings of love on the part of the man, and on the part of a woman it might involve some hopes of improving her fortunes. Last but not least, there was the matter of religion. Confronted with all these difficulties, many people in Montaillou preferred, at least to begin with, to take advantage of the public tolerance of concubinage.[1]

Another illegitimate couple was formed by the temporary union between Alazaïs Guilhabert, daughter of a sheep-farmer of Montaillou, and Arnaud Vital, the shoemaker and satellite of the Belots. Alazaïs Guilhabert (i.413): *I was very fond of Arnaud, with whom I had established a dishonourable familiarity; he had instructed me in heresy; and I had promised him to go and see my mother to persuade her to agree that my young brother* [he was very ill] *should be hereticated.*

This is an interesting case: retrospectively Alazaïs agreed that her affair with the Cathar shoemaker was morally debatable ('dishonour-

1 i.244. A distinction was made between publicly keeping a concubine and having a more or less secret affair with a mistress.

able'). But at the time she did not think it anything she needed to hide or be ashamed of, and Arnaud Vital remained on friendly terms with Allemande Fauré, his mistress's mother.[1]

Moreover, we should note that this was a real love affair. True, it was a matter of inclination rather than passion: Alazaïs uses the word *diligere* and not *adamare*. But in the matter of love, Montaillou allowed a wide range of variations. Béatrice de Planissoles, for example, felt a real, burning, requited passion for the young *vicaire* who consoled her second widowhood.

On the subject of irregular unions, we should also take into account various supplementary episodes and the escapades of the priest, Pierre Clergue. But as far as our four couples here are concerned, their youthful pranks did not prevent the four ladies from finding husbands. After her concubinage with Pathau and her thrilling adventure with the priest Pierre Clergue, Béatrice de Planissoles married Othon de Lagleize, which, far from being a fall, represented a kind of social advancement. As for Gauzia Marty, Alazaïs Guilhabert and Vuissane, they married three very respectable farmers from the Pays d'Aillon called Bernard Clergue (the *bayle*'s namesake), Arnaud Faure and Bernard Testanière respectively.

Note that these ladies' lovers were mostly Cathars and determined heretics.[2] Likewise, Martin François, who apparently lived in concubinage with a woman in Limoux, must have been delighted to hear the Authiés preach in his own house on the subject 'marriage is nothing' (ii.12–13). When all was said and done, Catharism was very tolerant towards irregular unions. At least, Catharism as it was understood in Montaillou. It railed against legal marriage; strict abstinence from sex it reserved to the goodmen alone; and it left ordinary believers free, *de facto* if not *de jure*, in the matter of morals, by virtue of the famous maxim, *since everything is forbidden, everything is allowed*.[3] Even so, it

1 i.414. See also the friendly complicity between Mengarde Clergue's sister and Guillaume Clergue's concubine. Guillaume was Mengarde's son and the priest's brother (i.222).

2 Such is the case with Bernard Belot, Raymond Ros and Arnaud Vital. Pathau Clergue is not listed as a heretic, but Pierre Clergue, who succeeded him in Béatrice's favours, was as heterodox as anyone could be.

3 i.224–5. The argument of the sophist Pierre Clergue is based on the following two ideas. (a) Making love is in any case a sin for a woman, whether with her husband or with a lover. With her husband it is even worse, because they do not know that they

would be wrong to explain the sexual customs and behaviour of upper Ariège in Fournier's day as the local implantation of a heterodox ideology, tempting though this hypothesis may be. Amilhac the priest was no heretic, but he was almost as much of a fornicator as Pierre Clergue, the Albigensian and double agent. It is true that heresy did nothing to restrict concubinage in Montaillou; perhaps it encouraged the practice. But it certainly did not invent it. It had been there for a long time, finding its justification, primary or secondary, in the dearness of dowries, the difficulty of marriage and the overriding need not to dissipate the family *domus* by rash and costly alliances. Heresy was only one more reason for concubinage. Moreover, it flourished in many other parts of the Pyrenees never infected with the ideology of the goodmen, and where little or nothing was known of Catharism. In the diocese of Palhars, for example, the priests had for a long time been able to live with their concubines, enjoying the blessing of the local bishop. As for the ordinary peasants, concubinage fitted easily into their system of farming and household management: your maidservant was also your mistress, and she worked all the harder if she was spurred on by false promises of marriage. Conversely, a farm worker was always glad to plough his mistress's field. He did so either for love, or merely in accordance with the common pooling of land between couples (i.456; ii.126).

Concubinage in Montaillou was accompanied by contraceptive precautions which were more or less efficient, birth control obviously being more sought after by lovers than by husbands. For example, Béatrice de Planissoles, at the beginning of her relationship with Pierre Clergue, was haunted by the fear of having an illegitimate child (i.243–4): '*What shall I do if I become pregnant by you?*' she said to the priest. '*I shall be ashamed and lost.*'

Clergue had an answer for everything. He told his sweetheart that he had a special herb which acted as a contraceptive, both masculine and feminine. He said: '*I have a certain herb. If a man wears it when he mingles his body with that of a woman he cannot engender, nor she conceive.*'

Béatrice, a real country girl despite her noble extraction, asked:

---

are sinning. Therefore, ladies, take lovers. (b) In any case, if one is received by a *parfait* on one's deathbed all one's sins are done away with. Why worry about sinning then? (Clergue's anarchical extremism is not typical of the average outlook of the ordinary people of upper Ariège, even if they were Cathars.)

'*What sort of herb? Is it the one the cowherds hang over a cauldron of milk in which they have put some rennet, to stop the milk from curdling so long as the herb is over the cauldron?*'

The reference to rennet is very relevant. Since the days of Dioscorides and of Magnino of Milan, his thirteenth-century successor, the rennet of a hare was thought to be a contraceptive. Béatrice did not see it as a contraceptive, but as something which made cow's milk or a man's semen curdle, thus producing either cheese or a foetus. Pierre Clergue's magic herb prevented this solidification, and thus acted as a contraceptive.

Béatrice gave some more details about the famous 'herb': *When Pierre Clergue wanted to know me carnally, he used to wear this herb wrapped up in a piece of linen, about an ounce long and wide, or about the size of the first joint of my little finger. And he had a long cord which he used to put round my neck while we made love; and this thing or herb at the end of the cord used to hang down between my breasts, as far as the opening of my stomach* [sic]. *When the priest wanted to get up and leave the bed, I would take the thing from around my neck and give it back to him. It might happen that he wanted to know me carnally twice or more in a single night; in that case the priest would ask me, before uniting his body with mine, 'Where is the herb?'*

I was easily able to find it because of the cord round my neck; I would put the 'herb' in his hand and then he himself would place it at the opening of my stomach, still with the cord between my breasts. And that was how he used to unite himself with me carnally, and not otherwise.

Was the object in question in this fascinating lovers' game simply a magic amulet? Or was it a kind of pessary, as the vague reference to the *opening of the stomach* may suggest? Who knows. The fact is that the herb 'worked'. Or at least, and it amounts to the same thing, Béatrice believed that it did.

Clergue exploited his mistress's fear of pregnancy.

One day, said Béatrice, *I asked the priest: 'Leave your herb with me.'*

'*No*', he said, '*I won't, because then you could be united carnally with another man, and thanks to the herb avoid becoming pregnant by him!*'

The priest said that out of jealousy of Pathau, his cousin, who had been my lover before him.

So contraception, as far as we know, was regarded by Pierre Clergue and his rivals in Montaillou as a way of attaching a woman to them, not as something which liberated the opposite sex. Nor did Béatrice protest.

The fear of giving birth to an illegitimate child was a general anxiety in Occitan culture. It was particularly acute among the nobility, to which after all Béatrice de Planissoles belonged. A bastard, automatically described as a lout or a bumpkin, detracted from the noble race to which the woman who conceived him belonged. More important still, the husband's legacy was diverted to the posterity of the lover. 'Husbands fondle the little louts and imagine they are surrounding their own sons with loving care.' Marcabru comes out very strongly on this point, and is followed by other troubadours, such as Cercamon and Bernard Marti.[1] This preoccupation was certainly one of the reasons why the Languedoc poets often suggested Platonic models for extra-marital love. It is true that there were many distinguished bastards among the nobility of Foix. Apart from these inevitable 'mistakes', the nobles remained theoretically hostile to illegitimacy because it jeopardized the already precarious purity of blood. Béatrice echoed this fear when she said she would be ashamed and lost if she became pregnant by the priest Clergue. Pierre Clergue himself was a villager by origin, not noble, a peasant even: he acted according to values which were more lax. But he certainly understood his mistress's arguments. He knew very well that old Planissoles, her father, would blush with shame at the idea of seeing his daughter, a widow, made pregnant outside marriage (i.244, 245): '*I would not want to make you pregnant, as long as your father Philippe de Planissoles is alive,*' said Pierre Clergue to Béatrice. '*Your father would be too ashamed.*' (Shame, as we shall see, was one of the chief factors in morals in Ariège in those days.)

Nevertheless, the tiresome father could not live forever. Pierre was not averse to the idea of giving his mistress a child once the old man had departed. '*When Philippe is dead, I am quite willing to make you pregnant,*' he told her (i.245). When there was no longer any surveillance on the part of the noble line, Pierre was quite ready to return to the peasant scale of values which tolerated the procreation of bastards.

There were plenty of bastards in Montaillou.[2] More, proportionally, than were to be found in the seventeenth and eighteenth centuries, for more of them were engendered, and when they were about to be born no one thought, as they did later, of exporting them to the towns. Only

---

1 See R. Nelli (1963), pp. 108–09.
2 See also iii.267–8 for the many bastards, both of priests and laymen, in the Junac area.

occasionally did people resort to the deferred form of infanticide which consisted in putting them out to nurse. (See however the case of Raymonde Arsen. She put her bastard baby out to nurse so as to become a servant in the *ostal* of the Belots. From time to time in the Belot *ostal* she would take care of the legitimate baby of the family.)

The moral and social status of bastards in the village presented them with problems which were not completely insoluble. In general, the noun which described them was a term of insult: '*You old bastard*', cried Bernard Clergue to Allemande Guilhabert (ii.294) when she refused to carry out his orders and make her daughter go back on evidence compromising the Clergues in the eyes of the Inquisitor. Among the bastards known to us, one, Pathau Clergue, was a brutal character. But the psychological difficulties arising out of his status did not prevent him from being the official lover of the ex-*châtelaine*, who had previously yielded to his violent approaches. As for the female bastards, who were relegated to the rank of servant or beggar, they seem in general to have occupied the lowest stratum of Montaillou society. As we have seen, Brune Pourcel was a poor girl, looked down on by her natural father, Prades Tavernier, although he was rich (a former weaver) and a proud *parfait*. Brune was some time a servant in the Clergues' house, some time established on her own account as a bride and mother and finally a widow, but always begging and borrowing (i.382ff.; i.385). The other bastards known to us from the Pamiers records seem to have married without any great difficulty into the local peasantry. Mengarde, the natural daughter of Bernard Clergue, lived for a long while in the great house belonging to her father, where she acted as servant in charge of the bread and the linen. Subsequently she married Raymond Aymeric, who lived in Prades d'Aillon, a neighbouring village.[1] We do not know much about the fate of the other bastards mentioned in the Fournier Register. What became of the natural children of Bernard Belot and his sweetheart Vuissane? We do not know. They probably died young. As for Arnaud Clergue, all we can say about him is that he married into a local farming family, the Liziers, of Montaillou,[2] and that he provides

1 i.416. See also the case of Guillot, bastard son of the priest of Mérens. Despite his natural father's comparatively comfortable position, Guillot was a mere goatherd, employed by Na Ferriola of Mérens (iii.163).

2 ii.227. Arnaud Clergue also took on the job of doing the errands of his uncle, the priest, in the village (i.476).

one more example of the libidinous proclivities of the Clergue family, rash when it came to concubinage, prudent, in order to preserve the *domus*, when it came to marriage. We have also seen that Pierre Clergue's first cousin, Fabrisse Rives, Pons Rives's wife, was a bastard: the priest took advantage of this and of his relationship to deflower Fabrisse's daughter, Grazide, who was none other than his own niece. Her, too, he married off into the Lizier family, a convenient receptacle for the iniquities of the Clergue *domus*.[1]

Permissiveness, comparatively widespread in Montaillou and productive of bastards, was still not promiscuity. The inhabitants of Montaillou did not couple like 'rats in straw'. Arnaud de Verniolles rates incest, the deflowering of virgins and adultery as more guilty even than sodomy (iii.42). Incest, including incest with the concubine of a cousin, interfered with the sacred links of lineage. It was therefore natural that it should be severely condemned, even while it was indulged in occasionally. The deflowering of virgins was also a great matter, involving responsibility and therefore sin. In a village which though permissive still did not tolerate complete abandon, it might oblige the deflowerer to face up to his responsibilities – in upper Ariège, virginity was sometimes subjected to the jurisdiction of *matrones*, who could carry out an inspection and make an official report (iii.56). Whoever committed a crime against a virgin had either to enter into some sort of concubinage with his 'victim' or else find her some other solution in the form of a husband. Or else both, one after the other. The two things might remain compatible for a long while, so long as the seducer could intimidate the former virgin's family and husband (i.302).

As we have seen, in one case of this kind, that of Grazide Lizier, the husband was complaisant. But such accommodating behaviour only helps us to draw the bounds of 'laxity' in Montaillou. There was a proverb popular in upper Ariège which ran:

> Tout temps et tout temps sera
> Qu'homme avec femme d'autrui couchera.[2]

1 i.302. See also Chapter IX. On bastards, who were quite numerous among the bourgeoisie in upper Ariège, see, for example, ii.197, and ii.209 (bastards of the Authié-Teysseire family).
2 There will never be a time in any of our lives when men don't sleep with other men's wives.

But it does not do to take proverbs too seriously. Pierre Clergue could trick Pierre Lizier openly, and Pierre Benet too (i.329), because his power as a rich priest was irresistible in the case of these poor husbands and their docile wives. But for ordinary mortals things were not so easy. Husbands were heavy-handed and might even go so far as murder, and wives needed to be careful and not indulge in the liberties they might freely enjoy as girls or widows. In Montaillou, permissiveness often stopped on the steps of the altar, and only returned at the husband's deathbed. Béatrice de Planissoles's reaction to the advances made by her steward, Raymond Roussel, are typical in this respect (i.219).

'*Let us run away and go among the good Christians*', said Roussel.

Béatrice replied: '*But when my husband finds out that we've gone, he will come after us; and he will kill me.*'

Bold and passionate as she was during her two widowhoods, Béatrice showed a touching fidelity to her two husbands while they were alive. She committed only two minor infractions of the marriage contracts: the first, her rape by Pathau, was involuntary, and the second was an isolated occurrence and of little significance (i.239).

Judging from the parts of the Register which deal with Montaillou, the restraint of married women is remarkable in comparison with the sort of conduct to be seen among young girls, widows and unmarried maidservants. It was only in the refuge in Catalonia that the virtuous behaviour of married women became less evident. There, mothers of families whom the hazards of the exodus had long separated from their husbands might permit themselves a new, illegal liaison without necessarily being certain that their husbands were dead. This is what Bélibaste suggests in speaking to his concubine, Raymonde, of her absent husband, Arnaud Piquier (iii.188): '*Alive or dead, Arnaud is not likely to bother us much here.*'

But back in Montaillou, where couples lived together and marriages were comparatively stable, wives were on the whole virtuous. At least until they became widows (i.491). The case of Grazide Lizier was an exception.[1] To a lesser extent, husbands were virtuous too. As far as we

---

1 The village of Tignac supplies other exceptions. In his own house, Arnaud Laufre of Tignac found his wife, Esperte, in bed with his brother Bernard. Arnaud interrupted them just in time (ii.131; see also i.283). But, on the whole, unlawful sexual activity occurred at least ten times as often among girls, widows and unmarried maidservants as among wives.

know, the Don Juans of Montaillou were bachelors, though the shoe-maker Arnaud Vital remained an impenitent womanizer even after he married.[1] Pierre Authié, a connoisseur of upper Ariège, considered that in that region most sexual activity took place within marriage. He told Sybille Pierre, the sheep-farmer, '*it's still within marriage that people make love most often*'.[2]

1 ii.411. For the imprecations of the troubadours against fickle husbands, see R. Nelli (1963), p. 110.

2 Even poor illegitimate servant maids like Brune Pourcel and Raymonde Arsen ended up by finding husbands. There were few spinsters in Montaillou and upper Ariège.

CHAPTER XI Marriage and love

Despite certain irregularities in the system, marriage remained the centrepiece of the demographic edifice in Montaillou; not one woman in the parish was left a spinster for ever. The philosophy of marriage in upper Ariège and in the Aude part of Languedoc was summarized in a masterly fashion by Bélibaste for the benefit of his own little flock. Guillaume Bélibaste, son of the patriarch of Cubières, had become the Cathar holy man of Morella. So there was no reason why he should adopt the Catholic theology which governed the institution of marriage. On the other hand, he knew it was no use hoping that simple Cathar believers would ever adopt the ideal of absolute chastity which the Albigensians preached in theory. He also rejected the anomalous Nietzscheism professed by certain Cathars, the priest Clergue chief among them. So Bélisbaste had to be satisfied with prosaic lay justifications of marriage like those which subtended the daily round of life in his own country. '*It amounts to the same*,' he said (iii.241; ii.59), '*and the sin is the same, to know one's own wife carnally or to do the same with a concubine. This being so, it is better for a man to attach himself to a definite woman than to fly from one to another like a bee among the flowers: the result in the latter case is that he engenders bastards; moreover, when a man frequents several women, each of them tries to lay hold of something, and between them all they will turn a man into a pauper. But when a man is attached to one woman, she helps him to maintain a good* ostal.

'*As for incest with women of one's own blood or related through marriage, that is a shameful act, and I in no way advise believers to indulge in it* . . .

'*So you two want to get married? If you mutually desire one another, all right. Promise you will be faithful to one another, and serve one another in times of health or sickness. Embrace one another. I now declare you united in marriage! Well, there you are! No need to go to church!*'

This is a key passage. It forbids incest, not only with blood relations, which went without saying, but also with women related to one through marriage. Monogamy – which in practice meant marriage – on a basis of fidelity and mutual service and desire is presented by Bélibaste as the key to the preservation and prosperity of the *ostal*. A mistress takes, while a wife, with her dowry, gives. Marriage is thus explicitly linked to the *domus*, itself the fundamental value of Pyrenean societies.

Thus marriage in Montaillou involved much more than a mere agreement between two individuals. A wife, says Lévi-Strauss, is always given to her future husband by another man. In Montaillou this gift proceeds not only from one man, but from a whole group of men, together with several women. Raymonde d'Argelliers is an interesting case. She was by no means a young girl at the time of her second marriage to Arnaud Belot, and yet the affair was arranged by relations and friends, together with the local clergy. Raymonde herself was treated merely as the object at stake, with no power of individual decision. *After the murder of my first husband, Arnaud Lizier of Montaillou*, she says, *I remained a widow for nearly three years. As a result of the negotiations conducted by the brothers Guillaume, Bernard and Jean Barbès of Niort, the brothers Bernard and Arnaud Marty of Montaillou, Pierre-Raymond Barbès, priest of Freychenet, and Bernadette Taverne and Guillemette Barbès of Niort, I married Arnaud Belot of Montaillou, then aged about thirty : he was the brother of Bernard, Guillaume and Raymond Belot of Montaillou.*[1]

Raymonde d'Argelliers had been living in Montaillou for a long time, because of her first marriage to Arnaud Lizier. But she did not contemplate marrying again without the interposition between her and the man of her choice of several groups of brothers, who for reasons of friendship or kinship were in a position to conclude the agreement. Not all Montaillou marriages used so many intermediaries. But it was rarely a matter just for the two people concerned. The go-betweens were often a father, mother, brothers, friends, lovers, relations, an aunt or the priests. Pierre Azéma of Montaillou more or less offered his daughter to Gauzia Clergue on a platter, in order that she should marry one of Gauzia's sons and consolidate their two *domus* or the common *domus* which would arise out of the marriage. Rixende Cortil, widow of Pierre Cortil of Ascou, suggested her daughter Guillemette as a possible wife for the shepherd Jean Maury of Montaillou. Jean Maury was interested because, as he said, the two families had in common their heretical beliefs, transmitted to Jean by his father and to Guillemette by her mother. Did the fact that Rixende acted in this way break the rule by which a woman is always given to a man by another man ? Yes and no. This offer on the part of a mother, not the only one known to us, was made during a light meal the family was taking at the house of Rixende's

1 iii.63. Niort and Freychenet are in the present departments of Aude and Ariège respectively.

father. Those present included the father, his wife, Rixende's son and grown-up married daughter and Rixende herself; also Jean Maury. So the gathering was really a family venture designed to attract the shepherd, though the marriage did not in fact take place. Other examples of negotiations by intermediaries include Bélibaste's giving Raymonde in 'marriage' to Pierre Maury. The priest Pierre Clergue did the same for Grazide, who became the wife of Pierre Lizier. The priest of Albi in Catalonia negotiated with Esperte Cervel, mother of Mathena, to bring about a marriage between the girl and Jean Maury. The Belot brothers arranged their sister's marriage. Even when the ceremony was as quiet as possible, absent members of the family were not forgotten. *'Don't forget to speak about my marriage to my uncle, the other Pierre Maury,'* said Pierre Maury to Bélibaste before he 'married' Raymonde (iii.189). Poor maidservants, on the other hand, tended to gravitate away from their native *domus*; perhaps they were freer than the daughters of comfortably-off farmers to move about and make their own marriage decisions.

A marriage might be the cause of a whole collective expedition. When a marriage was planned between Arnaud Sicre's sister and Arnaud Maury, son of Guillemette of Montaillou, part of Bélibaste's little group made the long journey to the north. It would have been a typical endogamic marriage between partners who were both natives of Ariége and Cathars; but the long journey ended badly, with the travellers falling into the trap set for them by the Inquisition.

A Montaillou wedding was preceded by a betrothal period during which the young man, desirous of pleasing his future wife's *domus*, lavished presents, if he could afford it, on his future mother-in-law.[1] To fix the date of the wedding a *parfait* was consulted, and he indicated which phase of the moon was most favourable (i.291). A wedding invitation to some outside person was a significant gesture. The invitation might be either accepted or refused, but in any case the answer was significant. *'If we marry our son Jean to the woman he loves, we shall send for you for the wedding day,'* said Guillemette Maury to Bélibaste (iii.189). *'No,'* said he, *'I will not be present at a marriage between those who have not the understanding of good.'* Among the relations and friends at weddings, some received a more formal invitation than others. These were the witnesses and sureties: thus six women – sisters, mother-in-law, friends

1 ii.271. And for further details on betrothal: i.248, 254.

and wives of friends, or servants – were the witnesses and sureties for Raymond Belot and Guillemette Benet (i.371, 455). These six ladies were important members of feminine society in the Pays d'Aillon.

A distinguished guest might dance at a wedding, as Guillaume Authié did at Béatrice de Planissoles's first marriage, to Bérenger de Roquefort. Marriage was the great event in the lives of the peasant women of Montaillou. They preserved their wedding dresses carefully until they died. When Guillemette Piquier, Pierre Maury's sister, ran away from her husband, she took with her in her bundle of clothes her wedding garments and a sheet (iii.154).

Marriage in Montaillou was a serious social act and a commitment, a costly investment, but later it was supposed to bring in rewards in proportion. To marry and have children was at least to risk ruin. As Emersende Marty said to Pierre Maury, who was younger than she was and still a bachelor (iii.182), '*My boy, you have neither daughter nor son, nor anyone to look after except yourself; so in this part of the world you could live without having to work too hard.*'

But if marriage was a threat in the short term, in the middle term, fifteen years or so later, it was a promise of wealth, security and happiness because of the hopes, or illusions, offered by the unfolding of the family cycle, transforming children from 'parasites' into protectors. A wife also brought a dowry and looked after her husband in his old age. Bélibaste actually complained more than once that the wife of a dying man refused to leave the marriage bed: the *parfait* could not administer the *consolamentum* because of the impurity of a feminine presence (iii.189).

Local endogamy was the rule in fourteenth-century Montaillou; the men and women of the village married among themselves. There were very few immigrants from outside. People went away from Montaillou to live elsewhere or during the migrations, but people hardly ever came there from elsewhere to live. We have no parish registers to give accurate figures on this endogamy, but the statistics which can be derived from the Fournier Register are eloquent:[1] 'Out of sixty-three women in Montaillou, seven only married outside the community; only one came from another village. Out of fifty known couples, forty-three consisted

1 I gratefully acknowledge here my indebtedness to the work of F. Giraud, in his Diplôme d'Etudes Supérieures (Paris) thesis on Montaillou.

of a man and a woman who both came from Montaillou, and only seven
involved one person from Montaillou and another person from another
village.' If we add to this a few unions not included by Giraud, including
those involving the men of the Maury family in Catalonia, we find 80
per cent of the natives of Montaillou marrying within their own parish.
According to Giraud, moreover, five out of seven of the other villages
which supplied Montaillou with some marriage partners were less than
ten kilometres away. Montaillou may have been a nest of vipers, but at
least they kept themselves to themselves.

The village may be consider a *connubium*, an endogamous unit, which
among other reasons explains the heretical and linguistic particularism
of the community. As Arnaud Sicre remarked one day, Montaillou and
the Pays d'Aillon had their own language, Occitan but with special
peculiarities.

Despite the high rates of emigration on the part of shepherds and
Cathars, the exogamy rate was low. In the first place, many of the shepherds considered themselves too poor or too free to get married and they
remained bachelors. Secondly, many of the exiles preferred to marry a
payse – a fellow-countrywoman from Montaillou or, failing that, from
elsewhere in the mountains of Ariège. Three men of the Maury family
lived south of the Pyrenees, but only one of them married – for love – a
Catalan girl. The other two, Pierre and Jean, married women who came
from Tarascon-sur-Ariège and Junac respectively. The emigrants from
the Comté de Foix felt ill at ease among the Catalans: *The people of this
region are too proud*, said Bélibaste (iii.189). To marry their daughters,
according to him, was to risk having to break off relations with one's
family in Ariège. Catalan pride was a kind of subtle discrimination against
the immigrant workers and an additional reason for seeking a wife
among the diaspora from back home. Some men made the long journey
back in search of a wife and then returned with her to Catalonia. As Jean
Pellissier related in 1323, *Pierre Maurs fled from Montaillou after the
Inquisition's first round-ups* [about 1308]. *He settled in Catalonia, and has
remained there ever since. But two years ago he came back to Montaillou to
take a wife, and he married the daughter of Guillaume Authié of Montaillou, who is now in prison in Carcassonne for heresy. He lived in the
village up till the beginning of this winter ; then quite recently he went back
again to Catalonia.*[1] Similarly Bélibaste and his friends went north to

1 iii.76. This Guillaume Authié was not the Cathar missionary but his namesake.

seek a wife for one of their number. But they were caught by the henchmen of the Church, and never came back.

But there was also an endogamy of conscience: the Cathar peasants had a tendency to marry among themselves. Bélibaste's followers believed (ii.66), *It is better to marry a woman who is a believer* [i.e. heretic] *and who has only her shift than one with a big dowry who is not a believer.* We have already seen Arnaud Vital telling Vuissane Testanière that Bernard Belot will never marry her, despite the fact that she has worked for him and given him children (i.456), because she does not share his Cathar beliefs. The same attitude is to be seen towards the marriage of Raymonde d'Argelliers to Arnaud Belot. Raymonde was suspected of having been involved in the murder of her first husband, Arnaud Lizier, whom his fellow-citizens in Montaillou reproached with being a strict Catholic who hated the heretics (iii.65). So Raymonde was strongly suspected of Cathar sympathies. Her second marriage, to Arnaud Belot, was a mystery. Arnaud was as poor as Job (all his possessions put together scarcely amounted to 15 *livres tournois*), he had no trade, she did not love him passionately, she did not even know whether he was a Cathar (iii.64). So why on earth did she marry him? She still could not say.

Marriage between Cathars or Cathar sympathizers was not merely a cultural model in Montaillou but also a real practice. The big local Albigensian farming *domus* – the Clergues, the Belots, the Benets, the Forts, the Maurys, the Martys and so on – exchanged their boys and girls in marriage.[1]

This endogamy of conscience did not act as an additional limit on the marriage market, for in fact the two endogamies, Cathar and local, overlapped and even more or less coincided. The Montaillou *connubium* had upper social limits. A noble lady like Béatrice de Planissoles might recruit one or two lovers among the villagers of Montaillou and elsewhere, and have friendly relations with the ordinary people. But when it came to marriage she chose noblemen, or at least a priest. We have also glimpsed other social and occupational barriers to marriage: Pierre Maury, a shepherd of Montaillou, had doubts about marrying Raymonde Piquier, daughter of a rich blacksmith's family in Ariège.

1 See the marriages between Bernard Belot and Guillemette Benet, Bernard Clergue and Guillemette Belot, Raymond Clergue and Esclarmonde Fort, Guillaume Marty and Raymonde Maury, Bernard Marty and Guillemette Maury, etc. (in the last case two brothers married two sisters). See i.370, 430, and above, Chapters II and III.

The smallness of the Montaillou *connubium* raised the problem of incest and intermarriage. Catharism, freely interpreted, incited some to go beyond the usual limits.[1] Bélibaste, who was no ascetic, deplored these practices. *Many believers*, he said (iii.241), *imagine that it is no shame to know carnally women to whom they are related or connected by marriage; when they do this they think they do no shame, because they think that at the end of their life they will be received by the goodmen and that thus their sins will be done away with and their salvation assured. I consider this kind of incest wicked and shameful.* Raymond de l'Aire, a peasant of Tignac who was both a materialist and an atheist, explained that the taboo on incest did not apply to second cousins (ii.30): *To sleep with one's mother, sister or first cousin is not a sin, but it is shameful. On the other hand, to sleep with second cousins and other women I do not consider a sin, nor a shameful act either; and I hold firmly to this view, because in Sabarthès there is a proverb which says, 'With a second cousin, give her the works'.* According to Pierre Maury, incest was prohibited between mother and son, brother and sister, and first cousins, all of whose bodies 'touched' naturally. The taboo did not apply to cousins who were the offspring of first cousins and those who were unrelated, all of whose bodies were permitted to 'touch' carnally (iii.149).

The ban on sleeping with a first cousin was sometimes broken, though the case was usually one of concubinage rather than marriage, and indirect rather than direct. Fabrisse Rives, the priest's first cousin, regretted that he knew her daughter Grazide carnally. She kept telling her, not always with much conviction (i.326), *'Do not commit sin with the rector, because you have a good husband and the rector is my own first cousin.'*

Yet the ban on sexual and marital relations between first cousins was so strong in Montaillou that an affair with the mistress of a first cousin was regarded as impure! As we have seen, Vuissane Testanière discouraged Arnaud Vital's attentions by saying (i.458), *'I am your first cousin's mistress.'* Similarly the gossips of Montaillou alleged that the priest Pierre Clergue *had committed incest* with Béatrice de Planissoles. This was an allusion to the fact that Béatrice had been the sweetheart of the bastard Pathau, the priest's first cousin (i.310, 238).

1 In general, the smallness of the villages in Ariège helps to explain why the prohibition of incest was scarcely applied except to first cousins (ii.130). There was not much choice.

For the ban on incest to work, a person had to know who his relations were.

'*Did you know*,' demanded Jacques Fournier of Grazide Lizier, rebuking her for having committed 'incest' with Pierre Clergue, '*did you know that the priest was first cousin – illegitimately it is true – of your mother, Fabrisse?*'

'*No, I did not know*,' answered Grazide, perhaps not altogether truthfully. '*If I had known I would have forbidden the priest to know me carnally.*'[1]

The refugees in Catalonia tended to be even more ignorant of their family tree. Some girls from Montaillou did not know who their cousins were. One day in San Mateo Pierre Maury asked his cousin Jeanne Befayt, daughter of his aunt Emersende Maury, to cook him some eggs. She replied, cantankerously (iii.173–4): '*I'd rather give you a gumboil!*'

'*Cousin*,' said Pierre Maury, '*don't be so bad-tempered!*'

'*What!*' cried Jeanne in amazement '*How are you my cousin?*'

'*I am the son of Raymond Maury of Montaillou.*'

'*Why didn't my silly old mother tell me that the last time you were here?*'

Jeanne melted and went and got Pierre some eggs and wine. In this case her initial ignorance led only to rudeness. In other circumstances it might have led to incest.

With all these prohibitions, was it possible to marry for love? The troubadour tradition has it that passion existed only outside marriage. But it would be wrong to take that literally. Pierre Bourdieu has studied, for the years 1900 to 1960, a village in Béarn where the choice of marriage partner was just as limited as among the people of Montaillou. He found that the impulse of the heart often coincided with other imperatives. He notes that in Lesquire, the village he studied, 'happy love, i.e. love which is socially approved and thus likely to succeed, is nothing but that kind of *amor fati*, that love of one's own social destiny, which, by the apparently hazardous and arbitrary paths of free choice, unites partners already socially predestined for each other.'[2] In Montaillou long ago, as in Lesquire now, it was possible to love passionately within apparently

1 i.302. Incidentally, Grazide, whose relation to the priest was first cousin's child and not first cousin, was in fact outside the prohibition as usually practised.
2 P. Bourdieu, *Annales*, July 1972, p. 1124.

rigid structures which predisposed towards and presided over the choice of a marriage partner.

True, it was more likely to happen outside the village – in Catalonia, where manners were freer and children more independent of their parents. Thus Jean Maury, son of Guillemette Maury of Montaillou who was a refugee in San Mateo, passionately loved (*adamat*, iii.189) a local girl there called Marie, though she was not a heretic. The marriage was a great success. *For our family*, said Guillemette (ii.188–9), *Marie is a daughter-in-law after our own heart. All that we want, Marie wants, and does it too.* But Guillemette still did not give up the old Montaillou principle by which the impulses of the heart had to be reconciled with the wishes of the families of the couple concerned. The same day as she testified to her daughter-in-law's goodness, she put a young visiting priest in his place on a similar subject (ii.188).

'*Why don't we give your son Arnaud a wife?*' asked the young man innocently.

'*No!*' said Guillemette. '*We will not give him a wife this year! Not until we find people or a woman whom we can trust. We don't know the people.*'

The marriage of another Jean Maury, Pierre Maury's brother, is another instance of love and fate being reconciled. Jean had been expelled from one place because he did not have the right to graze his sheep unless he married a local girl. He and his sheep therefore moved away, and he went to Albi near Tarragona to find a certain monk who was looking after some property for him. In Albi he was told that the monk was in Juncosa, not far off, and at Juncosa he found not only the monk but a girl (ii.487). He did not fall romantically in love with Mathena Cervel, but he was very fond of her; 'she pleased him'.

Through the good offices of a priest – priests often arranged marriages – Jean and Mathena became man and wife. Both were refugees in Catalonia, and both were from Foix, he from Montaillou and she from Tarascon. Both belonged to the Cathar tradition, though he had more or less rejected it.

Although in Montaillou itself to marry for love was more difficult, we have already seen how Bernard Clergue, the *bayle*, fell passionately in love with his future wife, Raymonde Belot. His brother Pierre, the priest, made fun of him for it. In 1321, Bernard Clergue related (i.273–4): *More than 12 years ago, during the summer, I was madly in love with Raymonde, who is now my wife : I wanted to go into the Belots' house*

*... but I noticed, under the gateway of my house, my brother, the priest
Pierre Clergue. At that, I did not like to go into the Belots' house, for my
brother the priest laughed at me because I was madly in love with Raymonde
'Belote'.*

The *bayle*'s passion for his intended overflowed on to the whole Belot
ostal, in particular his future mother-in-law, Guillemette, on whom he
lavished gifts of wine. When old Guillemette died, Guillemette Benet
said to Alazaïs Azéma (i.462), *'No need to weep for her. Guillemette
"Belote" had all she wanted. Her son-in-law did so much for her that she
never lacked for anything.'* Bernard was so fond of old Guillemette that
when she was near to death he urged her to practise the *endura*. In other
words, he encouraged or obliged his mother-in-law to die of hunger to
be sure of saving her soul.

As for Bernard's marriage, he was quite a young man, and because of
his wealth and his position as *bayle* he was one of the best matches in the
village. He could afford to marry for love and the best families in
Montaillou were ready to offer him their daughters. This multiplication
of possibilities increased the probability of actually falling in love. Such
cases were not rare among the rich farmers spoken of in the Fournier
Register. Raymond Pierre, a large-scale sheep-farmer in the village of
Arques, was very fond of (*diligit*) his wife Sybille, who returned his love
(ii.415). Their mutual regard was suspended when they quarrelled over
the question of hereticating their sick baby. Then, once doctrinal agreement was restored, Raymond began to love his wife again. Still, many
marriages were arranged by the family or friends of the people concerned without much attention being paid to their feelings. We have
seen how Pierre Maury was the object of two marriage projects, in
neither of which were his views much consulted.

In the upper classes too there were many arranged marriages: it is
likely that in Béatrice de Planissoles's first two marriages less attention
was paid to the heart of the lady than to the requirements of rank and
lineage. There were even planned marriages where the groom had never
even met the bride. Bertrand de Taix, knight, says: *I was very disappointed by my wife, for I thought I was marrying the daughter of Pons
Issaura of Larnat; but in fact she was the daughter of Maître Issaura of
Larcat.*[1] It was very annoying. The first Issaura, of Larcat, was a good
Catholic, while the second Issaura, of Larnat, was a Cathar sym-

1 iii.322. Larnat and Larcat are both in the present department of Ariège.

pathizer. So instead of being able to enjoy long heretical conversations with his wife, Bertrand de Taix was doomed to more than twenty years of conjugal silence. This kind of mistake could not happen in Montaillou itself, where all families were in direct contact with one another and everyone knew everyone else. But one married a *domus* rather than an individual marriage partner. A love match, though conceivable and not too rare, was far from being always possible.

The important thing was that marriage for love did sometimes happen – for men. But as to the feelings felt by women towards the person who aspired to their hand, the situation was less rosy. In very rare cases the record does speak of young women who married according to the dictates of their heart. The Register, however, speaks of quite a number of young men who did so. But in the institution of marriage as it then was, the woman was regarded as an object – an object loved or an object beaten, as the case might be. The historian finds himself faced with an area of cultural silence on this subject. It is probable, and sometimes proved, that the young men in love whom we find in the Register aroused similar feelings in the girls they married. But references are scarce. Rightly or wrongly, in upper Ariège the man was supposed to possess the initiative or even the monopoly in matters of love and affection, at least in the realm of courtship and marriage.

It was rare for the women of Montaillou to use the word love in a romantic sense (*adamare* or *diligere*) when speaking of their feelings towards a man. They never talked of love in that way in relation to marriage or an affair designed to end in marriage. Like the troubadours, they regarded real love as something outside legal marriage. As we have seen, both Béatrice de Planissoles and Alazaïs Guilhabert talk of passionate love only in connection with concubinage, not with reference to their husbands.

So when courtship aimed at marriage, the initiative in love, whether it was a question of passion or of inclination, belonged mostly to the man. Everyone looked upon this as quite normal. When Béatrice de Planissoles collected her daughter Philippa's first menstrual blood as a talisman, it was to ensure that the girl's future husband would be so madly in love with her that he would never think again of any other woman (i.248). As for Philippa's feelings for the man, Béatrice says nothing about that. Nor did she go into her own feelings towards her own two husbands.

In fact, the idea of a loving pre-marital courtship had no great meaning, at least for the girls, in a village where many women were married very young. The important thing was, as Bernard Clergue realized, to woo the mother-in-law. Guillemette Maury of Montaillou, Pierre Maury's younger sister, was married off by her father to the carpenter Bertrand Piquier of Laroque d'Olmes when she was well below the age of eighteen. She was a Cathar sympathizer and he a strict Catholic, and the marriage turned out badly. Guillemette ran away twice, once briefly to her father's house in Montaillou, and once for good. Grazide Lizier was married at fifteen or sixteen. One little girl was promised in marriage to Pierre Maury when she was only six. There were serious thoughts of marrying Philippa, Béatrice de Planissoles's daughter, as soon as she began to menstruate; an obscure passage (i.248) speaks of a betrothal and even a husband, though the marriage was never celebrated or consummated. Béatrice herself was married young, probably in her twentieth year or earlier. Raymonde Maury, another of Pierre Maury's sisters, was married at eighteen at the latest to Guillaume Marty, who also came from Montaillou. Esclarmonde Clergue, née Fort, was perhaps married at the age of fourteen. Pre-nuptial and conjugal manners were summary or even rough. Sexual permissiveness was relative and reserved chiefly for widows or poor girls and maidservants, for whom a career as a concubine was available until they managed to find a husband.[1]

On the other hand, the men do not seem to have married young in Montaillou. The boys mentioned in the Fournier Register as being between fifteen and twenty are still bachelors. For men, marriage seems to have been a serious matter, not be taken on before the age of about twenty-five, when one had some position in life. Bernard Clergue was *bayle* of the village and father of a bastard daughter when he was struck by his grand passion for Raymonde Belot. Bernard Belot already had a number of illegitimate children when he married a girl who was not their mother. The marriages planned for Pierre Maury could not have taken place until after he was thirty. Arnaud Vital the shoemaker sowed plenty of wild oats before he married Raymonde Guilhou. Raymond Roussel did not marry the sister of Pierre Clergue (the priest's namesake) until long after he had enjoyed himself as steward of the château of Montaillou and Béatrice's Platonic lover (i.338). Arnaud Belot was well

1 As well as cases previously referred to, see that of Rousse Gonaud (iii.278).

over thirty when he married Raymonde d'Argelliers (iii.63). Jean Maury did not marry Mathena Cervel until he had spent years as a migrant shepherd, both adolescent and adult, on both sides of the Pyrenees; he must then have been at least twenty-five (ii.469–70).

In short, husbands in Montaillou were generally fully adult and they often married young innocents. The girls were beginners; the men were settling down. This difference in age in a world where people died young soon produced a crop of young widows. With one husband in the grave, women prepared to go through one or even two more marriages.

CHAPTER XII Marriage and the condition of women

The position of a young bride in Montaillou and the other villages of the region was not a particularly attractive one. Every married woman could expect a fair amount of beating some time or other. An ambiguous proverb was popular in Occitania in the 1320s (iii.243):

> Qui bat sa femme avec un coussin
> Croit lui faire mal et ne lui fait rien.[1]

Other more explicit texts show that while the man in Montaillou possessed the initiative in courtship he later on claimed the right to violence. We may disregard the somewhat special case of the woodcutter Bernard Befayt, who gallantly beat up his own wife in order to protect his mother-in-law (iii.178). The reaction to Guillemette Clergue's black eye is indicative of the sort of behaviour expected from husbands. Through some accident or infection, Guillemette had a bad eye and set off to find some quack to cure it. On the way she met Prades Tavernier, the weaver and *parfait* of Prades d'Aillon. Tavernier asked (i.337): '*Hey, Guillemette, what happened? Did your husband beat you?*'

'*No,*' she answered, '*there's just something wrong with my eye.*'

But Guillemette Clergue was certainly afraid of her husband. One day she was reaping corn with her mother, Alazaïs, in a field which belonged to Bernard Rives, Guillemette's father and Alazaïs's husband. The two women began to talk about the goodmen.[2]

'*They save souls, they do not eat meat, they do not touch women,*' said Alazaïs.

'*Never tell my husband we have been talking about that,*' Guillemette said, '*for if he found out he would kill me. He hates the heretics.*'

Guillemette told Jacques Fournier himself how frightened she was of her husband (i.341).

---

1 The man who beats his wife with a cushion thinks he is hurting her but isn't doing anything.

2 i.334–5. The field in question is in a place called *alacot* or '*à la coste*', meaning 'on the hill', which is below the old village and where the present village stands. Topographically, the present village is on the same spot as the outlying parts (*barris*) of the old village, which were built after the time of Fournier's Register and before the nineteenth century.

'*Did you tell your husband you had ever seen the heretic Pradès Tavernier?*' asked the Bishop.

'*No*', she answered. '*I was too afraid he would ill-use me if I told him.*'

We have already seen how Pierre Maury's sister Guillemette was treated by her husband.

From this point of view, women of the nobility or the bourgeoisie were no better off than their country sisters. However urban or aristocratic their husbands, they also were heavy-handed. Béatrice de Planissoles was afraid her first husband would kill her if she committed adultery with the steward. (She was also afraid of her brothers, who illtreated her during her affair with Barthélemy Amilhac.) As for the bourgeoisie, one example concerns the daughter and son-in-law of the great Pierre Authié himself.

'*Arnaud*,' said Authié to his son-in-law Arnaud Teisseire as they walked together in the square at Ax-les-Thermes, '*you don't get on well with your wife, my daughter Guillemette; you are harsh and cruel to her; and in that you are acting against Scripture, which bids man to be peaceful, gentle, and tender.*'

'*It's your daughter's fault*,' answered Arnaud, who did in fact beat his wife.[1] '*She is bad-tempered and a gossip. And take care yourself not to be caught by the jaw, because of your heretic's long tongue.*'

Guillaume Ascou, a good Catholic of the village of Ascou, called his wife Florence a 'sow'. He suspected her of having contacts with the Cathars (ii.365). '*Sow! . . . You and your accomplice Rixende, that leper and heretic, the wife of Pierre Amiel of Ascou, they ought to burn both of you.*'

Raymond Sicre, the witness of this scene, went on: *And Guillaume d'Ascou, furious, went to bed and covered his head, uttering threats against his wife. Hearing these, the said spouse left the house by a bedroom door and went away.*

Certain enlightened Cathars who knew their Bible, like Pierre Authié, advocated more humane treatment of women (ii.213). But as far as the institution of marriage was concerned, the peasant civilization of upper

---

1 ii.213, 197. The Register records more cases of wives than of children being beaten. The relationship between parents and children, which belongs to the order of nature, seems to have been better and more cordial in upper Ariège than the relations between husband and wife, which derived, at least initially, from a social choice.

Ariège at that time was very misogynous. Pierre Authié himself, despite his affection for his daughter, generally considered women as something base (ii.409). Bélibaste, who married and unmarried his mistress to Pierre Maury within the space of a few days, never made any mystery of his male chauvinism and masculine imperialism. According to him, the soul of a woman could not be allowed into Paradise after her death; she had to be reincarnated as a man, however briefly, before that could happen.[1] One day Bélibaste said to Pierre Maury and Raymonde (iii.191), '*A man is worth nothing if he is not his wife's master.*' Pierre Maury, a faithful interpreter of Montaillou philosophy, was not behind-hand when it came to speaking ill of the ladies: '*Women are devils,*' he said to his employer, Sybille Pierre (ii.415), who had dared to nurse her heretic baby. '*The soul of a woman and the soul of a sow are one and the same thing – in other words, not much,*' said Arnaud Laufre of Tignac (ii.131), insulting a local woman. In more concrete terms, when the men gathered round to have a drink before a meal, women were excluded from the group (iii.155).

Women might be beaten, or they might be subjected to an oppressive silence. The silence could be reciprocal. See the cases of Guillemette Clergue, Raymonde Marty, Béatrice de Planissoles and Raymonde Guilhou. This taciturnity was not due to ideological differences alone. The women did talk among themselves, but out of earshot of their husbands. They feared them even when they loved them.[2]

But the women of Montaillou were clever tacticians and had occasional successes. One way of getting their own back was through 'matriarchy'. A matriarchal situation arose when it was a woman who succeeded, even temporarily, as head of a family, when the male master of the household died or withdrew. The absence or unsuitability of a male successor might give rise to such a situation, when normally a son-in-law would marry a daughter who would continue the family line. He might be adopted by his father-in-law. He would thus become an integral part of

---

1 ii.441–2. The Waldensians of Pamiers, who were more worldly, were less anti-feminist on this point than the Cathars of upper Ariège, more rustic and doctrinally more eccentric. Raymond de la Côte, a Waldensian of Pamiers, did not think that women would be born again as men; *Everyone*, he said (i.88), *will be born again in his or her own sex.*

2 *I fear and love my husband very much* (Sybille Pierre: ii.424).

the new *domus* to which he was admitted. But his position would be delicate vis-à-vis the name and person of his wife. The tribulations of Guillaume de l'Aire of Tignac are relevant here (ii.129). *He took a wife at Lordat, and because of his wife's family, into whose house he entered, he was afterwards called Guillaume de Corneillan; this Guillaume is believed to be still alive, and still living in Lordat.* Another case was that of Sybille Baille, of Ax-les-Thermes. By inheritance, Sybille was owner of a house in Ax, and her children referred to it (ii.21) as the '*maternal* ostal'. Sybille was married to a notary in Tarascon, Arnaud Sicre, but being the owner of a *domus* she was not as humble and submissive as most wives in the Comté de Foix. Arnaud, a determined anti-Cathar, was unfortunate enough to displease the strong-minded Sybille, who was still young and who drove him without ceremony out of the house in Ax, where he had come to live with her as her husband.[1] Arnaud was reduced to working as a notary in Tarascon, and his wife, after having expelled him in such a cavalier fashion, did not scruple to send him their son, also called Arnaud and now aged seven, to be educated. Sybille was an active Cathar. Her sons sometimes used their father's name, Sicre, and sometimes their mother's name, Baille, and Arnaud Baille-Sicre was to demonstrate, in his career as a spy, entirely devoted to getting back the maternal *domus*, how seriously he regarded himself as belonging first and foremost to the *ostal* of his mother.

Another example is that of Guillemette Maury. She was a near relation of Pierre Maury (though not to be confused with the Guillemette Maury, wife of Bertrand Piquier, who was Pierre's sister). She married Bernard Marty of Montaillou, who had a *domus* there. With the persecution of 1308 and the exodus, the Martys fled from Montaillou and wandered from town to town in Catalonia, from one temporary dwelling to another. Meanwhile Bernard Marty died. The Marty's two sons were now almost grown up and in the prime of youth. So mother and sons went and settled in San Mateo, a more 'lucrative' town (iii.169). They earned a comfortable living there and were able to buy an *ostal*: around the house, which had several bedrooms, there grew up a farm, with a courtyard, a garden, a cornfield, vineyards, pastures, an ass, a mule and sheep. Guillemette used to entertain twelve or fifteen guests at a time. The family earned extra money by working the wool from their sheep

1 ii.28. See also the case of Cicarde, another strong-minded woman, also from the group of leading citizens in Ax-les-Thermes (i.290).

and hiring themselves out to other farmers at harvest time. Occasionally they even had employees of their own. The new *ostal* had nothing to do with the late Bernard Marty, who was quite forgotten. Guillemette became 'Her Grace, Madame Guillemette' (ii.28). She reverted to the name of Maury, her married name lapsing into disuse. Her two sons were known as Jean and Arnaud Maury, not Marty. As in every matriarchal system, the mother's brother, Pierre Maury (uncle and namesake of our shepherd), played an essential role in the household. But Guillemette remained its head. She accepted or refused proposed marriages for each of her grown-up sons. She reigned over the one reception room which served as drawing-room, dining-room and kitchen combined.[1]

Montaillou, Prades d'Aillon, Mérens, Belcaire, all mountain villages in Foix or the Pays de Sault, offer other examples of widows or dominant women who inherited a house from their own family, or created one for themselves, or simply ran it after the death of their husbands. These matriarchs are recognizable by the fact that their names, given a feminine ending of -a, are preceded by the particle Na (i.e. *domina* – madame or mistress). In Montaillou, old Na Roqua was one of the mothers of the Cathar Church and adviser to the heads of families (i.458). Na Carminagua was also the head of a house in Montaillou (iii.75). In Mérens, Na Ferriola owned a house and a flock of goats; she was a heretic and employed shepherds (ii.461, 477; iii.163). In Prades d'Aillon, Na Ferreria was a healer of eye diseases (i.337). In Belcaire, the blacksmith Bernard den Alazaïs (i.e. de Na Alazaïs) was probably descended from a matriarch of this type, either his mother or an earlier forebear. Like Na Ferreria, he possessed interesting traditional secrets, in his case concerning the fate of souls after death. Were these secrets inherited? Has matriarchy, in western society, been the best preserver of traditional thought? Whatever the case, a woman acquired consideration and respectability when, with the coming of age, she gradually ceased to be regarded as a sexual object. The change of life brought power.

Another possibility, limited but real, of comparative emancipation was provided by certain occupations which were accessible to women,

---

1 See also the case of the nobleman Bertrand de Taix and his mother: she was the owner of the family manor (*terre*) while her son was merely its master in reserve until she died (ii.312–13).

though they did not necessarily have the monopoly of them. We have already seen Fabrisse Rives making a living as a wine-seller in Montaillou (i.325-6). Not much of a living, because there were so few people in the village. Alazaïs Azéma sold cheese. At Laroque d'Olmes, and beyond the Pyrenees, the inns along the roads and at the fairs frequented by the people of Montaillou were run by hostesses.

For the most part the weaker sex really was weak, confronted with the powers arrogated to themselves by men. But they were not completely defenceless.

In her own house a woman certainly worked hard. But her duties themselves gave her some power. And when she grew older there were compensations to be looked for from other members of the family, apart from her husband. Husbands, their desire now weaker, did not hesitate to call their wives old women, old heretics or old sows.[1] But vis-à-vis her children, nieces and nephews an elderly woman was in an exalted position. Oppressed as a wife, she was revered as a mother. No Protestantism would ever wipe out the cult of the Virgin.

Although the Cathar peasants might refer to Mary as a tun of flesh in which Christ was shadowed forth, they were, inside their own families, respectful and affectionate sons. Pierre Clergue, who respected nothing else, loved and revered the memory of his mother. Guillaume Austatz, farmer and *bayle* of Ornolac, respected his mother and addressed her as 'vous'. It was from her that he got his half-heretical, half-materialist views.

There were bad sons too, in upper Ariège. The son of Stéphanie de Chateauverdun tyrannized over his old mother. But many passages show that between 1300 and 1320 Montaillou demonstrated the typical Mediterranean pattern of a young wife oppressed by an older husband eventually becoming an elderly mother venerated and respected by her male children. The daughters also surrounded their mother with filial love. Ava, Philippa, Esclarmonde and Condors, Béatrice de Planissoles's daughters, wept when they thought of the danger of her being arrested (i.257), thus rewarding her for the affection she had always manifested towards them (i.246).

1 Old noblemen were just as badly behaved in this matter as old peasants (iii.328). But when an elderly noblewoman was called an old woman by her husband she did not hesitate to answer him back.

Among the peasants, daughters showed deference to their mothers, who continued to render them material services even after they were grown-up and married. *One day*, says Guillemette Clergue (i.337), who was in the power of a violent husband, *I needed to borrow some combs to hackle the hemp, so I went to my father's house. And when I got to the door of the house I met my brother bringing out the dung. So I asked my brother: 'Where is madame my mother?'*

'What do you want with her?'

'I want some combs,' I said.

'Mother is not here,' said my brother. 'She won't be back for a long time.'
I would not believe my brother and tried to enter the house. Then he put his arm across the door and prevented me from going in.

This remarkable passage shows Alazaïs Rives, the mother, fetching and carrying water for her husband's *domus*, yet being addressed as 'Madame' by her grown-up daughter. Although this family was a nest of scorpions, the links between its members were thus ritualized. The brother addresses his sister as 'vous', though this does not stop him from treating her roughly. As for the maternal uncle, Prades Tavernier, he demanded greater respect from his illegitimate daughter, Brune Pourcel, even than that which Guillemette gave to Alazaïs. As we have seen, he made Brune worship him on her knees.

Another honoured mother was the mother of Vuissane Testanière. Vuissane, Bernard Belot's young mistress, renounced her Cathar beliefs after the shock of Arnaud Vital's attempted rape, but hastened to add that her re-conversion to strict Catholicism was also due to her mother's influence. Jean Pellissier adopted Cathar ideas because of his aunt Maura's influence (iii.79). She had regaled her young nephew with heretical talk one day when she found herself alone with him in a hut full of oats.

True, there were some old or mature women who were strongly challenged by younger ones, including their own daughters. There were Homeric battles, sometimes descending to blows and the use of weapons, between Jeanne Befayt and her mother, Emersende Marty. But these quarrels were an example of the cultural distintegration that arose from emigration to Catalonia, where the Roman faith prevailed. In Montaillou, before the exodus, Emersende was respected by her daughter. Bélibaste himself held her in high esteem. *She has seen more than twenty heretics*, he said (ii.64, 75). *She knows and sees the good better than we do.*

And in Montaillou itself an old woman like Guillemette 'Belote', who had grown old in the heretic tradition, was highly regarded among her co-religionists, their sympathizers and the villagers as a whole.

The young peasant women as well as the old had some defences against their husbands' real or possible violence. Some of them were very quarrelsome themselves. Pierre Maury's sister, who ran away from her husband twice, the second time for good, was regarded by the heretics she afterwards mixed with as caustic, sharp-tongued and always ready for a row (iii.155). In the village of Bouan (present-day Ariège), Maître Salacrou might shout and bawl whenever there were heretics in his house (ii.425) but he made absolutely no impression on his wife or his daughter Blanche. They were both good Cathars and continued to entertain the *parfaits*. Women were generally regarded as quarrelsome, both against men and among themselves. Fabrisse Rives (i.325): *With Alazaïs Rives we used to quarrel often. We only stopped quarrelling the day when each of us found out the little heretical secrets of the other, which put us in a position to betray one another before the Inquisitor. So then we stopped quarrelling.*

Coercion on the part of husbands was not the only explanation of the comparatively smooth running of Montaillou society. Sociologists have underlined the importance of the code of honour as a regulator of human groups. With reference to Andalusia, Pitt-Rivers has pointed out the fundamental role of *vergüenza*, which combines shame, modesty, care for one's reputation and feminine honour. This group of sentiments protects women's virtue, held so precious by their husbands. Woman possesses, according to Pitt-Rivers,[1] a limited quantity of *vergüenza*, and once it is lost it cannot be found again. The quantity of *vergüenza* possessed by a woman can only diminish, never increase. It is an externalized, not an internalized value, inherited and passed on from one generation to another. A sense of *vergüenza* is well developed among the women of the lesser nobility whom we encounter in Montaillou, and contributes as much towards the preservation of marital fidelity as fear of husbands or of the rod. For example, Béatrice de Planissoles tries to avoid even the suspicion that she might be having an adventure with her steward (i.222), for fear that her husband should think that she has done something dishonourable (*inhoneste*). This is clearly an 'externalized'

1 Pitt-Rivers (1961).

point of honour, seen in terms of other people's judgment rather than the verdict of one's own conscience. '*If I go with you to Lombardy,*' Béatrice says to the steward, '*people will say we have left the country to satisfy our lust.*' Elsewhere she says she is afraid of being disparaged by her two lovers if, as a widow, she gives her favours to more than one man at a time. While still a widow she talks of the shame which would be brought on her lineage, particularly her father, Philippe de Planissoles, if she became pregnant outside wedlock. The whole family was affected by the misbehaviour of one of its women. Thus Béatrice's brothers recalled her so severely to her duty when she was with Barthélemy Amilhac that she had to leave their village, where she had been temporarily living. The same thing was found among the lower classes in Montaillou. Pierre Maury entrusted his sister Guillemette's honour to Guillaume and Bernard Bélibaste (iii.155). *After dinner, Bernard and Guillaume said to Pierre: 'We will take as good care of your sister as of ourselves: she herself will behave so that we surround her with affection and honour.'*

And the sister promised in her turn: 'All I have to do I shall do well.'

The amount of feminine reputation available to be lost was quantitatively less among mere peasants than among the nobility. But the notions of dishonour, and above all shame, were at the centre of rural morals in upper Ariège.

Marriages generally came to an end through the death of one of the partners, usually the man. In all traditional societies, widows are almost always more numerous than widowers. This was particularly marked in the Pays d'Aillon, whether in Prades or Montaillou. One reason for this was the customary disproportion of age between husband and wife. Among the nineteen females from Prades and Montaillou questioned by Jacques Fournier, seven were married women with husbands still alive and twelve were widows. The latter were not necessarily poor, for several of them lived with their grown-up unmarried sons, or with a married couple which included one of their sons. Some widows exercised real spiritual and family authority among the group of rural Cathar sympathizers, both male and female. This was true of the three Fates of Montaillou, all great friends, Na Roqua, Guillemette Clergue and Guillemette 'Belote'. They often acted as directors of conscience to the villagers, and their coterie was an essential element in the feminine society of the place. In Catalonia, Emersende Marty and Guillemette Maury were also widows who exercised ideological influence. Sometimes widows married again. Béatrice de Planissoles, a good match among the nobility, and Raymonde Lizier, whose first husband was murdered, did so quite quickly, one with a squire and the other with a poor farmer. In other cases it was more difficult, and sometimes concubinage was a temporary though unsatisfactory and 'dishonourable' solution. Lovers were not all that easy to come by.

In many ancient societies the remarriage of widows involved the reversal of a taboo. When a widow remarried she was taking a man away from the group of husbands available for the girls. There was often a charivari, a deliberate hullabaloo, which acted as a ritual for reproving and then forgiving the widow's action. In Montaillou we find no trace of charivari, but widows were the object of a kind of sexual taboo, though this was easily got round by the bolder spirits. When Pierre Clergue made dishonourable propositions to Mengarde Buscailh of Prades, she replied indignantly (i.491), 'No, I will not. It would be a great sin. Don't forget I am a widow!'

Divorce, or at least separation, was in theory another way in which marriages could end. In Montaillou itself the women were too timid and well kept under by the rigid *domus* system to turn out their lords and masters. But some men did not hesitate to threaten their wives with expulsion, or even to carry out the threat. Fabrisse Rives was one of those who were turned out. To begin with, she lived with her husband, Pons Rives the farmer, and, interestingly, also with his father and mother, Bernard and Alazaïs Rives (i.339–40). Bernard Rives was a quiet character under the thumb of his son Pons, who was virtually the head of the *domus*. The operative people in the household were Pons Rives and his mother, the overbearing and shrewd Alazaïs. They were both Cathars. Fabrisse's arrival caused trouble, for she was not a heretic. She even told the priest, who could not have cared less, that there were goodmen in the village (i.324). The husband and mother-in-law soon saw that the young wife was going to interfere with their Catharism. '*It was the Devil who brought you into our house,*' said Pons to Fabrisse.

So he drove her out of the *ostal*. She simply carried on as an independent woman, the wine-seller of the village. She brought up her daughter Grazide as best she could, but both women were soon drawn into the orbit of the Clergue *domus*, Fabrisse as a dependant of the *ostal* of

Bernard Clergue, who did her various services, and Grazide as the priest's mistress.

Fabrisse Rives was driven out of her husband's house because she was not a heretic. A similar but converse misadventure almost befell her sister-in-law. Guillemette Rives was the daughter of Bernard Rives, and Pons Rives's sister. She married Pierre Clergue, namesake and relative of the priest. Guillemette was a friend of the heretics, her husband their enemy. She therefore avoided talking about her Cathar acquaintances, and one day, she relates (i.346), *My husband threatened me : 'If you go to the houses of those who welcome the goodmen, I will kill you or drive you out!'*

In all, the Register provides only two cases, or one and a half, of separation. The break-up of a couple was very rare in Montaillou, because of the strength of family structures; only ideological differences were enough to lead to such an extremity. One case of separation and one threat of separation out of some fifty couples young and old in one parish is not much. To these should be added the rather special case of Raymonde Clément, wife of Pierre Fauré, who left her husband's *domus* and went back to her own people because he was impotent.

Expulsion or the threat of expulsion always came from the husband, not the wife. But outside Montaillou, in the small towns of Ariège where there were the beginnings of urban or artisanal liberty, and beyond the Pyrenees in Catalonia, we do find women from Ariège who took the initiative in separating themselves from their husbands. Here, too, the causes of the rupture were ideological and religious, but they took effect in a more modern way. As we have seen, in Ax-les-Thermes Sybille Baille the Cathar drove out her husband, Arnaud Sicre the elder, a Catholic notary. In Laroque d'Olmes, a small town with fairs and markets, Guillemette Maury, the shepherd's sister, twice took the initiative of running away from her husband's home. Raymonde Marty of Junac, a blacksmith's daughter, realized that the circumstances of the exodus had finally separated her fate from that of her husband, Arnaud Piquier, trout-fisher in Tarascon. So she decided to join up with the *parfait* Bélibaste.

Whatever happened, even in the boldest cases, the *domus* never quite lost its power. Even if the husband was impotent it was the wife who left the common *ostal*. Sybille Baille would never have been able to drive out her husband if she had not possessed her own matriarchal *domus*. In

Montaillou itself, Pons Rives could permit himself to drive away his wife, Fabrisse, because he was backed up by the presence of his parents. In upper Ariège itself the rare separation of a couple (never actual divorce in due form) was not a sign of individualism but a demonstration of the insurmountable predominance of the *ostal*.

CHAPTER XIII

Childhood and other ages in life

As was normal under the *ancien régime*, the peasant family in Montaillou was a large one. Mengarde and Pons Clergue had four sons and at least two daughters known to us. Guillemette Belot had four sons and two daughters. Guillaume and Guillemette Benet had at least two sons and three daughters. Raymond Baille had four sons, but no daughter is mentioned. Pierre and Mengarde Maurs had four sons and one daughter. There were four Marty brothers. Alazaïs and Raymond Maury had six sons and at least two daughters.

There were smaller families. Bernard and Gauzia Clergue had only two known children, a son and a daughter. Two couples, Guillemette and Raymond Maurs and Bernard and Guillemette Maurs, had two sons each, as well, probably, as daughters unknown to us in name or number. From the information available, eighteen couples emerge who were in the process of completing, or had completed, their family in the demographic period 1280–1324, the time roughly covered by the Fournier Register. These eighteen families, complete and incomplete, gave birth to a minimum of forty-two boys and twenty girls. The number of girls is clearly under-estimated or under-recorded. The figure for boys certainly does not take into account losses from infant mortality, the deaths which occurred between birth and the end of the first year of life. It also leaves out an indeterminable fraction of juvenile mortality, especially between one and five years of age. Even so, this gives us a mean of 2.3 boys per couple. So, taking into account various imponderables, it is reasonable to assume 4.5 legitimate births, including boys and girls, per family, complete or incomplete,[1] a fertility rate equal

---

1 The couples in question here are: Pons Clergue and Mengarde (four boys, two girls: Guillaume, Bernard, Pierre, Raymond, Esclarmonde, Guillemette); a couple whose head, unreferred to elsewhere, was called Bar (three sons and two daughters: Pierre, Raymond, Guillaume, Mengarde, Guillemette; see i.418); Bernard Rives and Alazaïs (one son, two daughters: Pons, Raymonde and Guillemette, who married one of the Clergues); Pons Azéma and Alazaïs (one son: Raymond); Pierre Azéma and Guillemette (one son: Raymond); Bernard Clergue (the *bayle*'s namesake) and Gauzia (one boy, one girl: Raymond, Esclarmonde); Bernard Clergue, *bayle* of Montaillou, and Raymonde (no children); Belot senior (Christian name unknown) and Guillemette (four sons, two daughters: Raymond, Guillaume, Bernard, Arnaud, Raymonde and, according to i.371, Alazaïs); Guillaume Benet and Guillemette (two

to that of the prolific inhabitants of Beauvaisis in modern times. The illegitimacy rate in Montaillou was higher.

One explanation of the size of Montaillou families is the early age at which girls married. Moreover our figures are chiefly concerned with the Cathar and endogamous group of big farming families, allied among themselves, which dominated Montaillou around 1300. For reasons which are perhaps fortuitous, the few Catholic families in the village, for example the Azémas, recorded fewer children and fewer marriages than the heretics.

There were limits to this fecundity. The richest family, the Clergues, in Pierre and Bernard's generation, seem to have practised certain kinds of birth control (magical herbs, or perhaps *coitus interruptus*). Pons Clergue's many sons left several bastards but no legitimate child, though there were other Clergues in the village to carry on the name. As for the lower ranks, the shepherds tended not to get married. More generally, the last generation with which we are concerned, that which married between the round-up of 1308 and the interrogations of 1320–25, was greatly disturbed. Many people were put in prison and the circumstances may have led some couples to practise abstinence or contraception. At all events, during the decade beginning in 1310, which

---

sons, four daughters: Raymond, Bernard, Alazaïs, Montagne; and, according to i.400, Gaillarde and Esclarmonde); Raymond Baille and X (four sons; Pierre, Jacques, Raymond, Arnaud); Vital Baille and Esclarmonde (one son: Jacques); Pierre Maurs and Mengarde (four sons and one daughter: Arnaud, Guillaume, Raymond, Pierre, Guillemette); Raymond Maurs and Guillemette (two sons: Pierre and Bernard); Bernard Maurs and Guillemette (two sons: Raymond and Pierre); the four Marty brothers, the names of whose mother and father are unknown: Guillaume, Arnaud, Bernard and Jean; X Testanière and Alazaïs (one son and one daughter: Prades and Vuissane); Raymond Maury and Alazaïs (six sons and two daughters: Guillaume, Pierre, Jean, Arnaud, Raymond, Bernard, Guillemette and Raymonde); Jean Guilhabert and Allemande (one son and three daughters: Guillaume, Alazaïs, Sybille and Guillemette, according to i.403, ii.256 and ii.482 and 484). I have left out the very old groups, like those of Pons and Guillaume Clergue, which were already decimated by death, not only among infants and children but also among adults and elderly people. I have also left out very young couples only a small part of whose procreative life fell within the last years of the Fournier Register; moreover, these were greatly disturbed by the Inquisition. Finally, I have left out the wives who were widowed early and took refuge in Catalonia. It goes without saying that the records we are dealing with have only a very indirect and unintended demographic value.

was also economically unpropitious, fertility in Montaillou seems to have declined.

Between 1280 and 1305, however, there was in Montaillou, as elsewhere, a baby boom. Large groups of two brothers or even four all living together were very common (i.193, 203). A high birth rate was taken for granted. If you lost one child and were not too old, it was very likely that you would have more and these, according to a far-fetched Cathar interpretation of metempsychosis, might be the means of restoring to a mother the souls of her previously lost children (i.203).

My fellow-sponsor, Alazaïs Munier, says Guillaume Austatz, *bayle of Ornolac, was sad; in a short time she had lost all her four sons. Seeing her desolate, I asked her the cause.*

'*How could I be other than unhappy,*' *she asked,* '*after having lost four fine children in so short a time?*'

'*Don't be upset,*' *I said to her,* '*you will get them back again.*'

'*Yes, in Paradise!*'

'*No, you will get them back again in this world. For you are still young. You will be pregnant again. The soul of one of your dead children will enter into the new foetus. And so on!*'

We see that Guillaume Austatz did not think it strange that a woman should have eight pregnancies in all.

The countrymen of this period were well aware of the population pressure of the 1300s, resulting from, among other things, the high fertility rates discussed above. *Where,* it was asked (i.191), *would there be room to put all the souls of all the men who are dead and of all those who are still alive? At that rate the world would be full of souls! The entire space between the city of Toulouse and the Mérens Pass would not be enough to hold them all!* Fortunately, explained Guillaume Austatz, God had found a simple remedy. Every soul was used several times. *It emerged from a human body which had just died, and entered almost immediately into another. And so on.*

In theory the Cathar dogma professed by many of the people of Montaillou, though little known to them in detail, was hostile to marriage and procreation. The most sophisticated Cathar peasants, and *parfaits* or pseudo-*parfaits* like Bélibaste, were acquainted with this point. Bélibaste himself (ii.48), who wanted *through virginity to transport the seed of this world into the next,* would not have *any man join himself carnally to a woman; nor would I have sons or daughters born of them. For if people would hold to barrenness, all God's creatures would soon be gathered together* [in heaven]. *That is what I should like.* Similarly, we have seen Pierre Clergue of Montaillou making use of contraception, perhaps magical. But how many people in the village of the yellow cross were capable of such refinements? In any case, the duty of barrenness was incumbent only on the goodmen, not on mere 'believers'. So the peasants of Montaillou, even when they were sympathetic to heresy, continued to produce numerous children. There was enough land, especially pasture, to provide them with employment when they grew up. Moreover, Catalonia, which as Bélibaste said (ii.42) *lacked neither pastures nor mountains for the sheep*, welcomed surplus youth from Montaillou with open arms. They easily found jobs there as shepherds and muleteers. In these circumstances, why worry? A *domus* rich in children was a *domus* rich in manpower; in other words, rich, pure and simple. This explains the large number of sons produced by the big farming families of Montaillou – the Belots, the Maurys, the Martys and so on. Only the last generation of Clergues, wealthy enough not to have to descend to manual labour, were not interested in producing a large number of workers. So, both in theory and in practice, they could afford views favourable to contraception and hostile to marriage.

The large number of children produced by most Montaillou families were not immediately profitable. First they had to be brought up, fed and, to begin with, suckled.[1] In rural circles it was rare to put a child out to nurse. Wet-nurses were employed only by the well-off nobility: one of the ladies of Chateauverdun, who joined the heretics, entrusted her child to a wet-nurse. At one stage of her career a peasant girl might quite naturally become a wet-nurse to noble infants: Rousse Gonaud, a girl from the mountains, was first servant maid to a nobleman, then wet-nurse to the wife of another nobleman. Betweenwhiles she must have been made pregnant. Subsequently she became the mistress of a village *bayle*, with whom she lived. She ended up as the lawful wife of a farmer.[2]

In Montaillou itself, as far as we know, wet-nurses were only resorted

1 There is virtually no information on natal and pre-natal practices in Montaillou. Recovery from childbed seems to have been accompanied by a ceremony in the local shrine to Mary (i.223). Noble families had long been using cradles (i.221).
2 iii.278. All Rousse Gonaud's career was set in pro-heretical circles.

to by poor girls forced to get rid of their babies in order to work as servants. As we have seen, Raymonde Arsen transferred her baby from one country wet-nurse to another before going to take up employment at the Belots'. There she from time to time looked after a child of one of the Belot daughters.[1] Anyhow the commercial demand for milk was not very great in Montaillou, and might sometimes be exceeded by supply. One day in about the year 1302, around Easter, Alazaïs Rives went to see Brune Pourcel, a poor, rather stupid bastard girl already referred to (i.382): *Alazaïs told me to take my son Raymond to her house. I was nursing him at that time, and he was about half a year old.*

'*In my* ostal,' said Alazaïs, '*there is a woman from Razès who has too much milk . . .*'

'*Never,*' I answered. '*Her milk would be bad for my son.*'

Finally, giving way to my neighbour's insistence, I took my son to her house and there, indeed, I found a woman from Razès: she was sitting warming herself by the fire.

But apart from such special cases, it was usual for mothers to nurse their own babies in Montaillou, as in similar villages. This was true even among the richest farming families. The nursing period might be quite long. Perhaps children were not weaned until after they were two years old as with some peasant children in modern times. Sybille Pierre was the wife of a rich arable and sheep-farmer, and her son was still being fed at the breast at the age of *one or two years* (ii.17). Breast-feeding produced temporary barrenness, and thus caused longer intervals between births, but whether this was due to physiological processes or merely to sexual taboos during lactation we do not know.

After marriage, pregnancy was accepted as normal, natural and a thing to be desired. Outside marriage, feelings towards a prospective bastard were ambiguous but not necessarily devoid of affection. Pierre Clergue's first impulse was to say, '*I am a priest and I do not want a child.*' Béatrice's answer: '*What should I do if I become pregnant? I should be dishonoured.*' And then gradually their feelings change: the priest ends up by saying to his mistress, '*After your father's death, we'll have a child*'.[2]

1 i.370. See also Agnes Francou, nurse to the Waldensian Raymond de la Coste. She suckled him after his mother's death, and then spent the rest of her life with him (i.125).
2 i.225, 243, 244, 245.

In many Montaillou families, a child started its life as a Cathar foetus. It soon became possessed of a soul, and thus took on considerable value, including emotional significance. For, as the Albigensian Vulgate known among the peasants of the Pays d'Aillon said, 'The world is full of old souls running madly about'. If these souls came from the body of some- one who had been wicked, they immediately entered through the opening *in the belly of any female animal – bitch, rabbit or mare – who had just conceived an embryo not yet supplied with a soul.*[1] But if the wandering soul came from the body of someone whose life had been innocent, it could enter into the womb of a woman, and take possession of a newly- conceived human foetus.

So, in Cathar Montaillou, a foetus was bound to be good since it was immediately provided with an innocent soul. This was one more reason why it should be loved by its mother from the womb. '*But I am pregnant. What should I do with the fruit I bear, if I ran away with you to the heretics?*' said Béatrice de Planissoles to her steward (i.219). This senti- ment was not exclusive to ladies nobly born. Alazaïs de Bordes, a simple peasant of Ornolac, says (i.193): *The other day we were crossing the Ariège in a boat, and the river was in flood; we were very frightened of being wrecked and drowned. Especially me; for I was pregnant.* The subsequent dialogue shows clearly that Alazaïs's fear was not for herself but for her unborn child. Is it by chance that the Fournier Register mentions con- traception but never deliberate abortion?[2]

In such conditions the birth of a child could become a matter of care and anxiety. But, culturally and emotionally, it was still felt as a funda- mental happiness: Jacques Authié, in a homily delivered to Pierre Maury (iii.130), makes the Devil say, '*You will have children. And you will rejoice more for one child, when you have one, than for all the peace you now enjoy in Paradise.*' Satan is supposed to be speaking to angels in Heaven, doomed to fall. But what he says reflects the spontaneous attitude of the villagers, who were in favour of birth and friendly towards infants, an attitude against which official Catharism laboured in vain. Pierre Maury himself, and many others with him, knew that a baptism was a source of merriment and joy, transmuted into solid friendships (iii.185).

1 ii.35. See also i.220, for Raymond Roussel's opinion. The Waldensians of Pamiers also thought a foetus had a soul (i.88).

2 The single reference is to a spontaneous abortion, genuine or imaginary (i.519).

Babies in Ariège were made a great fuss of by their mothers from their earliest days. Raymond Roussel, a country steward, described clearly practices which were not regarded as new in the first half of the fourteenth century. *Alicia and Serena were ladies of Chateauverdun. One of these ladies had a child in the cradle and she wanted to see it before leaving* [she was going to join the heretics (i.221)]. *When she saw it she kissed it ; then the child began to laugh. She had started to go out of the room where the infant lay so she came back to it again. The child began to laugh again ; and so on, several times, so that she could not bear to tear herself away from the child. Seeing this she said to her maidservant : 'Take him out of the house.'*

Her journey was to bring her to the stake.

Despite what some writers have said about love of children being a comparatively recent phenomenon, this was undeniably an ambiance of affection, and the death or even illness of a young child, or separation from it, could be a source of sorrow and real suffering for parents. Especially, of course, for the mother. *In our village*, says Pierre Austatz, *bayle* of Ornolac (i.202), *there lived in her house a woman called Bartholomette d'Urs (she was the wife of Arnaud d'Urs, of Vicdessos). She had a young son, who slept with her in her own bed. One morning when she woke up she found him dead beside her. She started to weep and lament.*

'Do not weep,' I said. *'God will give the soul of your dead son to the next child you conceive, male or female. Or else his soul will find a good home somewhere else.'*

For offering this easy consolation, the *bayle* of Ornolac was to spend eight years in prison, and then to be condemned to wear the double yellow cross (i.203, 553).

There are many examples in upper Ariège of the sorrow of country parents at the death of their offspring. It is true that within the framework of the *domus* system, love for children was not, in the last resort, entirely disinterested. Bélibaste suggested as much when exhorting Pierre Maury against remaining a bachelor (iii.188). Alazaïs Azéma was more precise still, reporting on the feelings of Guillaume Benet, a farmer of Montaillou, on the loss of his son (i.321). *When Raymond Benet, son of Guillaume Benet, died, I went after a fortnight to Guillaume Benet's house. I found him in tears.*

'Alazaïs,' he said, *'I have lost all I had through the death of my son Raymond. I have no one left to work for me.'*

All Alazaïs could say was: '*Cheer up; there's nothing we can do about it.*'

But if a male child meant a strong right arm to Guillaume Benet, he also meant much more. Guillaume loved Raymond for himself. And he was somewhat consoled to think that Guillaume Authié had hereticated his son before he died. So the son was in fact happier than his father, left behind in this vale of tears: '*I hope,*' said Guillaume, '*that my son is in a better place than I am now.*'

When Guillemette Benet of Montaillou lost a daughter and was weeping for her, Alazaïs Azéma tried to console her (i.320). '*Cheer up, you still have some daughters left; and anyhow you can't get the one that is dead back again.*'

To which Guillemette replied: '*I would mourn even more than I do for the death of my daughter; but,* Deo gratias, *I have had the consolation of seeing her hereticated on the night before her death by Guillaume Authié, who hurried here in a blizzard.*'

Sincere as all this affection was, it was also ritualized, socialized and shared. So were the condolences offered to a bereaved parent by friends and neighbours. The difference there might be between a father's and a mother's love is shown in the story of the Pierre family, an episode which has the additional interest of dealing with a little girl less than one year old. Despite the infant's extreme youth, it was undoubtedly the object of emotion. Raymond Pierre was a sheep-farmer in the village of Arques, a terminus on the migration route used by the people of Montaillou. He had one daughter, Jacotte, by Sybille his wife (iii.414–15). Jacotte, not yet a year old, was seriously ill, and her parents decided, so much did they love the child, against all the rules of heresy, to have her hereticated before she died. In theory it was not right to hereticate anyone so young: Jacotte *did not have the understanding of good.* But Prades Tavernier, the *parfait* who undertook the ceremony, was laxer than the Authiés and thought there was nothing to be lost by it.[1] So he started to administer the *consolamentum*: *He performed a lot of bows and elevations,* and placed that rare object, a book, on the child's head. Once these rites were accomplished, Raymond Pierre could say to his wife, '*If Jacotte*

---

1 iii.144. In fact, Prades Tavernier, a villager by origin, not a bourgeois like the Authiés, was influenced by the pressure of Catholic behaviour, and administered the *consolamentum* to a baby in just the same way as a Roman priest would administer baptism in the same circumstances.

dies, she will be an angel of God. Neither you nor I, wife, could give our daughter as much as this heretic has given her.'

Full of joy and disinterested love, Raymond Pierre left the house to see Prades Tavernier on his way. Before going, the *parfait* told Sybille not to give the baby any milk or meat. If Jacotte lived, all she was to have was fish and vegetables (ii.414). For a child of that age, and in the dietetic conditions of the period, this was risky. In fact, what it amounted to was that after the father and the *parfait* left, Jacotte would be doomed to imminent death by a process similar to the *endura*, or final fast.

But there was a hitch. Sybille Pierre's love for her little girl was essentially warm and physical, not spiritual and sublime like that of Raymond. So, relates Sybille, *when my husband and Prades Tavernier had left the house, I could not bear it any longer. I couldn't let my daughter die before my very eyes. So I put her to the breast. When my husband came back, I told him I had fed my daughter. He was very grieved and troubled, and lamented. Pierre Maury* [Raymond Pierre's shepherd] *tried to console his master. He said to my husband, 'It is not your fault.'*

And Pierre said to my baby, 'You have a wicked mother.'

And he said to me, 'You are a wicked mother. Women are demons.'

My husband wept. He insulted and threatened me. After this scene, he stopped loving [diligere] *the child; and he also stopped loving me for a long while, until later, when he admitted that he had been wrong.* (Raymond Pierre's change of heart occurred at the same time as all the inhabitants of Arques decided collectively to renounce Catharism.) *My daughter Jacotte,* Sybille concluded (ii.415), *survived this episode for a year; and then she died.*

All this shows that there was not such an enormous gap, as has sometimes been claimed, between our attitude to children and the attitude of the people in fourteenth-century Montaillou and upper Ariège. Another example is the case of Raymond Benet's new-born son, who was not expected to live. Perhaps his mother was already dead. Guillemette Benet, who lived in the same village as her brother, tells the story (i.264). *Raymond Benet of Ornalac had a new-born son who was dying. He sent for me when I was going to the woods to gather firewood, so that I could hold the dying child in my arms. So I did hold it from morning until evening, when it died.*

There are, of course, some differences between our attitude to our children and the affection felt by the peasants and especially the women of Montaillou towards their offspring. But they probably loved their children just as intensely as we do, and perhaps even spoiled them too.[1] Of course, parental love had to be divided up among a greater number of children than today. It also had to adapt itself to a higher rate of infant mortality. Lastly, many couples seemed to be comparatively indifferent to very young infants.[2] But this indifference was less marked than has recently been claimed.[3]

The first stage of childhood in Montaillou and the neighbouring villages covered the period from birth to weaning. We do not know whether weaning took place between one and two years, or nearer the age of two. Nor do we know whether children were swaddled. A cradle is mentioned in connection with the child of a noble family in Chateauverdun (i.221). It is worth recalling that at a time when there were no perambulators or bottles, the links of dependence between infants and their mother, wet-nurse or the maidservant who looked after them, were much closer than they are nowadays. Infants were usually breast-fed, and in general spent much more time in their mother's arms. For example, Guillemette Clergue says (i.335), *One holiday I was standing in the square at Montaillou with my little daughter in my arms when my uncle Bernard Tavernier of Prades came up and asked me if I had seen his brother.* Raymonde Arsen remarks (i.371), *At a family reunion organized for the wedding of Raymond Belot, I was standing by the hearth holding in my arms the baby daughter of Alazaïs, Raymond's sister.* This dependence

1 I think I have said enough to counter the point of view expounded by Madame B. Vourzay, who writes that 'children were of little account' for the people of Montaillou. (Vourzay (1969), p. 91). It is true, as she rightly says, that grown-ups in upper Ariège were afraid that children might betray them to the Inquisition. But in my view this did not affect the general feeling towards children.

2 There is little mention of the death of infants in Montaillou itself, though such losses must have been frequent.

3 There is not enough information available for us to go into the question of the attitude of grandparents. But, to take a few examples, Béatrice de Planissoles was an attentive grandmother (i.249) and a dead grandmother came back as a ghost to embrace her grandchildren in bed (i.135). The Fournier Register tells us nothing about grandfathers: men were much less likely to live long enough to become grandparents. But see iii.305 for the interest taken by Raymond Authié (namesake of the *parfait*) in a suggestion of marriage concerning his granddaughter, Guillemette Cortil.

continued in other forms after weaning. It is probable that infants under a year old did not sleep in their parents' bed for fear of their getting smothered. But children of over one or two might spend many nights in their parents' or their mother's bed. Sybille Pierre, the wife of a rich farmer, relates (ii.405): *It was the time at which people generally go to bed. I myself was in bed with my daughter Bernadette, who was about five years old.* We have just seen how Bartholomette d'Urs, a peasant woman, burst into tears on waking one morning to find beside her the corpse of her little son, who had died in the night (i.202).

Country children in general did not go to school; there were few schools and no reason why they should go to them. But there was one schoolboy in the area: Jean, who was under the tuition of the priest (i.243). The boy's chief function was to act as Pierre Clergue's messenger, or as go-between for his rendezvous. But in the little villages of the lowlands and the Ariège valley some schools functioned fairly regularly, catering for the sons and daughters of noblemen or leading citizens. The ecclesiastics who ran these establishments were often subjected to severe temptation by the pupils' mothers (i.251–2). There were schools of a higher intellectual level in comparatively important towns such as Pamiers.

If the peasants had no access to schools, how was their culture handed down? First of all, through work performed in common. The boys would dig the turnips with their father and the girls would reap the corn with their mother. As they all laboured together, the older people would talk to the youngsters. Tongues were equally active around the family board. It was in his own house that the weaver Raymond Maury recounted the Cathar myth of the Fall to his children, who were shepherds. Children were often used to take messages, denounce people or supply information. This obliged them to take responsibility and exercise their memories.

Raymond Pierre, related Pierre Maury, *sent a poor child to fetch me. The boy's Christian name was Pierre; I don't remember his surname. Pierre said to me: 'Come to Raymond's house. He wants you.'*

Elsewhere Pierre Maury says (ii.39): *A little boy showed me the house of the Moslem fortune-teller whom I wanted to consult on the subject of Guillemette Maury's sheep.*

Mengarde Buscailh relates: *One day around Easter, when I came back from the fields to have the midday meal in the house where I lived with my husband and brother-in-law, I noticed that someone had been kneading dough in the trough. I asked a little girl of eight, called Guillemette, who came from Mérens and whose surname I do not know, 'Who has been kneading dough?'*

And the little girl, who lived with us, answered, 'It was Brune, Bernard de Savignan's wife, who was kneading bread for two men.' One of the two men was none other than Prades Tavernier, the *parfait*.

Another instance of a youthful messenger being sent some distance and having to make use of his memory is given by Barthélemy Amilhac (iii.129). *The Monday after the Feast of St James, Béatrice de Planissoles sent a child from Belpech* [in present-day Aude] *to look for me, and he came to Mézerville, where I was then living* [as serving priest]. *And the child said to me, 'A lady in Belpech who is your friend sent me to ask you to come and see her there.'*

But I, said Barthélemy, *couldn't think of any lady I knew in Belpech. So I asked the child, 'Can you describe the shape of the woman who sent you?'*

And the child began to describe what the woman looked like. And I understood from his description that it must be Béatrice. So right away I went to Belpech, where I found Béatrice in her house near the château.

Béatrice was used to employing children as go-betweens. It was Jean, Pierre Clergue's young pupil, who had earlier escorted her *on a very dark night* to the Church of Saint Peter in Prades, in the sanctuary of which the priest had installed a bed for them to make love in (i.243).

Children were usually sent to bed early. When a family had guests to dinner and then entertained them round the fire, the children were not to be seen. Bernadette, Raymond Pierre's six-year-old daughter, was put to bed before the meal (iii.122, 129).

From birth to two years of age the documents refer to a child as *infans*, or more usually *filius* or *filia*. From two to twelve years, the word *puer* was applied generally. Towards thirteen or fourteen at the latest, the records switch to the term *adulescens* or *juvenis*. In Montaillou this corresponded to an occupational change. At twelve or soon after, Jean Pellissier, Jean Maury, Pierre Maury and Guillaume Guilhabert began to keep their fathers' sheep, or those of an employer who took on the boy as an apprentice.[1] Twelve years was also the age of reason, according to

1 i.410; ii.444–5, 470. This rigorous 'youth' lasted up to the age of twenty or twenty-five (ii.122).

the Cathar missionaries. '*It is at twelve years of age, and more especially at eighteen, that a man may have the intelligence of good and of evil and receive our faith,*' said Pierre Authié to Pierre Maury (iii.124). Pierre Maury himself confirmed this point of view (iii.143). *Gaillarde, Guillaume Escaunier's sister, and wife of Michel Leth, and Esclarmonde, his other sister, aged about twelve, were believers in the heretics.*

The Inquisition rounded up everyone in Montaillou over the age of about twelve.

But although boys might enter a profession at this age, when girls grew to be twelve or so they did not become shepherdesses. In Occitania, unlike the Lorraine of Joan of Arc, all the shepherds were male. Sooner or later they would have to migrate with their sheep and that was not a woman's job. But, of course, there was a rite of passage into adolescence for girls as well. When menstruation began, a mother would talk frankly to her daughter. Béatrice de Planissoles looked her daughter Philippa straight in the eye and asked her what was the matter (i.248). Philippa's friends and relations then began to look for a husband for her.

In Prades d'Aillon, a bigger and more cheerful village (more advanced, too, for the people there played chess), young people of fifteen and over formed a specific age group, with their own dances and games at festival times. It may well be that the young men and women of Montaillou also formed one or two groups of their own. But under the stifling *domus* system, such groups could not have much independent existence. There was nothing like the confraternities of young people which flourished in Provence in the seventeenth century. Moreover, the girls married too young to remain long in such groups. As for the young men, after the age of eighteen they were soon incorporated in the group of adult males. This group, although divided against itself, was the predominant group in Montaillou.

When it came to old age, there was a different pattern for men and women. In their thirties, men were in their prime. In their forties, they were still strong. But after about fifty a man was old in those days, and his prestige, unlike that of an elderly woman, did not increase with time.

Old men were rarer than old women, and the few who did survive in Montaillou were not surrounded with the respect and affection lavished on such old ladies as Na Roqua, Guillemette 'Belote', Mengarde Clergue and many another stout old dame in the Pays d'Aillon or the Catalan diaspora. Old Pons Clergue had no authority over his son the priest, and though he might deplore, he could do nothing about his activities as an informer. When he died, Pons Clergue had long since ceased to be the head of his *domus*. Pons Rives too trembled before the grown-up son who had taken command of the *ostal*. When his daughter wanted to borrow a mule, he could not grant her request without asking his son's permission (i.339–40).

The Fournier Register does not provide many statistics on mortality. Madame B. Vourzay has worked out the way twenty-five exiles in Catalonia met their death. None of them was old. Almost half were from Montaillou. All twenty-five lived in Catalonia between 1308 and 1323, the limits of our information about them. Out of the total of twenty-five, nine (36 per cent) died of some illness – a higher proportion than normal. One died in a work accident. Eight were arrested by the Inquisition, and of these two died at the stake. The other seven survived, but we do not know what became of them afterwards.[1] If we concentrate on the twelve people out of this group who came from Montaillou, we find that four of them died of illness, four were arrested and four survived. But the rates and causes of mortality among the emigrants in Catalonia does not necessarily reflect the pattern among the people of Montaillou itself.

Unfortunately, no Catholic records were kept at that time which might enable us to see how death was distributed, by age, among the population as a whole. We have to make do with the partial data relating to the *consolamentum*, the Cathar ceremony administered to believers on their deathbeds. As far as I can tell, eleven people of Montaillou were

---

1 The following is Mme Vourzay's list, with corrections by me concerning Emersende Maury and her daughter Jeanne Befayt. The names of the people from Montaillou are given in italics.

Fatal illnesses or accident

Bernard Bélibaste, died in hospital at Puigcerda; Raymond de Castelnau, fell ill and died at Granadella; Raymond Maurs, fell ill and died at Sarreal; *Bernard Marty* (husband of Guillemette, née Maury), died in the mountains at Orta; Bernard Servel, died at Lérida; Guillaume Marty of Junac, died in Catalonia; probably another Marty brother, died in Catalonia; Bernard Befayt, died in an accident in the forest; *Emersende Maury* and her daughter *Jeanne Befayt*, died in an epidemic (iii.214).

Arrested by the Inquisition

Guillaume Bélibaste and Philippe d'Alayrac, burned at the stake; *Pierre and Jean Maury*, brothers, and *Guillaume and Arnaud Maurs*, brothers, arrested; Esperte Cervel and Mathena Cervel, mother and daughter, arrested.

Survived and not imprisoned

The family of *Guillemette Maury*, consisting of herself, her two sons, Arnaud and the other Jean Maury, and her brother, i.e. the other Pierre Maury (*four people* in all); Raymonds and Blanche Marty and Raymond Issaurat.

'consoled', or, as it says in the records, hereticated on their deathbed. We do not know the age of three of them – Raymond Banqui, Raymond Bar and Raymond Maurs. Five others were young or quite young and their names were as follows:

Guillemette Fauré, née Bar, Pierre Fauré's young wife.

Esclarmonde Clergue, daughter of Bernard Clergue (the *bayle*'s namesake) and of Gauzia his wife; she fell ill and was hereticated in her father's house where she subsequently died, in the presence of Guillaume and Raymond Belot and of Guillaume and Guillemette Benet, all stalwarts of local Catharism.

Alazaïs Benet, daughter of Guillemette Benet and young wife of Barthélemy d'Ax; mortally ill, she was hereticated in her mother's house by Guillaume Authié, in the presence of Guillemette Benet and of Guillaume and Raymond Belot (i.473). She died during the night.

Raymond Benet, young son of Guillemette Benet (i.474). He too died in his father's house, a few months after his sister. He was hereticated with his own full consent by Guillaume Authié, in the presence of Guillaume and Guillemette Benet, his father and mother, and of Guillaume and Arnaud Belot and Arnaud Vital (the latter three had escorted the *parfait* to the house).

Guillaume Guilhabert, a shepherd about fifteen years old. He had been spitting blood, and was hereticated in the presence of his mother, together with three other women of the village, and Guillaume Belot.

Then there were three older, or definitely elderly people:

Guillaume Benet, husband of Guillemette Benet, who died in his own house 'on the Feast of Saint Michael in September', his daughter having died in the winter and his son at Whitsuntide. He was hereticated by Guillaume Authié in the presence of his wife Guillemette Benet and his son Bernard, and of Guillaume and Raymond Belot and Bernard Clergue. The ceremony took place in the part of the house where the cattle slept and where the sick man's bed had been brought, probably for the warmth (i.474, 401).

Na Roqua, an old matriarch of Montaillou. She was seriously ill, and her heretication took place in the presence of Guillaume Belot, Guillaume and Raymond Benet, and Rixende Julia, who may have been related by marriage to the Benets (i.388). After Na Roqua had been hereticated, three of the village women (Brune Pourcel, Rixende Julia and Alazaïs Pellissier) watched over her deathbed. She refused to take food, and died after two days. Alazaïs Pellissier and Brune Pourcel prepared her for her shroud, and then she was buried in the graveyard of the local church.

Guillemette Belot, mother-in-law of Bernard Clergue, the *bayle*.[1] Most of the people in this short list – five as against three – were still young. This confirms the suggestion, seen in the figures relating to the Catalan refugees, that illness took a heavy toll of young people in Montaillou.

A more complete count, including all those from Montaillou and other places who died a natural death and were hereticated at an age which can be roughly assessed, gives a proportion of eight 'young' to seven 'old'. Thus Esperte Cervel of Tarascon saw nothing unusual in her own experience (ii.454). *I had three children. Two of them were boys. They died in Lérida. And the third, Mathena, was about three when her brothers died. When my sons died, one was about eleven, the other about seven. The elder died six or seven years ago. My husband died the same year.* In Montaillou itself, Guillemette Benet lost her husband and two children within a year. Alazaïs Munier, the young fellow-sponsor of Guillaume Austatz, *bayle* of Ornolac, said (i.193), *I lost four children in a very short time.* In a very brief space Jeanne Befayt, her mother and her husband all died; the women were both struck down by infection (iii.213) after the man had been killed in a work accident. In Junac, a certain Fabrisse, whose surname is unknown, and her daughter nick-named 'Bonne femme', who was hereticated and therefore could no longer have been a baby, both died in the same year, 1303 or there-abouts, in an epidemic, one at Epiphany and the other at the Feast of the Purification of the Virgin (iii.267–8). A number of deaths in upper Ariège between 1300 and 1305 seem to have been caused by infection, perhaps transmitted in time of famine and weakness.

Pierre Goubert tells us that in Beauvaisis under Louis XIV out of every four children born one died before reaching the age of one year,

1 i.462. In addition, the following were given the *consolamentum* in places other than Montaillou: old Raymonde Buscailh of Prades (i.494, 503); Mengarde Alibert of Quié, mother of a grown-up married daughter (ii.307); the mother of a married man in Ax (ii.16); Arnaud Savignan of Prades, old enough to be a grandfather (iii.149); a still very young man of Junac (iii.267); two heretic babies, against all the local Cathar rules. The person who broke these rules was the *parfait* Prades Taver-nier, and the infants 'consoled' were the children of Sybille Pierre and Mengarde Buscailh respectively.

and another died between one and twenty-one. Thus infant and juvenile mortality combined amounted to 50 per cent. We have no such figures for Montaillou in the fourteenth century, and all we can say is that mortality among children, adolescents and young adults was probably high.

The Register does not reveal whether between 1300 and 1320 people in Montaillou died of hunger. It speaks only of exodus, not of death, as the consequence of food shortage. *I left the country because of famine*, said Esperte Cervel (ii.453). *Because things were so dear, our family had no longer enough to live on.*

On the other hand, the records do give evidence of epidemics. Several people might died almost simultaneously in the same family, especially in the early 1300s.[1] But epidemics are never referred to as such. Perhaps it was not until after the wave of plagues after 1348 that the rural consciousness was gripped by the dread of contagion. The classification of illness was very elementary and based merely on the symptoms which affected different parts of the body – and, even then, usually the external parts. It was a matter of symptomatology rather than etiology. When her children died, Guillemette Benet was suffering from 'ear-aches'. Raymonde Buscailh, according to her daughter-in-law, died of a 'flux of the womb'. The shepherd Raymond Maurs fell ill after eating some chitterlings. He got a barber to bleed him, recovered slightly, walked fifteen kilometres, fell ill again and died a few days later. The young shepherd Guillaume Guilhabert *was gravely ill and spitting blood*. Guillemette Clergue says: *I had the disease commonly called 'avalida' in my right eye.* Aude Fauré of Murviel suffered from *the falling sickness of Saint Paul*, which may have been epilepsy or convulsionary hysteria. Raymonde, Bélibaste's concubine, had a bad heart, and was threatened (by a Saracen soothsayer) with rabies and the falling sickness. The shepherd Bernard Marty, after spending a fortnight in the house of his

1 At the beginning of the first decade after 1300 the shepherd Bernard Marty visited the noble Castels brothers in their house at Rabat (three of them were legitimate and the fourth a bastard). All four were in bed, one in the kitchen, another in the cellar and the remaining two in the barn beside the courtyard. Three at least of the brothers (the 'legitimate' ones) were to die very soon afterwards (iii.281). The effect of epidemics was made worse by the fact that a deathbed was the occasion for social intercourse (ii.260; iii.189, etc.).

employer Guillaume Castel, was *ill with fever*; no further details are given. Arnaud Sicre's elderly aunt had gout and could not walk. The vocabulary of insult includes scrofula, fistulas of the thigh, ulcers and abscesses.

Skin diseases were rife and included the itch, ringworm, scabies, leprosy, St Anthony's Fire and St Martial's Fire, which could be treated at the sulphur baths at Ax-les-Thermes. They might even serve as a pretext for a pilgrimage to upper Ariège, theoretically in search of a cure, in fact in order to meet the *parfaits*. *I would have liked to go to Sabarthès, to meet the goodmen in secret*, says Bertrand de Taix, a noble of Pamiers and a long-term sympathizer with Catharism (iii.313). *So I scratched my arms as hard as I could, as if I had scabies; and I lied to people and said, 'I ought to go to the baths at Ax.'*

But my wife [she was very anti-Cathar] *said, 'No, you're not going to the baths.'*

And she would say to people who came, 'Don't go praising the baths at Ax. It will make my husband want to go there.'

If anyone disappeared suddenly from the uplands, local rumour had three possible explanations for his flight: either he was in debt, or he was a heretic or he was a leper. In the latter case, he had to go down to Pamiers or Saverdun and enter one of the leper colonies there.

Doctors might visit Montaillou from time to time. Or patients would go down to consult them in the town. *My daughter Esclarmonde had seen many doctors since she fell ill, but not one of them has cured her*, said Gauzia Clergue, though she was only a simple peasant woman who dug her own turnips (iii.360–61). Having ruined herself for her daughter's sake with doctors of the body, Gauzia decided to send for a doctor of the soul, a *parfait*.

The nearest 'real' doctor to Montaillou was Arnaud Teisseire, in Lordat. He acted as a kind of intellectual-of-all-work. He had patients as far away as Tarascon, but he also acted as a notary, ranging the country-side to make people's wills, which he kept in an office which also served him as a bedroom. He was Pierre Authié's son-in-law and was regarded in upper Ariège as a man who had had a good life and never failed to enjoy himself (ii.219). Nevertheless he did not do much to lower the mortality rate up in the mountains. The people of Montaillou resorted to a village healer, Na Ferreria of Prades d'Aillon, when they had something wrong with their eyes.

But it was not really illness that mattered in upper Ariège; that was only an epiphenomenon. What mattered was death. Death unadorned, without fine phrases, falling like an executioner's knife, without warning – or at least without any warning recorded by our witnesses.[1]

In a region as divided as this one was, fanatical and contradictory religious convictions continued their battle right up to the gates of death. Dying Catholics would try to drive away any passing *parfait*, while he would do his best to hereticate them before they died. '*Stop harassing me, you devils*,' Arnaud Savignan of Prades d'Aillon said three times to the over-zealous local Albigensians who tried to take advantage of his weakness and administer the *consolamentum* (ii.140). Jean Maury, a vacillating Catholic but not a Cathar, had to defend himself even more firmly against Guillemette Maury, who, when he was gravely ill, tried to have him 'consoled' by Bélibaste. She then intended to have him embark on the *endura* (ii.484). But Jean said to Guillemette: '*It is for God to decide the day of my death, not me. Stop talking to me in this way or I shall have you taken* [by the Inquisition].'

We have already seen how a dying Cathar sent away the priest who tried to administer the Eucharist to him on his deathbed (i.231). Guillemette Belot, though dying and enfeebled by the *endura*, cried out when she saw the priest of Camurac bringing her the Sacrament (i.462), '*Sancta Maria, Sancta Maria, I can see the Devil.*' In upper Ariège, whether you were a Cathar or a Catholic, you were always the devil to somebody.

Death in Montaillou was, of course, attended by certain prescribed social activities. These mainly concerned the women, and were organized in terms of the *domus* system. They entailed ritual laments on the part of daughters and daughters-in-law when their mother or mother-in-law was dead or dying or even merely in danger. The Mediterranean *lamentu* is much older than Catharism, or even Christianity. But in Montaillou it was structured by the *domus*, and so did not include the women of the village as a whole. The *parfaits* tried to end this practice, which conflicted with their own salvationary myths. When Guillemette

---

1 On the suddenness of death, and the absence of any warning recorded in the Fournier depositions, Mme Vourzay gives an excellent series of passages from the Register. Equally striking is the suddenness of cures, when they do occur. The idea of convalescence did not exist. As soon as any one recovered from an illness he took to the road again or went out ploughing once more. See ii.484 and above, Chapter IV.

Belot, an old woman enfeebled by the *endura*, was on the brink of death, the village people expected to hear the ritual complaints of her daughters. But they heard nothing. Two women of the parish, Raymonde Testanière and Guillemette Azéma, expressed their astonishment (i.462). *'If Guillemette Belot is so weak and near to death,'* they said, *'how is it we do not hear her daughters weeping?'* To which Guillemette Benet replied: *'Silly fools! Guillemette "Belote" doesn't need to be wept for – her son-in-law has seen to it that she lacks for nothing.'*

As we have seen, Bernard Clergue had his mother-in-law hereticated and saw that she entered upon the *endura*.

Sometimes the women's wailing, which might of course be sincere, accompanied the mere prospect of death. Béatrice de Planissoles's daughters, at the family *ostal* in Varilhes, set up a clamour when they learned that she was in danger of being arrested (i.257). The laments of daughters and daughter-in-law continued after the death and followed their mother to the graveyard.[1] Mourning might be purely ritual, without tears, or genuine, with tears. In either case, the mourning was expressed in socialized forms. *When my mother-in-law died*, said Mengarde Buscailh (i.490), *I went to the funeral and uttered loud laments. But my eyes were dry, for I knew that she had been hereticated before her death.*

As elsewhere, women watched over the dying. They played a major role in preparing the dead for burial, and in preserving locks of hair and nail-parings from the corpse. After the burial, which took place soon after death and was attended by a large crowd, they would comment and gossip on the matter. The funeral itself was an illustration of the contrast between men and women in upper Ariège. The toll for the dead was different according to whether the deceased was a man or a woman. Local Catharism, which was very anti-feminist, tried to make death into a masculine affair. We have already seen how the people who attended the *consolamentum*, apart from the sick person and the *parfait*, were often men, pious local Cathar militants, such as the Belot, Clergue and Benet brothers. But one day a good Catholic rounded on the son of a Cathar doctor and told him that women too had a right to resurrection after death (ii.202).

Death also offered an opportunity to remind people of rank. Mengarde

1 But a man who lost someone near to him was supposed to show discretion in his lamentations (ii.289).

Clergue, who was 'rich', was buried in the church, under the altar of the Virgin of Montaillou. But the vulgar herd were buried in the graveyard outside the walls, which was occasionally allowed to lie fallow to prepare space for further batches of dead.

Over and above the social structures surrounding death, there was the primordial anguish which haunted the dying person and his nearest and dearest. This dread was not concerned so much with death in itself as with salvation in the after-life.

For good Catholics (and there were such, even in Montaillou, though the Fournier Register is not concerned with them), to make a good end was to throw oneself on the will of God. We have seen how Jean Maury the shepherd, almost on the brink of death, refused to lend himself to the virtual suicide of the *endura*.[1]

The Cathars of Montaillou were not very different from the Catholics when it came to preoccupation with salvation. They differed about means rather than ends; about earthly intercessors rather than about the heavenly object to be attained. According to Pierre Maury, the mendicant friars could not save souls. All they were fit for, after having given a man the last sacraments, was to sit down at table and guzzle (ii.29, 30). Pierre Maury concluded: '*Let us resort to the* parfaits*! They at least can save souls.*' The same belief is repeated on every page of the Fournier Register, whenever it is a question of *consolamentum* or *endura*. And the *parfaits* were always there to supply the demand whatever the weather, except in heavy rain.[2]

So the peasants of Montaillou were able to prepare themselves consciously for imminent death, on condition that illness left them a minimum of awareness. They accepted in a spirit of responsibility the risks inherent in the *consolamentum*, in other words, the prospect of a painful *endura* which added to the natural suffering of illness the pangs of hunger and, for those who were toughest and held out longest, of thirst.[3]

1 ii.484. In general, there is no evidence in the Register of any tendency towards suicide as we understand it. But the *endura* was really tantamount to a peculiar form of suicide. It was regarded as a purely religious act, designed to ensure salvation. But we cannot say how far the subconscious entered into it.

2 A heavy Mediterranean downpour was more likely even than snow to deter the goodmen from hurrying across country with the *consolamentum* (iii.308).

3 i.488. The records for survival in a state of *endura* were thirteen days and thirteen nights (iii.131), and a fortnight (i.235). Compare, in the seventeenth century, four-

Raymond and Guillaume Benet, son and husband respectively of Guillemette Benet (i.474), both willingly agreed to be 'consoled', and, if they survived, to 'endure' on their deathbeds. But in each case a mercifully rapid death supervened: both died during the night after being 'consoled' by Guillaume Authié.

Guillemette Belot and Na Roqua, old peasant women of Montaillou, were not so lucky. But they were equal to their ordeal. In the middle of her *endura*, Guillemette Belot refused the help of a priest who brought the Eucharist (i.462). Na Roqua held out heroically against hunger and thirst. *Fifteen or seventeen years ago*, said Brune Pourcel (i.388), *one dusk, at Easter, Guillaume Belot, Raymond Benet (the son of Guillaume Benet) and Rixende Julia, of Montaillou, brought Na Roqua to my house in a* bourras [a rough piece of canvas]; *she was gravely ill and had just been hereticated. And they said to me: 'Do not give her anything to eat or drink. You mustn't!'*

That night, together with Rixende Julia and Alazaïs Pellissier, I sat up with Na Roqua. We kept on saying to her, 'Speak to us! Say something!'

But she would not open her lips. I wanted to give her some broth made of salt pork, but we could not get her to open her mouth. When we tried to do so in order to give her something to drink, she clenched her lips. She remained like this for two days and two nights. The third night, at dawn, she died. While she was dying, two night birds commonly called gavecas [owls] *came on to the roof of my house. They hooted and when I heard them I said: 'The devils have come to carry off the late Na Roqua's soul!'*[1]

Equally edifying was the deathbed of Esclarmonde Clergue of Montaillou. She was the daughter of Bernard Clergue, the *bayle*'s namesake, and of his wife Gauzia, a peasant couple. While Esclarmonde was still young she married a certain Adelh of the village of Comus in Ariège. Guillaume Benet, godfather and protector of the young woman and a fellow-sponsor of Gauzia, said: *It is a good marriage, and Esclarmonde has made a good beginning.* But unfortunately Esclarmonde fell seriously ill. So, as was the custom, she came back to her father's *domus* to die. Her

---

teen days entirely without food in time of famine: see Le Roy Ladurie (1966), p. 499.

[1] See also ii.426, for the deathbed of Huguette de Larnat who, while suffering the pains of the *endura*, cried out and asked those around her (in particular the *parfait* who was watching over her last moments, hidden in a barrel), *'Will it soon be over?'*

bed was put by the fire in the kitchen; her mother tended her devotedly and slept with her at night while the father slept alone in the bedroom next door. Gauzia loved her daughter, but in the end she wanted God to take her, for she had ruined herself paying for medicine and doctors.

As Esclarmonde's godfather, Guillaume Benet regarded himself as responsible for her salvation, and he persuaded Gauzia to have her hereticated. All that remained was to ask for the young woman's consent. She gave it willingly. Too weak to speak much, she lifted up her arms towards her godfather. The *parfait* Prades Tavernier was, with some difficulty, sent for. As always, the heretication ceremony was attended by men and women of the Belot and Benet clans. The *consolamentum* took place in the kitchen on a Friday evening, at the time when people were usually in their first sleep. Esclarmonde's father, snoring in the next room, did not know what was going on. Raymond Belot, following the rule, brought a wax candle with him, so there was no need to light the kitchen fire in order to be able to see. It was Lent, and the room where Esclarmonde lay dying was cold. But the well-being of the soul was more important than that of the body. The *consolamentum* was administered and the *parfait* was rewarded with a tip (iii.364–5); he then left. There now arose the problem of the *endura*. Gauzia Clergue's reactions were the normal reactions of a loving mother. She protested against the masculine rigours of a fast which, in the case of her daughter, would mean suicide.

'*Do not give your daughter anything more to eat or drink, even if she asks for it,*' said Raymond Belot (iii.364).

'*If my daughter asks me for food or drink, I shall give it to her,*' said Gauzia.

'*In that case you will be acting against the interests of Esclarmonde's soul,*' she was told.

Fortunately the question did not arise. Esclarmonde Clergue died the next day, towards the hour of terce, without asking for food or drink. Was this due to heroism? Or to weakness? We do not know. But before her *consolamentum* and death, the young woman showed a touching concern for her salvation.

A similar concern, similarly tempered by a mother's love, is to be found in the case of Guillaume Guilhabert, a young shepherd of Montaillou.[1]

1 The facts about Guilhabert are divided up among various witnesses and scattered from i.390 to i.430.

At fifteen, an age when most young shepherds were scrambling over the mountains more nimbly than their fathers, Guillaume Guilhabert had to leave his flock. He was spitting blood; perhaps he had tuberculosis. He took to his bed, where friends older than he was, such as Guillaume Belot and Raymond Benet, both Cathars, had a strong influence over him. Guillaume Belot, a militant Albigensian, was connected in a number of ways with the Guilhabert *domus*, which welcomed the influence of his strong personality and of the Belots in general. The links between the two families were reinforced, as was usual in Montaillou, by fellow-sponsorship and, indirectly, by concubinage. Guillaume Belot was the fellow-sponsor of Arnaud Fauré, recently married to Alazaïs Guilhabert, young Guillaume Guilhabert's sister (i.429). Alazaïs herself, in her giddy youth, just before her marriage to Arnaud, had been the mistress of the shoemaker Arnaud Vital, great friend and frequenter of the Belot brothers. Arnaud Vital was to be an ideological as well as a sexual link between the Belots and Guilhaberts (i.413).

All the circumstances conspired to bring about Guillaume Guilhabert's heretication. He was already very much weakened by illness. (Incidentally, his family in general seem to have been afflicted by bad health. Guillemette, Guillaume's sister and the wife of Jean Clement of Gébetz, was also ill in bed in her father's *domus*, having left her husband's *ostal* (i.329). She was sleeping in the Guilhaberts' kitchen, on a bed not far from her brother Guillaume's deathbed. And her baby was sleeping with her!) Guillaume Belot did all he could to persuade young Guillaume to be 'consoled'. Alazaïs, Arnaud Fauré's wife, also wanted her brother to be hereticated, both because of her own beliefs and because it was a way of ending a family quarrel between her husband and her father, Jean Guilhabert. Jean had not handed over Alazaïs's dowry. Arnaud Fauré supported the pleas of his wife, Allemande Guilhabert (his mother-in-law) and Guillaume Belot (his fellow-sponsor). But the mother, Allemande Guilhabert, though she loved her son dearly, was also thinking of the future of her *domus*, which would be endangered if her son's *consolamentum* was betrayed to the Inquisition.

'*Comrade* [socie],' said Guillaume Belot to Guillaume Guilhabert (i.422–3), who was visibly growing weaker, '*would you like me to go and get a doctor to save your soul?*'

'*Yes*,' answered Guillaume, '*I should like that very much. Go and find a good Christian who will receive me into his faith and into his sect, and who will help me to make a good end.'*

'*My son*,' said Allemande, '*do not do that; it's enough that I should lose you, for I have no other son. I don't want to lose all my possessions as well because of you.*'

'*Mother*,' said Guillaume, respectfully addressing his mother as 'vous' though she addressed him as 'tu', '*I beg you, let a good Christian come and save my soul.*'

'*My son, do not do it!*'

'*Mother, I implore you, agree to what I ask; do not put any obstacles in the way.*'

Finally Allemande gave in. Guillaume Belot told her that thanks to the powerful protection of Pierre Clergue the priest, who was secretly a Cathar, the Inquisitors would not bother any people in Montaillou who were involved in heretication (i.414).

So Guillaume Guilhabert was 'consoled' by the *parfait* Prades Tavernier in the presence of all his relatives – his sisters, his mother and his brother-in-law. He died soon afterwards. Prades Tavernier was rewarded with a jar of oil and a few sheepskins.

Na Roqua, Guillaume Guilhabert and others like them extended the frontiers of courage. But such idealism caused tension. As we have seen, some of the women of Montaillou put up a certain amount of protest: '*Am I to let my child die of hunger?*' '*If my son's heretication is discovered, shall I lose everything I possess?*' But Catharism was very strong in Montaillou, and elsewhere defection from the ideal was even more marked. Villages like Quié, Arques, Junac and even Prades were not so united in their heresy. Some individuals there might be temporarily won over to the *consolamentum*, but they afterwards rebelled against the rigours of the *endura*. As we have seen in the case of Sybille Pierre of Arques, mothers were particularly apt to protest (ii.414, 415). And a league away from Montaillou, in the village of Prades, when Mengarde Buscailh's two- or three-month old baby was very ill and her brother-in-law, Guillaume Buscailh, suggested that the child should be 'consoled' and then subjected to the *endura* '*so that he should become an angel*' (i.499, 219; iii.144), Mengarde replied, '*I will not refuse my child the breast, as long as he is still alive.*'

At Ax-les-Thermes the mother of Guillaume Escaunier, a farmer, was given the *consolamentum* and then consigned to the *endura*. This was her children's doing, and she rebelled against it (ii.15, 16). She was a farmer, and loved meat more than heaven (iii.143). She demanded food and insulted the daughter who thought it her duty to refuse it. At Junac, Bernard Marty, seriously ill, was 'consoled' by Guillaume Authié and managed to last out through the *endura* for two days and two nights, taking nothing but water. But on the third day he gave up. His brother and sister, who had been supervising his fast, also yielded and let him have bread, wine and meat (iii.264–6).

Sometimes, when the demands of heresy were too rigorous, a Catholic death seemed to offer a solution. Mengarde Buscailh considered it for a moment for her baby. And Raymonde, Mengarde's mother-in-law, was besieged on her deathbed by the *parfait* and the priest alternately (i.494–507).

To return to Montaillou itself, all the cases of heretication known to us among countrymen and countrywomen, young and old, show the same attitude towards death. The main problem is that of salvation; the dread of annihilation, as such, does not seem to arise. Sometimes the concern with the soul's salvation is socialized, as in the case of Guillaume Guilhabert, who was hereticated in the midst of his friends and relations. In the case of Na Roqua, the struggle for salvation was apparently carried on in solitude. This attitude to death was cultural in origin, emanating from the group of *domus*, and under the virtually collective pressure of the villagers, Prades Tavernier was even forced to break the Cathar rule and give the *consolamentum* to people no longer in possession of their faculties and even to infants.

But while this concern with salvation was both cultural and collective, it was also Christian, and even Catholic in the traditional sense of the term. And this despite the difference in the choice of mediators. These country folk were no Huguenots to speak direct to God for themselves. They needed a mediator, a priest for those who remained orthodox Catholics, a goodman for those who no longer had confidence in the rectors and Minorite friars they considered to be corrupt. If possible, everyone, Cathar and Catholic alike, died surrounded by the members of his *domus* and of his family. The great thing was not to die alone – and to be saved.

CHAPTER XV

Cultural exchanges

For information about the mental outlook of the peasants of Montaillou
the Fournier Register, though not entirely comprehensive, is of outstanding value. One reason for this is the fact that it focuses on one
village, though at the same time it throws important corroborative light
on neighbouring parishes. Another reason for the Register's importance
is sociological: the Cathar heresy, one of the reasons for Fournier's
inquiries, was no longer, in the years 1300–20, an urban or noble
phenomenon. It had withdrawn into the country, among the peasant
people of the mountains. There it hid and survived, fostered by an anti-
clericalism exacerbated by the growing burden of tithes. Catharism here
existed in a state of hibernation because of a tradition of cultural transmission by which children took over their parents' ideology. Because of
this, for a quarter of a century Catharism experienced a modest revival
in the country which would have been impossible in the towns, vigilantly
watched over by the mendicant orders, the Minorites and the myrmidons
of the Inquisition. In this rural concentration the Albigensian heresy
provides an opportunity for the study not of Catharism itself – that is
not my subject – but of the mental outlook of the country people. The
concentration of heterodoxy among the peasants was very marked at the
beginning of the fourteenth century: so much so that those engaged in
non-agricultural activities, especially artisans, often regarded as the
supporters par excellence of new ideas, only occasionally played this
role in Montaillou and other villages in the Comté de Foix. The shoemaker Arnaud Sicre, *who makes the best shoes in the world out of a single
piece of leather* (ii.184), was only a false Cathar, though a genuine
informer. As for the weaver Prades Tavernier, who became a *parfait*, he
chose this dangerous career partly because, among other reasons, he was
tired of weaving (*fatigatus de texando*).[1] But between 1300 and 1320 in
upper Ariège, heresy was no longer the province of weavers and spinners;
it had become, like cheese, a product of the land. It was also encountered
often among blacksmiths' families, such as those of the Cervels and the
Martys in Tarascon and Junac. Although Bélibaste might describe as
gavets (mountain people from the north) the naive believers in the idols

1 i.339. See also iii.187 for the only weaver whom Bélibaste honours with his
company, though he was not a heretic.

and miracles of the Roman faith, it was (apart from a few country artisans who did act as leaders) peasants like himself, shepherds like Pierre Maury, and important peasant *domus* like those of the Benets, the Belots, the Forts and the Clergues, who together provided the social soil on which heresy experienced its last flowering. And this last flowering acts as a kind of photographic developer, revealing the mental attitudes of a whole rural community.

It acts all the more strongly because in Montaillou itself, from 1300 to 1320, the heretics contaminated the major part of the population. Elsewhere, in other 'infected' villages – in Sabarthès, in Capcir and in the southern Narbonnais – the heretics were only a minority, sometimes a very small one. Even so they might polarize the general anti-clerical frustration and thus influence the community as a whole.

So this entire peasant culture is refracted or at the best reflected by the Fournier Register. There is no need to underestimate this evidence because those who provided it were mere peasants. As we have seen, the word 'peasant' might be used in moments of anger as an insult, but the Register as a whole shows the country folk as by no means stupid, fond of abstract thought and even of philosophy and metaphysics. We see them conversing quite freely with heretic missionaries and jurists from the town, in exchanges which bring out the agility of Occitan speech and, despite differences in wealth, the lack of social distance between the countryman on the one hand and, on the other, the nobleman, the priest, the merchant and the master craftsman, in a world where manual labour, especially craftsmanship, was not despised.[1] (Craftsmen acted as

1 On the absence or at least unimportance of social distance, see the noblewoman embracing the peasant woman (i.300); the *châtelaine* frequenting the village women without any suggestion of paternalism or do-gooding; the wife of a trout-fisherman becoming the friend of the squire of Junac (iii.61); the Bélibastes, rich but simple farmers, receiving as guest, without thinking anything of it, the proxy of the Archbishop of Narbonne; and Bernard Clergue, connected in his daily and conjugal life with the peasantry of Montaillou and at the same time with the highest authorities of the Comté de Foix. It was precisely this absence of social distance in Montaillou and the Comté de Foix which made socio-religious conflicts so tragic.

Despite the prestige attached (in upper Ariège), to not working with one's hands, it is striking to see the way sons of 'good families', whether or not compelled to it by reverses of fortune, became artisans without considering themselves dishonoured. See the case of the shoemaker Arnaud Sicre, a notary's son, and the case of the Authiés, who came from a notary's family too but adopted the trade of tailor without a qualm.

cultural intermediaries and interlocutors in general between the peasants and other, higher social groups such as the nobles, the legal profession and the merchants.) Moreover, even between themselves the villagers were always talking and discussing things, in the fields, at mealtimes and above all around the fire at night, sometimes until cockcrow.

It was a very live culture despite, or perhaps because of, the attacks, the searches and the round-ups of the Inquisitor. But it was endangered when it emigrated to the towns of Catalonia, for there it was menaced not so much by harassment pure and simple as by disintegration as the result of distance, solitude and the dispersal of the faithful. These were in danger of getting stuck there and growing old without young children and sometimes without resources. The danger of deculturation came above all from the blandishments of the surrounding society, steeped in Catholicism. The younger generation of emigrants, born in the old country but brought up in Catalonia, were not immune from these rival attractions and sometimes engaged in bitter conflict against their parents, even descending to blows, a state of affairs which would have been unthinkable in upper Ariège. Peasant Catharism was rapidly eroded in Catalonia, threatened by a radically different ambiance and by the urbanization of the emigrants.[1] So it is in Montaillou itself that we can best study the mentality of its people in all its genuine freshness.

How far was cultural transmission in Montaillou and other villages of the same type due to books and writing? The preaching of the Authiés, decisive for Montaillou, was essentially based on the influence of books.

Pierre and Guillaume Authié, says the peasant Sybille Pierre (ii.403), *were clerks; they knew the law* [as notaries]; *they had wives and children; they were rich. One day, Pierre, in his house, was reading a certain passage*

---

1 Mme B. Vourzay has made a special study of this aspect of the emigration into Catalonia. See Vourzay (1969), p. 103 for relationships with shopkeepers; pp. 80, 81 and 127 for the poverty and social decline of single women; pp. 85 and 102 for discrimination due to Catalan pride; pp. 100 and 124–5 for the break-up of families; pp. 104 and 117–18 for the tendency for the emancipation of women to break up the closed *domus* imported from upper Ariège and Montaillou; pp. 100 and 123 for the fall in the number of emigrants, who died frequently and rarely reproduced; and p. 81 for the conflict between generations caused by the emancipation of the young people.

in a book. He told his brother Guillaume, who happened to be present, to read the passage.

After a moment, Pierre asked Guillaume: 'How does it strike you, brother?'

And Guillaume answered: 'It seems to me that we have lost our souls.'

And Pierre concluded: 'Let us go, brother; let us go in search of our souls' salvation.'

So they got rid of all their possessions and went to Lombardy, where they became good Christians; there they received the power of saving the souls of others; and then they returned to Ax-les-Thermes.

We can only guess what the book was that lay behind the Authiés' Cathar vocation. But one thing is certain: in the legal circles which gave rise to the economic and juridical renaissance of the thirteenth and fourteenth centuries, books were not entirely absent. There were even small libraries, some of them incubating heresy. The spread of the use of paper and the wide written use of the Occitan language could only favour these dangerous tendencies, also stimulated by the professional activity of the notaries, among them the Authié clan which exercised so much influence in Montaillou.

Fourteen years ago, related in 1320 Pierre de Gaillac of Tarascon-sur-Ariège (ii.196), once employed as a clerk by Arnaud Teisseire, doctor at Lordat and son-in-law of Pierre Authié, *I lived for half a year in the house of Arnaud Teisseire, writing out the contracts deposited in his office; one day when I was looking through his papers to find his books of notes, I found a certain book written on paper in the vulgar tongue and bound in old parchment. I spent some time reading it. In it I found arguments and discussions in the vulgar tongue concerning the theories of the Manichean heretics and of the Catholics. Sometimes the book agreed with the views of the Manicheans and disagreed with those of the Catholics; and sometimes the opposite. While I was reading the book, my employer, Master Arnaud Teisseire, came in; suddenly, and in a fury, he snatched the book out of my hands; he hid it; and during the following night I heard him beating his wife and Guillaume, his bastard son, because I had managed to find the book. Whereupon, blushing and ashamed, I went back home to Tarascon-sur-Ariège. The third day Master Arnaud came to fetch me; and took me back with him.*

This passage reveals the danger inherent in books themselves. Some peasants ended up thinking that everything which was written down must be heresy. *One night*, said the stock-farmer Michel Cerdan (iii.201), *during the night before full moon, I got up before dawn, in summer, to lead my cattle to pasture; I saw some men in a meadow behind the house of Arnaud Teisseire reading something written, by the light of the moon; I am sure they were heretics.*

In the region of Aude and Ariège there was a small 'socio-economic base' for the making of books. Leaving aside Pamiers, which was an intellectual centre, quite unimportant villages like Belpech (in present-day Aude) and Merviel (Ariège) might contain a parchment-maker or a 'scriptor' of books (i.256; ii.91). Small as their production was, it sufficed, through the agency of the goodmen, to 'infect' Sabarthès and the Pays d'Aillon. The process was speeded up when paper arrived to supplement parchment. So there were some links between learning and popular culture, and these were helped by the circulation of a few books, though of course such interaction was much slower and more fortuitous than nowadays.

Nevertheless, books remained rare and precious. The respect felt for them by the illiterate people of the village paralleled their touching reverence for learning and for people who were educated. Guillemette Maury of Montaillou, exiled in Catalonia, was overcome with admiration for the *parfait* Raymond Issaura of Larcat (ii.63): *He can preach very well, he knows many things about our faith*. Urged on by Guillaume Bélibaste, she actually adored the Cathar Bible itself, composed by God in Heaven.[1] And so a goodman without his books was a soldier without his gun. The *parfait* Raymond de Castelnau – he was about forty, tall, of a ruddy complexion, white-haired and with a Toulouse accent – told the shepherds of Montaillou how sorry he was because *I have left my books at Castelsarrasin* (ii.475).

One of the reasons why books were so highly regarded was that almost no one had access to them. Apart from the goodmen themselves, only the priests owned or borrowed books or were able to read them. The priest Barthélemy Amilhac owned a book of hours which, when he was in

---

1 ii.45, 46. The peasants, although illiterate, regarded scripture (in every sense of the word) as an essential reference. See the anxious question of Raymond de Laburat, a Catholic farmer excommunicated for non-payment of tithes: '*Is excommunication to be found in any scripture?*' he asked a priest (ii.318–19). Similarly a miller (i.152): '*The Resurrection is a proven fact, because the priests say it is written in the records and the books.*'

prison, earned him the mockery of the Albigensian Bernard Clergue (ii.283). It was this book that Barthélemy thought of pawning or selling to finance his flight to Limoux with his mistress (i.247). Pierre Maury met a Gascon priest, of whom all we know is that he came from a rich family, was thirty years old, had grey-green eyes and brown hair and owned the *book of the faith of the heretics* bound in red leather (ii.188, 383, 483, 484). In Junac, a village of peasant farmers and mountain blacksmiths, the perpetual *vicaire*, Amiel de Rives, possessed a *book of homilies*, or at least read such a book, though it might have belonged to his parish church (iii.7–10). He extracted from it heretical views which he subsequently used in his sermons, in the presence of his parish priest, the local lord, and a large number of his parishioners. In Montaillou itself part of the prestige and charismatic power of the priest Pierre Clergue derived from the fact that for some time he had in his possession a 'calendar' called, again, the *book of the heretics*, or *book of the holy faith of the heretics*, lent to him by Guillaume Authié (i.315, 375; i.292; ii.504). The various names by which this one book was referred to suggests that it was some kind of calendar 'followed or preceded, within the same binding, by a short edifying text'.[1] The popular literature of the early eighteenth century was to include many 'little blue books' which similarly mingled calendar, almanac and religious text. At all events, this one book, part of the circulating library of the Authié brothers which contained three volumes (i.375, n. 159), did not remain long with the priest. After giving various public lectures from it around the fire in people's homes, Pierre Clergue returned the book through Guillaume Belot to its rightful owners. But its temporary presence in the Clergue *ostal* was an event in the village of Montaillou, and attracted the attention of four witnesses, among them Raymonde Arsen, an illiterate servant maid. The shepherd Jean Maury, for his part, suggests that it was this 'calendar' which brought about the complete conversion to Catharism of the four Clergue brothers, the priest chief among them (iii.504). Indeed, the impact of such a book could not have been negligible in the house of Bernard Clergue, generally regarded in Montaillou as a learned man (i.302). For his brother the priest, who by definition had a certain amount of intellectual equipment, the influence of the written word was something which went without saying.

Sometimes other books circulated among the people of Montaillou,

1 See i.375, n. 159.

thanks to goodmen such as the ex-weaver Prades Tavernier. *One day,* says Guillemette Clergue (i.340–41), *I intended to take my mule to the fields to collect turnips; but first I had to give it some hay. So I went into the barn where my mother kept hay and straw, to get some. But I hid from my brother, for he might stop me. And right at the top of the said barn I saw Prades Tavernier sitting: by the rays of the sun, he was reading in a black book the length of someone's hand. Prades, taken by surprise, got up as if he meant to hide, and said: 'Is that you, Guillemette?'*

And I answered: 'Yes, Monsieur, it's me.'

But the reading of suspicious books was not only practised in solitude in Montaillou. Now and then the goodmen would share the benefits with the illiterate peasants around the fire of their *domus*. *One evening,* said Alazaïs Azéma (i.315), widow and peddler of cheese, *at the time when I used to frequent the heretics, I went into the house of Raymond Belot not knowing that there were heretics there that day. In the house, sitting by the fire, I found the heretics Guillaume Authié and Pons Sicre; also present were Raymond, Bernard and Guillaume Belot, the three brothers, together with their mother, Guillemette 'Belote'. Guillaume Authié the heretic was reading a book and also speaking to those present . . . He referred to Saint Peter, Saint Paul and Saint John, the Apostles; so I sat down on a bench beside Guillemette; the Belot brothers were sitting on another bench; and the heretics on a third. Until the end of the sermon.*

In slightly larger, more urban and more distinguished villages than Montaillou there were sometimes, beside the priest and the *parfait*, some ordinary laymen who were literate and could read Occitan or even Latin. *Nineteen or twenty years ago,* said Raymond Vayssière of Ax-les-Thermes (i.285), *I was sunning myself beside the house I then owned in Ax (I later sold it to Allemande, the mistress of the present priest at Junac); and four or five spans away, Guillaume Andorran was reading aloud from a book to his mother Gaillarde. I asked: 'What are you reading?'*

'Do you want to see?' said Guillaume.

'All right,' I said.

Guillaume brought me the book, and I read: 'In the beginning was the Word. . . .

It was a 'Gospel' in a mixture of Latin and Romance, which contained many things I had heard the heretic Pierre Authié say. Guillaume Andorran told me that he had bought it from a certain merchant.

The number of books in circulation in the fourteenth century was of course infinitely smaller than in the eighteenth. But the contrast between town and country later noted by Nicolas Rétif was already marked. In the local town of Pamiers the homosexual Arnaud de Verniolles read Ovid; there were Jewish refugees, Waldensian residents and school-masters, each with his own small but daring library. But only a few works of edification, Catholic in the lowlands, Cathar in the mountains, ever penetrated as far as the villages. And indeed it was the new presence of the occasional Albigensian volume that encouraged the modest triumphs of heresy in upper Ariège.

In Montaillou there were several strata of literacy. At the top there was a literate and 'charismatic' élite, whose only representatives were the Authiés and a few other *parfaits* like Issaura or Castelnau who circulated among the Catalan diaspora. These men had access to what Jacques Authié called the double scripture: the bad scripture which emanated from the Roman Church, and the good scripture, the scripture which saved, known to the goodmen and proceeding from the Son of God (iii.236; ii.504).

A literate élite, constituting the second stratum, knew something of Latin but possessed no specific charisma. The Register contains quite good descriptions of this élite in villages other than Montaillou but similar to it: in Goulier (Ariège) one Bernard Franc, a farmer (i.352), who planted his millet just the same as everyone else, was also a clerk in minor orders and knew some Latin. *One Sunday four years ago*, said Raymond Miégeville of Goulier (i.351), *Mass had just been said in the church of Saint Michael in Goulier. I had remained behind in the sanctuary by the altar, together with Arnaud Augier, Guillaume Seguela, Raymond Subra, Bernard Maria and Bernard Franc, all of Goulier. Then Bernard Franc and Arnaud Augier, who were clerks, began to argue in Latin; and the rest of us, the laymen, whose names I have just given, could not under-stand what they were saying to one another. Suddenly, after the discussion in Latin, Bernard Franc started to speak in the vulgar tongue; and he said: 'There are two Gods! One good, the other bad.'*

We protested.

Thus for a peasant like Raymond Miégeville the distinction between Latin and the vulgar tongue corresponded quite simply to the contrast between cleric and layman. Similarly, in Ax-les-Thermes, the local people assumed that the priest was able to write (in Latin) to his bishop (ii.358). The same was true in Montaillou for Pierre Clergue the priest, and his successor or substitute, Raymond Trilh (ii.239).

Below the latinist clerics, who might well be only ordinary farmers, there was another cultural level – that of the more cultivated laymen, able to read a text so long as it was written in the vulgar tongue, Occitan. These people were described as *sine litteris*, without letters (i.e. Latin letters). Ordinary people regarded them as distinctly inferior to the Latinists. Witness the condescending tone in which the sheep-farmer Raymond Pierre speaks of the ex-weaver Prades Tavernier (ii.416; i.100), elevated to the rank of *parfait* though no one was very sure that he had the requisite knowledge. *Pierre, Guillaume and Jacques Authié,* said Raymond Pierre, *are wise men; many people are very fond of them. Anyone who makes them presents does himself good. So the Authiés are overwhelmed with presents, and lack for nothing. On the other hand, André Prades Tavernier is not so highly regarded; he is ignorant of letters. He has much less knowledge and fewer friends than the Authiés. That is why he is poor; so people have to give him presents in order that he may have clothes, books and all the rest.*

A final barrier separated the few individuals who were literate in the vulgar tongue from the common herd of illiterates. This barrier, too, was a cultural reality, but it appears not to have caused friction or to have wounded anyone's pride: the people on both sides of the frontier all really belonged to the same world.

But the number of actual illiterates raises problems about the transmission of ideas derived from books. Out of some 250 inhabitants in Montaillou, no more than four were definitely literate;[1] even an ex-*châtelaine* like Béatrice was illiterate, unlike her daughters. She was unable to write love-letters to her sweetheart, who knew how to read and write, and was reduced to sending him messages by word of mouth through a little boy.

All this being so, the purely oral transmission of books was of supreme importance. Out of some dozens of heretical meetings that we know of in

---

1 They were Pierre Clergue the priest; his pupil (*scolaris*); Bernard Clergue; and Prades Tavernier, who stayed for long periods in the village though he did not really belong to it and came from the neighbouring parish. Clergue the priest, his pupil, and perhaps also Bernard Clergue, reputed to be learned, probably also knew some Latin. In all, the literacy rate was about 1·6 per cent, including perhaps two or three with a smattering of Latin.

Montaillou and elsewhere, only two are clearly seen to have been held by *parfaits* actually using books. The other meetings were entirely 'verbal', the *parfait* speaking to the believers and sympathizers without any reference to written matter. Most of the time, books only appeared at Montaillou in order to be placed for a few minutes on the head of some-one dying, in the last stages of the *consolamentum*. Outside Montaillou there is evidence of books being used as objects upon which witnesses, friends or fellow-conspirators pledged their truthfulness.[1] In the absence of written records the memory, both visual and auditory, was highly developed among the people of Montaillou. Hence also the importance of preaching and of eloquence in general. *When you have heard the good-men speak*, said Raymond Roussel (i.219), steward of the château of Montaillou, *you can no longer do without them, you are theirs for ever*. Pierre Authié, like his son Jacques, was said to have *the mouth of an angel*, though their pupil, Guillaume Bélibaste, was thought to be com-pletely undistinguished in this respect (ii.406, 28–9).

There were other connections between what was written and what was oral. For example, an idea in circulation in peasant and artisan circles of upper Ariège asserted that the world was eternal. There was of course a basis for this notion in folklore, but it also owed something to written culture, both literary and philosophical, retransmitted to the people by such instructors as the quarrier Arnaud de Savignan of Tarascon-sur-Ariège, who flouted Christianity by claiming that the world had no beginning and would have no end. He quoted two sources: the local proverb about men always sleeping with other men's wives, and the teaching of his master, Arnaud Tolus, overseer of the schools at Tarascon (i.163, 165). Tolus's teaching was probably based on books.

Another example is the way the influence of the troubadours was passed on. According to the Fournier Register, though this evidence is only negative, Montaillou and similar villages were not directly affected and, apart from noblemen's castles, troubadour influence is seen only in Pamiers. But even in this urban context poems were transmitted chiefly by word of mouth: people whispered Pierre Cardenal's *cobla* to one another in the choir of the church at Pamiers (iii.319).

---

1 The Inquisition made witnesses and accused persons swear on the Gospel (ii.358 and *passim*). The friends of the homosexual Arnaud de Verniolles swore on some sacred book (iii.14–50). Less sophisticated people swore on their own head, or on bread and wine or on flour.

Attitudes and ideas were also transmitted directly: from father to son, mother to daughter, aunt to nephew, or older brother or cousin to younger brother or cousin and so on. Pierre Maury remarks (iii.174): *My father's house in Montaillou was destroyed three times for heresy; and there is no question of my making up for it; I must remain faithful to the beliefs of my father.* Similarly Jean Maury, Pierre's brother, says (ii.470): *I was then twelve years old, and looked after my father's sheep. One evening, going back to my father's house, I found sitting by the fire my father, my mother, my four brothers and my two sisters. In the presence of my mother and brothers and sisters my father said to me: 'Philippe d'Alayrac and Raymond Faur are good Christians and goodmen. They are men of good faith. They do not lie.'*

Another instance of a parent passing on religious attitudes to his child is offered by the case of Pierre Maury and his proposed marriage, later, to a little girl at that time aged six.

'*And how do you know,*' asked Pierre (iii.122), '*that Bernadette, when she is grown up, will have the understanding of good?*'

'*The little girl's father,*' answered Bernard Bélibaste, '*will bring her up so well that, with the help of God, she will have the understanding of good.*'

Guillaume Austatz was won over to heretical ideas partly through the influence of his mother, who had been subject to direct propaganda on the part of Pierre Authié (i.203–04). Mother and son used to discuss the Cathar missionary's ideas during long evenings round the fire, or on the way to and from Carcassonne. And many others, like Jean Pellissier and Vuissane Testanière, had been exposed to heterodox influences on the part of an aunt, a mother, a husband and so on (i.461, 469; ii.86, 87).

Generally speaking, cultural transmission rarely operated through a peer group. As we have seen, it is doubtful whether there was an effective group of young people as such in Montaillou. Basically, the right to transmit or retransmit culture was something acquired either through age or through social superiority (the priest vis-à-vis his parishioners; an employer vis-à-vis his employee; the owner of a pasture vis-à-vis the lessee). The older generation in general taught the younger generation.

It could be a father, mother or aunt who in this respect enjoyed the privilege of age; but it could also be a husband, an older person or merely an employer. *My cousin Raymond Maulen*, said Pierre Maury (iii.110), *came to an agreement with Raymond Pierre* [a sheep-farmer] *that I should live with him* [as a shepherd] *in his house so that the said Raymond Pierre could bring me to share in the belief of the heretics*. The brothers Belot, still young bachelors, taught Catharism to their younger comrades (*socii*) such as Pierre Maury and Guillaume Guilhabert, aged between fifteen and eighteen.

Raymond de l'Aire of Tignac gives an example of the ideological respect paid by youth to age (ii.129): *Twenty years ago or thereabouts I had bought some standing grass or hay from a meadow situated near Junac and belonging to Pierre Rauzi of Caussou. We arranged to meet on a certain day in the meadow in order to cut the grass. When we met there, he coming from Caussou and I from Tignac, Pierre Rauzi began to whet his sickle to cut the grass. And as he whetted his sickle, he said: 'Do you believe that God or the blessed Mary are something – really?'*

And I answered: 'Yes, of course I believe it.'

Then Pierre said: 'God and the Blessed Virgin Mary are nothing but the visible world around us; nothing but what we see and hear.'

As Pierre Rauzi was older than I, I considered that he had told me the truth! And I remained in this belief for seven or ten years, sincerely convinced that God and the Virgin Mary were nothing but this visible world around us.

Raymond de l'Aire was in the habit of accepting what older people told him. One day when he was looking after the mules with his name-sake and fellow-citizen Guillaume de l'Aire of Tignac, Guillaume sent one of the mules to graze among the corn (it was the month of May and the corn was already quite high). When Raymond objected, Guillaume replied (ii.129): *'There's nothing wrong with that. The mule has a good soul, just like the owner of the field. So it might as well eat wheat, just like him!'*

Raymond must have been a child or adolescent at the time. *I believed all that,* he said later, *because Guillaume de l'Aire was older than I.*

There was no intrinsic reason why Raymond should not believe Guillaume. Raymond, an unwitting materialist, believed that the souls of animals were just as good as those of men, since all souls were merely blood.

It was rare for cultural transmission to act in the other direction, from the younger to the older. We have already seen how Jeanne Befayt, re-converted to the Roman faith during the exile in Catalonia, met with little sympathy from her mother, Emersende, an old Albigensian peasant woman from Montaillou. Cathar mother and Catholic daughter actually came to blows. Even when a male child was a priest and thus endowed with a certain cultural superiority, his influence on his mother and father might be extremely limited. *One holiday, in Montaillou*, said Guillemette Clergue (i.335–6), *I was standing in the village square with my little daughter in my arms ... Near my father's house, in the sheepfold adjoining it, was Guillemette Jean, wife of Pierre Jean of Prades, and my mother's sister. She called me ... and said: 'I would have liked to speak to my brother Prades Tavernier* [the *parfait*] *... The heretics or goodmen save souls ... But the priests persecute the goodmen.'*

Then my aunt said: 'If ever my son Pierre Prades, who is a priest and who now lives at Joucou [present-day Aude], *knew that I had come here to speak to Prades Tavernier, he would never set eyes on me again or do me any good turn.'*

And indeed, said Guillemette Clergue, *the priest Pierre Prades later sent for his mother, Guillemette Jean, to come to Joucou, and there she ended her life. The priest did so because he had realized that otherwise my aunt would join the heretics.*

In this case the influence of the son, although he was a priest, could only be effectively exercised by force.

In the case of Raymond de Laburat, a peasant farmer of Quié, the influence of the clerical son did not even achieve so much. Raymond, who had Cathar contacts, was violently anti-clerical, largely because of his objection to the tithe on sheep. In a moment of exasperation he cried (ii.328), *I wish all clerics were dead, including my own son, who is a priest.*

The general rule, by which the influence of a father on his son prevailed over the prestige usually attaching the clergy, operated in the case of the elderly Cathar Pons Clergue, who would have nothing to do with the ultimate pro-Catholic machinations of his son Pierre. Even though an elderly father might let himself be bullied by his sons, he would not be converted to their ideas when they differed from his own. A peasant might let himself be led by the nose ideologically by his wife or mother-in-law. But never by his son.[1]

Perhaps this pattern, based on that of the *domus* where the authority of the older generation was sacrosanct, was one of the reasons for the great success of the Authiés' propaganda. The Cathar missionaries from

[1] The conflict between generations dealt with here concerns parents who remained Cathars and refused to be influenced by children who had returned to the Catholic fold.

Ax-les-Thermes did not act as young men trying to convert people of the same age or older. The three of them, Pierre and Guillaume Authié (brothers) and Jacques Authié (Pierre's son), together formed a distinguished travelling phratry-cum-*domus* going about to convert other *domus*, less distinguished but sure of their rights. Thus the process of conversion preserved the principle which subordinated sons to fathers and the younger to the older.

Social life was very active in the Montaillou of the early fourteenth century, but Montaillou itself, little affected by the influence of the Minorites which was more evident in the lowlands to the north and in Catalan villages like Puigcerda in the south,[1] had none of the lay fraternities common in Toulouse and other large towns. Pierre Clergue, the parish priest, carried out his professional duties with a certain amount of conscientiousness. He administered the sacraments, but was too absorbed in extra-curricular activities among his lady parishioners to have either time or inclination to organize any religious confraternities. Nor is there anything to show that the priests of neighbouring villages, less extravagant in their behaviour than Pierre Clergue, set up any such organizations in other villages in upper Ariège. This sort of activity was more in the line of the mendicant friars, conspicuous in this part of the world by their absence. So, for want of other outlets, social exchanges operated chiefly, though not entirely, through the *domus*. And, in the *domus*, the chief occasion for social exchanges was round the fire at night.

An example of such a gathering at Ascou near Ax-les-Thermes is an exact parallel to similar gatherings in Montaillou itself. One evening Raymond Sicre, of the village of Ascou, who had just had a particularly successful row with his wife – he had called her an 'old sow' (*truiassa*) – calmed down and went out to cast an eye over his sheep (ii.365–6). He went by the house of Jean-Pierre Amiel, probably the head of the *domus*, who lived there together with his mother, Rixende Amiel. (Six years previously Rixende had left the village together with her husband Pierre Amiel: rumour had it that this was because Pierre was a leper, though others said that both of them were heretics. However that might be, Rixende had returned some time later alone, to live without her husband in her son's house. Pierre Amiel had vanished, none knew where or how.)

1 See below, Chapter XIX.

Raymond Sicre saw lights burning in the Amiel *domus*, which meant there must be guests. Raymond had not been invited, so to satisfy his curiosity he opened the door. He could not see who the guests were because of a rough curtain (*bourrasse*) hanging behind the door, so he went in and eavesdropped on what was going on. The subject of conversation at the moment was food, and in particular bread.

'*I am afraid you did not like the bread I made for you,*' Rixende Amiel was saying to her guests. '*We mountain women have no fine sieves. And we don't even know how to knead good bread!*'

'*Nothing of the sort,*' replied an unknown guest, '*your bread was extremely good.*'

'*I am delighted you enjoyed it,*' answered Rixende.

Raymond Sicre had to know who the Amiels' unknown guests were. His method of finding out shows the ramshackle nature of the cottage where the party was being held.

I went to the corner of the house, which was near the door. And with my head I lifted up a part of the roof. I took good care not to damage the roof covering. I then saw [in the kitchen] *two men sitting on a bench. They were facing the fire, with their backs to me. They had hoods over their heads and I could not see their faces.*

'*This is excellent cheese,*' said one of them.

'*They make very good cheeses in these mountains of ours,*' said Jean-Pierre Amiel.

'*No,*' said the other, not very politely, '*there are better cheeses in the mountains of Orlu and Mérens.*'

Then the other stranger said: '*The fish you gave us was just as good as your cheese! Really excellent!*'

'*Yes, indeed,*' said the other visitor, '*better and fresher than those I usually get in the valley of Ascou and the valley of Orlu.*'

'*The person who sent me that fish did a good deed,*' said Rixende. '*And Gaillarde d'Ascou has been very kind to me too. She prepared the oil for the fish. She prepared it in secret, and in great fear! She would be a very good woman, better than all the other women in the village. But she is terribly afraid of her husband.*'

'*Gaillarde is an excellent woman,*' agreed one of the men in blue hoods. '*But her husband is a miserable peasant, a lousy crop-eared hypocrite.*'

'*Gaillarde's husband is an excellent man,*' said Rixende. '*He is very pleasant to talk to. And he is a good neighbour; he doesn't harm anyone else's crops, and he won't let anyone else harm his.'*

After a pause, during which wine was handed round, the two visitors began to guide the conversation towards their own propaganda.

'*It would be a good thing if the people of Ascou and Sorgeat had a church. Then they wouldn't need to go down to the church in Ax-les-Thermes,'* said the first.

'*No,'* said the second, '*I don't agree. It's better if the people of Ascou have only the church at Ax. Otherwise it would be too expensive. Anyhow, the priests at Ax and in other places don't teach the inhabitants of Ascou as they should. They make them eat grass, as a shepherd makes his sheep eat grass when he gathers them under his crook.'*

'*The priests teach the people very little,'* rejoined the first visitor. '*Not half of their parishioners go to hear them preach or understand anything of what they say.'*

We do not know any more of what passed between the two Amiels and the two hooded visitors. Fifteen years later, Raymond Sicre had forgotten, and in any case he soon left his observation post in the corner of the roof to go and see to his sheep (ii.367). But the scene shows what an evening round the fire was like in Ascou and Montaillou. There was talk of food, and gossip about the neighbours and the parish. The two hooded guests were Cathar missionaries. One was none other than the notary Pierre Authié, who was well versed in people, manners and customs. He was something of a peasant himself, since he had his own herd of cattle. So he found no difficulty in taking part in popular conversation and orienting it towards anti-clerical themes, leading up to a Cathar sermon.

Homilies of this kind were common at evening gatherings both in Montaillou and among the exiles in Catalonia. In the little Cathar colony south of the Pyrenees there might be social exchanges among peasants and artisans at various times of the day. Ordinary meals or snacks in the morning or at noon, and dinners with twelve or fifteen guests might provide an opportunity for conversation tinged with ideology. Someone would unhook the ham from the rafter, someone else would hurry to the market to buy some fish for the *parfait*. Then the woman of the house would set about scaling the fish, and the rest would turn towards Bélibaste and demand: '*A speech! A good speech!'*

But the evening meal was ideologically the most important. As in the

New Testament parable of the wedding at Cana, the best wine would be put aside for the evening.

We ate the smallest of the fish, said Arnaud Sicre (ii.37), *and the heretic* [Bélibaste] *said to Pierre and Guillemette Maury: 'Keep the biggest fish for dinner, when Arnaud and Jean Maury, Guillemette's sons, and Pierre Maury, Guillemette's brother, will have come to join us.'*

Another evening Jean Maury, the shepherd's brother, arrived carrying a dead sheep over his shoulder. He had stolen it for the reunion dinner at Guillemette Maury's.

After dinner there would begin the long country-style evening around the fire. Those present included the hostess's two grown-up sons when they were not out keeping their sheep, together with her friends and relations, including Pierre Maury. There would also be a little group of passing *parfaits*, or some merry priests with their women, some poor beggars, or some women card-combers employed by Guillemette in the little carding shop which she had set up. The newcomers, to create a good impression, brought their own wine with them (ii.24).

Discussion would range over various topics. When only friends were present, the subject could be heresy. The veterans of Catharism would go over old memories: tricks played on the Inquisition by some woman heretic cleverer than its myrmidons; plots to murder a traitor or a bad daughter like Jeanne Befayt; or merely the problems of marrying off a son, questions of health or of removing a spell from some sheep which had been bewitched. The evening lasted until the embers were covered with ashes. The weaker brethren, remembering that they had to get up before dawn to go back to their sheep, would already have retired long since, two or three to a bed.

But it is in Montaillou itself, and in other villages in Aude and upper Ariège, that we see most clearly the regional customs prevalent at such evening gatherings. In the *domus* of the Belots (i.319 and *passim*), the Authiés were frequent visitors and often enlivened an evening with their eloquence, sitting with their hosts on benches round the fire. There were merry evenings, too, in the house of Pierre Maury's parents; together with their many children, they enjoyed themselves greatly at Christmas in 1304 or 1305 (iii.147 and n. 451). In Raymond Pierre's house at Arques, the Aude terminus of the migration route, Pierre Maury attended a big dinner in the kitchen, followed by an evening to which a *parfait* contributed (iii.122, 124). Master Pierre Girard, proxy of the Archbishop of Narbonne, made no bones about sitting down to dinner with rich farmers at the Bélibastes' house in Cubières (iii.139). The dinner at the Bélibastes' was followed by an evening with a heretic, Master Girard having previously been invited to go to bed.

The best descriptions of such evening gatherings in Montaillou are those of Jean Maury, Pierre Maury's brother (ii.469 ff.). It was because the meetings he relates were honoured by the presence of a goodman that they were made the subject of inquiry by the Inquisition. Apart from that they were typical, not particularly grand occasions. In 1323 Jean Maury told of two dinners followed by evening sessions which took place at his home in Montaillou around 1307 or 1308. On the first occasion, Jean's mother and father were present, together with his four brothers, Pierre, Arnaud, Bernard and Guillaume (all four of whom were, like Jean himself, to have a taste of prison sooner or later). Jean Maury's two sisters, Guillemette and Raymonde, were also there, both destined to marry very young, one in Laroque d'Olmes, and the other in Montaillou. The party was completed by two *parfaits*, Raymond Faur of Roussillon and Philippe d'Alayrac, who had arrived at the beginning of the evening. We recognize the typical work method of the goodmen, whose propaganda was effected 'intra-*domus*', among the members of one or two families at the most.

At the time, Jean Maury himself was twelve years old and kept his father's sheep. He arrived in the kitchen when the others were already there. At dinner only the grown-up men of the family – the father and his eldest son, Guillaume – sat at table with the two *parfaits*. The mother and daughters looked after everyone. The younger sons sat by the fire, respectfully munching the bread (probably blessed by the heretics) which their father sent across to them from time to time. The two *parfaits* were offered a modest repast of round loaves of bread and cabbage seasoned with oil. After dinner the men sat on a bench. The mother of the family, impure because she was a woman, sat on another bench. The children went to bed early, leaving the grown-ups to their serious discussions. One of the defects of education in Montaillou was that the young were thus excluded from general debate. Before he went to bed, Jean Maury just had time to notice that the conversation was monopolized, first by his father, then by the *parfait* Philippe d'Alayrac. Jean had to get up at break of day. Next morning he rose before it was light, and went off to tend his sheep.

There was another similar evening at the Maury house in Montaillou at about the same time (ii.469, 471). It took place in a very snowy January. The people present were much the same as before, and included the visiting Philippe d'Alayrac and Jean Maury himself, back as usual from a day spent keeping his sheep. There was the same segregation by seating: the *parfait* Philippe, Maury senior, his eldest son and their neighbour Guillaume Belot, who had escorted the heretic through the snow, all dined at table. The younger sons, the mother and the daughters ate and warmed themselves around the fire. Pieces of bread, blessed by Philippe, were passed from the table to the young men by the master.

There was no problem about lighting on such evenings. Since they took place in the kitchen, the fire provided light enough. Only when heretications took place in other rooms at night was it necessary to use a torch or a candle (i.436, 437). Heating too was provided by the kitchen fire, as late as Whitsuntide if necessary (iii.99).

The natives of Montaillou habitually drank water rather than wine. But they did take wine during these evening gatherings. It was predominantly the men who drank; the women and especially the girls pretended to be reluctant. Often the wine wasn't even offered to them. But things were easier in town and in the Catalan diaspora among the vineyards, and there it was a common thing, though usually restricted to men, to go to the local tavern for a drink and to fetch wine (ii.29, 33) to accompany a chat or celebrate a friendship. Evening gatherings in the mountains never degenerated into drunken orgies. The few cases of insobriety mentioned in the Fournier Register are urban, individual and sometimes merely simulated (iii.209; iii.14–50).

Convivial evenings in Montaillou were devoted to words rather than wine. The peasants of Ariège were connoisseurs of eloquence, even if they were no great orators themselves. We have seen how the exiles in Catalonia called on the *parfait* Bélibaste for a speech – though Pierre Maury noted that Bélibaste's skill at rhetoric was nothing beside that of Pierre and Jacques Authié. With his usual modesty, Pierre rated himself lowest of all. After a good fish dinner, Guillemette Maury and her guests would sometimes, for want of a *parfait*, ask Pierre to oblige them with a speech (iii.180): '*Come on, Pierre, a speech, a good speech!*' But Pierre always answered: '*You know I am no orator. I can't preach fine sermons.*'

This sort of cultural action in depth, practised on little groups of five to a dozen people, was not confined to artisan and peasant circles. Country priests had their own evening gatherings among themselves, with bitter battles of ideas. Both laymen and priests from various villages used to come and spend the evening around the fire with Amiel de Rives, perpetual *vicaire* of Junac. They talked about everything – the arguments in a book of homilies on the Resurrection of the body, whether or not the body survived after Judgment. Alazaïs, the priest's servant, was present at these discussions: despite differences in economic and social status, the social distance between employer and domestic was very much reduced during such evening gatherings. This was a world where a single room served as kitchen, dining-room and reception room.

CHAPTER XVI Social relationships

The *ostal* or *domus* was the chief unit in social relationships and cultural transmission, but there were other more general relationships.

If we begin with women, we find, not unexpectedly, that they are not organized as such, even at the monastic level. No women resembling nuns, whether bell-ringers or members of enclosed orders, were to be found except at much lower altitudes than the Pays d'Aillon: at Tarascon, at the confluence of the Ariège and the Vicdessos, Brune de Montels and Marie were enclosed nuns attached to the Church of the Virgin at Savart. There they entertained passing priests and pseudo-priests, offering them the characteristic dishes of the region. They were very harsh to the peasants who were excommunicated for not paying their tithes, and barred the door of the Virgin's shrine against them. But one cannot say that this pair alone constitutes a nunnery.[1]

In fourteenth-century upper Ariège there was, however, a certain sense of solidarity between women, sometimes tinged with anti-masculine feeling. *Gaillarde d'Ascou would be one of the best and bravest women in this village*, said Rixende Amiel of Ascou (ii.366–7), *if she wasn't so afraid of her husband*. More important were the special friendships between small groups of influential women, such as that which existed at Montaillou between the three matriarchs, Mengarde Clergue, Guillemette 'Belote' and Na Roqua (i.326, 328). They belonged to the leading, more well-to-do stratum of the village, and visited one another, took the sun together near the door to the cellar of the Clergue *domus* and sent parcels to whichever of them happened to be imprisoned by the Inquisition (i.229). They were the stoutest female militants among the Cathars of Montaillou. The other women influenced by heresy (we know of about ten in all) had been swayed by others: their own personal beliefs were not particularly strong, but they had yielded to the urgings of their relatives or of friendly *domus* already infected with heresy.

Another female quartet, less firm perhaps in its convictions, was formed by Gauzia Clergue, Guillemette 'Maurine', Guillemette 'Benete' and Sybille Fort. All four were heretics, great friends and wives of Montaillou farmers, members of the middle or lower middle

1 ii.316 and ii.33. See also the 'béguine' at Castlenaudary, with whom Blanche Marty of Junac took temporary refuge (iii.285).

class which formed the backbone of the village.[1] The bonds of friendship between them were reinforced by those of fellow-sponsorship.[2]

Such informal feminine networks existed before the coming of the Cathar missionaries, though they were widely exploited by them. Pierre Authié, for example, had a whole grid of female friends and sympathizers in upper Ariège, including Sybille Pierre, another married woman and a girl from Ax-les-Thermes (ii.425). Guillaume Authié specialized in preaching clandestine sermons to groups of women in Montaillou and Junac (i.477; iii.68-9, 273).

Social relationships among women transcended social class, especially in rural parishes. To avoid complete isolation, the *châtelaine* had to mix with the other local women; but she found it no hardship. Béatrice de Planissoles, formerly the *châtelaine* of Montaillou, had at least five close women friends in Dalou *in whom she could confide her secrets* (i.214, 215). They seem all to have been of the common people – the wives of peasants or even mere maidservants. (Such servants, who might sleep in their mistress's bedroom, would be her confidantes in love-affairs. They were half duennas and half bawds, and often knew things of which husbands were kept ignorant. To anyone they liked they were apt to reveal the secrets of the household which employed them (i.222, 256; iii.286), and were thus one of the main elements in the village's cultural and information systems.)

Both when she was living in Montaillou and afterwards in Prades, Béatrice used to make quite long journeys to Caussou and Junac. She went to see her sister, who had just had a baby. She also met Raymonde de Luzenac (i.237-8), *who clasped her to her bosom or embraced her because she was one of her relations*. In Montaillou itself she frequented even the most ordinary peasants, sitting round the fire with Raymonde Maury and Alazaïs Azéma, listening to the latest gossip, heretical or otherwise (i.234-7, 308). Sometimes she was so moved that she donated a sack of flour for the goodmen.

This kind of feminine relationship existed in town and in Catholic

---

1 iii.67-8 and iii.71. Guillemette 'Maurine' was in fact Guillemette Maury before her departure to Catalonia.

2 ii.224. For example, Mengarde Clergue was Guillemette Belot's fellow-sponsor. It may be noted also that Béatrice de Planissoles was the fellow-sponsor of Clergue the priest, son of Mengarde Clergue, which meant a further strengthening of the links between the former *châtelaine* and the group of Cathar matriarchs (i.253).

circles, as well as in the country, among Cathars. In Pamiers, the wife of the nobleman Guillaume de Voisins attended mass in the Church of St John the Martyr with a group of women friends. In the villages there might also be special bonds of affectionate patronage between noblewomen and countrywomen. Alazaïs Azéma of Montaillou – widow, cheesemonger and pig-farmer – bought supplies from Rixende Palharès, a cheesemaker of Luzenac who was mistress to a local nobleman (iii.496). Soon afterwards Alazaïs met one of Rixende's other customers, Raymonde de Luzenac, a noblewoman, who at once embraced her in the name of their common affection for Alazaïs's son, who aspired to be a *parfait* (i.313, 300).

The ladies did not merely indulge in idle gossip. Trade gave them the opportunity to exchange important information. Rixende Palharès, as well as selling cheese, was also a professional messenger, travelling ceaselessly from Limoux to Lordat, from Ax-les-Thermes to Tarascon. Alazaïs Azéma performed the same important office. *One day*, said Alazaïs (i.318), *I was going to Sorgeat to buy cheeses and I saw, sitting at the door of her house, Gaillarde, the wife of Raymond Escaunier. As Gaillarde was my cousin, I sat down beside her. And she said to me:* 'Cousin, do you know that the Authiés are back?'

And I answered: 'But where have they been?'

'In Lombardy,' she said. 'They spent everything they had there and became heretics.'

'And what are these heretics like?'

'They are good and holy men.'

'In the name of God,' said I, 'perhaps it is a good thing!'

And I went away.

No doubt the news soon spread. The mill was another scene for mainly feminine gatherings and exchanges. The usual division of labour in upper Ariège meant that it was the women who took the wheat to be ground, carrying it on mules and then bringing it back as flour (i.151). One day in 1319, in Ax-les-Thermes, the miller Guillaume Caussou was the only man among a crowd of women from the neighbourhood. Valentin Barra of Ax, who was related to the local pro-Cathar nobility, had just been murdered. Whereupon such supernatural sounds were heard at night in the churchyard where he lay that the priest dared not sleep in the church. This topic gave Jaquette den Carot the opportunity to deny the Resurrection of the body. '*Sancta Maria,*' she said, '*to*

*know our mothers and fathers after death! To return from death to life! ...
To come to life with the same bones and in the same flesh as that which we
have now! What an idea!* And she vowed she did not believe a word
of it. The miller, scandalized, replied that the Resurrection of the body
must be true *'because the Minorite friars and the priests have found it
written in the books and the records'*. And then, unable to face up any
longer to the crowd of women, Guillaume Caussou went back to his
work. A little girl of twelve, a priest's maidservant, was present that
day, and later denounced Jaquette den Carot as a blasphemer.

The fetching of water was another specifically feminine activity
which favoured the exchange of ideas. The women usually fetched
water, in jars balanced on their heads, from a spring at some distance
from the village. *Fifteen years ago*, related Raymonde Marty of Montaillou (iii.103), *I was coming back from fetching water with Guillemette
Argelliers of Montaillou. And Guillemette said to me: 'Did you see the
goodmen (in other words the heretics) in your father's house?'*

'Yes,' I answered.

'Those goodmen,' said Guillemette, *'are good Christians. They keep the
Roman faith which was kept by the Apostles, Peter, Paul and John, and
so on.'*

Other occasions for social exchanges between women might be in the
kitchen at evening time, before the men got home from work; in bed,
with three to a bed, two peasants and a noblewoman (iii.67; ii.291, 366);
during a delousing session (i.462–3; iii.288); in the village square
(i.335–7, 316); when there were corpses to be laid out, watched over,
buried and commented upon. (Between death-bed and burial, people
became the property of the women, as they had been, when alive,
during their infancy.) There were also the ordinary daily exchanges of
women lending things to one another, spinning together or merely
chatting.

This tide of feminine talk arising from every village dealt, among
other things, with this one's childbed and that one's heresy.[1] When
trying to appraise the importance of this chatter we should not forget
that peasant women in those days were generally neither more nor less
educated than their male counterparts. The long-lasting discrimination
introduced later by parish schools, meant chiefly for boys, was then

1 i.310: Alazaïs Azéma spreads the *rumour of Montaillou* about the dubious love-
affairs of Béatrice de Planissoles with Pathau and Pierre Clergue.

practically non-existent. So feminine conversation was then as sensible and serious as masculine exchanges. Women's inferiority was linked to their physical weakness and their specialization in what were considered inferior jobs (cooking, gardening, carrying water, childbearing, bringing up children).

It was at noon that the word really came into its own. When Guillemette Clergue went to her parents' house to get the mule to fetch corn from Tarascon she found the door closed. This was quite natural: the men were still in the field with the mule, collecting turnips. But the women of the neighbourhood were there, in the street and on their doorsteps (i.340). Sometimes one man on his own might go by and crack a joke or even make a dash at the women, who were, or pretended to be, duly frightened.

'*You're a rascal!*' they cried.

'*No worse than the Bishop of Pamiers!*' was the reply (ii.368, 258).

Social exchanges between women might be repeated every day: *In Montaillou*, says Alazaïs Fauré (i.416), *Guillemette 'Benete', Guillemette Argelliers, Gauzia 'Belote' and Mengarde, the priest's mother, went almost daily to the house of Raymond Belot.* The Belot household was a heretical one.

For women, speech was a way of getting back some of the power usually reserved to men. The bolder spirits among them would try to urge on the more timid to revolt, though the usual result was that the latter remained obedient to their husbands.[1]

Fourteen years ago, said Raymonde Marty of Montaillou, *I went to the house of my brother-in-law Bernard Marty of Montaillou.*[2] *Sitting at the door of the house I found Guillemette 'Benete' and Alazaïs Rives (wife of Bernard Rives). They said: 'Sit here with us for a moment, niece.'*

But I remained standing. And they said: 'You should give alms to the heretics. Not to give them presents (when you possess the goods of this world, in other words wool and your husband's other wealth) is to act badly! For the heretics are good men.'

'The heretics will not taste my possessions,' I answered . . .

'You are wicked! You have a heart of ice!' they said.

But I turned my back on them.

1 See ii.415 and i.338 for a friendship between two peasant women *against* men.
2 iii.107. Raymonde Marty was Guillaume Marty's wife and Pierre Maury's sister. This Bernard Marty should not be confused with Bernard Marty of Junac.

So while the men of Montaillou controlled the essential structures of power, the women might be said to play an important part in the secret service. Hence, perhaps, their inquisitiveness.

At the time when I lived in the house of Raymond and his brothers, said Raymonde Testanière (i.459–60), *the Belots built a new* solier *above their kitchen . . . I suspected that the heretics had come and were sleeping in the* solier. *So one day, towards the hour of vespers, after having fetched water, hearing people speak in low voices in the* solier, *I left the brothers Bernard and Raymond Belot and their mother, Guillemette, warming themselves around the fire, and went out into the courtyard. In the court-yard there was a big tall dungheap, from the top of which you could see through a chink in the wall what was going on in the* solier. *I climbed up on the dungheap, and through the chink I looked round the said* solier, *and in a corner of the room I saw Guillaume Belot, Bernard Clergue and the heretic Guillaume Authié, speaking to each other in low voices. Suddenly, Guillaume Clergue came along. I was frightened. I got down off my dungheap.*

'What were you looking for in the courtyard?' asked Guillaume.

'I was looking for the cushion which I put on my head to carry my pitcher of water,' I answered.

'Be off with you. It's time you went back into the house,' said Guillaume.

There are endless examples of this feminine curiosity in the Pays d'Aillon. Raymonde Capblanch told Emersende Garsin (i.278): '*In Prades, through a hole in a door, I saw Pierre or Guillaume Authié heretichate a sick man.*' Raymonde was so indiscreet on the subject that people were afraid the Inquisition would come and destroy her father's and mother's *ostal*. In Montaillou, Guillemette Clergue, going along the street one day with a pitcher of water on her head, saw two men dressed in green in the house of the Belots. She went back to get a better look. They immediately hid: so they must have been heretics (i.347). Alazaïs Azéma was even more unscrupulous: she stole quietly into the Belots' house to spy on a goodman (i.311). In Prades, Mengarde Savignan and Alazaïs Romieu were sent to bed – the same bed – by Gaillarde Authié, wife of Guillaume Authié the *parfait* (ii.149), so as to keep as secret as possible the evening ceremony in which Guillaume was to heretichate Arnaud Savignan, Mengarde's father-in-law, who was seriously ill. But Mengarde left the door ajar between her bedroom and the kitchen where the old man was dying. She put her eye to the crack and was able to follow the scene, dimly lit by the embers of the kitchen fire, smothered in ashes. At the funeral of Guillemette 'Belote' in Montaillou, the two groups of women, Catholics on one side and Cathars on the other, watched and eavesdropped on one another (i.462).

Men in upper Ariège were inquisitive enough, sometimes morbidly so. But their curiosity was nothing beside that of the women. It was not until the advent of more bourgeois stages of civilization, with their concern for privacy, that this kind of female spying decreased.

The women of Montaillou, especially the young ones, were also fond of firing off a series of questions at one another. Guillemette Clergue interrogates her sister-in-law Alazaïs Roussel (i.337-9): '*What has happened – did your husband beat you?... And where is my uncle* [Prades Tavernier] *going?... And where does he mean to sleep tonight?... And where is Master Prades Tavernier?... And why hasn't your mother, Alazaïs, come?... And why doesn't Prades Tavernier weave linen any more?*'

Guillemette Clergue, in another conversation, this time with her mother, as they are harvesting together, fires off another battery of questions (i.334-5):

'*And where is my brother Pons?*'

('*He has gone away with uncle Prades Tavernier.*')

'*And what is uncle Prades Tavernier doing with the lady Stéphanie de Chateauverdun? Why has he left his house and trade, and sold his possessions?*'

('*He and Stéphanie have gone to Barcelona.*')

'*And what do Prades and Stéphanie mean to do in Barcelona?*'

('*They have gone to see the goodmen.*')

'*And who are these goodmen?*'

('*They touch neither woman nor meat. They are called heretics.*')

'*And how can they be goodmen, if they are called heretics?*'

('*You are a silly, ignorant girl. They are goodmen because they send people's souls to Heaven.*')

'*And how can heretics send souls to Heaven, when priests hear confession and handle the body of the Lord, so that, it is said, souls may be saved?*'

('*It is plain that you are young and ignorant.*')

The dialogue then ends, and the two women continue to reap the corn in the family field at Alacot below the village of Montaillou.

Whether there was a specifically feminine system of values is obscured by the fact that the women of Montaillou, with a few notable exceptions, were passive rather than active elements in Cathar propaganda.[1] They accepted Catharism rather vaguely, as something come to them from without, because their husbands, fathers, brothers, lovers, friends, employers, cousins or neighbours had compromised or even trapped them into it. Often, except in the special case of the matriarchs, the women of Montaillou rallied to the heretic cause only temporarily and superficially; they had no intention of going as far as the stake. They felt strange and uncomfortable in their new, unorthodox identity, and resistance soon stirred in hearts steeped in traditional thought and full of irrepressible feeling. For example, Brune Pourcel, the poor bastard girl, allowed herself to be affected for a moment by the arguments of Alazaïs Rives, who told her that only the goodmen could save souls (i.383). But, as Brune related: *Even before I left the courtyard of Alazaïs's house, I came back to my own heart, and said to her: 'But how can the goodmen, who hide themselves, really save souls?'*

Béatrice de Planissoles, on a higher social level, beset by heretic propaganda, declared (i.238): '*No, I have not met the goodmen, and I can find no reasons in my heart why I should meet them.*'

Whether it was a question of spying on their male neighbours or remaining loyal to ancient beliefs, the women of Montaillou were more often than not governed by their emotions. Friendship between women was not usually competitive, but rather a matter of complicity.[2]

Social relationships between men were more comprehensive than those between women, and more important politically. We have seen these relationships at work in evening gatherings among friends, where

1 See the cases of Alazaïs Azéma, Raymonde Arsen, Brune Pourcel, Alazaïs Fauré, Allemande Guilhabert, Guillemette Argelliers, Guillemette Maury and Gauzia Clergue, all of Montaillou. Their meetings with, and adoration of, the *parfaits*, were far from spontaneous (i.311, 373–5, 386, 415, 423; iii.68, 99, 363).

2 It may be that the development of social relationships between men, resulting from the progress of the consular system in the thirteenth and fourteenth centuries, entailed a certain diminution of feminine influence. Perhaps that was the price that had to be paid for 'democratization'. We may recall that Bernard Clergue, the *bayle*, a typical representative of pre-consular power, did all he could to oblige the women of his mother-in-law's *domus*.

Catharism reinforced the age-long tendency separating men from women. Men also communicated among themselves at work in the fields, especially in the ploughing and harvest seasons (i.400 and *passim*). They might also meet together to play games or sing. At Prades d'Aillon, near Montaillou, seven or eight villagers, all men, came regularly to the house of Pierre Michel, nicknamed *Le Rouge*, to play at dice and chess. According to Raymonde de Poujols, Michel's daughter (ii.401), they were so absorbed in their games that *they did not even bother to go and see the* parfait *Prades Tavernier, who was hiding in my father's cellar*. Sometimes meetings between men took the form of musical evenings: a flute was a necessary part of every shepherd's equipment, and of one who was ruined it was said that he no longer had *even a flute* (ii.182). At an all-male dinner at the house of Hughes de Sournia on Assumption Day there were eight people present, including a young mendicant friar who was allowed to sit at the foot of the table (ii.123). Before the meal, for aesthetic rather than religious reasons, the young man was asked to sing the Ave Maria and when he gave his performance too pious a tone, the rest of the party told him off. Similarly, in Pamiers, it was in the choir of the church, perhaps reserved for men, that there was a whispered performance of the troubadour Pierre Cardenal's *cobla* against the priests (iii.328).

But more significant were the gatherings where the men of the neighbourhood met in the street, or in the village square under the elm tree, especially on Sunday. This was the Christianized form of the eternal Mediterranean assembly. The talk would be of women and, above all, of religion (i.475; iii.301). *That same year*, said Guillaume Austatz, the peasant *bayle* of Ornolac, in 1320, *after the heretic Raymond de la Côte had been burned near Pamiers, six men of Ornolac were gathered by the elm tree in the village square one Sunday; they were talking about the heretic's execution. I came up to them and said: 'Let me tell you, the man they burned there was a good priest.'*[1]

On another occasion, also in Ornolac, seven men (of whom four or five took part in the discussion just mentioned) were again gathered together in the village square (i.202). This time the subject of conversation was what happened to souls after death, and how large Heaven must be in order to accommodate the souls of all the people who died every day. (Perhaps there was an epidemic at the time.) Guillaume

1 i.208. Raymond de la Côte was a Waldensian who lived in Pamiers.

Austatz told the other seven men that Heaven was bigger than a huge house stretching from Toulouse to the Mérens Pass in the Pyrenees: so there was no immediate danger of a housing crisis in Heaven.

In 1323, Bernard Jean, the village priest in Bédeillac, described another masculine assembly (iii.51). *One holiday, I think it was the Sunday before the Feast of St John, after the midday meal, between nones and vespers, Arnaud de Bédeillac and I, and some other men of the village, I remember only three of their names . . . were under the elm by the churchyard. I was the only one sitting down, the others were standing. We were talking about the wheat harvest: 'It gave us some anxiety,' said one man, 'but thank God it turned out all right.'* (iii.51).

Arnaud de Bédeillac then said it was not God who watched over the harvest but nature alone. The priest was very shocked, and Arnaud turned on his heel and left.

Such gatherings were common in Bédeillac. A few days later there was another. *That same year*, said Adhémar de Bédeillac (iii.52), *Arnaud de Bédeillac and I, Bernard Jean the priest and some other men whose names I have forgotten, were under an elm tree in front of Bédeillac church, and we were talking about a certain spring in the diocese of Couserans. Someone said that in the olden days someone had fried some fish near the fountain, but the fish jumped out of the pan into the fountain and you can still see them there, fried just on one side!*

Whereupon Arnaud de Bédeillac remarked that God certainly produced a lot of miracles in those days. Bernard Jean the priest, who easily lost his temper, rebuked Arnaud, who only repeated his blasphemies. The village square in Bédeillac was an anticipation, in miniature, of a free-thinking café in the nineteenth century. At Goulier, a parish in Vicdessos, there were pro-Cathar discussions, and occasionally blows, between farmer-priests and ordinary peasants, sometimes accompanied by a few women, on the subject of the 'two Gods' (i.350–69).

Sometimes this kind of public debate between men was linked to similar discussions in the *domus* (i.350). But men could also act independently of family and personal connections. Raymond de l'Aire was a peasant of Tignac and a bold free-thinker: he denied, at one fell swoop, the Resurrection, the Crucifixion and the Incarnation. One day in the village square, talking with three or four or more of his fellow citizens (ii.132), he declared that the soul was only blood, that it was mortal, that there was no other world or age than our own, and so on. At this point Jacques Fournier pressed his questions further.

'*Did you speak of these errors to your wife, Sybille?*'

'*No.*'

'*Did you speak of them to your sister-in-law Raymonde Rey, who was for some time your concubine, despite the fact that she was your sister-in-law?*'

Again the answer was negative.

'*Or with your son, Raymond?*'

'*Not with him either.*'

Men also challenged institutions, especially those of the Church, which were debated much more frequently than lay institutions. In 1320 under the elm tree in the square at Lordat, five villagers were talking about the tithe on lambs, which would soon be due (ii.122).

'*We're going to have to pay the* carnelages,', said one of them.

'*Don't let's pay anything,*' answered another. '*Let us rather find a hundred livres to pay two men to kill the Bishop.*'

'*I'll willingly pay my share,*' said a third. '*Money could not be better spent.*'

The village of Quié, situated lower down than Montaillou but otherwise not very different, provides the clearest picture of these subversive male gatherings. Raymond de Laburat, farmer and vine-grower, gives a detailed account of the many informal masculine gatherings, large and small, which took place at Easter and on Palm Sunday, sometimes in the village itself, sometimes outside Savart church in Tarascon-sur-Ariège, which served Quié as parish church. The people of Quié also went to the local market there. Still in Savart, they might also meet near the cloth mill at Cabesses.[1] The role played here by the church at Savart shows how social relationships between men might act as a link between town and country.

The male half of the population regarded the village church as its own property, built as it was by their own labour, voluntary or forced. In it, bishops and priests were thought of as exercising only a kind of usufruct. '*The church and its bells belong to us,*' said Raymond de Laburat to a group of male villagers who had been excommunicated.

1 For Raymond de Laburat's evidence see ii.309–28. At only one of these meetings were a few women present.

'*We built it, we bought and put in it everything that was necessary. We keep it up. Woe to the Bishop and priests who drive us out of our parish church; who prevent us from hearing Mass there, and make us stand outside in the rain.*' Raymond de Laburat, like the rest of them, had been excommunicated for non-payment of tithes. He suggested that an unofficial Mass should be held out of doors (ii.311, 320).

All these masculine gatherings went to make up an unofficial community underlying the official community with its consuls, criers and other elected or co-opted functionaries (ii.453). Such informal groups defended traditional privileges against innovations imposed by the Church. When the bishop's agents and the consuls sent representatives to collect the tithes on cattle (ii.315), Raymond de Laburat said to a group of a dozen or so peasants: '*If only all the clerks and priests could go and dig and plough the earth . . . as for the Bishop, let him meet me in a mountain pass; we will fight out this question of tithes, and I shall soon see what the bishop is made of!*'

In Montaillou itself and the Pays d'Aillon in general, relationships of this kind between men were less in evidence than they were in Quié or Lordat. Perhaps this was because of the ideological dissension here, the fear of informers and the fact that church institutions were somewhat devalued. Moreover, Montaillou was the home of the travelling shepherds, and the most important meetings between men often took place outside the village – in the mountain passes, in the *cabanes* in the pastures at shearing or milking time, or in town, at the lamb or wool markets, rather than under the elm tree in front of the church.[1] Nevertheless, the communities of the Pays d'Aillon did have their own masculine slant. In Prades and Montaillou, official letters from the Bishop on the subject of heresy in the parish were read in the presence of a group of men, including leading citizens with the familiar names of Benet, Clergue, Argelliers, etc. The privileged position of such people vis-à-vis the community as a whole is underlined in the matter of

---

1 There are certain characteristic features of Montaillou – the highly developed social relationships between women, the absence, before 1320, of consular institutions, the comparative absence of public and official social relationships between men, and the strength of the traditional, seigneurial institution of the *baylie* – which suggest a logically structured whole in direct contrast to the more modern structures of villages which had consuls, highly developed public relations between men, and so on.

names. At Prades d'Aillon seven men at least were called 'Prades', a fact which brings out the quasi-tribal links between the male section of the population and the name and genius of the place.[1]

The evidence of social relationships between young people as such in Montaillou is very limited. One reason for this was probably the large number of young men involved in migration. Another factor was the disproportion in marriage age between the girls, who tended to get married while still adolescent, and the young men, who remained single until twenty-five or after. In general the division between men and women, was, if not more important, at least more consciously felt in Montaillou than the division between young and old. But there are some allusions to the way young people amused themselves. At La Bastide-Serou and at Junac, the children watching over the pigs and cattle played among themselves and ate the beet and turnips. They would slice a round of beet and one of them would elevate it like the Host, a parody also practised by witches in the Pyrenees in the sixteenth century. Young labourers harvesting millet would play pranks in the barn they used as a dormitory, where their employer had packed them in several to a bed. The game soon got past the stage of a mere pillow fight and one of the young workers, Pierre Acès, parodied the elevation of the Host and pretended a drinking glass was a chalice. The other young men were shocked. A few days later their employer dismissed Pierre Acès as a dangerous idler and chatterbox. One of the witnesses, threatened with a knife, informed on him, and he was brought before Fournier's tribunal (iii.455–6).

Probably these adolescent escapades, sometimes tinged with deeper cultural connotations, implied some awareness of young people as a special age-group. Aude Fauré, who lived with her husband in Murviel (Ariège) but came from Lafage (Aude), had not taken communion since her wedding at the age of seventeen or eighteen (ii.82–3). When her husband asked why not, she said, '*Because, in the village of Lafage, where I come from, the young men and women are not in the habit of receiving the Body of Christ.*' Perhaps, then, there was a kind of age-group from which one emerged at one's 'first communion', a rite of passage which took place at the age of nineteen or twenty and, in the case of girls, often

1 ii.239, 256; iii.504 and *passim*. See also ii.366 for the same phenomenon in the village of Ascou.

coincided with marriage. The young people liked singing, dancing and playing games, and sometimes invited recently married couples to join them. Guillemette Clergue, born and married in Montaillou, relates (i.338): *On the day of the Feast of St Peter and St Paul, after Mass and the midday meal, I went to play and dance with the other lads and lasses in the village of Prades; in the evening I went to my uncle's house in Prades for dinner.*

The boys seduced by Arnaud de Verniolles wrestled and danced before satisfying his desires (iii.42 and *passim*). But dancing was not a privilege confined to the very young. In 1296, at Béatrice de Planissoles's wedding, Guillaume Authié, already getting on in years, was one of the 'tumblers'. Later on he was popular in Montaillou because of his skill in leading the dance (i.218).

But social groupings existed other than those of age and sex. A tavern, in its most fully developed form, was run by a woman or a married couple. Most of its customers were men, but there were women too. The old stereotyped idea that taverns, like bars in the years 1900–50, were reserved for men, does not apply to upper Ariège in the fourteenth century or to the *ancien régime* in France in general.[1]

In Montaillou itself, and in most purely rural villages which imported wine, the tavern existed only in an embryonic form. Fabrisse Rives, for example, sold wine in Montaillou (i.325–6), but we do not know for sure whether she received her customers in a shop. Her main activity consisted in supplying wine on demand at the houses of other inhabitants of the village. As we have seen, her professional equipment was not very adequate.

Real taverns with public rooms were found only in the small towns, the larger villages and in other trading centres. There, on fair and market days, the country folk rubbed shoulders with men and women, priests and laymen from other regions and other social circles than their own. At Foix there was a big tavern run by Pierre Cayra; his wife, Gaillarde, measured out the wine. It was here that people from the towns and villages of the Comté de Foix – mostly men, but a few women too – commented on the execution of a Waldensian heretic, with its miraculous details. '*The condemned man threw up his hands to Heaven when*

1 When men and women drank together, either in a tavern or in a private house, the man was usually passing through and the woman was usually the hostess (iii.197).

the fire destroyed his bonds.' People like Bérenger Escoulan of Foix used to go round the various taverns in the town (i.174) collecting and distributing news. Tavern conversations would subsequently be relayed to the mountain villages, where it made its contribution to protest against the burning of heretics and the imposition of tithes (i.195). Certain taverns were known as meeting places for the heretics. *I went to Ax-les-Thermes*, says Guillaume Escaunier of Ax (ii.14), *and as I went through Coustaussa I stopped in a tavern and had a drink. Some of the customers knew that I was a believer and asked me: 'Where are you going?'*

'To Ax,' I answered. 'I am going to find a heretic to hereticate my mother, who is dying.'

Then a young man who was there (it was Pierre Montanier, I think) said to me: 'You need not go alone. I'll come with you.'

And we set off together for Ax.

But the tavern was only secondary. The great occasion which brought the villagers together, whether from their houses or from the pastures, was Sunday Mass. Even though taverns were sometimes frequented by peasants, they were chiefly an urban phenomenon. But the Mass was everywhere, sung or spoken (i.145) in every parish (except, as we have seen, where a village had no parish church of its own and the inhabitants had to go to the nearest town).

Even for unbelievers and heretics the Mass could serve a useful purpose. It might serve as a meeting-place for plotting a kidnapping (iii.151). For Catholics, it was of course the central point of their religious life. As Gaillarde Cayra, who helped to keep the tavern in Foix, said (i.169), *Our whole salvation consists in the Mass*. As regards Montaillou itself, even Cathar sympathizers like Pierre Maury and Béatrice de Planissoles, whether at home in Ariège or in exile, went to Mass quite regularly, or at least from time to time (iii.136). By a kind of dual belief which was not then regarded as shocking, they even showed a special Catholic piety to some particular saint, Béatrice offering coloured candles at the altar of the Virgin and Pierre Maury donating fleeces to the altar of Saint Anthony.

So although regular attendance was probably not universal in Montaillou, the Mass did bring together people of all ages and both sexes.

Hence its importance in propagating subversive ideas. Heresy was spread not only against but also through the Mass. The ideas in question might be derived from a book by some semi-intellectual priest, who then preached them to his illiterate parishioners. Amiel de Rieux, perpetual *vicaire* of Junac, preached a sermon which denied the Resurrection of the Body to a congregation of some fifty villagers (iii.19): '*You must know* [he used the singular pronoun, 'tu', as if speaking to a single individual] *that at the Last Judgment you will come to life again in flesh and blood. And so you will hear your judgment both in body and in soul. But after the Judgment your soul will go either to Heaven or to Hell; while your body will return to the grave and turn to dust . . . that is what I read in a book!*'

Of course there were some rural free-thinkers who occasionally maintained that the whole Mass, whether spoken or sung, was rubbish (i.145, 148). Nevertheless, even in a place like Montaillou, the Sunday Mass remained one of the chief occasions for communication both with the outside world and within the village itself.

The main social categorizations, by age and sex, contributed in fact to overall solidarity rather than division. In Montaillou, the domination by adult males did not provoke rebellion either among the women or among the young people. It was accepted and, as far as possible, shared with fairly good grace.

The real sources of division were the various village clans, divided one against the other and each incorporating for its own ends a series of other *domus* or parts of *domus*. At its worst this polarization could divide the village up into unequal halves. Between 1295 and 1300 Montaillou was dominated by the Clergue clan and its allies. As the priest himself said, this clan held the whole community *between its feet*. It was so powerful that it finally came to embody almost the whole local society. '*The priest Pierre Clergue protects us,*' Alazaïs Fauré told her mother, Allemande Guilhabert, to persuade her to have her sick son hereticated (i.413–14); '*of all the men in the village, there is not one who will denounce us.*' For the dominating families of Montaillou (the Belots, Benets, Clergues, Forts, Maurys, Martys and Rives), Catharism was a kind of togetherness. The three chief families (Belots, Benets, Clergues), the Clergues at their head, were reciprocally linked together by marriage. Bernard Clergue the *bayle*, romantically in love with Raymonde Belot, married her with a smaller dowry than he might have demanded with a richer girl, in view of his own social rank in the region. But, as he himself said (ii.427), he preferred to demonstrate in this way that there was a bond of love and of clan solidarity, as well as of belief, between the Clergues and the Belots.

The links between the Belots and the Benets were also consolidated by marriage. Guillemette Benet married Bernard Belot, whose mother, old Guillemette, saw the dangers in this union (i.455). '*Misfortune will come upon our* ostal *because of these Benets, who are on too good terms with the Authiés*', Guillemette told her son. Ultimately the old woman was right, but in the short term, before the Inquisition struck, the Benet family were the focal point of heresy in the village. It was in this *domus*, with the agreement of Guillaume Benet and his wife, that the Authiés stayed for the first time when they returned from Lombardy in 1300 (i.471). Once the Benet *ostal* had been contaminated, it infected the whole community with heresy. The Belot–Benet alliance, buttressed by the Belot-Clergue axis, built up an almost invulnerable Cathar front, supported by a wide network of other relationships. This whole structure was dominated by the Clergue family, thanks to its wealth and to the respective powers of the two brothers, Pierre the priest complementing Bernard the *bayle* who exercised local power in the village in the absence of the lord of the manor.

And yet, even then, at the very beginning of the fourteenth century, there was an opposition group in Montaillou. It consisted of two *domus*, the Liziers and the Azémas. The resistance put up by the Liziers did not last long. Anonymous assassins, perhaps in the pay of the Clergues, killed Raymond Lizier, the head of the *ostal*, a simple peasant *who was a good Catholic and hated the heretics* (iii.65; i.296). Perhaps the murderers were helped by Raymonde, née d'Argelliers, Raymond Lizier's wife. At all events, she married Arnaud Belot soon after Raymond Lizier's death. The circumstances of the murder were never cleared up and the funeral oration pronounced upon the victim was brief (ii.427): '*Raymond Lizier of Montaillou did not love the heretics. And they used him roughly. His corpse was found, recently killed, outside the château of Montaillou.*' It was a great relief to the Cathars. As Pierre Maury said (iii.162), '*Since Raymond Lizier's death, we have no more to fear from his house.*'

Much more formidable than the Liziers' was the *domus* of the Azémas, led by the old and terrifying Na Carminagua, Raymonde Azéma (i.460). One of her sons was a good Catholic, an unusual thing in Montaillou at this time. He was practically the only person in the whole place whom Guillaume Authié mistrusted (i.279). The orthodoxy of the other son,

Pierre Azéma, was more doubtful, and at first Pierre Authié regarded him as a friend of the heretics. Later the Clergues took advantage of this youthful error on Pierre Azéma's part to have him imprisoned at Carcassonne. Did Pierre Azéma return to Catholicism when he was older? Or did he enjoy the struggle for predominance for its own sake? Whatever the true explanation, when the Clergue family began to decline, Pierre Azéma was their main challenger and the chief candidate for supreme power in Montaillou.

The Azémas were peasants like the other inhabitants of Montaillou, but they were distant cousins of Bishop Fournier, and this lent them a certain modest distinction. Their friends in the village included the Pellissiers, the Fourniers and the family of Na Longa (iii.75), mother of Gauzia Clergue. Na Longa may have been the widow of Raymond Marty of Camurac; she lived in Montaillou, probably in the *domus* of her late father.

The Clergues, who feared no one, were nevertheless very wary of the Azéma family around 1305. Both the Clergues and Belots (i.460) steered well clear of the redoubtable Na Carminagua and her son.

But the Azéma family alone were not a real danger to the Clergues. It was only after 1305, when the Inquisitors at Carcassonne began to come into the picture, that things began to change. The Clergue faction simultaneously strengthened its position and began to disintegrate. Its leaders continued to protect their clients and friends as best they could. When Raymonde d'Argelliers, widow of Raymond Lizier, foolishly tried to tell Pierre Clergue the priest about the suspicious behaviour of certain female citizens of Montaillou whom she had seen in the company of a *parfait*, the priest soon shut her up. '*Something unpleasant will happen to you,*' he told her (iii.71), '*if you denounce Gauzia Clergue, Sybille Fort, Guillemette "Benete" and Guillemette "Maurine", who are better than you are. If you say anything whatever against these women, look out, or you will lose your body, your house and your possessions.*' Raymonde, whose husband had been killed by his fellow-villagers, did not need telling twice.

But repression grew more severe, and the system of protective patronage which the Clergues had established began to show some cracks. The Belot-Clergue alliance, for example, was shaken and almost destroyed. True, Bernard Clergue the *bayle* remained faithful to his youthful passion for Raymonde Belot, now his wife, and vice versa. At the worst, there were a few domestic rows between them (i.399), caused by

Raymonde's inability to follow her husband's ideological reversals. Raymonde, speaking on Bernard's behalf, personally threatened her fellow parishioners when they betrayed their clan loyalty and acted as informers to the Inquisitors of Pamiers (i.466).

But while the relationship between the *bayle* and his wife remained more or less intact, his connection with her family, the Belots, deteriorated. The Inquisitors of Carcassonne made use of the Clergues as their agents on the one hand, and on the other they persecuted the heretics, including the Belots. Such a situation was bound to cause trouble. As early as 1306, Bernard Clergue threatened his mother-in-law, Guillemette 'Belote', of whom he had once been so fond, that he would have her locked up in Carcassonne (i.347). He made similar threats to his brother-in-law, Guillaume, Guillemette's son. We do not know how serious all this was: Bernard Clergue was in the habit of talking like that, even to his own mother (ii.432). But Mengarde Clergue was revered by her other sons, and no harm came to her. In the case of Guillemette Belot, she soon found herself in prison at Carcassonne, though we do not know how far her son-in-law was implicated. It was only when she was on the point of death that Bernard Clergue relented, stood surety for her and brought her home from prison to Montaillou on a mule. There he had her hereticated, saw her embarked on the *endura* and supervised her death and funeral (i.416).

So it would be wrong to insist exclusively on the Clergue family's treachery. In order to live with the times they made themselves the standard-bearers of the Inquisitor of Carcassonne, but they nevertheless remained throughout faithful to their anti-Catholic convictions. Later on, in prison, Bernard Clergue made jokes about orthodox Roman practices (ii.283). But the world being what it is, the Clergues were sometimes obliged to go against the Cathar convictions of their clients. Often they used force instead of the gentler methods of their early days of domination, when they had acted in exchange for little presents and friendly services. They brought physical mutilation and exile upon some members of the Maurs family. Some young men whom they had formerly protected, disgusted by their complicity with Carcassonne, rose against them. Certain of the Maurs, the Maury and the Baille families slipped through the fingers of the *bayle* and the priest and became shepherds on the other side of the Pyrenees. This breaking up of the clan constituted a threat. Bernard Clergue reacted by bringing pressure to bear on those who remained and who could be intimidated. Making use of the peasant women of Montaillou, especially the widows and servant maids, he tried to build up again his family's power. He attempted, with menaces, to make Raymonde Arsen, Vuissane Testanière, Fabrisse Rives, Raymonde Guilhou, Grazide Lizier and, on a higher social plane, Béatrice de Planissoles bear false witness in favour of his brother the priest (i.466, 467, 468; ii.284, 291, 292, 293.) They would have none of it. Placed under house arrest by the Inquisition, then imprisoned in Pamiers, he continued to approach with promises and threats the women he met near his *domus* or in jail. In vain. '*Do you think anyone wants to go to the stake just to please you?*' asked Grazide Lizier (ii.291). Another, Fabrisse Rives, went one better (ii.293): '*I'd sooner Bernard were grilled than me.*'

In prison, during the year 1321, Bernard Clergue reflected on the terrible years when the network of fidelity which supported his clan gradually crumbled away. He decided, with reason, that the question of tithes had had a good deal to do with it. '*Bishop Jacques Fournier*', he said to one of his comrades in prison (ii.284), '*did us a great wrong; he organized all the repressive actions against the people of Sabarthès, because they refused to pay him the* carnelages . . . *he did this in order to seize the heretics' possessions.*'

'*And also the possessions of those who had never met a heretic in their life,*' said the other. '*It wasn't like that when the Inquisition at Carcassonne was dealing with us!*'

This passage shows how the Clergues maintained their supremacy in the village so long as they could rely on the Inquisition at Carcassonne, which only persecuted the heretics half-heartedly or partially, usually contenting itself with a few victims designated as a result of some vendetta on the part of the *bayle* or the priest, and not bringing all its weight to bear in favour of tithes. But after 1317 this compromise was a thing of the past. Jacques Fournier became Bishop of Pamiers and insisted that tithes be fully exacted, thus undermining the power of the Clergues even before he attacked them directly. Up till then the Clergues had collected the small amount of tithes exacted by the Church, not fleecing and sometimes even protecting the villagers. They merely extracted a small percentage for themselves and gave another share to their friends the goodmen.

But after 1317, when the Bishop demanded full payment of tithes, and again after 1320, when the Clergues were directly attacked, these reasonable arrangements ceased. The Clergues were no longer concerned with protecting their profits and preserving their friends. They were now struggling for survival, and without very much hope.

They did retain some friends, however, right to the end, including some loyal supporters from outside Montaillou. In Laroque d'Olmes, Pons Gary, Bernard Clergue's nephew, devotedly executed his uncles' ultimate skulduggeries (i.396). Pierre den Hugol, *bayle* of Quié, when he heard that Bernard Clergue had been arrested, declared before witnesses (iii.402): '*I am horrified; I would rather lose a ewe than know that Bernard Clergue is in prison.*'

While the Clergue clan declined, the Azéma clan rose. (We should speak of the Azéma clique rather than clan, for while the Clergues were an established majority around 1300–05, the Azémas represented only a strong minority).

Later, in the grim years leading up to the 1320s Pierre Azéma and his *domus* were supported by their cousin Jacques Fournier, and managed to build up in the village a network of friends and accomplices which for a time counterbalanced that of the Clergues. As early as the funeral of old Guillemette 'Belote', in about 1311, Guillemette Azéma, Pierre's wife, and Vuissane Testanière, an apostate from Albigensianism, defied almost face to face their Cathar neighbours Guillemette Benet and Alazaïs Azéma.[1] Pierre Azéma, to strengthen his party against that of the Clergues, did not shrink from suggesting exchanges of presents and services and even women. Women had helped to build up the influence of the opposite party. Pierre offered his daughter as future wife to the son of Gauzia Clergue, the priest's cousin (iii.70), on condition that Gauzia left the Clergue clan and joined that of the Azémas. She was also to abstain from making a certain denunciation harmful to the interests of the Azémas: '*You will thus strengthen both our houses,*' said Pierre (iii.367).

Pierre Azéma also tried to rally to his own cause certain families which had once been under the influence of the Clergues but had quarrelled with them and sent some of their members to safety in Spain. Partisan ambition made strange bedfellows. The Azéma *domus*, supposedly good Catholics, wooed persecuted Cathars who had once been

1 i.462. Alazaïs Azéma was a distant relative by marriage of the Azémas proper.

victims of the Clergues' intrigues. Conversely the Clergues, though they remained heretics in their hearts, became agents of the Catholic tribunal in Carcassonne. Behind all these apparent changes lay a continuous struggle for local power.

Vuissane Testanière was soon to be interrogated at the Bishop's tribunal in Pamiers. Pierre Azéma told her not to denounce Vital and Esclarmonde Baille, Raymonde Lizier, Gauzia Clergue and the Maurs brothers, all more or less implicated in heresy but belonging to families which had at some time been at loggerheads with the Clergues (i.468). Similarly, Pierre Azéma asked Gauzia Clergue to be careful with the Marty family, whom he was to make use of later. '*Do not inform on Emersende Marty*,' he said to Gauzia (iii.366). Like the Clergues, he too brought pressure to bear on the women. Did he know that they could not defend themselves? Did he act in this way because there were no male witnesses in the village who could be suborned, many of the men being dead, or in prison, or in exile? For whatever reason, Pierre Azéma tried to manipulate, and force to bear witness in his favour before the Inquisition in Pamiers, Vuissane Testanière, Na Moyshena, Raymonde Guilhou, Na Lozera and even Guillemette Benet, once an enemy of the Azéma clan but now stripped of the former glory of the Benet *ostal* (i.465, 468, 479; ii.226–7, 281). When the Inquisitor from Carcassonne, a friend of the Clergues, visited Montaillou, two of the village women, Na Lozera and Na Moyshena, complained that Pierre Azéma had terrorized them into making false confessions before his cousin, Bishop Fournier (ii.281).[1]

Pierre Azéma did not rely only on his friends in the village. Just as Pierre Clergue made use of the Inquisition at Carcassonne, so Azéma made use of the Inquisition in Pamiers. He also had well-placed accomplices in the small neighbouring towns. He was in league with the priest at Prades and with an unqualified lawyer, Pierre de Gaillac of Tarascon-sur-Ariège, who acted as an informer when the occasion served (ii.281, 287). Azéma knew that his party could not win a decisive victory over the Clergues unless he could get control of the local institutional powers. The Clergues themselves had annexed the offices of *bayle* and priest and

1 According to Jean Duvernoy (1966), p. 147 and note, Na Lozera was Grazide Lizier. I am inclined to think, since the term 'Na' denoted a matriarch, that Na Lozera was Raymonde d'Argelliers, widow of Arnaud Lizier and then wife of Arnaud Belot.

the influence of the castle. Pierre Azéma did his best to evict his rivals from these corridors of power. When his influence was at its height, he shamelessly manipulated the new representatives of authority – the *vice-châtelain*, the consul Bernard Marty and the *vicaire* Raymond Trialh, successor of the late Pierre Clergue (i.406).

The Clergue and Azéma clans were like two scorpions in a bottle. Doomed first to live and then to die together, they allowed themselves to be used to settle the respective accounts of their masters in Carcassonne and Pamiers. Even after he ended up in prison in Pamiers, Bernard Clergue still exercised some influence. He got his protectors in Carcassonne to imprison Pierre Azéma, whose past was not entirely unsmirched with Catharism. Master Jacques, the jailer in Carcassonne and a great friend of the ex-*bayle* of Montaillou, ill-treated Pierre Azéma once he was in his power, and his victim soon died (ii.281), thus ridding Bernard Clergue of the man he had always called a traitor. Bernard Clergue regarded Pierre Azéma as a traitor to Montaillou because he was a traitor to the Clergue clan, who had so long identified their own fate with that of the village itself (ii.285, 287–8).

But the ex-*bayle* himself was destined to meet a tragic end. Pierre Azéma's remaining protectors and accomplices in Pamiers paid Bernard Clergue back in his own coin. He was sentenced to the severest form of imprisonment and did not survive more than a month of being kept in fetters and fed on bread and water. He died at the end of the summer of 1324, soon after his brother the priest (i.405, and n. 164; ii.227, 281; iii.376).

The deaths of Bernard Clergue and Pierre Azéma did not end the struggle of the clans in Montaillou. The long-term predominance of the Clergues survived for a while: some members of the clan were among the chief inhabitants of Montaillou during the decade beginning 1320 (ii.255, 256).[1] But the Azéma clan had been more ambitious than its wealth and numbers warranted, and it seems not to have recovered from the death of its leader in prison in Carcassonne. Opposition to the Clergues revived, however, among the remainder of the Guilhabert *domus*, which Azéma had once tried to rouse against the Clergues (ii.255–7; i.406).

1 According to the relevant documents in the departmental archives of Ariège and the communal archives of Montaillou, Clergue was the commonest family name in the village from the fourteenth to the twentieth century.

The same sort of internecine conflict is seen in other villages in Ariège in the period 1300–20. In Junac, where the lord of the manor was actually resident, the local nobles acted for a long while as protectors of heresy and of the local farmers and blacksmiths who were Cathar sympathizers. But after the period 1305–10 the de Junac family, like many other leading citizens in the area, took fright at the increasing threats from the Inquisition. They tried to compromise with it. They broke with former protégés whose involvement in heresy was too obvious, and even terrorized ultra-Catholics who might denounce them. We have seen how Pierre Clergue caused a former friend to have her tongue cut out. The de Junacs all but strangled with their own hands the father of Bernard Marty, suspected of betraying them (iii.251–95).

It is possible that the same sort of thing happened in the village of Quié. There the dominant group, which included the priest and the consuls, tried around 1320 to make the villagers obey the Bishop. The Bishop wanted them to make an Easter candle weighing between 15 and 20 pounds – a ruinous demand (ii.324–6). Several peasants protested, Raymond de Laburat at their head (ii.324–5). The dominant group in Quié, though they now supported the Catholics, had been tinged with heresy in the past (ii.316, 324–5; iii.487) but they had switched loyalties, thus risking a conflict with their former supporters, who might subsequently regroup to form an opposition party.

At Caussou, also in upper Ariège, Philippe de Planissoles, Béatrice's father, was very deeply involved in heresy (iii.351). So was his family in general. It ruled over Caussou by means both of patronage and of violence, which sometimes went as far as murder. Philippe, who had worn the yellow cross, was reconciled late in life with the Church, which exempted him as a nobleman from paying the tithes and dues which the common people had to pay. So Philippe de Planissoles and his group of friends which exercised power in Caussou met with lively protest from a coalition of local tax-payers. '*They fleece us, and spare the nobility.*' This sort of anti-noble protest was very rare in upper Ariège. It is to be explained in the last resort as one of the consequences of the realignment of noblemen, leading citizens, *bayles* and manorial officials. They were often Cathars or Cathar sympathizers during the second half of the thirteenth century and the beginning of the fourteenth. But afterwards, at different dates in different areas, as repression grew, they closed their doors to the goodmen. Some of them may have remained Cathars, but only in secret and in their hearts. In about 1290, Bertrand de Taix, a nobleman of Pamiers said (iii.328): *I once knew a time when many noblemen in this region were believers in the goodmen and did not hesitate to speak freely on the subject . . . That time is past. The priests have destroyed these people and dissipated their fortunes.*

But if, by 1290, it was no longer the case that the noblemen of Pamiers joined with their popular and peasant followers in heresy, they did take up the cause again in upper Ariège, later, thanks to the revival of 1300 to about 1310. But here, too, there was ultimately a realignment of loyalty. Repression triumphed. The mountain nobility turned their coats, at least publicly and often in reality. Their former clienteles had great problems of readaptation. As we have seen in Montaillou with the Clergue and Azéma clans, people lost their bearings.

Conflicts between those who wielded manorial power (noblemen themselves or their representatives) and those they ruled were translated, in Montaillou, into terms of clan conflict. These conflicts were not permanent. The manorial judge and his colleagues only had to arrive for a few years (after 1300, for example) at a valid compromise on the question of tithes or on the tolerance of heresy in order to win the support of the great majority of the village. Needless to say, there was never any question of a revolutionary solution to these conflicts. The clan which aspired to domination did not seek to bring down the manorial authorities but only to annex them.

Social relationships in Montaillou can best be understood within the framework of regional historiography. Compared with similar communities in the region, Montaillou was late in becoming a consular municipality. There is no mention of a consul in Montaillou until the year 1321, and even then he plays only a subordinate role (i.406). The sense of community was scarcely developed at all. The Clergue clan represented what Madame Gramain has called the 'manorial party'. Bernard Clergue, the *bayle*, in the absence of the lord of the manor, represented manorial institutions and traditional, authoritarian methods of local government. The Azéma clan made use of the recently installed consulate, and Pierre Azéma shamelessly manipulated the consul Bernard Marty (i.408). The Azéma clan thus embodied the 'consular' party, favourable to Bishop Fournier and thus pro-French and pro-royal. The gradual changes in social and political life took place via the unending conflict between the local clans.

The study of Montaillou shows on a minute scale what took place in the structure of society as a whole. Montaillou is only a drop in the ocean. Thanks to the microscope provided by the Fournier Register, we can see the protozoa swimming about in it.

CHAPTER XVII

Concepts of time and space

In an important article, Jacques Le Goff has contrasted the two enemies, 'the time of the Church' and 'the time of the merchant'.[1] But where does the special time of the farmer, the shepherd and the craftsman come in? The first thing to be noticed is that the time of the humble people had been only partially annexed by the Church. Arnaud Sicre of Tarascon speaks of *the time it takes to say two Paternosters* (ii.27), but he is referring specifically to religious rites (heretical ones, as it happens). Normally, to indicate a brief lapse of time in Sabarthès, people used some vague expression like 'a short moment', 'a brief pause', 'a long pause' and so on. Or, less frequently, time was measured in terms of motion (*the time it takes to travel a league*, or *the time it takes to travel a quarter of a league*). This method was common with a great walker like the shepherd Bernard Marty (iii.257, 260 and *passim*).

Fixed points in time were indicated by references to meals (*prandium* or *cena* – that is, lunch or dinner), or to liturgical hours such as terce, nones or vespers. These liturgical references were mostly used by priests, *parfaits* and a few women of Catholic faith or leanings.[2] So daytime chronology was only partly Christianized. Nights remained an entirely lay matter, except in the case of a bigot like Bélibaste, who got up six times during the night to say his prayers. The people of Montaillou and Ariège in general indicated the divisions of the night by means of visual, aural or physiological references such as *after sunset, at nightfall, at the hour of the first sleep, at the hour half-way through the first sleep, at cock-crow,* or *when the cock had crowed three times.*

Church bells are scarcely ever referred to except when they ring for funerals or for the elevation of the Host during Mass; they seem not to have been used in Montaillou simply to mark the passage of time. Time was not money in the Comté de Foix. The people of Montaillou were

1 J. Le Goff (1960).
2 i.335; ii.38, 338; iii.51, 67, 360, 364. Among the women who used such expressions were Gauzia Clergue, Raymonde d'Argevilliers, Guillemette Clergue (all of Montaillou) and Bernadette de Rieux of Ax. The Waldensians of Pamiers also indicated time by means of the liturgical hours (i.104, 121), but in their case this corresponded to prayers which they actually said. The shepherd Pierre Maury refers occasionally to 'nones' (iii.135).

not afraid of hard work and could make an effort when necessary. But they did not think in terms of a fixed and continuous timetable, whether in their own fields or, in exile, in the workshops of Catalonia. For them the working day was punctuated with long, irregular pauses, during which one would chat with a friend, perhaps at the same time enjoying a glass of wine. *At those words*, said Arnaud Sicre, *I folded up my work and went to Guillemette Maury's house*. And Arnaud Sicre indicates several other similar interruptions: *Pierre Maury sent for me in the shop where I made shoes . . . Guillemette sent a message to ask me to go to her house, which I did . . . Hearing that, I left what I was doing.*

So work was not so absorbing that one couldn't bear to leave it. And this relaxed attitude was found generally, not only in the case of a distinguished shoemaker like Arnaud Sicre. The time of a craftsman seems still to have been very close to that of a farmer or shepherd. Pierre Maury, who had a reputation for competence, was always ready to leave his flock in the charge of his brother or a friend, perhaps for hours, perhaps for days or weeks. A good deal of time in Montaillou and upper Ariège was spent walking or taking a siesta, especially when it was hot.

At first sight it seems that there was a weekly division of time. Arnaud Sicre, a woman of Ax, Béatrice de Planissoles and the shepherds Bernard Benet and Bernard Marty all use the word, and the idea, of a 'week'. But in ordinary rural circles the term was avoided, as were references to the lunar calendar and the names of the days of the week, except occasionally for Sunday.[1] People spoke of eight days or fifteen days rather than one or two weeks. This usage corresponds to the idea of a quarter or half of a month. The people of Ariège were used in general to dividing things up into halves: they often referred to a 'half year' (ii.196; iii.283, 289). This had the additional advantage of lending itself to the usages of transhumance, which divided the year up into winter and summer pasturage.

The rhythm of the year was that of the twelve months and the four seasons, but these were not referred to very frequently. Dates were often

1 ii.201. Gauzia Clergue for example, does not say 'Monday', but 'the day after Sunday' (iii.360). It is an exceptional occurrence when the sheep-farmer Raymond Sicre of Ascou says 'Thursday' (ii.364). On the other hand, the scribes of the Inquisition, in their preambles, often use the names of the days of the week. Barthélemy Amilhac uses the term 'Monday' (i.256); but he was a priest.

fixed by reference to purely natural phenomena, not necessarily agricultural. *We were sitting, Guillemette Benet and I, under the elm*, says Alazaïs Munier,[1] *at the season when elms have put forth their leaves. It was on this occasion that Guillemette Benet said to me: 'My poor friend, my poor friend, the soul is nothing but blood.'* Harvests and other agricultural work also provided points of reference. *Raymond de la Côte*, said the Waldensian Agnès Francou, referring to the man who was later burned at the stake with her (i.125), *remained in Pamiers from the wine-harvest in 1318 to the Feast of Saint Laurent in 1319*. There are many specific references in Montaillou to the wheat and turnip harvests.

But these natural references are outnumbered by references to the Christian year. While the division of the day and of the night remained largely lay, the division of the year was largely ecclesiastical. All Saints, Christmas, Carnival and Lent, Palm Sunday, Easter, Whitsun, Ascension Day, the Assumption, the Nativity of the Virgin and the Holy Cross made up a universally known cycle. All Saints' Day was very important, naturally enough in a society much preoccupied with death and what came after death. Christmas was a family feast. Easter served as a pretext for feasts of lamb. The times between All Saints and Christmas and between Easter and Whitsun were referred to precisely as such.

Saints were honoured mostly during the period from the end of spring through summer to autumn. Both in the Pyrenees and in Catalonia there was a slack period between the beginning of November and the beginning of May. The reason for this seems to have been that the major feasts celebrated between Christmas and Whitsun were too numerous to leave room for much minor devotion. The year was divided up into one part dedicated to God and Christ and running from Christmas to Whitsun, followed by another part devoted to the Virgin Mary and the Saints and running from Whitsun to All Saints. The more Christian portion is clearly the first, given what we know about the pagan elements attached to the worship of the Saints and the Virgin.

Saints' days were linked to various collective activities, including cattle fairs. The Maury brothers were well-known visitors to the market at Ax-les-Thermes and the fair at Laroque d'Olmes, which occurred on Holy Cross and Saint Ciriac's Day respectively (ii.477–8; iii.148). Feast days meant holidays. The saints were the friends of the workers, including farmers and agricultural labourers. At the feasts which fell at

1 i.260. This Guillemette Benet is the namesake of the matriarch of Montaillou.

the end of the summer the shepherds came down from the summer pastures to join in the fun. Even the peasants who were Cathars did not dream of giving up these Catholic festivities. Only Bélibaste, an out and out Albigensian, carried heretic zeal as far as shutting himself up to work during holidays (ii.53).

Finally, it was the priest, who might possess a calendar, who was responsible, when necessary, for saying what day of the year it was. The day was defined not by a figure but by the name of a saint or a feast. The priest was thus the guardian of time.

The scribes of the Inquisition made use of a time expressed in figures, a modern time expressed to the exact day: *2 April 1320, 26 December 1321* and so on. This contrast between the definite time of the scribes and the vague time of the peasants was more marked still when it came to the demarcation of a large part of the year, or a group of years. Guillaume Austatz, though he was a *bayle*, did not say 'in 1316' or 'in 1301' but *three or four years ago, seventeen or eighteen years ago, it may well have been twenty years ago, twenty or twenty-four years since* (i.202; i.499; iii.271; and *passim*).[1] Other common expressions were *at the time when the heretics predominated in Montaillou, before the round-up by the Inquisition in Carcassonne*, and so on, just as we say 'before' or 'after the War', 'before' or 'since May '68'. The farther back an event, the vaguer the reference. A child was not six or seven months old, but *half a year* old; not a year or eighteen months old, but *between one and two* (i.382; ii.17). A few examples suggest that women preserved a more exact idea of the past than men. Béatrice de Planissoles is very precise about dates: *nineteen years ago on Assumption Day, twenty-six years ago in August*, she says, referring to her own past (i.218, 223, 232). Béatrice was a noblewoman, but the same phenomenon is seen among the peasants. The shepherd Bernard Benet refers to the death of Guillaume Guilhabert as having taken place *sixteen or twenty years ago*, i.e. between 1300 and 1305 (i.398). But a peasant woman, Alazaïs Fauré, says more precisely that the event took place *eighteen years ago*, i.e. in 1303 (i.410).

Whether precisely given or otherwise, rural time was always vague. The prevailing mental attitude was Merovingian, like that of Grégoire de Tours or the pseudo-Frédégaire. We have seen above how Agnès

---

1 Although the villagers could not read or write, they could, of course, count. They were, after all, repeatedly having to count their sheep.

Francou referred to the actual years 1318 and 1319 (i.125), but she lived in Pamiers and came from more sophisticated circles.[1] Up in the mountains there is only one case of such an exact reference. During Lent 1318, Bernard Cordier, then living in Tarascon, told his fellow-citizens what he had heard in his native town of Pamiers: '*There will be catastrophes in 1318 because of the birth of Antichrist.*'[2]

In these circumstances, history was absent or almost absent from Montaillou culture. All the people knew on the subject were a few scraps of eschatology derived from Christianity and various other beliefs. The Cathar myth of the Fall was extremely popular among the heretical sympathizers of Montaillou, but as far as Catholic tradition was concerned, little was known of the time covered by the Old Testament. Familiar conversation in the *domus* produced a few references to Adam and Eve, but none to the Flood or the Prophets. Catholic time, in upper Ariège, mentioned the Creation only briefly, and began in earnest with Mary, Jesus and the Apostles. It ended in some distant future, *when the world has lasted many years* (i.191). Then came the Day of Judgment and the Resurrection. These final prospects, though sometimes called in question, were often referred to around the fire in the evening. *About four years ago*, said Gaillarde, wife of Bernard Ros of Ornolac (i.191), *I was in my house at Ornolac, together with my fellow-citizen the wife of Pierre Munier. Guillaume Austatz* (*the* bayle) *came in, with other people whose names I forget. We sat around the fire and began to talk about God and the general Resurrection.*

When the inhabitants of Montaillou referred to historical events in the modern sense of the term, they were usually concerned with things which occurred after 1290, if not after 1300. There is one unique reference to the 1240s. This evokes the moving story of Alesta and Serena, heretical ladies of Chateauverdun who were captured, who removed their make-up and were burned at the stake, one of them having left her infant behind in order to go to Lombardy. Raymond Roussel, who recounts this story to Béatrice, tells it without any date, as if it were simply an old tale from the past (i.220–21).

1 See P. Aries (1954), pp. 119–21. Merovingian chroniclers, like the Montaillou peasants, did not use precise figures to indicate years.
2 i.160. There is another example where a peasant woman of Montaillou appears to be referring to the year 1320 (iii.336). But the context suggests that it was the Inquisition's scribe who inserted this date into the evidence.

Allusions to history proper, whether ancient or modern, are almost entirely absent from the records, whether these deal with Montaillou itself or with Ariège in general. Roman antiquity was known only in Pamiers, and then only just. There were schools in Pamiers, and a text by Ovid was read there. But the memories of the farmers scarcely went back further than the previous Comte de Foix, who had been kind to his subjects but an enemy to tithes and the Church. He died in 1302 (iii.331). Apart from a few very rare passages about, for example, the great age of some *genus* or lineage (ii.367, 368; ii.110), the witnesses whom Fournier interrogated took no interest in decades earlier than 1290 or 1300. It should be remembered, of course, that there were few elderly people among these witnesses. So the people of Montaillou lived in a kind of 'island in time', even more cut off from the past than from the future. *There is no other age than ours*, said Raymond de l'Aire of Tignac (ii.132).

This absence of a historical dimension went with a general use, in speech, of the present indicative tense, without logical connections with past and future. The narratives of Pierre Maury, Bernard Marty and many others are quite flat, without any direct revelation of the individuals involved. For hours we listened to Pierre Maury's reminiscences. They show us Arnaud Sicre the shoemaker; but it is only suddenly, just before the end, that we learn that he was an informer, only at the moment when he actually appears as one in the narrative.

Space, whether immediate, geographical, sociological or cultural, was basically linked to physical perception, especially that of the hand and the arm. Guillemette Clergue says (i.341): *I saw Prades Tavernier reading in the rays of the sun a black book as long as my own hand.* Raymond Vayssière says (i.285): *I was sunning myself behind my house, and four or five spans away Guillaume Andorran was reading a book.* Guillemette Clergue again (i.341): *Prades Tavernier, who was carrying four or five lambskins round his neck, walked along keeping a constant distance of a crossbow shot between himself and the road.* Longer distances are measured in terms of a league (ii.27), a stage of a journey (ii.43) or a stage of the migration. In the mountain village of Montaillou, people did not go simply from point A to point B; they went up or down (i.223, 462; iii.296; and *passim*).

But the people of upper Ariège were not very deeply concerned with space. Their notion of it was bounded by the two philosophical concepts of Montaillou, *corpus* and *domus*, body and house. The body was the measure of the world, in the first place, and when the world was too large to be measured by the body its place would be taken by the *domus*. '*If you want to have an idea of Heaven*,' said Guillaume Austatz (i.202), '*imagine a huge* domus *stretching from the Mérens Pass to the town of Toulouse.*'

Nor was space in Montaillou very definitely orientated. In later centuries the surveyors who drew up the land registers of Languedoc defined the fields in terms of the points of the compass, the prevailing winds, the positions of the sun, and so on. But in 1310 the people of Ariège did not describe a journey in terms of its general orientation but in terms of a series of towns along the way. '*To go to Rabastens*,' said Bélibaste to Pierre Maury (iii.151), '*you go first to Mirepoix, then to Bauville, and then to Caraman. And there you ask the way to Rabastens.*' The expressions rising sun, setting sun, north, south, east and west, are never used in the Register. The peasants of Montaillou spoke of going *towards Catalonia* (i.e. south), *towards the lowlands* (i.e. north), *beyond the mountains*, *towards the sea*, *towards Toulouse*, and so on.

Geographically, the basic perception was that of the locality or village – the *terra*. This word denoted both the manorial estate and the sub-region itself. We should not be misled by the word *terra*. The peasants and shepherds of Montaillou, preoccupied with their *domus*, were not obsessed with the land belonging to them in the way that farmers of all ages are sometimes supposed to be. Their method of production was domestic, and *terra*, for them, was not family land but the territory of the parish and, more generally, of the locality. People spoke of the *terra* of a village, or a group of villages or of any region with limits at once human and natural. *Terra* might also apply to a manorial estate, large or small, or even a whole principality. Everyone was conscious of the Comté de Foix as a political unit. But there was a clear distinction between, on the one hand, the uplands (centred not on Foix, the capital, but on Ax and Tarascon), and, on the other, the lowlands, dominated by the town of Pamiers, ecclesiastical, anti-Cathar and Dominican, surrounded by its rich cereal plains. The frontier between the upper regions, anti-tithe and pro-Cathar, and the lower regions, solidly Catholic, lay a few kilometres to the north of Foix along a transverse valley called the Labarre Pass. *The people of Sabarthès*, said Berthomieu

Hugon in 1322 (iii.331), *would like to come to an arrangement with the Comte de Foix whereby no cleric came up further than the Labarre Pass ... If the Comte de Foix were as good a man as his predecessor, the priests would not come up and demand* carnelages.

This distinction was accepted by everyone in Montaillou. Clergue the priest warned Béatrice not to go down to the 'lowlands' of Dalou and Varilhes, infested with Minorite friars. In prison in Pamiers, Bernard Clergue looked up at the mountains which blocked the southern horizon: up there among them was his *terra* of upper Ariège, made up of Sabarthès and the Pays d'Aillon, and above all of the manor of Montaillou of which he was *bayle*.

Upper Ariège, bounded in the north by the Labarre Pass, was bounded in the south by the line of the Pyrenean passes. A Bishop of Pamiers, the spiritual arm of the King of France, tried to extend his inquisitorial control as far as this line. The people of Foix lived *citra portus* (on the hither side of the passes), on the northern slopes of the Pyrenees, under the influence of French imperialism. The Spanish slopes of the mountains were called *ultra portus* (beyond the passes). '*Flee beyond the passes*,' said Pons Bol, the notary of Varilhes, to Béatrice de Planissoles (i.257), '*because on this side of them you will be caught by the Bishop.*' For the exiles in Catalonia, the main axis of the Pyrenees, which corresponded with the line of the passes running from east to west, was the frontier of freedom, beyond which the Kingdom of France began, in terms of oppression if not according to the letter of the law. For it was there that the activity of the Inquisitors began. *When we go through the passes and re-enter the Kingdom of France*, said the emigrés (ii.71), *all our hair stands on end*.

There were varying degrees of contact between the different localities and sub-regions. Montaillou had a permanent relationship with Prades, the neighbouring parish, and was linked to it both by a path and by bonds of inter-marriage (i.462). Camurac, on the other hand, another neighbouring community, hardly any farther away than Prades, had only very slight links with Montaillou, apart from the occasional visit of the priest of Camurac, bringing the last sacraments to some dying inhabitant of Montaillou (i.462). Montaillou had frequent contacts – commercial, cultural, social and friendly – with Ax-les-Thermes, chief town of the upper valley of the Ariège. The women of the Prades valley went to Ax to sell their hens and eggs and to get their yarn woven.

Mules laden with wheat went from Montaillou to the mills on the River Ariège in Ax and then came back again to the village laden with flour.

One day, said Guillemette Clergue (i.343), *not long before the general arrest of the people of Montaillou (apart from that, I don't remember when it was), I went to gather grass in the place called Alacot. On my way, I met Guillaume Maury with his mule; he was coming from Ax, singing. I said to him: 'You've been drinking. You are so cheerful.'*

'I've been to Ax to have the flour ground; I'm bringing it back on my mule,' he said.

'And how is it,' I answered, *'that when my husband goes to Ax to have the flour ground, he comes back to our* domus *completely exhausted with sleeplessness and flour dust?'*

'As a matter of fact,' said Guillaume, *'I didn't stay long at the mill. I took advantage of the journey to go and see the goodmen!'*

The seasonal migration created links between Montaillou and places a long distance away. In Arques, for example, in the present-day department of Aude, Sybille Pierre, a sheep-farmer's wife, knew all the Montaillou gossip. The two villages were 40 kilometres away from one another as the crow flies, but in fact they were brought close together because one was the summer terminus and the other the winter terminus of the migration circuit. They also exchanged servant maids and seasonal workers for the harvest (ii.427). In a sense, the Fournier Register is a great dialogue across space between the winter pastures in Catalonia and the summer pastures in Sabarthès.

Montaillou and the *terre d'Aillon* (Prades and Montaillou) were a part of Sabarthès. *Pierre Clergue is priest of Montaillou in Sabarthès* (iii.182). There was a lesser Sabarthès, centred on Ax and Tarascon and the shrine at Savart, which gave Sabarthès its name. And there was a greater Sabarthès, corresponding with the southern, mountainous part of the Comté de Foix itself and including (south of the Labarre Pass and north of the axis of the Pyrenees) the environs of Ax, Tarascon, Foix and the region of Vicdessos. Many passages show how the inhabitants of the various villages regarded themselves as living in Sabarthès.

'Aren't you from Sabarthès?' a young man asked Pierre den Hugol in a tavern in Laroque d'Olmes (iii.375).

'Yes, I'm from Quié.'

As well as gastronomic and other specialities, Sabarthès had its own language or at least dialects. This linguistic unity favoured inter-marriage. Mathena Cervel (ii.451): *My future husband Jean Maury had come to Juncosa* [in Spain] *to recover his sheep. When he learned that my mother and I were of the tongue of Sabarthès, he negotiated to marry me, although we did not even know each other.*

Goodmen and priests had at least one thing in common: they all preached, when necessary, in the vulgar tongue (i.454; iii.106). The people of Montaillou were very much aware of a local dialect spoken by about a thousand people at the most.

At San Mateo, says Arnaud Sicre (ii.21), *I was making shoes in the workshop of Jacques Vital, a local shoe-maker, when a woman came along the street, calling: 'Any flour to grind?'*

Someone said to me: 'Arnaud, here's a farm woman from your country.'
I asked the woman: 'Where do you come from?'
'Saverdun,' she said.

But as she spoke the tongue of Montaillou, I cut her short: 'You're not from Saverdun. You're from Prades or Montaillou.'

This exchange suggests that there was a difference between the language spoken in the lowlands (Saverdun, north of the Labarre Pass) and that of Sabarthès. Again, within the latter, there was something special about the dialects of Prades and Montaillou, which perhaps contained Catalan expressions. For the people of Montaillou, especially the shepherds, there was a sort of continuum between Occitania and Catalonia. No problem of comprehension was involved for them in going from Tarascon and Ax-les-Thermes to Puigcerda and San Mateo. Linguistically speaking, the Pyrenees scarcely existed.

People from Ariège took refuge in Lombardy, Sicily, Catalonia, Valencia and Majorca. Exile and the yearly migrations brought them into contact with the Moors of Spain. There were influences from the East, both Moslem and Christian. All the more remarkable, then, is the absence of 'French' influence in Sabarthès. The Inquisition at Carcassonne and Pamiers did undertake to act as the spiritual arm of France. France was far away, but its force was felt, hanging like the Sword of Damocles over the hot-heads of Sabarthès.

Apart from such indirect pressures, there was little French influence as such in the region. Many migrants continued to travel through the mountain passes of Ariège and Roussillon, coming from the north and going to Spain. But they were Occitans, not French-speakers from the Paris basin.

More decisive in the demarcation of the cultural space of Sabarthès were the currents of heresy. Despite the various tentacles which Catharism extended from time to time towards the north of Europe, it was by origin an Italian, Mediterranean and Balkan heresy, and came to the *pays d'oc* by means of a journey from east to west. Upper Ariège remained almost unaffected by Waldensianism, coming from central and eastern France, and by the *pastoureaux*, or peasant rebels, from northern France.

As far as we know, only one inhabitant of Montaillou ever had even the opportunity of going to the Ile de France. In 1321 Guillaume Fort was sentenced by the Bishop's court in Pamiers to go northward as a pilgrim to Vauvert, Montpellier, Sérignan, Rocamadour, Puy-en-Velay, Chartres, Notre Dame de Paris, Pontoise, Saint-Denis and to the Sainte-Chapelle. But before this sentence could be carried out, a second sentence, promulgated the following day, condemned him to be burnt at the stake. And so he was (i.453).

In one respect at least France was definitely present, and that was through its money. About 71 per cent of the coins used in the Comté de Foix were either *parisis* or, more often, silver *tournois* made in mints in some way connected with the monarchy in Paris. This was the first of many annexations. The farmers and shepherds of Montaillou and Sabarthès had now got beyond the primitive stage of a subsistence economy. They had a growing need of coins, and these, more and more, were French.

There was no question of aesthetic appreciation in fourteenth-century Montaillou. The peasants of upper Ariège had a feeling for beauty, but it was essentially associated with desire, pleasure and the agreeable sensations which come from the senses or from the heart's affections. They spoke of a *beautiful girl*, a *fine fish pie*, of *handsome men*, of *beautiful singing in church*, of *fine orchards in Heaven*. But they did not thrill at the contemplation of nature or the surrounding mountains. Nature and the mountains presented them with too many concrete problems.

But the village and the region had the feeling – a feeling tinged with anthropocentrism – that they shared in surrounding nature. The microcosm (man and his *domus*) was part of the macrocosm, in the centre of which was the *ostal*. The macrocosm stretched out to include the stars. As we have already seen, people kept bits of fingernail and locks of hair from a deceased head of the family in order to preserve the *domus*'s good fortune (*astrum vel eufortunium*). *Men should not swear by Heaven*, said Bélibaste (ii.200), *for they cannot cause a star to be large or small*.

The individual had his own *fatum* or destiny (iii.179). Catharism did not introduce the idea of fate into upper Ariège. But it so happened that popular theories on this subject fitted in very well with the goodmen's teaching on metempsychosis. Thus Bélibaste expounded his denial of free will to the Maury family (iii.179): '*When a man steals away someone else's possessions or commits evil, that man is none other than an evil spirit which enters into him: this spirit makes him commit sins and makes him abandon the good life for the wicked. Everything is full of souls. All the air is full of good and evil spirits. Except when a spirit has been dwelling in the body of a dead person who when he was alive was just and good, the spirit which has just escaped from a dead body is always anxious to be reincarnated. For the evil spirits in the air burn that spirit when it is among them; so they force it to enter into some body of flesh, whether of man or of beast; because as long as a human spirit is at rest in a body of flesh, the evil spirits in the air cannot burn it or torment it.*'

A similar conception of the world is expressed by Bernard Franca, of the village of Goulier in the parish of Vicdessos (i.350–70). Bernard

Franca was a priest and served Mass, but he was also a true peasant. He grew his own fields of millet and, jointly with his brothers, owned a house in the village street. He used to debate with his co-parishioners while working at the harvest; he took part in the informal gatherings outside the church on Sundays and feast-days. His sociability earned him a denunciation, a trial in Pamiers and a sentence which forced him to wear the double yellow cross.

Bernard Franca believed that everything that happened to anyone was bound to happen to him from all eternity. Human beings were not free, and consequently could not sin. Conversely, so-called good works were of no merit. Bernard Franca had professed his heterodox opinions for forty years. He had derived them simply from the local peasant philosophy of Sabarthès.

'*Was it some learned doctor who inspired these errors in you?*' asked Jacques Fournier in 1320 of Franca, now in his sixties (i.356, 357).

'*No*,' replied Franca. '*But it is commonly said in Sabarthès, when some good or some evil happens to someone, that "it was promised him" and that "it could not have happened otherwise" . . . Moreover, when I was taken prisoner I said: "What has to be will be." And then I added: "It will be as God wishes."*'[1]

The moon, though not so important as the stars or as the air and its spirits, was important in Montaillou when it came to arranging one act essential to the survival of the *domus*. This act was marriage.

Sixteen or so years ago, said Raymond Vayssière of Ax-les-Thermes in 1320 (i.291), *I was in the house of Raymond Belot of Montaillou; and we were talking (in general) about the time when marriages should be celebrated. Raymond said: 'When we wanted to give our sister as wife to Bernard Clergue, we went to see Guillaume Authié the heretic to ask his advice on the following question: when will the moon be propitious to marry our sister to Bernard? Guillaume Authié told us to fix the wedding on a day which he indicated to us. And so we did.'*

The people of Montaillou had recourse not only to the goodmen but also to ordinary soothsayers in order to choose the best time for a wedding or a journey, and so on. Béatrice de Planissoles made use of spells supplied by a converted Jewess (ii.40). The exiles in Catalonia consulted a soothsayer who found his predictions *in a book written in Arabic characters* (iii.207). This soothsayer used the swinging of a stick

1 The last two sentences quoted are in Occitan in the original.

or the intervals between footsteps in order to make predictions about illness in men or beasts, or about marriages. Less sophisticated were the premonitions derived from the flight of birds of ill omen – owls and magpies, for example. The sight of two magpies flying across his path was enough to deprive Bélibaste of what little courage remained to him: he lost the use of his legs, and foresaw the tragic fate awaiting him (ii.78; iii.210).

The relationship between men and animals in general was not always a good one in Montaillou. The shepherds had dogs, which migrated along with the sheep (ii.485). Isolated farms were sometimes guarded by big noisy hounds (iii.257). Ordinary, everyday relations between men and dogs may have been pleasant and affectionate – we do not know. But the word 'dog' was commonly used as an insult. Dogs might give you rabies. When the shepherd Jean Maury was afraid that he might have been poisoned, he gave the dishes prepared for him by his hostess to his own sheepdog to taste (ii.485, 288).

Cats were sometimes regarded as creatures of the devil. *When Geoffroy d'Ablis, the Inquisitor of Carcassonne, died,* said Guillemette Maury (ii.69), *he died at night and there was no witness of his death. But next day the people who found the body also found two black cats by his bed, one at each end. They were evil spirits keeping the Inquisitor's soul company.*

Rats also were often regarded with repugnance (iii.221). Bélibaste and Tavernier forbade the killing of all animals except rats, snakes and toads.

Grazide Lizier, a young peasant girl of Montaillou, made a distinction between different kinds of animals.

'*Grazide*,' said Jacques Fournier (i.304), '*do you believe that God made all the physical objects which we see in the world?*'

'*I believe*,' answered Grazide, '*that God created the physical things which are good for human beings to use, such as men themselves and animals that can be eaten or that are useful to man, such as oxen, sheep, goats, horses, mules; and also edible fruits of the earth and trees. On the other hand, I do not believe that God made wolves, flies, lizards and other creatures harmful to men; nor do I believe that he made the Devil.*'

Similarly, Bernard Franca (i.358): *On the one hand there are the works of the good God, Heaven, the earth, the water, fire, the air and the animals useful to men for food, for carrying, for work or for clothing; including edible fish! On the other hand, the bad God has made devils and harmful animals, such as wolves, snakes, toads, flies and all harmful and poisonous beasts.*

The horse was in the first rank of animals which might serve as a receptacle, according to the Cathar prophets of Sabarthès, for the successive reincarnations of the soul. In this respect a horse, or rather mare, came after a woman, but definitely before a female rabbit or bitch, and before an ox (or a cow). Bélibaste says (ii.35): '*When the spirits come out of a fleshy tunic, that is a dead body, they run very fast, for they are fearful. They run so fast that if a spirit came out of a dead body in Valencia and had to go into another living body in the Comté de Foix, if it was raining hard, scarcely three drops of rain would touch it! Running like this, the terrified spirit hurls itself into the first hole it finds free! In other words into the womb of some animal which has just conceived an embryo not yet supplied with a soul; whether a bitch, a female rabbit or a mare. Or even in the womb of a woman.*'

The predominance of the horse is underlined by a myth of which the people of Ariège, whether resident or in exile, left behind at least four versions (ii.36, 408; iii.138, 221). Two very simplified versions are recounted by Pierre Maury, who heard them from Bélibaste and Prades Tavernier. A third is related by Sybille Pierre of Arques, who had it directly from Pierre Authié. The fourth and most complete comes down through Arnaud Sicre, who, like Pierre Maury, had it from Bélibaste, who, like Sybille Pierre, probably had it from Pierre Authié in person.

A man had been wicked, and a murderer. When he died, his spirit entered into the body of an ox. This ox had a harsh master who did not feed him properly and who covered him with pricks from a big goad. But the spirit of the ox remembered that he had been a man. When the ox died, the spirit entered into the body of a horse. This horse was the property of a great lord, who fed him well. One night, the lord was attacked by his enemies; he got on his horse and rode across some rough rocky ground. At a certain moment the horse caught its hoof between two stones; it had great difficulty in getting it out again, and lost its shoe, which remained caught between the two stones. Then the lord went on riding throughout part of the night. As for the spirit of the horse, it still remembered that it had once dwelt in a human body. When the horse died, its spirit entered into the body of a pregnant woman and was incorporated into the embryo of the child she was carrying in her womb. When the child grew up, he achieved the under-standing of good. Later he became a parfait.[1] *One day, with his companion, he passed the very place where the horse had lost its shoe. Then the man, whose spirit had been in a horse, said to his companion: 'When I was a horse, one night I lost my shoe between two stones, and I went on unshod the whole night.'*

Then they both began to search between the two stones; and they found the shoe and took it with them.

Even after death, the knights of the Comté de Foix were still accompanied by their faithful steeds. *Three years ago,* said Arnaud Gélis, sacristan of a church in Pamiers (i.132), *two dead squires from the village of Dun appeared to me. They were cloven down to the navel because of the wound which had caused their death; yet they continued to ride their two cobs, which had followed them into the other world!*

Sheep, despite their stupidity, enjoyed a certain esteem. '*My son-in-law is inhabited by a good spirit, and is as gentle as a sheep,*' said Emersende Marty, referring to Bernard Befayt (ii.65). There was one mythical creature who was popular in upper Ariège and in the Pyrenees in general. Its story was told by a man from the diocese of Palhars to a man from Sabarthès, who passed it on in his turn (i.357, 363).

'*There is a bird called the pelican: its feathers shine like the sun. And its vocation is to follow the sun. The pelican had some young. It left them in the nest, so as to be able to follow the sun more freely. During its absence, a wild beast got into the nest and tore off the nestlings' claws, wings and beaks. After this had happened several times, the pelican decided to hide its radiance and to hide among its young so as to surprise and kill the beast when it next came into its nest. And this the pelican did. And the little pelicans were delivered. In the same way Christ hid his radiance when he was incarnated within the Virgin Mary; thus he was able to take the bad God prisoner and shut him up in the darkness of Hell. And thus the bad God ceased to destroy the creatures of the good God.*'

As for fish, the Cathars did not consider the flesh to be corrupt. Nor

---

1 The text actually says 'good Christian' (*bon chrétien*). In the language of those who appeared before Jacques Fournier's tribunal, this meant goodman or *parfait*. One version of this myth, in the same context (iii.138), makes a clear distinction between this good Christian or *parfait* and the people listening to him who were 'ordinary believers'.

could they lend themselves to metempsychosis, since they did not carry their young in the womb. Opinions differed about plants. Some peasants considered that it was God himself who made the wheat 'flower and swell'. They thought the Devil produced hail, thunder and storms. But other peasants were equally sure that when crops flourished it was due to Nature itself, or to the fertility of the soil, or to the presence of the *parfaits*, or to human labour or to dung.

The people of Montaillou and Sabarthès in general did not share the absolute dualistic belief that nature was the work of the bad God. They saw the hand of the bad God at work in cats, owls, wolves, reptiles, thunder and lightning. But they did not systematically regard the whole creation as Satanic. There was no definite distinction between the Creator and bountiful Nature (regarded by some as creature and by others as creator). This attitude adapted itself as required both to Catharism and to orthodox Catholicism.

The assignation of positive or negative roles to animals recalls an interesting paper by Edmund Leach[1] in which he compares insults based on the names of animals with the taboos arising out of the prohibition of incest. The people of Montaillou were in fact making similar comparisons when they praised a *parfait* for abjuring all relations with women and refraining from eating any kind of meat: they themselves abstained only from women who were close relations and from the meat of more or less domestic animals (dogs, cats, rats). There was, so to speak, one circle of animals, such as dogs and cats and pigs, which lived in an emotional, residential and even almost physical community with human beings. These, with the exception of pigs (the eating of pork nevertheless presented some problems), provided material for food taboos, insults and sometimes allusions to the Devil. Then came the circle of farm animals and those of the stable. These were slightly less close to man, whose relations with them were distant enough to be correct or even cordial, and in any case positive. The poultry yard, and even the kitchen garden, belonged to this circle: hens were well regarded in Montaillou, and even today the list of French endearments includes 'mon poulet' (hen), 'mon lapin' (rabbit), 'mon canard' (duck) and 'mon chou' (cabbage).

1 E. Leach, 'Anthropological aspects of language: animal categories and verbal abuse', in *New Directions in the Study of Language*, ed. E. Lenneberg, Cambridge, Mass., 1966.

A second fundamental dividing line marks off nature in the wild. Animals like wolves and vipers and even flies live in a state of more or less real hostility with man and his domestic beasts. Sometimes the hostility, though felt as real, was in fact purely mythical, as in the case of harmless snakes, toads, owls, magpies and so on.

Outside these categories the rest of nature, both vegetable and aquatic, was regarded as neutral or even positive towards man. Leach is certainly right in saying that insults and other pejorative expressions occur at various points of rupture between man and his zoological or natural environment: for example, the dog, in the circle of domestic animals, the one closest to man's *ego* and *domus*, and, in the circle of wild animals, the wolf, then much more of a practical reality than nowadays. Thus zoological insults and similar modes of abuse constituted a very useful procedure in Sabarthès, introducing strategic divisions into the continuum between man and nature.

The collective unconscious was indeed 'structured like a language'. Animal insults were part of a whole series of equivalences between beliefs about the family, society and brute creation. As to the latter, the people of Montaillou did not regard animals as machines, but as creatures with faculties that made them fit to be compared with human beings. In later centuries Rétif de la Bretonne and the curé Meslier, both connoisseurs of peasant philosophy, give examples of village attitudes to animals. 'Try and tell the peasants their cows are only machines', says Meslier. 'They'll just laugh at you.'[1]

The table opposite shows the system of implicit equivalences at work in upper Ariège.

A widespread current opinion holds that peasant and village religions are very strongly marked with magic, various kinds of pagan fall-out and thaumatergic and fertility rites.[2] There are glimpses among the inhabitants of Sabarthès of this practical kind of religion – the religion concerned with abundant harvests and the avoidance or cure of disease – but they are rare. Is this because the culture here was centred on the *ostal* rather than on the soil? Was it because the people's professed

1 Rétif de la Bretonne, *La Vie de mon père*, bk. II, ed. G. Rouger, Paris, 1970, p. 83; J. Meslier, *Oeuvres*, 3 vols., Paris, 1970.
2 See the chapter on 'The magic of the medieval church' in K. Thomas, *Religion and the Decline of Magic*, London, 1971.

TABLE OF EQUIVALENCES

LEVEL A (zoological)	LEVEL B (in relation to family and *domus*)
I Close domestic animals: pejorative, insulting, even diabolical, allusions (dogs, cats, pigs, etc.)	Family circle, governed by prohibition of incest; this circle is itself diabolic: *The devils are our brothers* (ii.200).
II Good animals of farm and stable. Cattle providing (aphrodisiac) butcher's meat.	Surrounding society, in the village and in Sabarthès as a whole: i.e. outside the family, and where the prohibition of incest does not apply (in Sabarthès, this freedom begins with second cousins). This area is populated by 'aphrodisiac' characters (those inviting sexual intercourse).
III Nature in the wild. – Hostile and negative circle: wolf, owl, etc. – Other animals, and vegetable and aquatic creatures (neutral or favourable)	More distant world, beyond the borders of Sabarthès: – World (hostile) – World (neutral or favourable)

religion was concerned with meditation on the after-life rather than with earthly existence? Whatever the reason, in Ax, Prades and Tarascon, God was the master of salvation rather than the power who brought rain or banished typhoid and tempests. We have no evidence of rogation processions designed to bring down the blessing of the Lord upon the fields.

True, a villager of Bédeillac might see the hand of God in a good harvest (ii.51): '*See*', he said to his friends, '*this year we were afraid we would have no corn, because it scarcely appeared above the earth, and then suddenly, thanks to Almighty God who does everything, our corn has prospered and we will again have enough this year.*' But such assertions were theoretical. They appear not to have entailed any special ceremonies designed to invoke God's aid.

Such fertility and similar rites as existed belong to magic rather than religion. '*Your beasts perish*', Guillemette Maury was told by a soothsayer from the region of Téruel (ii.39, 40), '*because a spell has been cast on them by someone who is jealous of your success as a farmer . . . but next year your flock will do very well.*' The soothsayer got his information from a book written in Arabic characters. The peasants of Montaillou believed in such divination precisely because Islam was not their own religion. They would not have dreamed of making the same use of either Catharism or orthodox Christianity. Béatrice de Planissoles is one example of many of the way they drew a line between what was magical and what was sacred. She distinguished between her devotion to the Virgin Mary, which she regarded as specifically religious, and the little purely magical devices, learned from some witch or baptized Jewess, which she used to help her win her lawsuits, to make her daughters' love affairs prosper and to cure epilepsy.

Religion and magic were not, however, entirely separate. It was easier for a priest than for a layman to bewitch a woman and make her fall in love with him. Baptism prevented a man from being drowned or being eaten by wolves. A goodman contributed to the fertility of the soil. Saint Anthony and Saint Martial were responsible for, and perhaps cured, certain skin diseases (iii.234). But the people of Sabarthès did not confuse the functions of a village healer like Na Ferreria of Prades d'Aillon with those of religion itself. Pierre Maury refused to believe in the old wives' tales which in his view had nothing to do with religion. This robust scepticism did not prevent him from having a keen sense of the divine and a permanent preoccupation with the salvation of his soul. He shared in the collective unconscious which was always, though often silently, concerned with ancient rural beliefs; but his conscious energy was directed towards Heaven and salvation.

To ensure their salvation in the other world, some of the inhabitants of Montaillou remained faithful to traditional Roman belief, while others regarded it as inadequate and turned for a time towards Catharism. But if there were differences of method, the main preoccupation was the same.

Bernard Gombert, a Cathar of Ax, expounded his attitude to Bernadette Amiel, his cousin (ii.32): '*The goodmen follow the path of God . . . they alone can save souls. And all those who are received into their sect before death go straight to Heaven, whatever wickedness or sin they have committed. The goodmen can absolve people of all their sins. As for the priests, they cannot absolve a man of his sins. Only the goodmen can do this.*' Bernard Gombert lived in a town, but the same view was found in the villages. '*A woman of Montaillou,*' said Béatrice de Planissoles to her lover (i.254), '*was gravely ill. She asked her children: "Please go and find the goodmen for me, so that they may save my soul."*

'"*If we go and find the goodmen for you,*" answered the children, "*we shall lose all our possessions.*"

'"*So,*" said their mother, "*you prefer your possessions to the salvation of my soul!*"'

The *parfaits* themselves were categorical. '*We goodmen,*' said Guillaume Authié to Raymond Vayssière of Ax-les-Thermes (i.282–3), '*can absolve anyone of his sins. Our power of absolution is equal to that of the Apostles Peter and Paul. Whereas the Catholic Church does not possess this power, because it is a bawd and a whore.*'

The shepherd brothers, Jean and Pierre Maury, were complex cases: in various degrees and at various times they accommodated both Catholic and Albigensian beliefs. But they never ceased to be out-and-out salvationists. Pierre introduced the subject in connection with a pair of excellent shoes he had bought at great expense for his friend Bélibaste. '*A pair of ordinary shoes would have done for Bélibaste,*' remarked Arnaud Sicre to Pierre (ii.38–9). '*He works sitting down in his workroom. Whereas you are always travelling up hill and down dale.*'

Pierre replied with a long speech on the soul, his own, Bélibaste's and others. He pointed out that in the building of a tower, more trouble is taken strengthening the base (the immortal soul) than the top (the mortal body). *'That is why I have given shoes, tunics, hose and cloaks to thirteen goodmen, of whom some are already before the Holy Father, so that they might pray for me . . . When he dies, Bélibaste's soul will certainly be saved; it will ascend to Heaven, borne up by angels.'* Pierre then went on to deal with the best way of absolving sin. *'It is no good confessing to the priests. They keep whores, and all they want to do is eat us up, as the wolf destroys the sheep . . . It is better to be received into Bélibaste's sect just before death . . . Then you are absolved of your sins, and in three days, after you are dead, your soul ascends to the Heavenly Father.'*

This point of view was of course challenged by the orthodox Catholics in Montaillou. Raymonde Guilhou, delousing Mengarde Clergue, cross-examined the Albigensian matriarch on the subject of salvation (ii.224).

'What are the goodmen like?'

'They are blessed and holy men,' answered Mengarde, *'People cannot be saved except at their hands.'*

'And how can that be?' asked Raymonde. *'Aren't men better saved at the hands of a priest who utters good words and who handles the body of Christ, rather than at the hands of the goodmen?'*

Some people expressed themselves crudely enough on this serious subject. Pierre Sabatier was a weaver of Varilhes, who despite certain vacillations had remained a Catholic; Varilhes was in the lowlands, and had been won back by the Roman Church. *About twenty-five years ago or thereabouts*, said Pierre Sabatier in 1318 (i.457), *I was talking to Bernard Massanes of Varilhes, now deceased (he later became my brother-in-law, and it was I who taught him the weaver's trade).*

'Why,' asked Bernard, *'do they hold a lighted candle over the mouth of those who are dying?'*

'The candle,' I answered, *'is to show that the souls of the dying who have confessed and repented of their sins are as bright as light; and so will go to God. But if the dying have not confessed or repented of their sins, you might as well put a candle up their arse as in their mouth.'*

In terms of the Roman faith, absolution of the dying and the redemption of sin were inseparable from Christ's passion. Raymonde Testanière, known as Vuissane, a maidservant of Montaillou, when asked by the Cathar shoemaker Arnaud Vital what she believed, answered (i.457): '*I believe in God and in the Virgin Mary, his mother. God endured suffering and death for the redemption of our sins.*'

We note that Vuissane's belief in the Redeemer does not involve any differentiation between Christ and 'God' in general. Her belief came to her from her mother, who warned her that the goodmen could not save souls (i.461): '*Do not believe, daughter, that a man of flesh, who produces excrement, can save souls. Only God and the Virgin Mary have that power.*'

The figure of the redeeming Christ was at the centre of all preoccupations with salvation. The relationship of a believer to Christ, fundamental for the understanding of the nature and intensity of religious sentiment in a community like that of Montaillou, might be meaningful, and based on fervent prayer, or might be almost imperceptible. Historians of Christian feeling have pointed out the change which took place in the Middle Ages in the attitude towards the figure of the Son of God. As Georges Duby has said, the Christ of the Roman age was the hero of the Parousia, 'Jesus returning on the Last Day, in all his glory, to judge the living and dead. In the thirteenth century there appeared the more learned figure . . . of Jesus the wise man. But the preaching of St Francis emphasized the Passion, and the theme of suffering developed throughout the fourteenth and fifteenth centuries, so that the royal crown was replaced by the Crown of Thorns.'[1] Similarly, Alphonse Dupront: 'Between the eleventh and fourteenth centuries we pass from a religion of God triumphant and executor of justice to a Christic religion of God suffering, a religion of the Passion . . . anxiously centred on Christ and his mother.'[2] For Delaruelle, this evolution is due to the original character 'of a religion which was anthropocentric, more concerned with salvation, however it was conceived of, than with the praise of God.'[3]

The 'Christic religion of God suffering' had certainly, by this period, reached the villagers of the Comté de Foix. In Merviel, almost at the same latitude as the Labarre Pass, which separated Sabarthès from the northern half of the Comté de Foix, a rich village woman, Aude Fauré,

1 Duby (1973), p. 108.
2 A. Dupront (1972), p. 494, in M. François, *La France et les Français*.
3 In J. Le Goff (1968).

lost the ability to pray to Christ, and even to look at Him, at the precise moment when the priest elevated the consecrated Host before the altar. Aude confided her woes to her aunt, Ermengarde Garaudy.

'*Aunt, how do you pray to God, and what prayer do you say when the priest elevates the body of Christ above the altar?*'

'*At that moment,*' answered Ermengarde (ii.87), '*I say the following prayer* [given in Occitan]: *Lord, true God and true man, Almighty, you who were born of the body of the Virgin Mary without sin, and who accepted death and passion on the tree of the true cross, you who were nailed by the hands and the feet, you whose head was crowned with thorns, you whose side was pierced with a spear, letting forth blood and water, by which we were all redeemed from sin, give me a tear of that water brought forth from you: so that it may cleanse my heart of all ugliness and all sin* . . . [The rest is in Latin] *Lord God of truth, you have redeemed me.*'

But the pious Ermengarde Garaudy of Merviel (she said another brief prayer in Occitan every morning when she got out of bed) was very much more advanced than the ordinary peasant population of the Comté de Foix. Common practice was limited to making the sign of the cross over food before eating and over the bed before sleeping, the reciting of the Lord's Prayer, the Ave Maria, and 'other prayers', genuflecting in church, the Easter communion and fasting during Lent (for the most zealous, on the vigils of certain Apostles).

Pierre Sabatier, the weaver of Varilhes, was more typical. His religious equipment consisted of a few basic elements of Catholic dogma and a few very external practices, though these were conscientiously performed. Sabatier believed in the saving virtue of confession and contrition before death: this was the fundamental common denominator at that time of all religious belief in the Comté de Foix. Despite his attacks on the rapacity of the priests, whom he accused of saying Mass only for the offerings they got out of it, *he always believed the sacraments of the Church and the articles of faith to be true.* When he wished to show that he lived up to the ideal of an ordinary Christian, or of the general notion of that ideal, he said (i.145): *I am a good Christian, Catholic and faithful. I pay tithes and first-fruits, I give alms to Christ's poor, I go on pilgrimages like a good Christian; last year I went with my wife to the Virgin of Montserrat; and this year, again with my wife, to Saint James of Compostella.*

Was Christianity in Montaillou and Sabarthès more like that of

Ermengarde Garaudy or that of Pierre Sabatier? It was probably closer
to the works of the second than to the prayers of the first. The 'Our
Father' was often their only prayer, and that was addressed not to
Christ but to God the Father.[1] Amiel de Rieux, vicar of Unac, taught
the Creed, which dealt with the Trinity and accorded an important
place to God the Son (iii.9): *I expounded the Credo in the vulgar tongue
during my Sunday Mass, article by article.* Arnaud de Savignan, a
cultivated and perhaps heretical stone-mason of Tarascon-sur-Ariège,
knew the Creed, the Pater Noster, the Ave Maria and seven Psalms
(i.164). But apart from the Pater Noster these seem to have been
unknown to the peasants and shepherds of Montaillou.

Whereas the priests made the inhabitants of the towns recite the
Paternoster, the Ave Maria and the Miserere as penance for their sins
(ii.111; iii.36), they imposed only the Pater Noster upon the people of
Montaillou. As we have seen, there was probably a small élite in the
village which understood the Lord's Prayer. But for most of the people
of Montaillou and Sabarthès it was simply a prayer recited by the
priest in church, and valid for supporters of all faiths. It is probable
that many ordinary believers in the established Church themselves
recited the Lord's Prayer but the exercise was probably more of a
repetition than a meditation.

The influence of the mendicant orders was much less strong in
Sabarthès than in the lowlands. So the habit of intense, frequent and
fervent prayer is rarely encountered in Catholic circles in the uplands
of Foix. It is more frequently encountered among the heretics in the
region, especially among the *parfaits*. Bélibaste got up six times each
night, in his drawers, to pray. Those who shared his bed in crowded
inns made him sleep on the outside so that he would not disturb them.
There was no question of their imitating him. He himself did not ask
them to follow his example. On the contrary, he told them not to pray,
for their mouths were soiled by the impurity of their lives and would

---

1 It seems, however, that the peasants did indulge, though briefly, in personal
prayers. The bells summoned them to do so. *The bells are good*, said Guillaume
Maurs, the Montaillou shepherd (ii.178), *because they incite men to pray*. The
mention of bells in Montaillou in the period 1300–1320 suggests that they appeared
here earlier than in other southern regions, where certain villages acquired them
only in the second third of the fifteenth century (see Fliche, *Histoire de l'Eglise*, Paris,
1934–ᅠ, vol. XIV, p. 732).

stain even the words of the Lord's Prayer. As Pierre Maury said (ii.37): *No one should say the Paternoster except our lords the goodmen who are in the path of truth. The rest of us, when we say the Lord's Prayer, sin mortally, because we are not in the path of truth: for we eat meat and sleep with women.*

In Montaillou, the most obvious manifestation of relationship with Christ was seen in various references to the Cross. Guillaume Maury, Pierre's brother, had Cathar leanings like all his family. But when, on 15 August 1308, imprisoned with other villagers in the château of Montaillou, he wanted to denounce Pierre Clergue the priest for having given supplies of grain to the goodmen (ii.173), he *swore by the cross.* The Maurs brothers, also Montaillou shepherds, were not always 100 per cent Catholic, but they did not neglect to make the sign of the cross before eating (ii.181). Pierre Maury, though a heretic, was so lavish with the sign of the cross that Pierre Authié was shocked and suggested a parody (ii.284, 422): '*In summer, Pierre, you can flap flies away from your face; and as you do so, you can also say: here is the forehead and here is the beard, here is one ear and here is the other.*' The Cathar shoemaker, Arnaud Vital, protested against the respect which the natives of Montaillou showed for the Cross: '*It is worthless, it is the sign of evil*', he said to Vuissane Testanière (i.457). At the sight of all the wooden crosses scattered over the countryside, Bélibaste cried (ii.53; ii.410), *If I could, I would chop them down with an axe; I would use them as wood to boil the pots.*

Single or double yellow crosses, made of material, reminded those who had dabbled in heresy and yet been spared prison on what side the true faith was to be found. The Fournier Register shows forty-eight sentences of imprisonment in all, as against twenty-five people condemned to wear the yellow cross. Out of these twenty-five, seventeen had been sentenced to imprisonment in the first instance. In Montaillou itself, seven men and women escaped incarceration only to have to endure the infamy of wearing the yellow cross. It would be a great psychological ordeal, and the victims went to considerable lengths to lighten it. *On holidays,* said Arnaud de Savignan, heretical stonemason of Tarascon (ii.440), *I wear the yellow crosses openly on my cloak, but on other days, especially when I am working, I do not wear the crosses, because I am in my tunic or shirt. When I come home from work, I put on my mantle and therefore wear the crosses; but sometimes I wear them hidden; and other times I walk through Tarascon without wearing them, in my tunic.*

The annual fair at Ax-les-Thermes was held on Holy Cross Day (ii.477-8, 363). But frequent as all these references were, for the people of Montaillou the crucifix remained virtually unoccupied. In Sabarthès, only a minority of zealots, supported at a distance by the mendicant monks, went in for macabre meditation upon Christ's suffering on the Cross.

Christ, more often called 'God', was more frequently present in Sabarthès through the Eucharist. The 'sacrament of the altar', the 'body of the Lord' or the 'body of Christ' was a familiar presence in the parish church. The big bell was rung at the moment of the Elevation, and the people in the church fell on their knees, lowering their hoods (iii.60; 235). It was also a familiar presence in the highways and byways, where the priest carried the last sacraments to the dying. The Eucharist was an element of lowland civilization which early penetrated the Pays d'Aillon. As we have already seen, the first communion was an important rite of passage. After the first communion, people used to communicate once or several times a year. Gaillarde Ros, a pious informer of Ornolac, speaking of the local *bayle* Guillaume Austatz, a rich peasant, former usurer and free-thinker of his village, says (i.192): *I have lived in Ornolac twelve years and never seen Guillaume Austatz take communion! Not even during times of illness. Nor on holidays. And yet, at those times, people usually do take communion. But if Guillaume had done so, I would have known. Think, I have often seen him going into the church. And do not forget that I am his mother-in-law's sister.*

The four communions a year – at Easter, Whitsun, All Saints and Christmas – imposed as a penance on Aude Fauré, may be regarded as a maximum (ii.104). In the ordinary course of events there was no question of frequent communion. There was also a kind of terminal or panic communion, resorted to by individuals when they thought they were on the point of death, and by people in general at times of epidemic.[1] In Montaillou itself, the most resolutely Cathar section of the population probably did not go to communion; the priest Pierre

---

1 See ii.100, for a woman seizing the opportunity to take communion herself when a priest is visiting a sick person's bedside.

Clergue no doubt turned a blind eye. But even if at certain times, as between 1300 and 1307, most of the people in the village might have been regarded as sympathetic to the Cathars, the number who actually abstained from communion was probably only a minority. Believers in heresy did not hesitate to pretend to take communion when necessary, for, as Bélibaste said, *To eat a little biscuit never did anyone any harm* (ii.55). Elsewhere, the numerous free-thinkers among the peasantry of Sabarthès, and such deviants as homosexuals, might go for twelve years or so without taking Easter communion (iii.46). The refusal to take the last sacrament constituted a moment of great drama in the death-struggle of a Montaillou peasant suffering the *endura*. The dying person, wishing to be saved only by the goodmen, would try to drive the priests away from his bedside, calling them devils, peasants or boors (i.462).

Paradoxically, one of the most striking examples of the general respect for the body of Christ is the attitude of Raymond de Laburat, an anti-clerical peasant of Sabarthès. He said he would be glad to see all the clergy, from the Pope to ordinary priests, go off to the Crusades to be destroyed by the Saracens. He would be even more delighted to see the churches razed to the ground. Then Mass would be celebrated on the land and in the fields, and the peasants who, like him, had been excommunicated and driven out of the churches, would at last have the great happiness of seeing the body of their divine Master in the open air (ii.311).

Propaganda in favour of the Host made use of all possible resources, including the sort of anecdote made popular by the author of the Golden Legend. Ermengarde Garaudy told Aude Fauré (ii.84) how '*a woman cooked a girdle cake which a priest then consecrated on the altar. When she saw this, the woman burst out laughing.*

'"*It seems the girdle cake I made has become the body of Christ. That makes me laugh.*"

'*But she wanted to take communion just the same. So the priest prayed God to perform a miracle: and when the priest gave the woman communion, the cake-cum-Host took on the appearance of a child's finger and the consecrated wine in the chalice looked like coagulated blood. The woman was terrified! She communicated all the more devoutly.*'

Mass, as distinct from communion itself, continued to play an essential role. The many people who had been excommunicated for non-payment of tithes were excluded from Mass, as an example. Former heretics, condemned to various penances, were castigated between the Epistle and the Gospel. People in general came to Mass dressed in their best, especially on feast days (ii.440; i.338).

But people did not worry too much if they forgot to go to Mass – at least from time to time, on ordinary Sundays. Béatrice de Planissoles, after she had moved to the lowlands, where attendance at Mass was more strict than in Montaillou, was surprised to be rebuked by the *vicaire* of her new parish and told to go to church more regularly (i.214–15). The fact that in a village of considerable size like Unac in Sabarthès there were only about fifty people at an ordinary Sunday Mass shows that there was a certain amount of absenteeism which shocked no one.[1] There is nothing surprising about this lukewarm attitude. Specifically Christian piety was always the attribute of an élite in the Middle Ages and even when, in times of panic, this élite grew very numerous, it still remained urban rather than rural, and did not include the mountain dwellers. The love of God as a person was little known and little practised in the uplands of the Comté de Foix. There were a few exceptions, of which Bernard Franca was one (i.352). He was a cleric and a thinker who knew a little Latin; in church he reminded his fellow parishioners that love was at the base of all charity and that only those alms are valid which are given *through love and not through fear*. He criticized legacies to the poor which were made only from fear of approaching death. But it was very rare for anyone to place chief emphasis on the love of God as such, based on the example and teaching of Christ. Pierre Authié, the *parfait*, preferred to emphasize the fact that the members of his sect, once received into Heaven, would love each other like fathers and mothers, brothers and sisters. Once again, it was the human ideal of salvation which came first.

1 iii.9. A not very clear passage suggests that in one rural parish in Sabarthès about half the people went regularly to Mass on Sunday (ii.367).

CHAPTER XIX Religion in practice

Throughout the high Middle Ages, men of the Church, including St Bernard and St Dominic, had passionately promoted devotion to the Virgin Mary. In 1254 the Council of Albi raised the Ave Maria to rank with the major prayers, the Credo and the Lord's Prayer, which were theoretically taught to everyone over the age of seven.

Such was the theory, but what of the practice? Among the middle classes of the small towns, the Ave Maria did indeed form part of a Catholic equipment.

'*And you, how do you pray to God?*' Bélibaste asked Arnaud Sicre, son of a notary of Tarascon and of a lady of Ax (ii.37, 54).

'*I cross myself,*' answered Sicre, '*I commend myself to God who died for us on the cross, and to the Virgin Mary, I say the Pater Noster and the Ave Maria . . . I fast on the vigil of the Virgin.*'

'*The sheep bleats because it does not know how to speak,*' was Bélibaste's sarcastic answer. '*Let me tell you that the Ave Maria is worthless. It is an invention of the priests . . . As for your fasting, it might as well be the fasting of a wolf!*'[1]

In Montaillou itself, the small local élite, both noble and clerical, honoured the Virgin, at least with the external signs of piety. Clergue the priest had his mother buried under the altar consecrated to Mary. Béatrice de Planissoles, though she might sometimes forget to go to Mass on Sunday, did not neglect, when she rose from childbed, to dedicate a coloured candle made with her own hands to the local Virgin (i.223). The Assumption of the Virgin was the occasion for feasting among the nobility of the region (ii.123).

'Sancta Maria' was a common enough exclamation among the women of Sabathès (i.191, 194, 463), perhaps indicating the direction of their devotion. Among the peasants, it may be that some of them knew the Ave Maria as well as the Pater Noster. Some of them actually prayed to the Virgin. *I often reminded my brother Pierre that he ought to say the Pater Noster and the Ave Maria*, said Jean Maury, a shepherd of Montaillou who had learned the prayers in question from his mother,

1 Note that, unlike the Cathars of upper Ariège, the Waldensians of Pamiers had a high regard for the Ave Maria (i.104–05).

while his father represented heretical influence in the family; Jean himself remained half Catholic (ii.446, 449).

In 1334 Rixende Cortil, daughter of a villager of Vaychis and wife of a villager of Ascou, recounted an experience dating back sixteen years (iii.308): *One holiday, I went to the church in Ax and knelt at the altar of the Blessed Mary and began to pray to her. Guillemette Authié, wife of Amiel Authié (now dead), was beside me. When she heard me praying she said: 'Stop praying to Mary. Pray rather to Our Lord.'*

But I went on praying to Mary!

We do not know whether Rixende's prayer was actually the Ave Maria. In Montaillou, according to the two Testanières, mother and daughter, the Virgin Mary was not limited to her orthodox role of intercessor, and could also be redeemer in her own right (i.457, 461). This idea was probably quite general, and included the actual Adoration of the Virgin. The customers in a tavern in Foix, discussing the burning at the stake of a Waldensian, commented (i.174), '*He commended his soul to God and to the Blessed Mary . . . he adored them both in courtly fashion; so he is not a heretic.*'

At this period there were not many place-names in Occitania referring to the Virgin Mary, but there were pilgrimages and of course churches dedicated to her. The annual pilgrimage to the church of Sabart or Savart in Tarascon took place on 8 September, the Feast of the Nativity of the Virgin. Other places of pilgrimage to the Virgin Mary referred to in the Fournier Register are Montserrat in Catalonia, Le Puy, Racamadour and, very occasionally, Notre Dame de Paris. The Nativity of the Virgin was another notable day in the shepherds' calendar: *My brother Pierre Maury*, says Jean Maury (ii.486), *sold his sheep that same year at Morella fair, which is held on the Nativity of the Virgin.* There were pilgrimages, too, to the Blessed Mary of Montgauzy, also in the Comté de Foix. Gaillarde Ros, a peasant woman of Ornolac, had been robbed of money and other articles. So she went to implore Saint Mary of Montgauzy to get her things back for her. She set a tall candle before the altar and prayed to the Virgin to put it into the robbers' hearts to give back the stolen goods (i.192–7). But Saint Mary was not regarded merely as some Saint Anthony of Padua, there just automatically to restore lost objects. Aude Fauré (ii.95), when she realized that she no longer believed in the real presence of the Body of

Christ, *turned to her nurse and said: 'Pray God to put in my heart to become a believer again.'*

And while the nurse prayed to God as best she could, Guillemette, servant in Aude Fauré's ostal, came in. 'Guillemette', said Aude, 'pray to the Blessed Virgin Mary of Montgauzy and ask her to enlighten me that I may believe in God.'

Guillemette, after having knelt, carried out her mistress's order. And when she had prayed, Aude was immediately enlightened, and believed firmly in God, and she still believes in him today, according to what she says.

Some of the Cathars tended to take a mystical view of Mary. Bélibaste identified her with the Albigensian Church, or the congregation of the faithful (ii.52–3; i.282). Pierre Authié told Pierre Maury that *'the Mother of God was quite simply good will'* (ii.409). Pierre Clergue, while he might ridicule the official Virgin of the Catholic Church, still showed his veneration for the terrestrial Virgin of Montaillou. Undoubtedly, in the Pays d'Aillon and upper Ariège in general, the Virgin Mother was of the earth. Fertility cults both human and agricultural, which at first sight seem conspicuous by their absence, were unspoken rather than non-existent and, in fact, incorporated in the cult of the Virgin. Written texts and even people's minds may have been silent about them, but they nevertheless continued to underlie the more abstract superstructures of Montaillou's religion.

There were some ninety holidays each year, including Sundays and feast-days. The latter often involved some folkloric or even pagan elements. It is not always easy to distinguish the magical from the devotional in these observances.

Twenty-six years ago, said Bernard Marty the shepherd in 1324 (iii.276), *I said to my father on the day of the Epiphany: 'I am going to keep vigil in honour of Saint Julian, patron of our church in Junac.'*

Then the local châtelain, *who was present, made fun of me. 'Oh, so you're going to shed light onto your walls?'*

The reference is to Saint Julian the Hospitaller. Saint Anthony, the great Egyptian hermit and father of monasticism, was popular among the shepherds, who often offered him a fleece.

But the saints most frequently mentioned are the Apostles. E. Delaruelle has shown how devotion to the Apostles developed in the West after the eleventh century, linked to the discovery of the 'apostolic life' and gradually being incorporated 'into the realm of popular devotion'.[1] Pierre Maury was told by his co-parishioners (iii.120): *'The good people and good Christians came into this country; they follow the path followed by the Blessed Peter and Paul and the other Apostles, who followed the Lord ... We ask you: would you like to meet the good Christians?'*

Pierre answered: 'If the goodmen are as you say, if they do follow the path of the Apostles, why do they not preach publicly, as the Apostles did? ... Why are they afraid for truth and justice, when the Apostles themselves were not afraid to suffer death for such a cause?'

The regional councils in Occitania ordered the feasts of the twelve Apostles to be celebrated, and these instructions were on the whole followed in the region with which we are concerned (i.121). Saint Dominic had been to Occitania and preached the apostolic life both in words and by example. Saint Peter was the most popular of the Apostles. At both Prades d'Aillon and Montaillou, the two local churches in each place were dedicated to Saint Peter and to the Virgin, as were the two churches in Savart.

'Oh! Oh! How can we do such a thing in the church of Saint Peter?' said Béatrice de Planissoles, in Prades, when she entered the local church where her lover the priest had prepared a bed for the two of them for the night. To which the lover replied (i.243): *'Much harm it will do Saint Peter!'* Guillaume Bélibaste tried to make his little clique of admirers worship him *like a Saint Peter* (iii.258), to the point where Jean Maury observed: *'You make a very bad Peter.'* In both Prades and Montaillou the peasant girls put on their best clothes and gave their sweethearts a good lunch on the local Feast of Saint Peter and Saint Paul; afterwards they went out and danced in the square (i.338).

But in all this homage to the Apostles, the country people's chief preoccupation was salvation. The *parfaits* always insisted on the connection between the apostolic life and the saving of the soul. *'The goodmen alone follow the path of truth and justice which was followed by the Apostles'*, said the farmers Raymond Pierre and Bernard Bélibaste to the shepherd Pierre Maury (iii.122). *'They do not take other people's possessions. Even if they find gold or silver on their path, they do not "lift" it and put it in their pockets; they follow the faith of the Apostles: a man is better saved in the faith of the heretics than in any other faith there is.'* Pierre Authié remarked (iii.123): *'I shall set you in the way of salvation,*

1 E. Delaruelle, in J. Le Goff (1968), p. 149.

as Christ set his Apostles, who neither lied nor deceived . . . We will let ourselves be stoned, as the Apostles were stoned, without denying a word of the faith.' Guillaume Authié emphasizes the apostolic purity of those who can save in speaking to Bernard Marty, a young shepherd and son of a blacksmith (iii.253): *'The goodmen save souls . . . they alone! They eat neither eggs nor meat nor cheese; they follow the path of the Apostles Peter and Paul.'* He expresses a similar idea to Raymond Vayssière of Ax (i.282–3): *'The parfaits of our sect have as much power to absolve sins as had the Apostles Peter and Paul . . . those who follow us go in the end to Heaven, and the others to Hell.'*

The shepherds of Sabarthès did not pray to the Apostles as such, but they were glad to encounter holy men of flesh and blood who seemed to them to resemble Christ's companions.

All Saints' Day was a particularly important feast in the Sabarthès calendar. It marked the day of departure of the flocks towards their winter pastures (ii.479). It was one of the few vigils in the year when Bernard Clergue, an uncompromising Cathar, condescended to fast. *But you could see by his face that he did not like it*, remarked Barthélemy Amilhac, his fellow-prisoner (ii.283). All Saints, the eve of All Souls, was the prelude to a great upsurge of piety in Montaillou.

About twenty-two years ago, said Gauzia Clergue (iii. 356–7), *on the morrow of All Saints, I took a big piece of bread to the house of Pierre Marty, to give to him as alms. It was the custom in Montaillou on that day.*

'Take this bread for redemption of the souls of your mother and father, and your other dead relatives,' I said to Pierre.

'To whom shall I give it?' he asked me.

'Keep it for yourself and for those of your domus, *and eat it,'* I answered.

'It is for God', said Pierre.

And I went away, saying to Emersende, Pierre's wife, whom I met as I went: 'The alms I have given you counts as a good deed, because you are a friend of God.'

Such an incident is revealing of a characteristic combination of two strands of popular culture: traditional observances and a preoccupation with salvation.

As for the actual use of the sacraments, baptism was almost universally practised, not only because of its religious value, which was challenged by the goodmen (i.282; ii.410). We have already seen how it was believed to act as a protection, and how it led to the establishment of friendships among the sponsors. These friendships sometimes helped to spread Albigensianism. *I had gone to Arques to the house of Raymond Pierre, who was my fellow-sponsor,* said a Sabarthès farmer (ii.9), *and we began to talk about the heretics, and my friend said that the heretics were good men, that they possessed the true faith . . . as for my mother, she had established a great friendship with her own fellow-sponsor and with this woman's sister . . . who was later burned for heresy.*

According to orthodox Catholic theology, reaffirmed by the thirteenth-century Popes, baptism obtained the remission of original sin. The idea of original sin was not completely unknown in the Pays d'Aillon. Mengarde Buscailh, an ordinary peasant woman of Prades, near Montaillou, said: *The baby I am suckling is Christian* [i.e. baptized], *and has committed no sin; except what he derives from me.* But this allusion is unique as far as the rural witnesses in the Fournier Register are concerned.[1] Although the meaning of baptism derived from the idea of original sin, this dogma was much less familiar to the peasants of Montaillou than that of transubstantiation or the remission of sins through penance, notions which lay behind the sacraments of communion and confession. People usually went to communion, and to the confession which preceded it, once a year.

'*Do you wish to make confession to me?*' Arnaud de Verniolles asked a young villager then living in Pamiers (iii.27).

'*No,*' replied the boy. '*I have already confessed this year . . . And anyway you're not a priest!*'

In Montaillou itself almost everyone went to confession at least once a year. On several occasions the shepherds Pierre and Jean Maury and Guillaume Maurs remarked on their annual confession of sins; and yet these men were never more than lukewarm towards orthodox Catholicism, and two of them at least were heretics for long periods. Every year before Easter Pierre Clergue the priest used to hear the confessions of his flock, though he did not believe in this sacrament (i.224). When peasant women who sympathized with Cathars went to confession with the rest they said nothing about their connections with the goodmen and the 'believers'. *I make confession of my sins,* said Raymond Marty (iii.104; Béatrice de Planissoles said much the same, i.232), *except that*

1 Outside rural circles, and among the Waldensians of Pamiers, the notion of original sin was a familiar one (ii.245; i.51).

which I have committed in heresy; because I do not think I have sinned in committing it. Also Raymonde, wife of Arnaud Belot (iii.71): *I make confession of my sins, except those I have committed in heresy, for I am afraid of losing all my possessions if I reveal that. But I have repented of these heretical sins, and by way of penance, which I inflicted on myself without the help of any confessor, I did not wear a shift for two winters.*

So the people of Montaillou did not necessarily tell all in the confessional, for as Bélibaste said (ii.38–9), they were expected to tell their secrets to a priest who might afterwards laugh about their foolish sins with his friends (iii.229). But everyone knew that confession, in order to be valid, had to be accompanied by sincere feeling. Guillaume Maurs related (ii.103) how *the priest who heard my confession would not let me take communion because of the hatred I bore in my heart towards the priest of Montaillou.*

Many heretics in Sabarthès made 'blank confessions', kneeling before their confessor but saying nothing of their sins (ii.196). There were also 'joke confessions', where the priest could not help laughing, and took advantage of his position to seduce his female parishioners. Sometimes confession was used for informing: Gauzia Clergue, making confession to the rector of Prades, denounced her Cathar friends in Montaillou (iii.357; ii.200). Nevertheless, confession was more highly regarded than many of the other sacraments, and even for heretics might always offer the means of salvation. *On my husband's instructions I went with some others to weed the corn in our fields on the other side of the river Ariège,* said Alazaïs de Bordes, a peasant of Ornolac (i.196). *We were very frightened when our boat crossed back again, for the river had risen very high. When I set foot on dry land again, I took refuge, trembling, in Guillaume Austatz's house.*

'*Why were you so frightened?*', he asked me.

'*Because I was afraid,*' I answered, '*of dying suddenly without being able to make confession; and I prefer to die in another manner, with confession!*'

Another witness, also a heretic, said (ii.245): *Not all the water in a tank, or even in the whole world, could wash away sin, unless there is confession and penance first.* So, undermined though it was by the ravages of Albigensian propaganda, confession remained almost universal among a population which, whether it was orthodox or heterodox, was preoccupied with its own salvation.

While first communion and marriage acted as rites of passage, other sacraments seem to have been almost unknown in the upland villages. For example, there are no instances of confirmation. There is good reason for this: the Bishop, who would have performed the ceremony, rarely left Pamiers and his inquisitorial tasks, and in any case was not eager to travel among the mountainous areas of his diocese. The Bishop did once get as far as Ax-les-Thermes, to 'reconcile' the church there after it had been polluted by murder (ii.108). But the Register makes no mention of confirmation, which was supposed to bestow on the recipient the gift of the Holy Ghost. Were it not for the enthusiasm with which Whitsun was celebrated, it would be tempting to think that this silence indicated that for the people of Montaillou the third person of the Trinity was of very minor importance.

Another sacrament which was absent from upper Ariège, as from many other parts of the west at this time, was extreme unction. People in danger of death, unless they were strict Cathars, wanted to make confession. The priest would come to their bedside and question the dying person on the articles of faith, especially the Real Presence. If the answers were satisfactory, the sick person would take communion (i.239–40). But there was never any question of anointing with holy oil.

The saying of Masses and prayers for the repose of the souls of the dead was a practice more common in the towns than in the villages and among the nobles rather than the peasantry. General remembrance of the dead was observed, in Sabarthès as elsewhere, on Ash Wednesday. Though in Montaillou itself this ceremony seems to have been eclipsed by the festivities of All Souls.

Of religious practices in addition to the sacraments, pilgrimage was regarded by the peasants of the Comté de Foix as one of the duties of a 'good Christian'. The pilgrimages performed by the people of Montaillou were usually local, and they also gladly gave alms to pilgrims visiting the Virgin of Montaillou (i.255). In return for such charity, Béatrice de Planissoles was given a berry called *ive*, which was supposed to cure epilepsy. She tried it on one of her grandsons, but the baby showed much more improvement when its mother took it on a pilgrimage to the Church of Saint Paul (i.249).

Going on a pilgrimage was regarded as so natural that a wife running away from her husband could throw off her pursuers by saying, *I am going with my brother on a pilgrimage to Romania* (iii.151). But the people of Montaillou itself did not usually go on distant pilgrimages. Those who went to Saint James of Compostella usually did so under compulsion, wearing on their backs the yellow crosses of the Inquisition.

Fasting was another religious practice which was widely observed; to refuse to fast was to court the anger of the orthodox. '*If you're not careful I'll fling your plate of meat all over you*,' said Bernard Austatz of Lordat to his brother Guillaume, a bold thinker in perfect health who was not observing Lent (i.195). The fact, though, that the custom of Lent was so generally followed enabled the goodmen to move about more freely, because during this season they could openly consume their favourite food, which was mostly fish (ii.71). The Montaillou shepherds, even those who were Cathars, seem to have abstained from meat both during Lent and on Fridays (ii.382). Even an anti-Catholic like Bernard Clergue fasted, though with reluctance, on the eve of All Saints (ii.283).

Sometimes people failed to fast through ignorance. *I do not know what the fast days of the Church are, apart from Lent and Friday*, said Guillaume Baille, a migrant shepherd of Montaillou (ii.382). Peasants most committed to heresy or anti-clericalism made a point of flouting the rules about fasting. *I don't like fish. I prefer goat's liver*, said one villager of Montaillou. Guillaume Austatz, a sturdy and hard-working farmer, said proudly (i.198), *For five weeks during this Lent I ate meat. I could have abstained from doing so without physical risk, while I was occupied with household affairs and with those of the threshing-floor.*

In the last resort, apart from individual peculiarities, people's attitudes to fasting tended to correspond to the ideologies which divided their society. *Twenty-three years ago*, said Gauzia Clergue of Montaillou in 1325 (iii.330–61), *during Lent, I was coming back one day, the day after Sunday, from gathering beets in one of my fields; and on the way I passed Guillaume Benet.*

'*Have you had lunch?*' *he asked me.*

'*No*,' *I answered.* '*I am fasting.*'

'*Well*,' *said Guillaume*, '*yesterday, Sunday, I was invited to Ax-les-Thermes, and I had a very good lunch. At first I hesitated about it. So I went to see the goodmen to ask their advice.* "*Anyway*," *they said*, "*it's just as great a sin to eat meat out of Lent as in Lent. It soils the mouth just as much. So don't you worry about it.*" *And so I accepted that excellent meat lunch.*'

But I, said Gauzia Clergue, *did not agree. Meat in Lent or out of Lent: from the point of view of sin it is not at all the same thing.*

The mendicant monks – Minorites or preaching friars – though very active at this period in other parts of Occitania, were conspicuous in upper Ariège by their comparative absence. People of Montaillou had heard of them, but they had to go a long way actually to see them. Vuissane Testanière confessed to a friar that she had listened to heresy in the house of the Belots; but the friar lived in Puigcerda, in Catalonia, miles away from her home in Montaillou (i.459). Pierre Maury enjoyed the sermon of a mendicant monk who set people's consciences on fire, but this was in Arques, in the present department of Aude (iii.123). Béatrice de Planissoles had important contacts with the Franciscans, but only after she had gone down into what Pierre Clergue called *the low countries among the wolves and dogs of Catholicism.*

After I went to live in Crampagna [lower Ariège] *with my second husband,* said Béatrice (i.232), *I was able to hear the sermons of the preaching friars and the Minorites. I renounced the errors of heresy; I made confession in a confessional to a Minorite friar from a monastery at Limoux* [present-day Aude], *in the Church of the Virgin of Marseillan. Near there, I went to see my sister Gentile, who had married in Limoux and lived there.* Note that Gentile was a devout Catholic, and that the confession took place in a 'confessional', whereas back in Montaillou the priest had heard confession simply behind the altar to the Virgin (i.224).

Despite their official ideal of poverty, the two new orders of Minorites and preaching friars were on the whole mistrusted in the mountain regions. Pierre Maury criticized them for being rich and gluttonous and covered with embroidery. With their urbane sermons, the preaching friars were more at home in the wealthier and more advanced towns of the lowlands.

So the field was clear for the ordinary secular clergy, especially the priest. Most parishes seem to have had a priest permanently in residence. Others apparently had to be content, at least temporarily, with a *vicaire.* Pierre Clergue, of course, was conspicuously resident in Montaillou. Pierre de Spera, his predecessor at the end of the thirteenth century, was also resident (i.223). Raymond Trilh, who succeeded Clergue after his death, was called the '*vicaire*' of Prades and Montaillou, so perhaps the new priest himself was absent (i.466; ii.239).

But residence was not a guarantee of competence. Amiel de Rieux, perpetual *vicaire* of Unac, would discuss learned books with his colleagues from neighbouring parishes; like Pierre Clergue, they could quote from Saint Augustine. But some parish clergy were well below this level: Adhémar de Bédeillac, priest of Bédeillac, had forgotten the passages from the Gospels and other scriptures which according to him he had once quoted in an argument with one of his parishioners (iii.53).

Despite the ritual criticisms of the *parfaits*, the prestige enjoyed by the priests was shown by the way they were addressed. Even in prison, they were given the title of *Dominus* (ii.273–304). Some priests possessed a *domus* and a farm large enough to bring in money as well as esteem. But the prestige of the priest was not limited to the individual. There were 'races of priests', whose members, including both laymen and women, inspired both respect and, especially, fear. '*I shall not say anything to you, because you belong to a race of priests: that frightens me,*' said Emersende Marty to Gauzia Clergue (iii.357).

We have already seen the privileges a priest might enjoy with his female parishioners. It may be that immoral priests were only a minority among the clergy of Sabarthès, but they were numerous enough, and very much in evidence. Round the central figure of the parish priest there might be members of other strata, higher or lower in the hierarchy. In some rural parishes in Sabarthès one or more peasants in minor orders, perhaps even with a smattering of Latin, performed the duties which would be carried out two centuries later by choirboys. In Montaillou itself the only assistance of this kind was the priest's pupil, who as well as doing Pierre Clergue's odd jobs might also have had a few Latin lessons. But on the whole Pierre Clergue carried out his duties and enjoyed his power alone. Sometimes the priest of Montaillou would go down to attend a council in Pamiers.[1] This gave Pierre Clergue the opportunity to look up old acquaintances and old sweethearts. The powers of the Bishop were felt very strongly in Montaillou itself. At least during periods of crisis, the people were always going to Pamiers, either summoned there by the Bishop, or in order to throw themselves at his feet, or to be put in prison.

The Pope was not unknown to the peasants of upper Ariège. The inhabitants of Arques went to him to be pardoned for their heresy. In Montaillou itself, Guillemette Argelliers, née Caravesse, said that *the priests have learned what they say from the Pope, whom God has constituted his representative on earth* (iii.95). But it was the local priest who was in

1 i.234. In theory the council at Pamiers was supposed to meet twice a year, at least after the appointment of Fournier's successor. Before that date it met less often.

charge of the religious instruction of the peasants. This instruction could be given either through sermons or through the teaching of children or adolescents. The Council of Albi in 1254 ordered 'that the priests explain the articles of the faith to the faithful on Sundays and feast days' and 'that children be brought to church from the age of seven years to be instructed in the Catholic faith, and to learn the Pater and the Ave Maria.'

Between theory and practice there might be a gap. The goodmen claimed (ii.367) that *the priests do not do their duty, they do not instruct their flock as they should, and all they do is eat the grass that belongs to their sheep.*

But the evidence shows clearly that after Sunday Mass the country priest often preached in the vulgar tongue. It was thus that Amiel de Rieux preached to some fifty people, including a nobleman and a priest. He took advantage of the occasion to expound a few heretical 'errors', which shocked the more educated of his audience but left the majority unmoved (iii.9–13). Another village priest told his congregation that Christ ate and drank like everyone else but that *when he ate, he did not swallow* (iii.55). People of Sabarthès were still laughing years afterwards about this jest against the Incarnation.

However, this sort of deviance was exceptional: the majority of the priests in the Comté de Foix preached in accordance with orthodox Roman dogma. Barthélemy Amilhac, for example, was suspected by the Inquisitors of immorality, but not of unsound doctrine. And he taught the boys and girls of Dalou in the local church (i.252). Guillaume Austatz, *bayle* and farmer of Ornolac, gives similar evidence about the orthodoxy of what people heard in church. *Under the influence of Pierre Authié and my mother,* says Guillaume (i.206), *I ceased to believe in the Resurrection of the Body. But my conscience was driven hither and thither. In church I had heard sermons about the Resurrection; and the priest, Guillaume d'Alzinhac, who lived with my mother at Lordat, had taught me when I was young, and he had told me that men and women come to life again after death.*

The priest certainly played a critical role in the transmission of Catholicism. But in Montaillou itself there was a contradiction between Pierre Clergue's theoretically Catholic teaching and the basic heterodoxy and cynicism of one who admitted that he only carried out his duties in order to receive the income attached to them (i.227). Some

Catholic matrons, including the mothers of Vuissane Testanière and Jean Maury, tried as best they could to hand on to their children the torch of the Catholic religion. But in the absence of a genuine priest they stood little chance against the influence of the goodmen.

In addition to the prose teaching of the Church there was also singing – though all we know about it is that it existed (i.145–6) – and visual instruction. Churches might contain statues, pictures and stained-glass windows. In Sabarthès, church art usually took the form of roughly carved wooden statues, embodying popular piety and superstition. The *parfaits* deplored them: '*Do you believe these bits of wood can perform miracles?*' said Bélibaste to Arnaud Sicre (ii.54–5). Pierre Authié, talking to some farmers (ii.420), said, '*You carved with your own axes the statues of saints in the "house of idols"* [i.e. the church] *and then you worship them!*' Bernard Gombert of Ax-les-Thermes even maintained (ii.333) that *the Virgin is never anything but a piece of wood, without real eyes or feet or ears or mouth!*

Religious deviation usually manifested itself in the form of millenarianism, with its characteristic symptoms – doom-laden prophecies about the imminent end of the world, the expectation of a period when all things would be made new in a kingdom of heaven and earth and violent anti-semitism. But in the region with which we are concerned there was very little millenarianism: the larger villages and small towns were tinged with it, but rural areas remained unscathed. Bélibaste, in exile in Spain, might predict that '*people will rise up against people and kingdom against kingdom: a descendant of the King of Aragon will graze his horse upon the altar in Rome*' (ii.63), but Guillemette Maury from Montaillou only replied politely: '*And when will that be, sir?*'

The influence of the anti-Jewish *pastoureaux* rebels did not spread much beyond the areas of the Garonne and Toulousain. In Pamiers there were anti-Semites among the religious zealots: *I can recognize Jewish ghosts by their smell*, said Arnaud Gélis, expert in dialogues with the dead. In Montaillou itself there were no Jews, and in fact they were almost unheard of: the only mention of Jews in the village itself is a reference to a converted Jewess who gave Béatrice de Planissoles a few small magic recipes.

There is no doubt that before the period we are dealing with, both in Languedoc in general and in the Comté de Foix in particular, there were rumours current about the end of the world, or at least some levelling revolution. These derived some of their credibility from distant echoes of the Mongol invasions. Montanhagol the troubadour bore witness to this fear: 'See, the Tartars are coming from the East. If God does not prevent it, they will bring everything down to the same level: the great lord, the priests and the peasants.'[1]

In 1318 the roads between Pamiers and upper Ariège were full of popular anticipations of the end of the world. *That year*, said Bertrand Cordier of Pamiers (i.60–61), *I came upon four men of Tarascon, including Arnaud de Savignan, on the other side of the bridge, in the territory of the parish of Quié. They asked me: 'What's new in Pamiers?'*

'They say that the Antichrist is born', I answered. 'Everyone must put his soul in order; the end of the world is near!'

To which Arnaud de Savignan replied: 'I don't believe it! The world has neither beginning nor end . . . Let's go to bed.'

When Arnaud was rebuked by the Inquisition for believing that the world was eternal, he gave his lack of religious instruction as an excuse. *Because of my work in the stone quarries*, he said (i.167), *I have to leave Mass very early and I do not have time to hear the sermons.* But in fact his view was a very common one among the people of Sabarthès. Arnaud said (i.151), *I have heard many of the people of Sabarthès say that the world always existed and always would exist in the future.* Jaquette den Carot, a woman of Ax, used the same words as Arnaud de Savignan on the subject, talking to fellow-countrywomen at the mill (i.151–3): *'There is no other age but our own.'*

To reject the idea of the end of the world, the final Judgment, the future life and the general Resurrection was to refuse *ipso facto* any propaganda in favour of millenarianism, as taught in various manners by the *pastoureaux* and different ecclesiastics. Sabarthès, in what was a kind of avant-garde archaism, was resistant to the modern though deviant trends of Catholic sensibility. Such scepticism was not limited to small towns such as Ax and Tarascon. As we have seen, Arnaud de Savignan said that he found it all over Sabarthès, and the records give evidence of it in the small villages. In Montaillou itself, Béatrice de Planissoles was accused of having said *that peoples' bodies will be destroyed like cobwebs, because they are the work of the devil* (i.309). Here the Resurrection of the Body is rejected in accordance with a Cathar form of dualism, which

1 Nelli (1966), p. 245.

regarded the flesh as derived from Satan and therefore subject to decay. A similar scepticism is found in Guillaume Austatz, a rich peasant and *bayle* of Ornolac. One day, seeing a heap of bones being extracted from a newly dug grave in the village churchyard, he said to his fellow parishioners (i.206): '*How is it possible for the souls of the dead to come back one day in the same bones as were theirs before?*'

Béatrice de Planissoles, Guillaume Austatz and Arnaud de Savignan were to a certain extent members of an élite. But the people of Montaillou in general, and of other rural parishes, showed no undue enthusiasm about the doctrine of the Resurrection. *In Rabat*, says Bernard D'Orte, who lived there (i.258–65), *several of us were joking with Gentile Macarie (Guillaume's wife) outside her house in the village square. (It was the Feast of the Purification of the Virgin.) After we had been jesting for a little while, I said to Gentile, showing her my thumbs: 'Shall we come to life again with this flesh and these bones? What an idea! I don't believe it.'*

In Montaillou itself, and in Lordat, the teaching of the Authié brothers, which was popular, denied the Resurrection of the Body (i.206), and Arnaud Cogul of Lordat, running with the hare and hunting with the hounds, believed, with Rome, that bodies would rise again on the Last Day, and then, against Rome, that they would disintegrate again after the Last Judgment (i.378).

Thus, for all kinds of reasons, millenarian theories encountered scepticism among the élite of Sabarthès, hostility among the most enlightened peasants and indifference among the masses.

A much more dangerous deviation was disbelief, sometimes total but more usually partial, in some aspect of dogma. Such departures were widespread along the Ariège valley, which formed the cultural axis of Sabarthès. Raymond de l'Aire, of Tignac, was a peasant larger than life, always busy in the fields and meadows. He believed that the soul consisted merely of blood and therefore disappeared after death, and of course he denied the Resurrection. Heaven was when you were happy in this world, Hell was when you were miserable, and that was all. He was an uncompromising anti-cleric and maintained that the Bishop of Pamiers, like everyone else, had been brought into being by *fucking and shitting*. He went further: in the village square, in the presence of three of his fellow-citizens, he asserted that God too, in other words Christ, was created '*through fucking and shitting, rocking back and forth and fucking, in other words through the coitus of a man and a woman, just like all the rest of us.'*

'*If you don't stop it, I'll break your head open with my pick-axe,*' said Raymond Segui, horrified.

Raymond de l'Aire was consistent and did not believe in the virginity of Mary, who according to him was made pregnant by Joseph. He denied Christ's Crucifixion, Resurrection and Ascension. Not believing in the Eucharist, he went for years without taking communion (ii.130).

Like other peasants in Tignac, he did believe that animals had a soul, and agreed with a companion from Caussou (near Montaillou) with whom he was reaping a meadow, that '*God and the Virgin Mary were nothing else but this visible and audible world*' (ii.129).

He had no sense of sin, whether murder or incest. He was the lover of Raymonde, the sister of his wife, Sybille (ii.132). It was concern with his reputation rather than with his conscience that kept him from committing certain acts which were looked at askance.

Even in his own parish, which had known other eccentrics, Raymond de l'Aire was looked on with suspicion, as a former madman and practising witch. One day when he was ploughing his mistress Rodière's field below the village, the two unbroken steers he was imprudent enough to be using shied and threw off their yoke. '*Devil, put back the yoke,*' said Raymond. And it fell back into place (ii.126).[1] In his youth, Raymond had suffered attacks of madness lasting a couple of months, but for the past twenty years he had been quite sane, apparently, since he managed his own farm quite efficiently.

Jean Jaufre, another inhabitant of Tignac, related to Raymond de l'Aire, held to a certain muddled Cathar belief that it was the devil who made dangerous animals (ii.121). Arnaud Laufre, also of Tignac, had mixed with the Cathars: he compared the soul of a local woman with that of a sow which belonged to Raymond de l'Aire (ii.132). Guillemette Vilar, of the same village, was sceptical about indulgences (ii.122). Her fellow-villagers Jacques de Alzen and Raymond Philippe considered clubbing together to pay two murderers to kill the Bishop (ii.122), '*So we won't have to pay tithes on the lambs.*'

In the village of Ornolac, too, people believed the soul was made of

---

[1] There is probably a reference here to a semi-magical technique employed in the training of male draught animals. The diabolical element may have been introduced either by the accused himself or by the person who informed on him.

blood. For Guillaume Benet, namesake of a woman of Montaillou, the proof lay in the fact that when you cut off the head of a goose, blood spurted out, and at the same time the life ebbed away. Alternatively, the soul was wind, for a dying person's last breath was merely the soul escaping, to wander wailing through the darkness until it found its final rest.

For Raymond Sicre of Ascou, who raised both cows and cereals, the soul was neither blood nor wind, but bread. This meant unfortunately that it was subject to decay; Sicre expounded his thesis before his fellow-villagers at a time when famine threatened.

The atmosphere of mental contestation created by the goodmen undermined the Catholic monopoly and opened the way to the emergence of pre-existing folklore elements, pre-Christian, non-Christian or anti-Christian. For example, traditional rural naturalism combined with Cathar belief to contradict the idea of a supernatural creation and divine intervention. For both Catharism and folklore, nature and matter were not and could not be the work of the good God. *It is the devil and not God who makes the plants flower and bear grain*, said an inhabitant of Ax-les-Thermes (i.283). Arnaud de Bédeillac told his fellow-citizens, under the village elm (iii.51, 60), '*The trees come from the nature of the earth and not from God.*' One snowy day, at noon, around the fire, Aycard Boret of Caussou told his friends (iii.346–7), '*The weather, following its course, causes cold and the flowers and the grain; and God can do absolutely nothing about it.*'

As we have seen, scepticism about the Eucharist could result merely in childish pranks. But in the case of Aude Fauré it was more serious. Aude Fauré lived in Merviel, a rural parish in the Comté de Foix, north of the Labarre Pass but near the northern border of Sabarthès. She was well-to-do, the wife of Guillaume Fauré, and employed one or two maids and a nurse. In Merviel she was addressed as 'Madame', but she remained very close to peasant circles, chatting familiarly with the maids, who also helped with the harvest on her farm. They used to come and see her when they came back from work (ii.98). She had a reputation for kindness, and gave alms to the local poor so generously that she deprived herself (ii.85).

She was born further north, in her father's *ostal* in Lafage, in the present-day department of Aude (ii.92). As with all the young people in her native village, she did not take her first communion until quite late –

at the age of eighteen or nineteen at the earliest, a whole year after her marriage.

Married at seventeen, neurotic, over-scrupulous, Aude Fauré had convulsions during which she tore off her clothes. She had attacks of guilt which she connected with some sin she had failed to confess before Easter communion. She was seized with remorse, and with an obsession with defilement. *Some women*, she said (ii.94), *told me that one night in a street in our village of Merviel, a woman had given birth to a daughter before she had time to get home to her* ostal. *And I could not stop thinking of the impurity which comes forth from the body of women when they give birth; every time the priest elevated the Host at the altar I thought that the body of Jesus Christ was soiled with that impurity . . . and then I thought that it was not the Body of Christ.*

By the time Aude was twenty-two she still believed in God, but not in the God who the priests said was contained in the sacrament on the altar. *Sometimes*, she said (ii.101), *I am mad; I cannot even pray to God and the Blessed Mary!*

Finally, Aude confessed her woes to her husband (ii.83–6): '*Sancta Maria, Monsieur! How can that be, that I cannot believe in Our Lord? What is the matter? In church, when the priest raises the Body of Christ, I cannot even pray to it or look at it. When I do try to look at it, some obstacle [anbegament] rises up before my eyes.*'

Guillaume Fauré, a typical Occitan husband, showed little sympathy. When she said, '*God cannot forgive my sin, nor even help me,*' he replied: '*What, wretch! Are you in your right mind, to talk like that? You are lost! The devils will carry you off body and soul, and I will drive you out. If you are what you say you are. If you do not confess at once.*'

Her masochistic tendencies drove Aude Fauré to implore the Bishop to impose public penance on her (ii.95). She also sought out the rebukes of other women, including her aunt Ermengarde Garaudy (ii.88): '*What, traitress! You will sully with heresy an* ostal *and a place which up till now were free of heresy. You are lost if you do not confess. Away with you!*' It was as if Aude were deliberately creating a repressive father and mother in the persons of her husband and aunt. The atmosphere of morbid hysteria affected not only Aude Fauré but also her female relations and servants. A confessor failed to cure her. It was only through the intervention of the Virgin, at the prayer of the women of the Fauré family, that she got better.

Disbelief among the men took the form of hatred and mockery as well as sexual, psychological and social non-conformism. Aude Fauré experienced her loss of faith in a form which might have seemed almost metaphysical if she had not been neurotic to start with.

But the hard core of religious deviation was the Albigensian heresy.[1] The frontier between believers in Catharism and believers in the ortho-dox Roman dogma was vague and easily crossed in both directions, by the same people. They did not hesitate to *fish from both banks* (ii.109). Much depended on the changing network of friendly or professional relationships between individuals. Pierre Maury (iii.209, etc.): *I want to use what I earn from my work to do good to both sides. Because really I do not know which of the two beliefs is the more valid. Although, in fact, I support rather the faith of the heretics. But that is simply because my com-munications and relations with the heretics are greater than with the others.*

In Montaillou and Sabarthès the Albigensian doctrine was an extreme manifestation of the point of view which considered the world as evil. Despite doctrinal differences, for example on the Incarnation, there was no absolute contradiction between the views of the Cathars and the almost equally radical views entertained by certain people who remained Christian in the orthodox sense of the word.

The people of Montaillou were almost all, including the priest, influenced by the goodmen. Thus, when they were in an Albigensian mood, they believed in the existence of God, creator of good spirits, and in the existence of the Devil, creator of the world and of sinful and perishing flesh. In this context, Christ could not have existed in earthly flesh, for incarnation would automatically have Satanized him.

The shepherds of Montaillou were fond of discussing theology, but the Cathar sympathizers among them, though they did not always realize it, were uncertain about several points of doctrine – for example, the question whether Satan co-existed from all eternity with God, as was believed by the 'radical' dualists whose influence had become so strong in Languedoc. A more 'Christian' view was that God himself created the Devil, who in turn created evil and the world: this was a kind of modified dualism. There are passages in the evidence of the Maury

1 Though Catharism was re-introduced into Sabarthès, and into Montaillou in particular, by the Authié brothers after 1300, various passages (e.g. i.219, 357) show that heresy had been constantly present in the area since the thirteenth century.

brothers and other inhabitants of Montaillou which lend themselves to either interpretation.

The Catharism of Montaillou was first and foremost a story, a myth. It was told over and over again, with variations, around the fire. To begin with there was the Fall. The Devil succeeded in leading astray some of the spirits surrounding the good God in Heaven. They fell from Heaven and were imprisoned here below by their seducer in vestures of earth, bodies of flesh, shaped in the clay of oblivion (iii.132). These fallen souls sped madly from one deceased body to another, one vesture of decay to another, a soul being sometimes incarnated first in animals and then in men; *until*, said Pierre Maury (iii.220), *it arrives in a body where it is saved, because then, being finally hereticated, it is brought to a state of justice and truth. Then, when it leaves that last tunic, the soul in question returns to Heaven. But until they are hereticated, spirits are condemned to wander from tunic to tunic.* Thus the metempsychosis of Catharism, by which fallen and suffering spirits wander over the earth, is the equivalent of the Purgatory of the Roman faith.

All the evidence of the Fournier Register suggests that in Montaillou those who believed in the myth and ritual of Catharism experienced it as an extreme and heroic variant of Christianity and not as a non-Christian religion. It was simply 'true' Christianity as opposed to what Guillaume Belot considered the pseudo-Catholicism of the *Pharisees* (i.473). The Cathar believers may have been doctrinally wrong but they were convinced in their hearts that they were Christian.

The goodmen of Sabarthès, who acted more or less as constant mediators between 'believers' and God, were not merely pure beings responsible for saving the souls of the villagers. They also performed a social function, helping to integrate contradictory elements among the people they influenced. They worked in a society which was under-administered, segmentary and in danger of disintegrating, *domus* fighting against *domus*, clan against clan. The Authiés, together with their less well-born counterparts, Bélibaste and Prades Tavernier, had connections not only among the heretics but also among the bourgeoisie and to a certain extent the nobility. They were thus able to strengthen respect for social values, appeasing violence without having recourse to repressive counter-violence. They witnessed oaths. They showed an ostentatious, almost exhibitionist, respect for the crops, vineyards and wives of other people, thus paying homage to the rights of property.

Morals were on the whole lax in Sabarthès. Much lip-service was paid to Christian ethics, but people reserved the right to disregard them until the final setting-to-rights before death. The marvellous invention of the *consolamentum* enabled people to lead a life which was not one of anomy, it is true, but of liberty, governed by custom rather than ethics.

The less wholesome, pure and moral the country was, the more it had need of real saints. The holy lives of a few goodmen made up for the free and easy ways of the masses. They maintained contact between the small locality, with its less than fully Christian fabric, and the great God of 'real Christianity', from whom all would one day have to seek salvation.

CHAPTER XX

Morality, wealth and labour

Jean Chelini[1] has summarized the basic principles of the anomy inherent in Catharism: 'There is a two-tiered morality. For the greater number, no restrictions and total liberty of life and manners. For the *parfaits*, an ascetic and élitist morality . . . and the responsibility of reconciling the other believers (sinners), on the brink of death, with the principle of good, this reconciliation being obtained through the *consolamentum*.'

But until this moment all was permitted: *Pierre Clergue told me*, said Béatrice de Planissoles (i.225), *that both man and woman can freely commit any sin they like during their life. And do whatever they please in this world. Provided only that at the end they are received into the sect or into the faith of the good Christians. Then they are saved and absolved of all the sins they have committed in their life . . . thanks to the laying on of hands of these good Christians, as it is received on the brink of death.*

But Clergue's interpretation of the Cathar ethic was extreme and over-simplified. The *parfaits* were much more careful and considered this attitude harmful, for reasons both circumstantial and doctrinal (i.386).

It is difficult for any society to live in a state of anomy or disorder. Underlying current religious opinions in Sabarthès, whether Catholic or Cathar, was a permanent moral system functioning simultaneously as a system of values (*ethos*) and a body of customary behaviour (*habitus*).

This morality was only partly based on a deeply felt sense of sin. This feeling did exist, sometimes in such extreme cases as that of the hyper-sensitive Aude Fauré. But equally influential was the general agreement or interpersonal consensus on what was socially shameful.

Raymond de l'Aire of Tignac said aloud what others thought without always explaining it to themselves. His arguments came under three heads (ii.130):

1 *I am a great alms-giver. But not for the love of God. It is rather to win a good reputation among my neighbours. To have the reputation of being a good man . . . Similarly, when I confess, it is not because I believe in sin, but in order to win the reputation of a good man with my priest and my neighbours.*

2 *I believe neither in sin nor in the redeeming power of good works; in my*

1 Chelini (1968), p. 253.

opinion, incest with mother, daughter, sister or first cousin is not even a sin; incest is merely a shameful act [turpe].

3 To sleep with my second cousin? For me, that is neither a sin nor a shameful act. There is a common proverb in Sabarthès which says: 'With a second cousin, give her the works'.

When he stresses the importance of local custom as distinct from general law, Raymond de l'Aire echoes a widespread feeling affecting both morality and politics: *The Bishop exacts tithes from us by virtue of the law; but we, the people of Sabarthès, refuse them in virtue of our customs,* said Guillaume Austatz, *bayle* of Ornolac (i.209).

The idea of shame was equally widespread in upper Ariège. According to Raymond Vayssière of Ax-les-Thermes (i.277–8), *Simon Barra had two sisters for mistresses, one after the other. He even boasted about it to Pathau Clergue of Montaillou and to me. I said to him: 'It is a great sin.'*

'No,' he answered, 'it is not a sin; but I admit it is a shameful act.'

Upon these words we sat down at table.

Guillaume Bayard, a magistrate of Sabarthès, went two better than Simon Barra. *He told me,* said Arnaud de Bédeillac (iii.155), *he had slept with four sisters, each pair from a different family. They were called Gaude, Blanche, Emersende and Arnaude.*

'How could you sleep with twice two sisters?' I asked.

'If I had slept with women close to me in blood,' answered Bayard, 'I would have committed a shameful act. But with two sisters! No, really. It's of no importance. Mere trifles.'

Round the fire one snowy day, several people told how *Raymond de Planissoles had for a mistress, one after the other, a certain Guillemette of Caussou and then her niece Gaillarde, who was at the same time a servant in Raymonde's house. What a terrible sin!*

'Not at all! There's no sin in that,' said Aycard Boret of Caussou, who was called a peasant for his pains (iii.346–7).

Sometimes I hang my yellow crosses up on a plum tree ... It is through shame [verecundia] that I avoid wearing them as much as possible, said a quarry-man of Ax. Poverty, the loss of one's house, economic failure or merely a descent in the social scale could be a source of shame, 'confusion', and loss of honour. They might make your neighbours respect you less: *I am generally little esteemed in Sabarthès because of my poverty,* said Arnaud de Bédeillac (iii.57). *I am impoverished and filled with confusion in our country through the fault of my mother (who caused me to lose my maternal* ostal), said Arnaud Sicre (ii.21, 29). When poverty was factual it was a source of shame. But as an ideal, or when it was practised for itself, it was admired.

Values were externalized; morality was based on neighbourliness and reciprocity (ii.107): *Do not pick grass from other people's fields; conversely, do not throw on other people's fields the weeds you have uprooted from your own field.*

A man was expected, especially if he belonged to the élite of the village or region, to be not only a good neighbour but also courteous. He ought to like jesting, which vents the spleen and fosters conviviality. These were the virtues which brought success to men like Pons Baille and Guillaume Authié. The latter had everything that might be pleasing: a beautiful wife, children, wealth and good humour (i.313). Sometimes, though, in that age of iron, it was necessary to use not the courtesy and respect for others of Guillaume Authié but the cynicism, brutality and truculence of Pierre Clergue.

Was society in Montaillou and Sabarthès especially delinquent? As far as theft and crimes against property went, the externalized ethic of the *ostal*, which prescribed the mutual respect of possessions, was relatively effective. In confession, people accused one another of minor thefts of fruit and hay. Jean and Pierre Maury were rebuked by Bélibaste and Pierre Authié on a few occasions for having taken a lamb or a few sheep from another flock which had mingled with theirs. The Virgin of Montgauzy was called upon to find an object, perhaps money, stolen in Ornolac. At the fair, a weaver might have some of his cloth stolen (i.156–7). There is occasional mention of forgers and highwaymen – but there were few highways and little cash. In Montaillou itself, where everyone knew everyone else and strangers were easy to find, crimes against property would have been very difficult to commit. True, mutual trust was far from being total, and doors might sometimes be locked. People and flocks might trample on other people's fields; the poor women who 'borrowed' hay or wood or sieves to sift their flour did not always ask before they did so. But apart from such irregularities, the people of Montaillou on the whole respected other people's property.

The Clergues and the Azémas might confiscate a field or a flock belonging to someone weaker than they were. But in theory such confiscations had a 'legal' foundation, and were effected in the name of the *bayle*, the Comte or the *châtelain*, on the pretext of the fight against heresy, though in reality as part of the local conflict between factions.

Crimes against the person – violence and revenge – were more common. Particularly notable are the depredations of local lords, and above all their *bayles*, against the people they administered, though the records stress the misdeeds of a criminal minority among the powerful.

In Montaillou the Clergues, *bayle* and priest, had Mengarde Maurs's tongue cut out as punishment for denouncing them. They were apparently mixed up in the murder of Arnaud Lizier. In Junac the local lords and *châtelains* strangled, or caused to be strangled, the blacksmith Pierre Marty, suspected of having denounced them as Cathars. Afterwards they were able to set up again as good Catholics, since no one now dared say a word against them. Informers ran a great risk of being murdered by the families of their victims. One was thrown off a bridge, another was threatened with the same fate (ii.65, 423).

Crimes committed by the great often remained unpunished. For years the Clergue family enjoyed impunity, thanks to their powerful connections in Carcassonne. The Planissoles too, guilty of murder by strangling, went scot free.

'*Raymond de Planissoles*', said Raymond Bec of Caussou to Aycard Boret, the accomplice of the Planissoles (iii.347), '*committed a very great sin when he strangled and killed Pierre Plan, whom he then buried in the garden of his father, Pons de Planissoles. And Raymond ought not to have aggravated the sin by deflowering Gaillarde, his own servant!*'

'*Indeed,*' answered Aycard Boret, '*Raymond and I did murder that man and bury him in unconsecrated ground. But neither Raymond nor I are afraid of having sinned. In fact we confessed it all to the proxy of the Comté de Foix, Guillaume Courtete, and came to an arrangement with him.*' We know, from another deposition, that Courtete was venal (iii.381).

Against a background of inquisition and repression the great were able to murder people when they had the power, in order to avoid being denounced, imprisoned and put to death themselves. It was a question of kill or be killed.

The shepherds tended to fight both among themselves and against the people living along the route of their migrations; sometimes the fighting might lead to a death. But it would be incorrect to talk of any real and fundamental antagonism between the nomad shepherds and the sedentary town-dwellers.

To kill a man was still a very serious matter, especially for people of the lower classes, unprotected by influential relationships. To slay someone usually meant depriving the body of burial in consecrated ground and depriving the victim of the possibility of receiving the last sacraments. This might mean depriving his soul of rest and happiness, condemning it to Hell or wandering and preventing its final resurrection. In such circumstances, corpses were apt to protest. *When Valentin Barra was assassinated*, said the women and the miller of Ax-les-Thermes (i.151, 156), *he made such a row at night in Ax churchyard that the local priests dared neither sleep in the church beside the cemetery nor leave the place.*

There is only one murder recorded for a whole generation in Montaillou, a village of 250 inhabitants. While men and women of the people were ready enough to threaten death, they were more reserved when it came to putting the threats into execution. Their violence was symbolic rather than factual. People carried knives or swords, but in general did no more than brandish them. Hired assassins were not unknown, but they were poor creatures who pocketed the money and did not carry out the murder. Perhaps they knew that their employers did not really want them to. Except in isolated cases, popular resistance to the Inquisition itself was passive, non-violent, almost non-existent. Between individuals themselves, delinquency directed against property was small and easily controlled, most of the time, through the village *bayles*.

In this connection we may recall the relative but nevertheless modest sexual permissiveness which reigned in the village of Montaillou. It may have come within the sphere of delinquency, but at the worst it went only as far as a couple of cases of rape or threats of rape. We have also seen that hard work did not rate very high in the scale of values. The actual morality of the *domus* of Montaillou was very different from that created later by Protestant and Catholic, Puritan and Jansenist Reformations, both kinds intolerant of sex and anxious to make people work. Whether they were Catholics or Cathars or in between, the people of Montaillou were not yet afraid either of sex or of idleness.

The villagers of Montaillou and their brothers in Sabarthès, Christians and Cathars alike, felt a deep, evangelical repugnance towards 'wealth'. This was in accordance with the society they lived in, where population trends, the small volume and weak growth of net production and the unequal distribution of goods created a permanent fringe of poverty. Condemnation of ostentatious wealth and the power which accompanied it seems to have been general. Clergue the priest, as a good Cathar, criticized marriage because the Church's wedding ceremonies are *nothing but secular pomp* (i.225). Temporal power, like women, the world and money, is also a gift of the Devil. One version of the Albigensian myth of the Fall, related by the shepherd Jean Maury (ii.490), has the Devil saying to the good spirits whom he wishes to seduce: '*I will give you wives whom you will love dearly . . . with one bird, you will take another, with one animal another animal. I will make certain among you into kings, or counts, or emperors, or lords over other men.*'

Ordinary Catholics, just like the Cathars, regarded wealth and the pleasures it brought as an inevitable source of sin. '*Come, Master Arnaud Teisseire,*' said a Pamiers jailer to the doctor of Lordat, dying in his cell and refusing to confess his sinful life (ii.219), '*you have wallowed in such opulence! And you have lived in such splendid fashion! And you have had so many temporal pleasures! How could you be without sin?*'

In the uplands of Foix, wealth meant possession of temporal goods, and also power, influence, knowledge and a network of friends and dependants. But of course most people were comparatively poor and powerless. When Bernard Clergue, in prison, asked Jacques Fournier to tell him the names of those who had informed against him, Fournier replied (ii.302): '*Give you the names of those who denounced you? Come, come! It would be too dangerous for the poor, weak men who deposed against you. Think, Bernard, of your power, your knowledge, the weighty threats you have already made against certain people, and of the multitudes of your friends.*'

But in Montaillou only beggars, wandering or otherwise, were regarded as actual paupers. The really poor also included those whose personal wealth was less than the value of a house (in other words, less than 40 *livres tournois*) and who had neither land, nor draught animals, nor a real flock nor an *ostal* in the real sense of the term, and who did not have any craft or skill to make up for it. The category might also include the head of a family who had lost his house because it was destroyed or confiscated by the Inquisition. Also regarded as poor were those who sought jobs as shepherds or day-labourers; farm servants, domestics, younger sons of rural families; bastard girls and those who worked for wages in the villages. This must have included in all at least 20 to 25 per cent of the local population.[1] But we need to distinguish, like Charles de la Roncière,[2] between those who were 'poor to themselves' and those who were 'poor to other people'. Many among the lower strata of the peasants of Sabarthès regarded themselves as poor, but alms were usually given only to beggars, migrants or peasants reduced to want by the destruction of their houses by the Inquisition. Anyone who was poor but had employment as a labourer or farmer was not regarded as 'alms-worthy' (iii.356).

Poverty in itself was not an ideal among the mountain folk. But the anti-wealth attitude was very widespread. It distinguished, however, between lay wealth, which was little challenged, and clerical wealth, the subject of great popular protest. Bélibaste to the Maurys of Montaillou (ii.25, 26, 56): *'The Pope devours the blood and sweat of the poor. And the bishops and the priests, who are rich and honoured and self-indulgent, behave in the same manner . . . whereas Saint Peter abandoned his wife, his children, his fields, his vineyards and his possessions to follow Christ.'* Bélibaste rounded off his diatribe with the usual references to the clergy's sexual depravity (ii.26): *'The bishops, the priests and the Minorite and preaching friars go to the houses of rich, young and beautiful women; they take their money and, if they consent, they sleep carnally with them, putting on appearances of humility the while.'* The *parfaits* contrasted *the Church which fleeces* with *that which forgives* (iii.123). Against the pomp of Rome, Bélibaste set a minimal organization of a non-militant Church without walls (ii.53): *The heart of man is the Church of God, the material Church is nothing.*

These ideas found echoes in the villagers of Montaillou and their friends the migrant shepherds. Pierre Maury, for instance, vented his feelings on the subject (i.29–30): *The Minorite and preaching friars? No! They call themselves little or 'minor', and they are big. Instead of saving the souls of the dead and sending them to heaven, they gorge themselves at banquets after funerals. And then they own too many silks. And do you think that their great houses were built by the labour of their own hands? No, these friars, they are wicked wolves! They would like to devour us all, dead or alive.*

1 See Mollat (1974), I, p. 22. His percentages apply to the mountains of Provence and to rural Languedoc. He had no figures for Montaillou itself.
2 Quoted by Mollat (1974), vol. II.

The Church was fatter than it looked; its gizzard was bigger than its heart. Instead of adopting Gospel poverty, it devoured the money of the faithful. One means of doing this was through indulgences.

One day, said Pierre Maury (iii.238), *I gave twelve Barcelona pennies to a collector from the Hospital of Roncevaux. When he saw me doing this, Guillaume Bélibaste said: 'Pierre, you have lost your pennies! You would have done better to use them to buy yourself some fish . . . The indulgences of the Pope cost a lot, but they are not worth much!'*[1]

In 1321, Guillaume de Corneillan of Lordat said (ii.121–2): *Two years ago, towards the Feast of Whitsun I was warping some linen (or was it hemp?) for Guillemette Vila, wife of Arnaud Cogul of Lordat. A collector came along; according to what he said, he was in a position to give us a lot of indulgences. Afterwards, when he had left us, Guillemette said to me: 'Do you think a man can give indulgences or absolve anyone of his sins? No, no man! God alone can do so.'*

'But,' I ventured, 'perhaps the Pope, the prelates, the priests . . .'

'No,' interrupted Guillemette. 'No one. Only God.'

On another occasion, Guillemette Vila upbraided the priest for trying to sell a series of indulgences in church at cut prices (ii.122). Bélibaste had no words strong enough to attack the retailers of indulgences who went from door to door with their wares, taking one farthing's profit for themselves for every thousand pardons, which they had bought whole-sale in Rome, where the Pope would sell a few tens of thousands of days of indulgence for 10 to 20 *livres tournois*, half the price of a house (ii.24–6).

Parallel to the protest against indulgences was the rebellion against excessive begging, and the offerings demanded by parish priests on major feast days. *Bernard, vicar of Ornolac, complained that the people of the village made fewer offerings than usual for the feast of Easter. Guillaume Austatz (in the course of a conversation with other villagers, in the house of a woman who lived in Ornolac), declared: 'The priests can only exact a theoretical offering. It is enough to give them one small coin, and we have done all we have to do'* (i.196).

Similar resistance was offered when the Bishop and the priest ordered the villagers to make a waxen candle for Easter, weighing three pounds. *'We will make one weighing a quarter of a pound only, with tallow instead*

1 The Cathars in the Comté de Foix were much more radically opposed to indulg-ences than were the Waldensians (ii.64).

of wax,' answered a few of the bolder peasants (ii.312, 314). As for tithes, they encountered psychological resistance among the people. *Last year*, said Jean Jauffre of Tignac (i.109), *we were in the upper story of a house, drinking and eating almonds, and we got talking about the lawsuits over the tithes between the ecclesiastics of the* archiprêtré *of Sabarthès and the laymen of the region* . . .

'*I only hope the priests don't get what they want from us,*' *said Arnaud Laufre of Tignac, in the course of our conversation.* '*If only all the priests in the world could be hung up by the jaw!*'

In Sabarthès the Church had adopted the disagreeable habit of excommunicating people for debt, above all for debt to the clergy, in other words non-payment of tithes, first fruits or *carnelages*. Some of the bolder spirits among the people, and sometimes even priests from the diocese of Palhars, where all eccentricities were allowed, would encourage the village protesters by saying (i.318), '*My good fellow, excommunication breaks no bones.*'

Resentment against excommunication for debt was accompanied by occasional animosity against usury. In a world of unequal but co-existing *domus*, the spirit of capitalist accumulation was comparatively unusual, and looked at askance. In the towns of the lowlands, usurers provoked anti-semitism. But in Sabarthès usury was neither very widespread nor greatly challenged. Guillaume Austatz practised it discreetly in his native village, but avoided doing so in Ornolac, where he was *bayle* (i.192). There was probably a very small amount of usury in Montaillou itself, but there is no reference to it in the Register. Tithes, debt for tithes, and excommunication for debt for tithes were the chief sources of anti-wealth sentiment in upper Ariège.

In passing we should note that popular protest against tithes and indulgences was not the only thing which linked the conquered Cathars of 1320 to the victorious Reformers of 1520 to 1580, whether German Lutherans or the Huguenots of Languedoc. Both movements were concerned with the Pauline theme of justification by faith.

According to Pierre Maury's deposition (iii.202), *On Christmas night, after we had feasted with Bélibaste, the holy man preached:* '*Baptism of water profits nothing,*' *he said,* '*because water has no virtue to save the soul. It is only faith which saves the soul.*'

Between 1300 and 1320, ordinary peasants of Sabarthès decried both 'works' and 'good works' (ii.130; i.356). Thus certain fundamental themes of the distant Reformation were already familiar in the mountains of Occitania in the early fourteenth century.

The hostility of the peasants of Sabarthès towards tithes, indulgences and all other ecclesiastical methods of extorting money was partly due to the frustration felt by country people towards those members of surrounding society who wielded wealth and power. But even the least sophisticated farmer was also moved by the teachings of the Gospel, according to which the rich were excluded from Heaven. As Raymond Roussel said to Béatrice de Planissoles (i.219), '*A camel cannot go through the eye of a needle ; nor can a rich man be saved. So there is no salvation for the rich : nor for kings, nor for princes, nor for prelates, nor for members of religious orders.*' This passage is interesting, in that it belongs to 1294, before the Authiés brought their propaganda to Sabarthès. Later, the shoemaker Vital said to his sweetheart Vuissane (i.457), '*The only ones who can attain salvation are the poor of the faith and of the sect of the good Christians.*'

Guillaume Austatz, *bayle* of Ornolac, believed that salvation through poverty would bring about the inversion of the social order after death (i.197, 207–08): *Those who have possessions in the present life can have only evil in the other world. Conversely, those who have evil in the present life will have only good in the future life.*

The rich were sometimes looked on as cowards, who preferred to save their possessions in this world rather than seek after salvation in the next. *Master Salacrou of Bouan*, said Sybille Pierre (ii.425), *liked the heretics well enough. But he moaned and groaned every time he had them in his house. He was rich, and he was afraid of losing his wealth.*

Rich and greedy priests were a special case. Not only were they themselves excluded from Heaven because of their deprivations, but they also deprived their parishioners of Paradise, because, unworthy as they were, they could not absolve sins. Sybille Pierre reported what the Authiés had said in a house in Ax-les-Thermes (ii.404): *The priests steal all men's possessions ; as soon as they have baptized children, they start to slip away, carrying the oil lamps and the candles. To say Mass, to do anything at all, they want money. They do not live as they ought ; that is why they have lost the power to absolve sins, both their own and those of others.* Thus poverty and salvation are inextricably linked.

The people of Montaillou did not praise all poverty indiscriminately. While Pierre Maury scorned the amassing of riches, he regarded poverty, from the material point of view, as *a disease* (ii.30). Raymonde Belot, Arnaud Sicre and Arnaud de Bédeillac are all 'confused' and 'irritated' because of the condescension shown on account of their poverty to the family of one and the husband of another, while the third is despised in his own person. Poverty itself was not so bad as impoverishment, which meant moving down the social scale. It was better to be poor in the long term, *pauper*, than to have become poor recently, *depauperatus*.

What was respected and revered, in contrast to wealth, cupidity and avarice, was the poverty which was voluntary, the state of being *poor of the faith*. In a conversation with her second lover, Béatrice de Planissoles said (i.255): '*In Montaillou, people commonly say that one ought to do good to all pilgrims and poor of the faith; and by "poor of the faith" they meant the heretics who were called, in the village, the good Christians.*'

To become *poor of the faith*, in other words a *parfait*, was to try to become poor in Christ, to follow the example given by Christ in the Gospel. *When a man becomes a goodman, that is to say a heretic*, said Bélibaste (ii.59), *he must send away his wife and children, and possessions and wealth. He thus conforms to the precepts of Christ, who wanted men to follow Him.* Needless to say, the problem of salvation was the central preoccupation of the *poor of the faith* in Montaillou, whether they were professional goodmen or ordinary people on their deathbed. Once they had been 'consoled', the dying, too, had detached themselves from all the goods of this world, including food.

Despite the differences between the Catholics of the lowlands and the Cathars of the mountains, the stress on voluntary poverty was a spiritual heritage possessed in common by the most dynamic elements among both groups. Hence the importance attached to giving alms. Whether they were given merely to help the needy, who were not necessarily vowed to voluntary poverty, or to hospices and hospitals, to be re-distributed to guests in want, the final object was always a spiritual one, sometimes invoking the love of God. *That night*, said Pierre Maury (iii.189), *we dined in the house of Guillemette Maury, in company with members of her family . . . and with a poor man to whom Guillemette had granted hospitality for the love of God.* Such attitudes might give rise to violent criticism of wills, 'passports to Heaven', in which legacies were designed to promote the testator's own salvation. According to Bernard Franca (i.352), *Legacies and alms which are bestowed by sick men are worthless, because they are not dictated by love but by fear. Only those alms are valid which are given by healthy men.* Nevertheless, few people were entirely disinterested, and gifts given to the poor in a spirit of human and divine charity had as their main object the subsequent welfare of the donor's soul. As always, some people were sceptical. Guillaume de Corneillan the younger, of Lordat (ii.121) recounted how *one Sunday last January, I was sitting up by the fire in his house with my father-in-law, Guillaume de Corneillan the elder. He told me that Bor of Tignac had spoken to him as follows: 'The priests talk nonsense when they tell us to give alms for the salvation of souls. All that is rubbish! When a man dies, the soul dies too. It is just the same as with animals. The soul is only blood....'*

Those who did believe in the survival of the soul and the existence of another world – and this was the case with the great majority of the country people – were concerned by the question of alms-giving. *I have sometimes doubted the value of indulgences,* said Pierre Maury (iii.238), *but I have never had the slightest hesitation about the value of alms.* Conversely, Guillemette Benet of Ornolac, who disbelieved entirely in the immortality of the soul, began to laugh when told that she ought to give alms for the salvation of her soul (i.262). Those who did believe, and who had the means to be lavish, might be almost excessive, like the over-scrupulous Aude Fauré. '*Madam,*' said a farm woman to her when she was rolling about in bed with convulsions and begging the Virgin to restore her faith in God (ii.98), '*what sin have you committed, then? Your alms-giving supports all the poor of the village!*'

To whom was one to give alms? Aude Fauré, the Catholic, gave to the local poor. Guillemette Maury, the Cathar, who was not so wealthy, invited a poor traveller to dinner. For those who stayed at home in Montaillou and were steeped in Albigensian orthodoxy, the best solution, while giving something to the local poor – beggars, migrants or heads of families ruined by the Inquisition – was to give chiefly to the *poor of faith,* the goodmen. As Rixende Cortil of Ascou said (iii.307): *The goodmen, thanks to the heretication they bestow, can send a soul directly to the Kingdom of the Father after death; to give alms to them is to obtain a great reward in exchange, far superior to what one obtains when one gives to other men.* Arnaud Vital of Montaillou expressed a similar view (i.457): *Alms for the goodmen, yes. For the Catholics, no.* And Alazaïs Guilhabert of Montaillou, too (i.124): *The goodmen saved the soul of my brother Guillaume the shepherd, who later died; in exchange it seems to me right, though my mother does not agree, to give them alms.* In

Montaillou it was sometimes the really poor, the *poor of life*, who took the bread out of their own mouths to give it to the *poor of the faith*, though these might already be gorged with the gifts of the faithful. Alazaïs 'Maurine' of Montaillou, wife of Raymond Maury and mother of Pierre Maury, told Béatrice de Planissoles (i.235–6), '*Poor as we are, my husband and I give alms to the goodmen. We abstain from food in order to give it them. We send them flour, the best flour.*'

Béatrice was astonished and asked Alazaïs whether the goodmen would accept food given in such circumstances. Of course, was the reply. Béatrice then decided to send some flour to the *parfaits* herself. Pierre Maury, Alazaïs's son, gladly deprived himself and sold a sheep in order to give six *sous tournois* to the goodmen he met in his travels (ii.416).

It was believed that the *poor of the faith*, laden with presents by the poor of the real world, ended up by becoming very rich. When the *parfait* Guillaume Authié collected gold and silver coins on his pastoral journey, he put them away in his chest, and from time to time he and his wife Gaillarde would amuse themselves by putting their heads inside the box and watching the money glitter in the dark (ii.417).

Often, however, alms-giving did relieve the genuinely poor. It also called down divine blessing upon the houses and crops of those who had been generous. To empty one's house to relieve the want of others was to fill one's barn.

The people of Montaillou were fond of having a nap, of taking it easy, of delousing one another in the sun or by the fire. Whenever they could, they tended to shorten the working day into a half day. Some, backed up by a comfortable dowry, neglected their manual tasks, or dreamed of neglecting them, in order merely to manage their estate.[1] But reality forced manual workers, in other words the great majority of people, to put their backs to the wheel at certain seasons of the agricultural year and at various stages of the transhumance.

At all events, work in itself was not a source of earthly consideration. For a peasant to farm his own land well was merely to show that he was

1 To run a house or a fairly large farm without actually working with one's hands was the dream of many poor peasants (iii.121). Conversely, while some individuals passed easily from the middle, non-manual classes to the position of craftsman or even shepherd, the downward transition could be difficult for a rich man (ii.59). This indicates the existence of an ideal, privileged world, where the rich are exempt from manual labour.

not mad (ii.126). The head of a household was expected to be a good neighbour, but not to kill himself with work.

Alms-giving and work tended to be mutually exclusive. '*One does not acquire merit by giving alms to me, because I am capable of working,*' said Emersend Marty of Montaillou to Gauzia Clergue, who gave her bread for All Saints' Day (iii.356). Alazaïs Fauré made a slightly different distinction (i.424): *Whoever does good to the goodmen gives alms of great value. For they are afraid to work lest they be taken prisoner* [by the Inquisition].

At the same time, the *parfaits* were also honoured because, unlike the good-for-nothing clergy, they worked. Pierre Maury said to Arnaud Sicre (ii.29–30): '*Do you think the preaching friars built their great houses with the toil of their own hands? No, of course not, but our lords* [the goodmen] *live by their own work.*' He was perhaps alluding to the fact that his friend Bélibaste earned a living by making combs. The people of Montaillou were vastly impressed by the fact that Guillaume Authié, though he had to lead a furtive existence, worked as a tailor, mending the tunic of Pierre Clergue the priest and making him a pair of trousers (i.315). Bélibaste even locked himself up and worked as usual during the feast days celebrated by the Roman Church (ii.53). Pierre Authié made a direct connection between work and salvation: '*We work and take pains,*' he said to Sybille Pierre (ii.406), '*not because we might otherwise be poor, but in order to save our souls.*' Jean Maury, during one of his heretical phases, would eat only what he had earned with his own hands, because *the Son of God said that man must live by the sweat of his brow* (ii.73). Guillemette Argelliers of Montaillou heard two *parfaits* say, in Raymond Maury's house (iii.95, 96, 97): '*The priests ought to live by the work of their own hands, according to the commandment of God. And not off the work of the people, as they do in fact. The priests, who expel people from the path of salvation, do all that in order to be well dressed and well shod, in order to ride on horseback and to drink and eat well.*' Guillemette was so struck by the Cathars' description of the priests' misdeeds that she told the two *parfaits*: '*If I was only sure you could do it better than the priests, I would let you save my soul.*'[1]

In general, there was nothing revolutionary about the idealization of poverty in Montaillou. The praise of poverty was quite compatible with

1 Pierre Dupont, a pig-farmer of Vaychis, regarded *working hard to earn one's living* as a virtue, whether in a Jew, a Christian or a Moslem (ii.158).

the efficient management of a *domus*, with the gifts made by a rich to a poor *domus*, with living by the sweat of one's brow, though without giving up the luxury of the siesta or a spell of relaxation in the sun. In one particular, however, the idealization of poverty was subversive. By setting up a poor Church as an image of salvation, it threatened the claims of the tithe-exacting priests. This idealization spared the establishments of wealthy laymen and noblemen, but turned against the established Church, which cost a lot of money yet did not save the soul. Sometimes the condemnation included recent capitalist accumulation, which undermined the *domus* hierarchy and was embodied in the practice of usury. Criticism was particularly severe against the mendicant orders; the preaching and Minorite friars came to symbolize the oppression of the innocent countryside by Pamiers, the Babylon of Foix. Wealth in itself was not the real object of attack. What the people of Montaillou hated was the unhealthy fat of the undeserving rich, clerics and mendicants, who exploited the village without giving in return any spiritual aid or even those services of help and protection habitually provided by a well-to-do *domus* or by wealthy local nobles.

Magic as such was not a central element in the mental outlook or practices of Sabarthès and Montaillou. But it was important as a technique, as a means to an end, the end being some action or object or information. This magic was connected with the traditional medicine of the healer, particularly the female healer; and such medicine was not necessarily ineffective. Magic in Montaillou also has connections with genuinely diabolical witchcraft, of which a few traces appear in Sabarthès, though only a few and those almost insignificant.

We have already seen that Prades d'Aillon had its female healer, Na Ferriera, though we know nothing about her techniques or recipes (i.337). Béatrice de Planissoles stressed the fact (i.249) that the various little potions and philtres she made use of were not spells.

As for sorcery itself, it was one thing to believe in the Devil and quite another to attribute to the Devil the occasional efficacy of old wives' spells.

It is clear that the Devil felt quite at home in Sabarthès. *Go to the Devil; be off with you, Devil; one day the Devil will carry everything off; Sancta Maria, I can see the Devil!* – such were the mildest exclamations of Cathar peasants at the sight of a Catholic priest, or of orthodox Catholics at the sight of a goodman. If a woman supposed by her family to be an Albigensian suddenly began to behave like a Catholic, she was said to be 'possessed by the Devil' (*indemoniata, dyablat*). Peasants who had dabbled in Albigensianism might see the world as radically evil, and so it was easy for them to see the hand of the Devil everywhere. One of them, carried away by the words of Arnaud Teisseire (ii.200), concluded that *the devils are our brothers.*

But the day was still far off when village magic would be equated with the conjuring of the Devil. In the early fourteenth century there were no witchhunts as such; the stake was reserved for Cathars.

It is true that the notion of making practical use of infernal powers was not entirely unknown in Sabarthès. Aycard Boret of Caussou replied sharply to a fellow-sponsor who queried Aycard's suggestion that he might have invoked the help of the Devil to have an enemy put in prison: (iii.348) '*Be silent, my good woman, for sometimes the Devil has more power than God, and I have no choice but to help myself, either with the aid of God or with that of the Devil.*' But Aycard Boret was a criminal, an accomplice to murder, and his was an isolated case.

There were cultural circumstances which accounted for this relative absence of devilry. Devils were everywhere in the uplands of the Comté de Foix, surrounding everyone. But it was not easy to enter into direct contact with them. As we shall see, even the 'messenger of souls', who had a monopoly in relationships with ghosts, could not speak face to face with the many demons who also dealt with ghosts.

Moreover, magic was especially a feminine province, and in the mountain villages of the early fourteenth century the cultural gap between men and women which was introduced by parish schools in the sixteenth century did not exist. Later, segregation by schooling made some boys literate but left most girls completely ignorant. They thus became, more than ever, the preservers of natural, non-scholastic culture, and also more and more suspect to the men. And mistrust of women soon turned into suspicion of witchcraft.

In Montaillou and Sabarthès, the establishing of diplomatic relations between the village of the living and the village of the dead involved the vast realm of myth and the marvellous, and also of miracles. The marvellous, based on the supernatural, is described quite objectively in the accounts given in the Register. Some of the narratives were directly communicated to the Inquisitor. Some were narratives of narratives, heard previously by a witness, and then repeated by him to Jacques Fournier. Of course, the marvellous was frequently present in the myths related in Sabarthès itself, myths which might be connected either with the official Church or with the Albigensian heresy.

Much rarer was the actualization of the marvellous in the form of a miracle. In Sabarthès, Catholic miracles belonged to the past. In Foix itself there was what appeared to be a heretic pseudo-miracle. When the Waldensian Raymond de la Côte was burned at the stake, and the bonds about his wrists were consumed by the flames, he was able to raise his hands and pray to God. '*That proves his soul obtained salvation,*' people said in the taverns of Foix (i.174).

But there was no Cathar miracle in the uplands of Montaillou and Sabarthès, with the possible exception of the strange lights which appeared during a *consolamentum* (iii.241-2, n. 490). This is rather remarkable: it shows that the Albigensian missionaries and the peasants they influenced (not to speak of the peasants they did not influence) actually rejected miracles, as if they wished to keep God out of the material world which they sometimes attributed to the Devil. In getting rid of God they also got rid of all kinds of supernatural causation: '*Do you believe that bits of wood can perform miracles?*' Bélibaste asked the shepherds of upper Ariège (ii.54–5). And he went on, taking care that Cathar miracles should not be confused with Roman ones: '*I'll perform miracles myself. But when I'm in the other world. Not in this world.*'

In the Comté de Foix myth remained within very narrow limits. It was often propagated by repetition, by the well-known method of examples (*exempla*).

In the context of Roman propaganda, a single *exemplum*, transmitted from one village woman to another, could give rise to whole series of *exempla*. Such was the story of the little cake used as a Host and the altar wine which were transformed into a child's finger and into blood respectively, for the edification of the sceptical peasant who had cooked the cake (ii.84; the story is also found in The Golden Legend). This *exemplum* is paralleled by a whole series of such structural transformations.

Among the Cathars, the teaching of the *parfaits* was full of *exempla*, and these were spread about by the farmers. Bernard Franca, the priest-cum-peasant of Goulier, presented the myth of the pelican as an *exemplum* or *istoria*.

Another very well-known *exemplum* was that of the two goodmen and the animal caught in a snare. Two *parfaits* were going through a forest when they came upon (in one version) a squirrel or (in another version) a pheasant caught in a trap. Instead of taking the animal and killing it in order to sell it or eat it just for pleasure, they set it free, out of reverence for the human soul which might be shut in the animal's body. They placed the equivalent in money beside the snare so that the hunter, who had to earn his living, would not lose by their action (ii.107; iii.306). Between 1300 and 1320 this *exemplum* was told as a true story around Montaillou, Ascou, Caussou and Tignac. The story of the lost horseshoe (see pp. 291–2) was equally popular.

But mythical ideas were largely concerned with the kingdom of the dead.

Guillaume Fort, a Montaillou farmer, said (i.447–8): '*In the past I did not believe in the resurrection of human bodies after death, although I had heard it preached in church. And I still do not believe in it! For the body of*

*a dead person is dissolved and transformed into earth or ashes. But I do
believe in the survival of the soul . . . the souls of the wicked will go "by
rocks and precipices"; demons will throw them down the cliffs from the
rocks.'*

'*Why do you believe that?*' asked Jacques Fournier.

'*Because*', said Guillaume, '*it is commonly said in the Pays d'Aillon and
de Sault that Arnaude Rives, a woman who lives at Belcaire in the diocese
of Alet, sees demons leading the souls of the wicked across rocks and slopes,
in order to throw the souls down from the rocks.*

'*Arnaude herself sees these souls! They have flesh and bones and all their
limbs: head, feet, hands and all the rest. They thus have a proper body;
and they are thrown down from on high by the demons; they howl aloud;
they grieve. And yet they can never die!*

'*Master Laurent, the priest of Belcaire, rebuked Arnaude Rives severely.
"Arnaude, how can you tell such stories!"*

'*But Bernard den Alazaïs, a blacksmith of Belcaire, said to the priest:
"I too have seen souls which go by rocks and slopes, and which are thrown
over precipices." At which the priest Laurent released Arnaude.*

'*I myself believed that both the man and the woman of Belcaire were
telling the truth . . . Moreover, all that is common rumour in the Pays de
Sault and d'Aillon.*'

Out of the nearby existence of this mountainous region which was
devoted to the souls of the dead, and which no ordinary living being
had access to, there arose a need for specialized intermediaries. These
were called *armariés* or messengers of souls. It was their job to establish
and maintain contact with the dead people surrounding the living.[1]

It would have been our good luck to have had the evidence of one
of these messengers of souls, male or female, operating in the region of
Montaillou. Unfortunately for us, though fortunately for them, the two
inhabitants of Belcaire did not come within the episcopal jurisdiction of
Jacques Fournier. But there are many indications, including recent folklore studies, which prove that tales about ghosts and their messengers of
souls are among the most general and long-lasting of all myths in the
Comté de Foix and the neighbouring region.

The deposition of Arnaud Gélis, a messenger of souls from the region
of Pamiers, brings out more clearly the allusions in the evidence given
by Guillaume Fort and others. Arnaud Gélis had seen the dead, and he

1 See Nelli (1969), p. 199.

undertook to deliver messages from them to the living and vice versa. He saw the other world with eyes of flesh.

Social strata, according to his observations, were as strongly marked there as among the living. But now the powerful got the worst of it. 'Great and rich ladies' continued to ride in carriages over hill and dale, just as they did in life; but the carriages were drawn by demons instead of mules. The silk sleeves which they had worn in Occitania since mulberry trees began to be cultivated in the Cévennes in the thirteenth century were now burned and shrivelled by their bony arms. Arnaud Gélis had also met knights who had been killed in battle: they rode on steeds like skeletons. Cloven down to the navel by the wounds which killed them, they bled and suffered in the morning; in the evening their wounds closed and their pains ceased until next day. It was not unusual to meet people who had been murdered, like Pons Malet of Ax, his face still covered in blood (i.131). There were also doctors who, although they were now dead, continued to lurk round the local leper hospital, and hooded monks, whose dress contrasted with the simpler white linen robes of the ordinary dead (i.134). Ecclesiastics who had had the misfortune to be rich might now be very uncomfortable: four huge dogs out of Hell tortured an archdeacon who had trafficked in farm rents (i.535). Bernard, late Bishop of Pamiers, could find no rest because he had reduced two of his faithful retainers to poverty.

There were divisions of age as well as of class. Some ages were conspicuous by their absence. There were no children under seven years old (or, according to another version, under twelve) among the multitudes of 'doubles' with whom the messenger of souls entered into contact. Children so young went directly from death to 'the place of rest', which the messenger could not visit. There was a violent conflict of generations between old people, who were very oppressed, and young people, who were very aggressive; the young were present in large numbers, for people died early in those days. The elderly dead were buffeted about and trodden underfoot by the youthful dead; or else they were so light that the wind blew them away like poppy-seeds, until they were trodden down again by the mass of other 'doubles' (i.134-5, 532, 543-5).

In that world, as in this, the very young men formed a special social group (i.542). There were also especially close links between women, more highly developed links than those between adolescents. The dead women went together, strong and beautiful in the wind; some were in rags, some were pregnant, some wore the rope of the Capuchins round their waists. They were out for revenge, great or small. They were supposed to possess information about both the living and the dead, and the living had no hesitation in consulting them about deceased relatives, through the agency of the professional messenger. A woman of Pamiers said to Arnaud Gélis (i.538): '*You go with the dead. So ask my dead daughter if my son Jean, who has left my house, is dead or alive. It's ages since I had any news of him.*'

The Jews were segregated in the other world. They were called dogs, swine. They stank. They walked backwards, whereas the other 'doubles' proceeded in the ordinary manner. They did not enter the churches, which were the normal gathering place for most of the ghosts. But the folklore of Foix, which had more pagan elements than Christian, was less harsh towards the Jews than was the Church of Rome: '*The Jews will one day be saved, and so will the heathen*', Gélis told his dead interlocutors, whereas the Catholic clergy doomed the Jews to eternal damnation, and even the Virgin Mary, so powerful and so merciful, could not save them.

Was all this a foreshadowing of the *danse macabre* of later ages? We are told that when the dead walked about the churches, they went hand in hand (i.535). But there is little in our texts about skeletons and decomposition, with which, after so much biological and psychological disaster, the following century was to be obsessed.

The souls of the dead had a proper body, with feet, head, hands and so on. This body was more beautiful than in real life, apart from the question of wounds and blood and ragged clothing. Nevertheless, Gélis maintained (i.135, 545) that *the life of us the living is better than that of the dead. Let us eat and drink as much as we can now.*

The dead felt the cold, and at night they would go to houses with a good supply of logs and light a fire in the hearth from the embers which the living had covered up before going to bed (i.128, 139, 537, 545, 548). The dead did not eat, but they did drink wine, and very good wine at that. At night they would go and empty the barrels in the finest and cleanest houses. (According to another version, the level of wine in the barrel did not go down.) Before the harvest, Gélis joined in veritable drinking bouts with the dead, in parties of over a hundred. He drank his share – it may have been this which earned him the nickname 'Bottler' (i.133, 139, 548).

But there was no question of the dead enjoying the pleasures of the flesh, or of family life in the full meaning of the term. They had no houses of their own, though they frequently visited the houses they used to live in as well as the homes of others. The fact that they had no *ostal* of their own gave them a sense of belonging to a larger community. Instead of being attached to the *domus* they were attached to the church. The dead were better parishioners than the living.

The normal state of the dead, before entering finally into their place of rest, was motion. They were always rushing from place to place. What a contrast to their lives before, when they were more or less rooted in their *domus*. They went about in order to do penance. The guiltiest among them, above all the usurers, were those who hurried fastest. Everyone, except the Jews, went from church to church, though their chief attachment was to the parish church near which they had lived and to the graveyard where they had been buried. They also went on pilgrimage. Some went as far as Saint James of Compostella, taking only five days for the journey. Others went to Saint-Gilles, Racamadour and so on. It was incumbent upon the living to leave the church lit up at night for the visits of the dead. The dead preferred oil-lamps to candles; they burned longer and more steadily.

So the ghosts' activity was interrupted while they went to church at night. It was resumed in the morning, when they left the church in procession in order to visit another. So, like the living, the dead might often be met with in the morning, after Mass, the traditional moment for general gatherings and social contacts. Gélis used to take advantage of this in order to talk to his 'clients' from the other world.

'*When you are walking,*' Gélis told his living audience, '*do not throw your arms and legs about carelessly, but keep your elbows well in, or you might knock a ghost over. Do not forget that we walk unwittingly among a multitude of ghosts; they are invisible to everyone but the messenger of souls.*'[1]

In all these stories there is very little mention of Purgatory. In 1320 it was a fairly recent theological discovery. Only one of Arnaud Gélis's dead interlocutors, Mâitre Arnaud Durand, went through its flames and all we learn from him is that it left vivid memories. He afterwards joined the other ghosts, going from church to church, awaiting his final rest (i.130, 131, 135).

1 i.134–5, 533, 534, 537, 543–5, 547, 548.

It was rest, not Hell, which predominated in Gélis's visions. Was this because the local people's sense of sin was not sufficiently developed? Did Hell seem to them too severe and final a punishment? Whatever the reason, it appears only as the underground dwelling-place of the demons, from which they emerge from time to time to persecute wandering souls or draw the carriages of the ladies. Nor does Gélis present a very clear view of Heaven. Heaven, in his account, exists only *after* the Last Judgment. Before this, the dead, like the living, still have their feet on the ground.

So, after a certain time spent in penitential wandering from church to church, the dead prepared for their second death. This meant their entry into the 'place of rest', which was also on earth, in a place which was agreeable but vague or even unknown. This 'second death' took place at All Saints. According to Gélis, it was sometimes heralded by angels. A group of these would come and choose out of the wandering crowd of 'doubles' those who had completed their penance and settled all their accounts and were ready to be admitted into the place of rest. This final departure was brought about and hastened by the Masses which the living had said for the dead, by gifts to the poor made for this purpose and by the payment of old debts left behind them by the dead. This exodus on the part of some of the ghosts aroused additional sorrow and lamenting among those left behind. Once they reached the place of rest, they were no longer in contact with the messenger of souls, and thus lost touch with the living.

The period during which the souls still wandered, and in which the messenger of souls could be an intermediary, might be quite brief and last only a few weeks (i.129).[1] During this time, some of the dead might go every Saturday and visit the *ostal* where their widow or widower still lived with their children. They might temporarily occupy their old bedroom, and so both house and chamber had to be kept in good order (i.137, 551). The dead might help their still-living relatives to sleep soundly, and were still concerned in the welfare of the household from which they had been snatched away. One dead mother repented not having persuaded a runaway daughter to return to her husband (i.131).

But for the living to help the dead to be admitted to rest was to

1 In some Occitan texts the wandering of the dead is presented as equivalent to Purgatory, while the place of rest at the next stage is equivalent to the Garden of Eden. Heaven itself is reached only after the Last Judgment.

shorten their own period of mourning. So Masses said for the dead were in the interests of both sides, not to mention the priests. When necessary, the dead would use Arnaud Gélis as intermediary to remind their living relatives of their duty in this respect. Gélis virtually acted as a tout for the local clergy – until Jacques Fournier came along and interfered (i.129, 135, 534, 551).

Arnaud Gélis himself was reasonably well off and probably owned his own house (i.128). He was not a glutton for work, and liked to sit in the sun (i.550). He was employed as a canon's servant and subsequently as an assistant sacristan. But his chief role, like that of the modern historian, was to act as mouthpiece for the dead.

Sometimes he might even act as intermediary, not between living and dead but between one dead person and another (i.134). Gélis carried out his functions as messenger of souls with professionalism and discretion, keeping his information to himself once he had imparted it to those concerned. For the Inquisition to suppress the messengers of souls was to encourage people to indulge in direct communications with ghosts, and there was then a danger of ghosts appearing in person to everyone everywhere.

The Church itself tried to replace the idea of ghosts with that of souls. According to Christian theology souls, after death, flew like arrows to Paradise, Hell or Purgatory. This again prevented the living from addressing their departed loved ones directly and there was a danger that, with their well-known love of the supernatural, they would be tempted to try themselves to speak with demons. (In the good old days of Guillaume Fort and Arnaud Gélis, demons might have had contact with the dead, but they were not in direct touch with men of flesh and blood.) The later developments opened the way to witchcraft.

The payments Gélis received for his services were not excessive. When he did not perform his errands satisfactorily among the living, the dead would requite him with a cudgelling (i.136, 544). The living paid him with a cheese or an invitation to a drink or a meal, or perhaps a little money (i.137, 538, 543, 544, 547). This was not unreasonable, considering the risks Gélis took vis-à-vis the Inquisition, into whose clutches he finally fell.

But for a long time his relationship with the official clergy was far from disagreeable. He often went to church, and his own utterances were influenced by what he heard from the pulpit and in the sacristy. He stood at the intersection of a certain supply and demand. He established a whole clientèle of living women who wanted to have Masses said for their dead husbands or fathers or children, and these he guided towards the priests of his acquaintance who asked nothing better than to recite offices for them, for a consideration. He did encounter a few sceptics among the living. But what he had to tell was so congenial to the mentality both of the masses and of the élite, and what he did was so genuinely useful, both domestically and socially, that he was assured of a good supply of faithful customers, most of them women (i.550).

Man had not only a soul, which most people believed to be immortal, but also a spirit. When someone was asleep and dreaming, the spirit might escape from his body. The people of Montaillou in general, and Pierre Maury in particular, were fascinated by the problem of dreams and by the *exemplum* of the lizard. Variations of this *exemplum* had been circulating for centuries. *Once upon a time*, said Philippe d'Alayrac of Coustaussa (iii.152), *two believers found themselves close to a river. One of them fell asleep. The other stayed awake, and from the mouth of the sleeper he saw emerge a creature like a lizard. Suddenly the lizard, using a plank, (or was it a straw?) which stretched from one bank to the other, crossed over the river. On the other bank there was the fleshless skull of an ass. And the lizard ran in and out of the openings in the skull. Then it came back over the plank and re-entered the sleeper's mouth. It did that once or twice. Seeing which, the man who was awake thought of a trick: he waited until the lizard was on the other side of the river and approaching the ass's skull. And then he took away the plank! The lizard left the ass's head and returned to the bank. But he could not get across! The plank was gone! Then the body of the sleeper began to thrash about, but it was unable to wake, despite the efforts of the watcher to arouse it from its sleep. Finally the watcher put the plank back across the river. Then the lizard was able to get back and re-enter the body of the sleeper through the mouth. The sleeper immediately awoke; and he told his friend the dream he had just had.*

'I dreamed,' he said, 'that I was crossing a river on a plank; then I went into a great palace with many towers and rooms, and when I wanted to come back to the place from which I had set out, there was no plank! I could not get across: I would have been drowned in the river. That was why I thrashed about (in my sleep). Until the plank was put back again and I could return.'

The two believers wondered greatly at this adventure, and went and told it to a parfait, *who gave them the key to the mystery : the soul, he told them, remains in a man's body all the time ; but a man's spirit or mind goes in and out, just like the lizard which went from the sleeper's mouth to the ass's head and vice versa.*

Every self-respecting Montaillou shepherd, whether in Sabarthès or in Catalonia, told the Cathar myth of the Fall over and over again (ii.33-4, 199, 407; ii.489-90; iii.130, 219 and *passim*). At the beginning of the story the spirits, seduced by the Evil One, fell straight through a hole in Heaven down to earth. Around the fire in the evening, the peasants went over the details. At first God did not notice what was happening, then he was surprised and did not understand, finally he grew angry and hastily put his foot over the hole in Heaven. But it was late, and many of the spirits had already fallen to earth, where they became the victims of feminine wiles and of the tunics of human flesh prepared for them by the Devil. Then began the lower part of the mythic cycle – metempsychosis. After various incarnations, both in the bodies of animals and in those of human beings, some souls would succeed in coming full circle. Having been the souls of *parfaits*, or of believers who received the *consolamentum*, they ascended after death into the Heaven from which they had originally fallen (ii.411 and *passim*). When all the good souls had left the earth and gone back to their home in Paradise, there would be no just men left on earth and it would be of no further interest. Then the end of the world became possible. The four elements would merge. Then, said the shepherds of Montaillou, echoing the brothers Authié, the sky would fall down on the earth, the sun and moon would go out, the sea would be consumed by fire and fire would be consumed by the sea. The earth would be a lake of pitch and sulphur: Hell.

Believers who had been 'consoled' now united in the great confraternity of those villagers of Montaillou who had attained salvation, and danced on the Last Day, trampling underfoot all the unbelievers, *as the lambs dance on the grass in the meadows, or on the stubble of the fields when they have been harvested* (ii.32).

What did the happiness of the souls of the just consist in, when they lived in Paradise? According to Pierre Authié (ii.411), *there every soul will have as much wealth and happiness as every other ; and all will be as one. And all the souls will love one another as if they loved the soul of their father or of their children.* Once again, the sacred is only the social, transfigured. Not a word about any beatific vision. For the people of Montaillou, Heaven would be one huge *domus*.

What was it that made a citizen of Montaillou 'tick' in the period 1290–1325? What were the fundamental motivations, the centres of interest which, over and above such basic biological drives as food and sex, gave his life meaning?

Our documents have enabled us to burrow beneath the rich but superficial crust of feudal and seigneurial relationships which for so long, in the absence of other evidence, nourished the histories that were written of early peasant communities. We have been able to penetrate beyond the community of inhabitants and the theoretical or actual municipal organization (which in any case was not of the first importance in Montaillou), beyond the tiny village 'élite'. We have got down to the basic unit, the unit of the people, the peasants, as reflected in our text. That unit, the *domus* or *ostal*, was at once building and family, the unifying principle that linked man and his possessions. It was thus the thing that counted most for the peasants, not yet obsessed, like their modern counterparts, with the problem of land.

Although this study has been confined to one village, Montaillou brings to mind the more general ideas of the philosophers and economists who have interested themselves in the methods of domestic production. Marx spoke of early economies in which the economic whole was really contained in each individual house, which formed its own independent centre of production. But Marx was thinking here of geographically scattered dwellings, which rightly or wrongly he took to be the rule in ancient Germania. In the case of heads of families each directing his own isolated house or farm, cooperation was necessarily reduced to a minimum. But in Montaillou the houses were close or even crowded together, and collaboration between *domus* presented no difficulty, though it took the comparatively restricted form of lending tools and utensils, common tending of the meadows, exclusion from fields with growing crops, the informal sharing of a well and so on.

More relevant for us are the ideas of Karl Polanyi.[1] They are based on Aristotle's theory, following Hesiod, concerning the *oikos* (house) and its *oikonomia* (administration or management). The *domus*, in Mon-

1 K. Polyani, *Primitive, archaic and modern economics*, Boston, 1971.

taillou as elsewhere, constituted a formidable reservoir of power or counter-power which could hold out with some degree of success against the external powers surrounding it.

Economically speaking, the *domus* was engaged in 'natural' rather than monetary relations with neighbouring *domus* and other economic units. These involved acts of reciprocity and symmetry (transhumance, barter, and acts of redistribution of agricultural surplus (chiefly in the form of tithes). But the *domus* had marked tendencies towards autarchy and subsistence economy. The lack of co-operation between neighbouring villages and even between the cellular economies of individual houses in Montaillou itself is striking. This tendency produced a loyalty to house rather than parish, and thus militated against the growth of a civic sense of community. Lastly, the *domus* also had intermittent but real contacts with the market: the sheep fair, the corn markets in Ax-les-Thermes and Tarascon, and so on. Considerations of faith rather than finance were likely to affect market dealings. A Cathar woman selling corn dear to a Catholic customer explained (ii.108): *I prefer to do favours to those who are of the faith* [i.e. supporters of heresy].

More generally, the case of Montaillou corresponds to the models put forward by the Russian economist A. V. Chayanov in his *Theory of Peasant Economy*,[1] and applying to rural life almost everywhere in the West before the time of Adam Smith. In this kind of society every *homo oeconomicus* is the organizer of one family economic unit in which employees play only a small or occasional part, and in which the overall economy is made up of the interrelations between the family units. The general features of the *domus* in the Pays d'Aillon correspond to those of this 'domestic system', with division of labour according to sex. The women are in charge of fire, housekeeping, cooking, gardening, greenstuff for the animals and for the family and the fetching of water. The men look after the fields and woods and flocks, with occasional female help which may be seasonal and migrant, or local and supplied by the family. As Rétif says,[2] in such a system the woman deals with 'indoor details' and the man with 'outdoor matters'. Production for the market is not neglected (mostly sheep, with poultry and eggs as a subsidiary contribution), but the main effort is directed towards the more or less

1 English translation, Homewood, Illinois, U.S.A., 1966.
2 Rétif de La Bretonne, *Les Contemporains*, vol. II, Paris, 1962, p. 205.

satisfactory subsistence of the family itself rather than towards 'the creation of accumulated surpluses'. The aim is not so much 'the extended reproduction of agricultural capital' as 'the production of usable values' such as food and clothing. Abundance is not asked for, but want can be avoided or dealt with. People are not necessarily lazy, but without the blandishments of surplus or the ever-increasing accumulation of capital there are no inordinate incentives to work. The peasant family, when it is large enough, with sons and daughters old enough to work, as well as adults, functions below its capacity. It thus exemplifies Chayanov's law that 'in a system of domestic production for use, labour intensity varies inversely with labour capacity in relation to the unit of production'. This refusal to over-exert oneself is reflected in all the naps taken, the time spent sitting in the sun and the many allusions to days off and saints' days. Childhood, which will eventually produce the labour that makes leisure possible, is at the centre of this domestic system, which therefore surrounds young children with love.

The absence of increasing surpluses makes usury and the infliction of heavy tithes difficult. In a society where almost everyone is poor without being too afflicted about it, and where no one aspires to ever-growing wealth, the real poor and the landless proletariat show little aggression. In Montaillou, lads whose probable lot is poverty simply go away with the migrating flocks to the masculine, bachelor civilization of the shepherds, and thus to a true market economy. The producer's ownership of the means of production is a rule of the system fairly closely obeyed in Montaillou itself: the men of the *domus*, even if they are not particularly well off, own a piece of land as well as their house; and when the poor shepherds grow older and return to the village they usually possess a few dozen sheep.

With the shepherds we emerge from the cellular universe of the *domus*. The young bachelors go off to the mountain pastures and Catalonia. As freelance employees they are more modern and emancipated than their fathers and brothers who stay at home. The shepherds, obliged but not unwilling to be lovers of Dame Poverty, sometimes manage to give their exacting mistress the slip. The Inquisition, detaching this wandering group from its base, confers a fascinating independence on Pierre Maury. The pastor's cabin contrasts with the villager's *domus*, just as true masculine friendship contrasts with parochial propinquity and all its rancour.

The harsh repression which fell on the village between 1308 and 1325 grew lighter afterwards, and finally disappeared. The Black Death struck in 1348, though its impact may have been comparatively light in upper Ariège. Then there were other plagues, and the ravages of different armies. By 1390, there were only twenty-three hearths in Montaillou, half or less than half than what there had been in 1300–20. But even though they were decimated, the leading families were still there, despite the Inquisition, despite epidemics, despite wars. The inhabitants of Montaillou in 1390 were called Benet, Clergue, Maurs, Ferrier, Baille, Fort, Azéma, Pourcel, Rives, Authié, Argelliers. There is only one name which may be new. So the *domus* held out. They were not adulterated by immigration; the mountains were too forbidding. Montaillou continued much as it was throughout the following centuries – in the 1970s there was still a Clergue in the local telephone directory. Now its people are abandoning the fields up in the mountains, and so threatening the stability of an ancient habitat which neither repression nor contagion was able to destroy. Montaillou culture was directed towards mere reproduction, self-preservation and the perpetuation of the *domus* in the world below. The only element of 'growth' which happened to manifest itself early in the fourteenth century had little to do with economics. It was concerned with the after-life and with a kind of spiritual transcendance, locally centred on the Albigensian idea of Heaven.

Jacques Fournier took it upon himself to remedy all that. Today Catharism is no more than a dead star, whose cold but fascinating light reaches us now after an eclipse of more than half a millenium. But Montaillou itself is much more than a courageous but fleeting deviation. It is the factual history of ordinary people. It is Pierre and Béatrice and their love; it is Pierre Maury and his flock; it is the breath of life restored through a repressive Latin register that is a monument of Occitan literature. Montaillou is the physical warmth of the *ostal*, together with the ever-recurring promise of a peasant heaven. The one within the other, the one supporting the other.

Selective bibliography

M. T. ANDRIEU, *La doctrine neo-cathare en haute Ariège*, thesis for D.E.S. (history), University of Toulouse, 1967

P. ARIES, *Le temps de l'histoire*, Monaco, 1954

M. BONNASSIE, unpublished *thèse d'état* on social history of medieval Catalonia, University of Toulouse – Le Mirail, 1972

G. BOUCHARD, *Le village immobile*, Paris, 1972

J. CHELINI, *Histoire religieuse de l'Occident mediéval*, Paris, 1968

M. CHEVALIER, *La vie humaine dans les Pyrénées ariègeoises*, Paris, 1956

E. DELARUELLE, *Dévotion populaire . . . au Moyen Age* (in LE GOFF, *Hérésies . . .*)

G. DUBY, *Fondements d'un nouvel humanisme, 1228–1440*, Geneva, Paris, 1973

A. DE DUFAU DE MALUQUER, 'Le pays de Foix sous Gaston Phoebus. Rôle des feux du comté de Foix en 1310' (Household rolls of the county of Foix in 1310), *Bulletin de la société des sciences, lettres et arts de Pau*, 2nd series, tome 28, 1898–9 (Foix, 1901)

A. DUPRONT, 'Vie et création religieuse dans la France moderne (14e–18e siècles)', in M. FRANCOIS, *La France et les Français*, Paris, 1972

J. DUVERNOY, *Inquisition à Pamiers*, Toulouse, 1966

J. DUVERNOY, 'La noblesse du comté de Foix au début du XIVe siècle', *XVIe Congrès de la Fédération des sociétés académiques et savantes, Languedoc, Pyrénées, Gascogne*, Auch, 1961. See also 'Nourriture en Languedoc à l'époque cathare', *ibid.*, *XXIVe Congrès*, published Carcassonne, 1970; 'Pierre Authié', *Cahiers d'études cathares*, 1970; and *Corrections* to his edition of Fournier's *Register*, Toulouse, 1972

L. FEBVRE, *Au coeur religieux du XVIe siècle*, Paris, 1957

L. FEBVRE, *Rabelais, ou le problème de l'incroyance au XVIe siècle*, Paris, 1942

J. FOURNIER, *Le Registre d'Inquisition de Jacques Fournier, evêque de Pamiers (1318–1325)*, Latin manuscript no. 4030 in the Vatican Library, edited by Jean Duvernoy, Toulouse, 1965, 3 vols

E. GELLNER, *Saints of the Atlas*, London, 1969

F. GIRAUD, *Hérésie et société paysanne à Montaillou*, D.E.S. thesis (history), University of Paris VII, 1971

D. GLASS and D. EVERSLEY (ed.), *Population in history*, London, 1965

J. GOODY (ed.), *Literacy in traditional societies*, Cambridge, 1968

R. HILTON, 'Medieval peasants', *Journal of peasant studies*, January 1974

J. LACAZE, *Les Vaudois d'après le Registre de Jacques Fournier*, D.E.S. thesis (history), University of Toulouse, n.d.

M. LAZAR, *Amour courtois et fin' amors*, Paris, 1964

J. LE GOFF, 'Au Moyen Age, temps de l'Eglise et temps du marchand', *Annales*, May–June 1960

J. LE GOFF (ed.), *Hérésies et sociétés*, Paris, The Hague, 1968

E. LE ROY LADURIE, *Les payspans de Languedoc*, Paris, 1966

C. LIMBORCH, *Liber sententiarum inquisitionis tholosanae, historia inquisitionis*, Amsterdam, 1962

M. MOLLAT, *Etudes sur l'histoire de la pauvreté*, Paris, 1974

R. NELLI, *L'erotique des troubadours*, Toulouse, 1963

R. NELLI, *La vie quotidienne des cathares du Languedoc au XIIIe siècle*, Paris, 1969

J. PITT-RIVERS, *People of the Sierra*, Chicago, 1961

A. RADCLIFFE-BROWN, *Structure and function in primitive society*, New York, 1965

D. DE ROUGEMONT, *L'amour et l'Occident*, Paris, 1939. (Various new editions in French and English)

J. M. VIDAL, *Le tribunal d'inquisition à Pamiers*, Toulouse, 1906

B. VOURZAY, *L'emigration des Cathares occitans en Catalogne, d'après le Registre de J. Fournier*, D.E.S. thesis, Aix, 1969

P. WOLFF, *Commerce et marchands de Toulouse*, Paris, 1954

Index of the main families of Montaillou

Compiled by Deirdre A. Jennings

Tabular index of the main families of Montaillou

The family tables I–XXVI are given in alphabetical family-name order. The heretics are denoted by an asterisk. An alphabetical list of all the peasants begins on p. 380 below.

I AUTHIE BROTHERS
Cathar missionaries (p. 244) from Ax-les-Thermes, converted to Catharism in Lombardy (p. 253) in 1300 (p. 267).

(a) PIERRE; his brother (b) GUILLAUME; PIERRE's son (c) JACQUES and daughter (d) GUILLEMETTE

(a) PIERRE*: his propagandist group method (p. 26); his nephews (called de Rodes, from Tarascon) denounced the village heretics in 1308 (p. 63); burned shortly after 1302 (p. 83); his profession: a clerk of law (p. 233); together with his son Jacques, schooled Guillaume Bélibaste [VI b] in heretical matters (p. 240); fathered Jacques and Guillemette (p. 193).

(b) GUILLAUME*: son-in-law of Arnaud Benet, brother of Guillaume Benet of Montaillou (p. 27); trust in Montaillou as a Cathar stronghold (p. 30); faithful frequenter of the Belot household (p. 45); married Gaillarde Authié (p. 63); Gaillarde's confessions at the Lent Inquisition of 1308 possibly led to the mass arrest of Montaillou (p. 63; cf. p. 256); danced at Béatrice de Planissoles and Bérenger de Roquefort's wedding (p. 160); imprisoned for heresy in Carcassonne in 1323 (p. 183); hereticated Raymond Benet (p. 211); his profession: a clerk of law (p. 233); lent Pierre Clergue (priest) the 'book of the holy faith of the heretics' (p. 236).

(c) JACQUES*: Pierre Authié's son (p. 83); preached to the shepherds (pp. 30, 84); taken by the Inquisition in 1305 (p. 88); master/mentor of Pierre Maury (shepherd) (p. 123).

(d) GUILLEMETTE: married Arnaud Teisseire (p. 193) who maltreated her (p. 234); Arnaud was a notary and the nearest 'real' doctor to Montaillou (p. 222); he had a bastard son, Guillaume, whom he also beat (p. 234); Arnaud's imprisonment and death in Pamiers (p. 331).

II AZEMA
Table of Pierre Azéma's family
Catholic, anti-Cathar household, consisting of the Azéma brothers, Pierre

and **Pons**, and their mother **Raymonde Azéma**, known as **Na Carminagua** (pp. 267–8).

(a)   **PIERRE**, married to (b) **GUILLEMETTE**; their son (c) **RAYMOND** and (d) unnamed daughter.

(a)   **PIERRE**: son of Mme **Carminagua** (p. 29); concerned with self-protection and the defence of the *domus* (p. 25); kept an anti-Cathar house (pp. 30, 35); together with **Pierre de Gaillac**, denounced **Pierre Clergue** (priest), for which they were jointly denounced as traitors by **Bernard Clergue** (*bayle*) (pp. 35, 268); cousin of **Bishop Fournier** (p. 59); had **Bernard Benet** incarcerated in the château dungeons for being an accomplice of the **Clergues** (p. 59); **Bishop Fournier** supported **Pierre's** *domus* 1300–21 (p. 271); anti-**Clergue** clan activist (pp. 271–3); imprisoned in Carcassonne through **Bernard Clergue's** contacts, where the jailor so ill-treated him that he soon died (p. 273).

(d)   unnamed daughter: offered by her father **Pierre** as wife to one of **Gauzia Clergue's** sons [X d] (pp. 25, 180), on condition that **Gauzia** left the **Clergue** clan and joined that of the **Azémas** (p. 271).

III AZEMA

Table of **Pons Azéma's** family

(a)   **PONS**, married to (b) **ALAZAIS**; their son (c) **RAYMOND**

(a)   **PONS**: son of Mme **Carminagua** (p. 29); good Catholic, mistrusted by **Guillaume Authié** (p. 267); distant cousin of **Bishop Fournier** (p. 268).

(b)   **ALAZAIS***: very active heretical conversationalist (p. 27); assisted **Brune Pourcel** with **Pons Clergue's** funeral rites (p. 31); called 'Madame' as mistress of a very important *ostal* (p. 35); received threats from **Guillaume Benet** and **Raymond Belot** should she denounce the **Authié** brothers (p. 50); one-time mistress of **Pierre Clergue** (priest) (p. 155); widowed, became a cheesemonger and pig-farmer (p. 253); messenger for the heretics (p. 253); spread the rumours concerning **Béatrice de Planissoles's** affairs with **Pierre Clergue** (priest) and **Pathau Clergue** [IX a], the priest's illegitimate cousin (p. 254).

(c)   **RAYMOND***: acting head of the household (p. 34); took food to the 'goodmen' (p. 162); aspired to be a *parfait* (p. 253).

IV BAILLE/SICRE

(a) **ARNAUD**, married to (b) **SYBILLE** (née **BAILLE**); their two sons (c) **BERNARD** and (d) **ARNAUD**

(a) **ARNAUD**: Catholic notary in Tarascon (pp. 195, 202); as a determined anti-Cathar he displeased his wife, who drove him out of her *ostal* (pp. 195, 202).

(b) **SYBILLE***: née Baille, of Ax-les-Thermes (pp. 90, 195); stock-raiser of Ax, separated from her husband, by whom she had two sons, **Bernard** and **Arnaud** (the informer) (p. 90); she was burnt at the stake for heresy (p. 90); the owner by inheritance of her own house (i.e. the maternal *ostal*) at Ax (p. 195).

(c) **BERNARD**: shared a bed in Barthélemy Borrel's house with **Pierre Maury** (shepherd), who was **Borrel's** employee (pp. 89–90) [Borrel, of Ax, was the brother-in-law of **Arnaud Baille Senior**, not (a), (p. 88); cf. Arnaud Baille the elder, of Montaillou, son-in-law of **Barthélemy Borrel** of Ax-les-Thermes (p. 115)].

(d) **ARNAUD**: this was the **Arnaud Baille/Sicre** (of Ax, p. 125) who became the chief informer to the Inquisition in his attempt to repossess the confiscated maternal *ostal* (pp. 33, 52, 90, 195); a shoemaker (p. 122); insinuated his way into **Guillaume Bélibaste's** colony of heretics in order to destroy it (pp. 130–1); apparently he had a sister who was promised in marriage to **Arnaud Marty** [XVIc] (p. 181); after his parents had separated his mother sent him to his father to be educated, when he was seven years old (p. 195); N.B. the children of this union used both the parental surnames (p. 195).

V BAILLE

Family 1
(a) **VITAL**, married to (b) **ESCLARMONDE**; their son (c) **JACQUES**

Family 2
(a) **RAYMOND**, married to (b) ?; their four sons (c) **PIERRE** (a shepherd, p. 75), (d) **JACQUES**, (e) **RAYMOND** and (f) **ARNAUD**

Family 3
(a) **GUILLAUME**: of Montaillou (p. 111); parentage unknown; migrant shepherd (*passim*); accused of heresy by his employer's family at Mérens (p. 11); described the life of the itinerant shepherds from his own experience (p. 111 *et passim*); not a heretic (pp. 11, 313).

VI BELIBASTE
(a) **GUILLAUME** (Senior); his sons (b) **GUILLAUME** and (c) **RAYMOND**; their relation (?) (d) **BERNARD**

(a) GUILLAUME*: the elder, the rich farmer from Cubières (pp. 83, 86); father of Guillaume Bélibaste, the *parfait* or pseudo-*parfait*, who was much loved by Pierre Maury (shepherd) (p. 83); lived with his three sons (Guillaume, Raymond (p. 87) and ?) and his two daughters-in-law (? and Estelle (p. 86)) and their children in the *domus* at Cubières (pp. 86–7).

(b) GUILLAUME*: the *parfait* – anti Pope, King of France, Bishop Fournier and the Lord Inquisitor of Carcassonne (p. 13); killed a shepherd, so had to leave the prosperous farm and fraternal *domus* at Cubières, becoming first a shepherd, then a *parfait* (p. 70); later settled down as prophet to a small Albigensian colony in Catalonia, where he became a maker of baskets or carding combs (pp. 70–1); in 1313 (?), Pierre Maury was presented to the Albigensian colony at San Mateo and Morella in the Tarragona region, which colony consisted of a small group of heretics from Montaillou and elsewhere who had gathered around Guillaume Bélibaste the younger (p. 94); he occasionally helped the team of shepherds led by Pierre Maury (p. 94); he and Guillemette Maury [XVI b] cheated Pierre Maury out of some sheep (p. 95); persuaded Pierre Maury to marry his own concubine, Raymonde Piquier, who was already pregnant, it seems, by Guillaume; and then dissolved the union, having thus suited his own ends, after a few days (pp. 97–102); had lived with Raymonde Piquier for a long time at Morella (p. 100); captured by the Inquisition (p. 102); took gross advantage of Pierre Maury's love for him, and of his powers as a *parfait* (Chapters IV–VII); burned at the stake (p. 218); an undistinguished orator, the pupil of Pierre and Jacques Authié (p. 240).

(c) RAYMOND*: son of Guillaume the elder (p. 87); believer in the heretics (p. 85).

(d) BERNARD*: stock-breeder in the region of Arques (p. 79); proposed the marriage of Pierre Maury (shepherd) to Maury's then employer, Raymonde Pierre's daughter, Bernadette Pierre (p. 79); important connections with heresy (pp. 80–1).

VII BELOT

The second wealthiest family in Montaillou; their *domus* was Cathar (p. 27), and was the focal point of heresy in the village, for it was here that the Authié brothers first stayed after their conversion to Catharism (p. 267).

(a) BELOT (no Christian name given), married to (b) GUILLEMETTE (old 'BELOTE'); their four sons (c) RAYMOND, (d) GUILLAUME,

(e) BERNARD and (f) ARNAUD; two daughters (g) RAYMONDE and
(h) ALAZAIS

(b) GUILLEMETTE*: often referred to as 'Belote'; effectively subdued
subversive anti-Cathar elements (p. 37); old friend of the matriarch
Mengarde Clergue (p. 43); hereticated before her death in 1311 (pp.
220, 269, 271); in 1306, her son-in-law Bernard Clergue (*bayle*)
threatened to have her imprisoned in Carcassonne, which fate befell her,
but Bernard Clergue stood surety for her and she was released (p. 269).

(c) RAYMOND*: first cousin of Raymonde Arsen [XXVI c] (p.42),
whom he asked to come and work as a servant in the *domus*, as his sister
Raymonde (g) was leaving to marry the *bayle*, Bernard Clergue (pp.
42–3).

(d) GUILLAUME*: Montaillou farmer (p. 28); godson of Guillaume
Benet (p. 45); was a shepherd (p. 69); died before 1324 (p. 77); his
brother-in-law Bernard Clergue threatened him with imprisonment in
Carcassonne (p. 269).

(e) BERNARD*: married Guillemette Benet (pp. 42, 45); imprisoned for
attempted rape on Guillaume Authié's wife (p. 45); first cousin and
landlord of Arnaud Vital (p. 46); had two illegitimate children by
Vuissane (Raymonde Testanière) who worked in the Belot *domus*
1304–07 (p. 46).

(f) ARNAUD*: married Raymonde Lizier [XIII b] who was eventually
imprisoned for heresy (p. 27); a widow of three years when she married
Arnaud (p. 180).

(g) RAYMONDE: married Bernard Clergue (*bayle*), a love-match (pp.
187, 220).

(h) ALAZAIS: married, had a child (p. 45).

VIII BENET

The third wealthiest family in Montaillou: Cathar *domus* (pp. 27, 28).
(a) GUILLAUME, married to (b) GUILLEMETTE ('BENETE'); their
three sons (c) RAYMOND, (d) BERNARD and (e) PIERRE; their four
daughters (f) ALAZAIS, (g) MONTAGNE, (h) ESCLARMONDE and
(i) GUILLEMETTE

(a) GUILLAUME*: brother of Arnaud Benet of Ax, who was the father-
in-law of Guillaume Authié (p. 27); it was through the Benet *domus*
that heresy was re-introduced into Montaillou in 1300 (p. 43); godfather of Guillaume Belot (p. 45); labourer-cum-farmer (pp. 118–19);

hereticated before his death by **Guillaume Authié** (p. 219); godfather of **Esclarmonde Clergue** [X e] (p. 226).

(b) **GUILLEMETTE***: a village matriarch, sometimes referred to as 'Benete' (p. 141).

(c) **RAYMOND***: hereticated by **Guillaume Authié** (pp. 211, 219); died (p. 210).

(d) **BERNARD***: would-be informer (p. 32); **Pierre Azéma** had him thrown into the château dungeons and his livestock seized and given to the Comte (p. 59); relegated on release to the status of a shepherd (p. 71); arrested several times by the Inquisition and on one occasion betrayed by **Alissende Roussel**, sister-in-law of his brother **Pierre** (e), possibly because she had been a temporary mistress of **Pierre Clergue** (priest) (pp. 71, 155).

(e) **PIERRE**: married **Gaillarde** (family name unknown); **Gaillarde Benet** and her sister **Alissende Roussel** had both been mistresses of the priest (pp. 71, 155, 157).

(f) **ALAZAIS***: hereticated before her death (p. 65) in her parental home by **Guillaume Authié** (p. 219); deloused her mother (p. 141); married **Barthélemy d'Ax** (p. 219).

(i) **GUILLEMETTE**: married **Bernard Belot** (pp. 42, 45); sentenced to life imprisonment, fetters and bread and water in 1321, although she had been saved from the Inquisition twelve years before by **Pierre Clergue** (priest), because of the strength of the inter-marriage connections (p. 56).

IX CLERGUE

The wealthiest family in Montaillou.
(a) PONS, married to (b) MENGARDE; their four sons (c) GUILLAUME, (d) BERNARD, (e) PIERRE and (f) RAYMOND; their two daughters (g) ESCLARMONDE and (h) GUILLEMETTE.

(a) **PONS***: his death and funeral rites (p. 31); a die-hard Cathar, alarmed at the depravity and spying of his son **Pierre** (e) (p. 60); had a brother, **Guillaume Clergue**, whose bastard son **Pathau Clergue** (p. 153) raped **Béatrice de Planissoles** (p. 150) and then kept her publicly as his mistress (p. 153); his brother **Guillaume** also had a natural daughter, **Fabrisse Clergue**, who married **Pons Rives** [XXIIIc] (p. 158).

(b) **MENGARDE***: called 'Madame' as the mistress of the most important *ostal* in Montaillou (p. 35); old friend of the other militant Cathar matriarchs, **Guillemette Belot** (p. 43) and **Na Roqua** (p. 251); **Raymonde Guilhou** (Arnaud Vital's widow) became her delouser, and through **Mengarde** was converted to Catharism (pp. 46, 61, 298); sent food to imprisoned Montaillou heretics (p. 61); son **Pierre (e)** had her buried in the church under the altar of the Virgin of Montaillou (p. 225).

(c) **GUILLAUME**: had a bastard son, **Arnaud Clergue** (pp. 56, 153); this **Arnaud** married into the **Lizier** family (p. 175); **Alazaïs Gonela** was **Guillaume**'s mistress (p. 163).

(d) **BERNARD***: *bayle* of Montaillou, tried bribery to release his brother **Pierre (e)** from the episcopal prison (p. 14); collected tithes for himself and for the superior powers (p. 21); prisoner of the Inquisition (pp. 54, 55); worshipped his brother **Pierre** as his 'god' and 'ruler' (pp. 35, 55, 60); deloused by old 'Belote' (p. 141); fathered a natural daughter, **Mengarde**, whom he used as a messenger to the heretics (p. 153), and as a servant in the *domus* (p. 42); married **Raymonde Belot**, whom he loved dearly, as he did his mother-in-law, old **Guillemette**, and the whole **Belot** *ostal* (pp. 153, 187–8); daughter **Mengarde** married **Raymond Aymeric** of Prades d'Aillon (p. 175); tried unsuccessfully to get many of the past mistresses of **Pierre (e)** to perjure themselves in the court of the Inquisition in order to save him (p. 270); imprisoned in Pamiers, having first been put under house arrest (p. 270); served only a month of his sentence (fetters, bread and water) before dying at the end of the summer of 1324 (p. 273).

(e) **PIERRE***: priest of Montaillou, and double agent (pp. 12, 65); arrested by the Inquisition and died in prison (p. 14); collected tithes for himself and for the superior powers (p. 21); organized his father's funeral rites (pp. 31–2); after the murder of the anti-Cathar **Arnaud Lizier**, took **Grazide Lizier [XIIId]** as his mistress (p. 29); was **Béatrice de Planissoles**'s business executive (pp. 35–6), and became her lover (pp. 39, 164–6); took **Raymonde Guilhou** as his temporary mistress (p. 46); carried out a vendetta against the **Maurs** *ostal* [XVII] (p. 50); official representative of the Carcassonne Inquisition (p. 58); buried his mother in the chapel at Montaillou (p. 61); took **Gaillarde Benet** and her sister **Alissende Roussel** temporarily as his mistresses (p. 71); **Grazide Lizier**, born of a bastard branch of the **Clergue** family, became his willing mistress at the age of fourteen years (p. 151); inherited the

XI DE PLANISSOLES
(a) PHILIPPE; his daughters (b) BEATRICE and (c) GENTILE

(a) PHILIPPE: friendly towards Catharism, was eventually condemned to wear the yellow cross (p. 160).

(b) BEATRICE: married the *châtelain* of Montaillou, **Bérenger de Roquefort**, who died young (p. 11); mistress to a bastard, then a Cathar priest and finally to an orthodox priest (p. 16); entertained superstitious beliefs (p. 32); married **Othon de Lagleize** and committed adultery with **Pierre Clergue** (priest) (p. 39); by 1308 she had been widowed twice (p. 64); took a young lover when quite old, the priest **Barthélemy Aurilhac**, who later threatened to denounce her to the Inquisition (pp. 131, 166–8); raped by **Pathau Clergue**, the bastard cousin of **Pierre Clergue** (priest) (pp. 150, 153); widowed the next year, became **Pathau Clergue**'s mistress and was publicly kept by him (p. 153); four daughters, called **Condors, Esclarmonde, Philippa** and **Ava** (p. 161); she and her lover **Barthélemy Aurilhac** imprisoned by **Fournier** in 1321, and both were released in 1322, though **Béatrice** had to wear the double yellow cross (p. 168).

(c) GENTILE: sister of **Béatrice** (p. 165); zealous Catholic, helped persuade **Béatrice** to conclude her affair with the Cathar priest (p. 165).

XII GUILHABERT
A heretical household (p. 28).

(a) JEAN, married to (b) ALLEMANDE; their son (c) GUILLAUME; their four daughters (d) ALAZAIS, (e) SYBILLE, (f) GUILLEMETTE and (g) RAYMONDE

(b) ALLEMANDE: maintained friendly relations with **Arnaud Vital**, her daughter Alazaïs's one-time lover (p. 171).

(c) GUILLAUME: a shepherd (p. 69); hereticated before his death (p. 32); died at the age of fifteen years (pp. 219, 228–9).

(d) ALAZAIS: married **Arnaud Fauré** (pp. 32, 228); **Arnaud Vital**'s mistress prior to her marriage (p. 228), and he had instructed her in heresy (pp. 46, 170); husband **Arnaud** employed **Pierre Maury** as a shepherd (pp. 77, 96); niece **Raymonde** (née **Clément**, p. 202) married **Pierre Fauré**, whose impotency caused her to leave home and live with **Alazaïs**, at which time **Pierre Clergue** tried, unsuccessfully, to importune her favour (pp. 154–5, 202); **Alazaïs** and her sister **Raymonde** had both been mistresses of **Pierre Clergue** (priest) (p. 155).

(f)   GUILLEMETTE: married **Jean Clément** of Gébetz (p. 228); left her marital home and was ill in bed in her father's *domus* (p. 278).

(g)   RAYMONDE: one-time mistress of the priest (p. 155).

XIII LIZIER

NOTE: The relationships between the members of this *domus* are not at all clear from the Register. Some references are inconsistent and contradictory. These are denoted by the symbol +.

(a) RAYMOND; (b) RAYMONDE (née D'ARGELLIERS); (c) ARNAUD; (d) GRAZIDE; (e) PIERRE; (f) an unnamed female member of the LIZIER family (who married **Arnaud Clergue**, bastard cousin of the priest)

(a)   RAYMOND: head of the *ostal*, a simple peasant who was a good Catholic and thus hated the heretics, for which he was murdered (p. 267); married to Raymonde (née d'Argelliers, see (b)) (p. 267).

(b)   RAYMONDE: née d'Argelliers, married to **Raymond Lizier** (a), her first husband, thus becoming **Raymond Lizier** (p. 267); widowed through her husband's murder (p. 267), though she was suspected of involvement in the crime (p. 267); referred to as **Raymonde d'Argelliers**, widow of **Raymond Lizier** (p. 268); she was threatened by the priest, **Pierre Clergue**, should she denounce four named female heretics (p. 268); referred to as **Raymonde Lizier**, very friendly with the confirmed heretical members of the **Belot** household (p. 27); three years after losing her first husband (p. 180) she remarried, this time to **Arnaud Belot**, changing her name from **Raymonde Lizier** to **Raymonde Belot** (p. 27); referred to as **Raymonde Belot** at the time when she made use of the **Benet** kitchen (p. 8); her second marriage is referred to as the marriage of **Raymonde d'Argelliers** to **Arnaud Belot** (p. 184); + 'After the murder of my first husband, **Arnaud Lizier** of Montaillou . . .' (p. 180); + **Raymonde** was suspected of having been involved in the murder of her first husband, **Arnaud Lizier** (p. 184); gave evidence to the court of the Inquisition in 1323 as **Raymonde Belot** (p. 8); ended her days in prison for heresy (p. 27).

(c)   ARNAUD: anti-Cathar who was murdered (pp. 29, 180); the *bayle* and the priest implicated in his death (p. 330); after his death, the house of Lizier came into the **Clergues'** sphere of influence (p. 29).

(d)   GRAZIDE: née **Rives**, daughter of **Pons** and **Fabrisse Rives** [XXIII c];

XV MARTY

The MARTY family of Montaillou (p. 101).
(a) PIERRE, married to (b) EMERSENDE (née MAURY); their daughter
(c) JEANNE

(a) PIERRE: husband of Emersende (pp. 113, 310).

(b) EMERSENDE*: married to Pierre Marty (pp. 113, 210); a refugee in
Spain together with Blanche Marty of Junac (p. 101); disapproved of
Pierre Maury's 'shot-gun' and short-lived marriage to Raymonde
Piquier [XIVc] (p. 101); distressed by Pierre Maury's disagreeable
life-style (p. 120); reproached Pierre Maury for his constant journeyings
because of the danger for everyone should he be caught, and so offered
him a refuge in her house in Catalonia (pp. 134–5); Pierre Maury's aunt
(p. 186); heretical sister of Guillemette Marty (née Maury) (p. 52);
conspired to murder her Catholic daughter, Jeanne Befayt (née
Marty) (p. 52); referred to as Emersende Befayt (p. 134), i.e. she
probably adopted her son-in-law's name, in the context of her continuing to live with her daughter Jeanne, despite the fact that Jeanne
kept attacking her (pp. 134, 242–3); delighted that Pierre Clergue, the
priest, had been arrested (p. 139); eventually Emersende and her
daughter Jeanne Befayt died in an epidemic (pp. 218, 220).

(c) JEANNE: Catholic daughter of Emersende Marty (p. 292); mother
conspired to murder her (p. 52); married Bernard Befayt (pp. 120,
292), thus becoming Jeanne Befayt; her mother would seem to have
assumed her daughter's married name when she went to live with her
(she may have been widowed), during which time Jeanne used to attack
her (pp. 134, 242–3), while Bernard beat Jeanne in order to protect his
mother-in-law (p. 192); Bernard Befayt, a woodcutter, died in an
accident in the forest of Benifaxa in Spain (pp. 120, 218); Jeanne
Befayt helped Pierre and Arnaud Maurs [XXIIc and f] to lead their
flock of sheep out of Montaillou (p. 104); Pierre Maury's (shepherd)
cousin (p. 186); died with her mother, Emersende, in an epidemic
(pp. 218, 220).

XVI MARTY

Family 3
(a) BERNARD, brother of Guillaume and Jean of Montaillou, married to
(b) GUILLEMETTE (née MAURY); their two sons (c) ARNAUD and
(d) JEAN

(a) **BERNARD**: died in the mountains at Orta (pp. 94, 218), not long before the winter of 1315–1316 (p. 94).

(b) **GUILLEMETTE***: (née Maury), the namesake of **Pierre Maury's** sister (pp. 94, 218), and their aunt (p. 181); widowed, so moved from Orta to San Mateo for ease of livelihood and to be near the **Bélibastes** (pp. 94, 195); thus became the head of the *ostal* at San Mateo, and so reverted back to the name of **Guillemette Maury** (p. 196); became a small farmer with vineyard and flock of sheep (p. 95); cheated her nephew **Pierre Maury** (shepherd) in a sheep deal (p. 95); was the sister of **Pierre Maury** (*not* the shepherd) (pp. 125, 196); Pierre (shepherd) and his sister, **Guillemette Maury**, not to be confused with their aunt and uncle, may have been named after them (p. 181); was urged on to adore the Cathar Bible by **Guillaume Bélibaste** (*parfait*) (p. 235).

(c) **ARNAUD***: an invalid (p. 99); with his parents, encountered other heretical Montaillou peasants/shepherds in Juncosa (p. 113); a marriage had been arranged for him with an unnamed sister of **Arnaud Sicre** (p. 181).

(d) **JEAN**: not a 'believer' (p. 181); married a non-heretic of San Mateo, while a refugee there, called **Marie**, and his mother greatly approved the match (p. 187), although the *parfait* **Guillaume Bélibaste** refused to preside at the wedding (p. 181); known as **Jean Maury** (p. 196).

XVII MAURS
A heretical family (pp. 28, 41, 74).
(a) PIERRE, married to (b) MENGARDE; their four sons (c) ARNAUD, (d) GUILLAUME, (e) RAYMOND and (f) PIERRE; their daughter (g) GUILLEMETTE

(a) **PIERRE**: lived next door to his brother Bernard Maurs [XIXa] (p. 41); his house was in open warfare with the priest (p. 41), this because of the priest's two-faced activities whereby **Guillaume** (d), **Arnaud** (c) and **Pierre** (a) were all imprisoned by the Inquisition in 1308, and only **Guillaume** was released (p. 50); imprisoned at Carcassonne with his sons **Pierre** (f), **Guillaume** (d) and **Bernard** (? may refer to **Bernard**, son of **Raymond Maurs** [XVIII d]) (p. 74).

(b) **MENGARDE**: Pierre Clergue (priest), acting through his brother the *bayle*, had her tongue cut out for 'false witness' against the priest (pp. 41, 50, 64, 72).

with his mother, **Guillemette Maurs**, was imprisoned by the Inquisition (p. 74).

(d) **PIERRE**: fled from Montaillou in 1308, after the raid on the local heretics by the Inquisition (p. 74), and settled in Catalonia before returning to Montaillou in 1321 to marry one of **Guillaume Authié's** daughters (pp. 74, 183).

XX MAURY
A heretical household (p. 28).
(a) **RAYMOND**, married to (b) **ALAZAIS**; their six sons (c) **GUILLAUME**, (d) **PIERRE**, (e) **JEAN**, (f) **ARNAUD**, (g) **RAYMOND** and (h) **BERNARD**; their two daughters (i) **GUILLEMETTE** and (j) **RAYMONDE**

(a) **RAYMOND***: weaver of Montaillou (p. 6); instructed his children in Catharism (p. 214); house was destroyed three times for heresy (p. 241).

(b) **ALAZAIS**: also called **Alazaïs Maurine** (p. 339).

(c) **GUILLAUME***: shepherd (p. 28); died before 1324 (p. 77).

(d) **PIERRE***: shepherd (p. 28 *et passim*); lost his 'fraternal portion' of the family *domus* (pp. 36, 123); 'kidnapped' his sister **Guillemette** (with her consent) from her bullying husband (p. 49); outlawed for heretical activity (p. 60); escaped the mass arrest of 1308 (pp. 63–4); looked after **Arnaud Fauré's** (his uncle, p. 129) and **Raymond Maulen's** (his first cousin, p. 79) sheep (p. 77); made first contacts with heresy through his brother **Guillaume** (c) and the **Belot** shepherds (pp. 77, 78); left home when eighteen years old, in 1300–01 (p. 78); his love affair with the non-believer **Bernadette den Asquinath** at Arques (pp. 78–79); first contacts with heresy while living in **Raymond Maulen's** house, while employed by **Raymond Pierre**, a staunch Cathar, at Arques (p. 79); **Bernard Bélibaste** tried to arrange a marriage between **Pierre Maury** and **Raymond Pierre's** six-year-old daughter, **Bernadette** [XXIIc] (p. 79); in 1302, had his first conversation with a *parfait* (p. 81), **Pierre Authié** (p. 82); greatly influenced by **Jacques Authié** (pp. 83–4); *chef de cabane* (p. 84); cousin of **Raymond Marty** [XVd] (p. 85); employed by **Barthélemy Borrel**, brother-in-law of **Arnaud Baille Senior** of Montaillou (p. 88 *et passim*); flirted with **Borrel's** maidservant, **Mondinette (Raymonde Isarn)** (p. 89); saved his sister from her husband's violence (p. 91); cheated in a sheep deal by his aunt, **Guillemette Marty (née Maury)** (p. 95); cheated out of some sheep by his friend **Guillaume Bélibaste** (*parfait*) (pp. 95–6); worked for **Raymond Boursier** of Puigcerda, together with his brother **Arnaud** (f), 1310–11 (p. 93); worked intermittently for his uncle, **Arnaud Fauré** (p. 96); worked for **Brunissende de Cervello** in 1319 (pp. 96, 97), who possibly became his mistress at this time (p. 98); very friendly with the **Bélibastes**, but was arrested soon after they were (p. 97); **Guillaume Bélibaste** (*parfait*) persuaded him to marry his concubine **Raymonde Piquier** [XIVc], but dissolved the marriage after less than a week (pp. 98–100); taken captive by the Inquisition, imprisoned in 1324 (pp. 102, 218); loved **Guillaume Bélibaste** more than his own brothers (p. 126).

(e) **JEAN**: shepherd (p. 38); always present at the family's Cathar meals (pp. 38, 248, 249); was offered as security by his brother **Pierre** on a sheep deal (p. 51); married **Mathena Cervel*** of Juncosa in Tarragona (pp. 105, 130, 187, 286), who was later arrested by the Inquisition with her mother **Esperte Cervel** (p. 218) [for the **Cervel** family tragedies see pp. 220, 221]; never a complete believer compared with his brother **Pierre** (pp. 125–6, 223); arrested by the Inquisition (p. 218); refused to be hereticated by **Guillaume Bélibaste** (p. 223).

(f) **ARNAUD**: joined brother **Pierre** in a team of shepherds working for **Raymond Boursier** of Puigcerda in 1310–11, then returned to Montaillou (p. 93).

(g) **RAYMOND***: imprisoned for heresy (p. 248).

(i) **GUILLEMETTE***: very unsatisfactorily married, at eighteen years of age, to **Bertrand Piquier** of Laroque d'Olmes, a carpenter (pp. 77, 91, 190); saved from her marriage by her brother **Pierre** (p. 49); after her rescue, Pierre entrusted her to the **Bélibastes'** care, but soon afterwards she was taken prisoner by the Inquisition (p. 91).

(j) **RAYMONDE**: married **Guillaume Marty** [XIVd] (pp. 77, 190).

XXI PELLISSIER
Non-heretical *domus* (p. 29).
(a) **BERNARD**, married to (b) **ALAZAIS**; their five sons (c) **JEAN**, (d) **RAYMOND**, (e) **GUILLAUME**, (f) **BERNARD** and (g) **PIERRE**

(b) **ALAZAIS**: together with **Brune Pourcel**, prepared **Na Roqua** for her shroud, after her heretication (pp. 219–20).

(c) **JEAN**: shepherd from the age of twelve years (p. 73); worked for **Bernard and Guillemette Maurs** (pp. 41, 73); orthodox Christian believer (pp. 28, 29); momentary conversion to Catharism while in the Maurs household (p. 73); employed by **Bernard Malet** and his sons at Prades (p. 74); adopted Cathar beliefs because of his aunt **Maura's** influence (p. 198).

(f) **BERNARD**: ploughboy, employed by **Bernard** and **Guillemette Maurs** and lived in their *ostal*, at the same time as his brother **Jean** (p. 41).

XXII PIERRE
of Arques
(a) RAYMOND, married to (b) SYBILLE; their three daughters (c) BERNADETTE, (d) JACOTTE and (e) MARQUISE

(a) **RAYMOND***: employed **Pierre Maury** as his shepherd (p. 79); substantial farmer and stock-breeder (p. 81); great friend of **Raymond Maulen** (first cousin of **Pierre Maury**, shepherd), and the two **Raymonds** together with **Bernard Bélibaste** set out to convert **Pierre Maury** to Catharism (p. 81, 242); he respected the **Authiés** as wise men, but esteemed **Prades Tavernier** less highly, even though he had **Prades** hereticate his sick baby daughter **Jacotte** (d) (p. 239).

(b) **SYBILLE**: mother also lived in the *ostal* (p. 81); sheep-farmer (p. 78); quarrelled with husband over the heretication of **Jacotte**, otherwise their marriage was a very happy one (p. 188); friend and sympathizer of **Pierre Authié** (*parfait*) (p. 252).

(c) **BERNADETTE**: although only six years old, a marriage was proposed between her and **Pierre Maury** (shepherd) by **Bernard Bélibaste** (p. 79); slept in her mother's bed (p. 214).

(d) **JACOTTE**: hereticated as an infant by **Prades Tavernier** (p. 211).

XXIII RIVES
A heretical household (pp. 27, 28).
(a) BERNARD, married to (b) ALAZAIS; their son (c) PONS; their two daughters (d) RAYMONDE and (e) GUILLEMETTE

(a) **BERNARD***: his *domus* housed the heretic's chapel, which was linked by secret passage access to **Guillaume Benet's** and **Raymond Belot's** *ostals* (p. 41).

(b) **ALAZAIS***: sister of **Prades Tavernier** (*parfait*) (p. 27), and thus the natural aunt of his bastard daughter **Brune Pourcel** (p. 8); terrorized by her son **Pons** (p. 34).

(c) **PONS***: married to **Fabrisse** (née **Clergue**), the tavern-keeper of Montaillou (pp. 6, 34); acting head of the *domus* (p. 34); friend of the *parfaits* (p. 34); drove his wife out of the house (p. 34); his wife **Fabrisse** informed **Pierre Clergue** (priest) of **Alazaïs Benet's** heretication (p. 65); **Pons** and **Fabrisse** had a daughter **Grazide**, whose virginity **Fabrisse** offered to the priest (p. 158); **Fabrisse** the natural daughter of **Guillaume Clergue**, brother of **Pons Clergue**, the patriarch (p. 158); the priest married **Grazide** off to **Pierre Lizier**, who left her a widow of twenty years of age (p. 159), though the priest remained her lover until about 1320 (p. 159).

(d) **RAYMONDE**: deloused her mother (p. 141); **Arnaud Vital's** mistress (p. 46).

(e) **GUILLEMETTE***: married **Pierre Clergue** (*not* the priest) [Xd] pp. 34, 192, 202); frightened of her husband (p. 192); friend of the heretics, but her husband was their enemy (p. 202).

XXIV TAVERNIER
(a) **PRADES**; his natural daughter (b) **BRUNE POURCEL**

(a) **PRADES***: weaver of Prades (p. 6); heretic (*parfait*) regarding tithes and religion (p. 21); brother of **Alazaïs Rives** (p. 27); had a bastard daughter, **Brune Pourcel** (pp. 32, 41); became a *parfait* (pp. 41, 76); demanded worship from his daughter **Brune Pourcel**, according to the Cathar rite (p. 42); orthodox *parfait* regarding dietary matters (p. 86); hereticated **Jacotte Pierre** (p. 211); hereticated **Esclarmonde Clergue** [Xe] (p. 227).

(b) **BRUNE POURCEL**: **Alazaïs Rives** her natural aunt (p. 8); assisted at **Pons Clergue's** funeral (p. 31); the bastard daughter of **Prades Tavernier** (pp. 32, 41); worked for the **Clergues** (p. 42); riddled with superstition (pp. 42, 226); assisted at **Na Roqua's** funeral (pp. 219–20).

XXV TESTANIERE
Non-heretical household
(a) husband, name unknown, married to (b) **ALAZAIS**; their son (c) **PRADES** and daughter (d) **RAYMONDE (VUISSANE)**

(b) **ALAZAIS**: helped to re-convert her daughter back to Catholicism (pp. 198, 307).

(d) **VUISSANE / RAYMONDE**: real name **Raymonde**, was employed in the **Belot** household 1304–07 by **Bernard Belot** [VIIe], by whom she had two children, one of whom was called **Bernard** (p. 45); had no Cathar tendencies, which led **Bernard Belot** to reject her for marriage with **Guillemette Benet** (p. 46); victim of attempted rape by **Arnaud Vital** while both living in the **Belot** *domus* (p. 46); thereafter renounced whatever Cathar beliefs she had adopted (p. 150).

XXVI VITAL

This couple may have been the 'houseless heretics' (p. 29), although they left the employ of the **Belots** and set up in their own *domus*, which prospered (pp. 39, 46–7).

(a) **ARNAUD**, married to (b) **RAYMONDE**; **ARNAUD**'s sister (c) **RAYMONDE ARSEN** (née **VITAL**)

(a) **ARNAUD***: shoemaker of Montaillou (pp. 5–6); parish guardian of the harvests (p. 42); brother of **Raymonde Arsen** (p. 42), née **Vital** (p. 45); heretic, and acted as a mountain guide for the *parfaits* (pp. 46, 75); village Don Juan: lover of **Alazaïs Fauré**, **Raymonde Rives** and **Alazaïs Gavela** (p. 46); **Bernard Belot** was his first cousin and landlord for a time (p. 46); attempted to rape **Vuissane (Raymonde Testanière)** in the **Belot** *domus* (p. 46); the consequences of his death (p. 46); cousin of **Bernard Vital** who lived in Val d'Arques (p. 81).

(b) **RAYMONDE**: servant in the **Belot** house (p. 46), where she met **Arnaud Vital** (p. 46); very unhappily married to **Arnaud** (p. 46); when **Arnaud** died, married **Bernard Guilhou** (p. 46); later she became delouser to **Mengarde Clergue** and her son **Pierre** (priest) and temporarily his mistress (p. 46).

(c) **RAYMONDE** (née **VITAL**): sister of **Arnaud Vital** (p. 42); sentenced in 1324 to wear the double yellow cross because of her connections with the heretics (p. 42); first cousin of **Raymond Belot** (p. 42), who asked her to replace his sister, **Raymonde Belot**, who was leaving the family *domus* to marry **Bernard Clergue** (*bayle*), by working as a servant in the house (pp. 42–4); had an illegitimate daughter called **Alazaïs** (pp. 44, 175); after her term of employment with the **Belots** she married **Prades den Arsen**, taking his name (p. 45); employed by the **Belots** to wash their and the *parfaits*' clothes (p. 143).

Alphabetical index of all the peasants listed in the family tables I–XXVI

Note : Where a peasant has no family table, the reference is given in parentheses to the relevant entry in which he/she appears.

ABOUT THE AUTHOR

Emmanuel Le Roy Ladurie is one of France's leading historians and professor of history at the prestigious Collège de France. He is the author, among other books, of *The Peasants of Languedoc*.

V-791	**REICH, WILHELM AND LEE BAXANDALL (ed.)** / Sex-Pol.: Essays 1929-1934
V-159	**REISCHAUER, EDWIN O.** / Toward the 21st Century: Education for a Changing World
V-622	**ROAZEN, PAUL** / Freud: Political and Social Thought
V-204	**ROTHSCHILD, EMMA** / Paradise Lost: The Decline of the Auto-Industrial Age
V-954	**ROWBOTHAM, SHEILA** / Women, Resistance and Revolution
V-288	**RUDOLPH, FREDERICK** / The American College and University
V-226	**RYAN, WILLIAM** / Blaming the Victim, (Revised edition)
V-130	**SALE, KIRKPATRICK** / Power Shift
V-965	**SALE, KIRKPATRICK** / SDS
V-902	**SALOMA, JOHN S. III AND FREDERICK H. SONTAG** / Parties: The Real Opportunity for Effective Citizen Politics
V-375	**SCHELL, ORVILLE AND FRANZ SCHURMANN (eds.)** / The China Reader, Vol. I: Imperial China
V-376	**SCHELL, ORVILLE AND FRANZ SCHURMANN (eds.)** / The China Reader, Vol. II: Republican China
V-377	**SCHELL, ORVILLE AND FRANZ SCHURMANN (eds.)** / The China Reader, Vol. III: Communist China
V-738	**SCHNEIR, MIRIAM (ed.)** / Feminism
V-375	**SCHURMANN, FRANZ AND ORVILLE SCHELL (eds.)** / The China Reader, Vol. I: Imperial China
V-376	**SCHURMANN, FRANZ AND ORVILLE SCHELL (eds.)** / The China Reader, Vol. II: Republican China
V-377	**SCHURMANN, FRANZ AND ORVILLE SCHELL (eds.)** / The China Reader, Vol. III: Communist China
V-971	**SCHURMANN, FRANZ AND NANCY AND DAVID MILTON (eds.)** / The China Reader, Vol. IV: People's China
V-89	**SENNETT, RICHARD** / Families Against the City: Middle Class Homes of Industrial Chicago 1872-1890
V-940	**SENNETT, RICHARD AND JONATHAN COBB** / The Hidden Injuries of Class
V-308	**SENNETT, RICHARD** / The Uses of Disorder
V-974	**SERRIN, WILLIAM** / The Company and the Union
V-405	**SERVICE, JOHN S. AND JOSEPH W. ESHERICK (ed.)** / Lost Chance in China: The World War II Despatches of John S. Service
V-798	**SEXTON, BRENDAN AND PATRICIA** / Blue Collars and Hard Hats
V-279	**SILBERMAN, CHARLES E.** / Crisis in Black and White
V-353	**SILBERMAN, CHARLES E.** / Crisis in the Classroom
V-850	**SILBERMAN, CHARLES E.** / The Open Classroom Reader
V-681	**SNOW, EDGAR** / Red China Today: The Other Side of the River
V-930	**SNOW, EDGAR** / The Long Revolution
V-902	**SONTAG, FREDERICK H. AND JOHN S. SALOMA III** / Parties: The Real Opportunity for Effective Citizen Politics
V-388	**STAMPP, KENNETH** / The Era of Reconstruction 1865-1877
V-253	**STAMPP, KENNETH** / The Peculiar Institution
V-959	**STERN, PHILIP M.** / The Rape of the Taxpayer
V-547	**STONE, I. F.** / The Haunted Fifties
V-307	**STONE, I. F. AND NEIL MIDDLETON (ed.)** / The I. F. Stone's Weekly Reader
V-231	**TANNENBAUM, FRANK** / Slave and Citizen: The Negro in the Americas
V-312	**TANNENBAUM, FRANK** / Ten Keys to Latin America
V-984	**THOMAS, PIRI** / Down These Mean Streets
V-322	**THOMPSON, E. P.** / The Making of the English Working Class
V-810	**TITMUSS, RICHARD** / The Gift Relationship: From Human Blood to Social Policy
V-848	**TOFFLER, ALVIN** / The Culture Consumers
V-980	**TOFFLER, ALVIN (ed.)** / Learning for Tomorrow: The Role of the Future in Education

VINTAGE CRITICISM: LITERATURE, MUSIC, AND ART

V-570 ANDREWS, WAYNE / American Gothic
V-418 AUDEN, W. H. / The Dyer's Hand
V-887 AUDEN, W. H. / Forewords and Afterwords
V-161 BROWN, NORMAN O. / Closing Time
V-75   CAMUS, ALBERT / The Myth of Sisyphus and Other Essays
V-626 CAMUS, ALBERT / Lyrical and Critical Essays
V-535 EISEN, JONATHAN / The Age of Rock: Sounds of the American Cultural Revolution
V-4   EINSTEIN, ALFRED / A Short History of Music
V-13   GILBERT, STUART / James Joyce's Ulysses
V-407 HARDWICK, ELIZABETH / Seduction and Betrayal: Women and Literature
V-114 HAUSER, ARNOLD / Social History of Art, Vol. I
V-115 HAUSER, ARNOLD / Social History of Art, Vol. II
V-116 HAUSER, ARNOLD / Social History of Art, Vol. III
V-117 HAUSER, ARNOLD / Social History of Art, Vol. IV
V-610 HSU, KAI-YU / The Chinese Literary Scene
V-201 HUGHES, H. STUART / Consciousness and Society
V-88   KERMAN, JOSEPH / Opera as Drama
V-995 KOTT, JAN / The Eating of the Gods: An Interpretation of Greek Tragedy
V-685 LESSING, DORIS / A Small Personal Voice: Essays, Reviews, Interviews
V-677 LESTER, JULIUS / The Seventh Son, Vol. I
V-678 LESTER, JULIUS / The Seventh Son, Vol. II
V-720 MIRSKY, D. S. / A History of Russian Literature
V-118 NEWMAN, ERNEST / Great Operas, Vol. I
V-119 NEWMAN, ERNEST / Great Operas, Vol. II
V-976 QUASHA, GEORGE AND JEROME ROTHENBERG (eds.) / America A Prophecy: A New Reading of American Poetry from Pre-Columbian Times to the Present
V-976 ROTHENBERG, JEROME AND GEORGE QUASHA (eds.) / America A Prophecy: A New Reading of American Poetry from Pre-Columbian Times to the Present
V-415 SHATTUCK, ROGER / The Banquet Years, Revised
V-435 SPENDER, STEPHEN / Love-Hate Relations: English and American Sensibilities
V-278 STEVENS, WALLACE / The Necessary Angel
V-100 SULLIVAN, J. W. N. / Beethoven: His Spiritual Development
V-166 SZE, MAI-MAI / The Way of Chinese Painting
V-162 TILLYARD, E. M. W. / The Elizabethan World Picture

VINTAGE BELLES—LETTRES

V-418	**AUDEN, W. H.** / The Dyer's Hand
V-887	**AUDEN, W. H.** / Forewords and Afterwords
V-271	**BEDIER, JOSEPH** / Tristan and Iseult
V-512	**BLOCH, MARC** / The Historian's Craft
V-572	**BRIDGE HAMPTON** / Bridge Hampton Works & Days
V-161	**BROWN, NORMAN O.** / Closing Time
V-544	**BROWN, NORMAN O.** / Hermes the Thief
V-419	**BROWN, NORMAN O.** / Love's Body
V-75	**CAMUS, ALBERT** / The Myth of Sisyphus and Other Essays
V-30	**CAMUS, ALBERT** / The Rebel
V-608	**CARR, JOHN DICKSON** / The Life of Sir Arthur Conan Doyle: The Man Who Was Sherlock Holmes
V-407	**HARDWICK, ELIZABETH** / Seduction and Betrayal: Women and Literature
V-244	**HERRIGEL, EUGEN** / The Method of Zen
V-663	**HERRIGEL, EUGEN** / Zen in the Art of Archery
V-201	**HUGHES, H. STUART** / Consciousness & Society
V-235	**KAPLAN, ABRAHAM** / New World of Philosophy
V-337	**KAUFMANN, WALTER (trans.) AND FRIEDRICH NIETZSCHE** / Beyond Good and Evil
V-369	**KAUFMANN, WALTER (trans.) AND FRIEDRICH NIETZSCHE** / The Birth of Tragedy and the Case of Wagner
V-985	**KAUFMANN, WALTER (trans.) AND FRIEDRICH NIETZSCHE** / The Gay Science
V-401	**KAUFMANN, WALTER (trans.) AND FRIEDRICH NIETZSCHE** / On the Genealogy of Morals and Ecce Homo
V-437	**KAUFMANN, WALTER (trans.) AND FRIEDRICH NIETZSCHE** / The Will to Power
V-995	**KOTT, JAN** / The Eating of the Gods: An Interpretation of Greek Tragedy
V-685	**LESSING, DORIS** / A Small Personal Voice: Essays, Reviews, Interviews
V-329	**LINDBERGH, ANNE MORROW** / Gift from the Sea
V-479	**MALRAUX, ANDRE** / Man's Fate
V-406	**MARCUS, STEVEN** / Engels, Manchester and the Working Class
V-58	**MENCKEN, H. L.** / Prejudices (Selected by James T. Farrell)
V-25	**MENCKEN, H. L.** / The Vintage Mencken (Gathered by Alistair Cooke)
V-151	**MOFFAT, MARY JANE AND CHARLOTTE PAINTER (eds.)** / Revelations: Diaries of Women
V-926	**MUSTARD, HELEN (trans.)** / Heinrich Heine: Selected Works
V-337	**NIETZSCHE, FRIEDRICH AND WALTER KAUFMANN (trans.)** / Beyond Good and Evil
V-369	**NIETZSCHE, FRIEDRICH AND WALTER KAUFMANN (trans.)** / The Birth of Tragedy and the Case of Wagner
V-985	**NIETZSCHE, FRIEDRICH AND WALTER KAUFMANN (trans.)** / The Gay Science
V-401	**NIETZSCHE, FRIEDRICH AND WALTER KAUFMANN (trans.)** / On the Genealogy of Morals and Ecce Homo
V-437	**NIETZSCHE, FRIEDRICH AND WALTER KAUFMANN (trans.)** / The Will to Power
V-672	**OUSPENSKY, P. D.** / The Fourth Way
V-524	**OUSPENSKY, P. D.** / A New Model of the Universe
V-943	**OUSPENSKY, P. D.** / The Psychology of Man's Possible Evolution
V-639	**OUSPENSKY, P. D.** / Tertium Organum
V-151	**PAINTER, CHARLOTTE AND MARY JANE MOFFAT (eds.)** / Revelations: Diaries of Women
V-986	**PAUL, DAVID (trans.)** / Poison & Vision: Poems & Prose of Baudelaire, Mallarme and Rimbaud
V-598	**PROUST, MARCEL** / The Captive
V-597	**PROUST, MARCEL** / Cities of the Plain
V-596	**PROUST, MARCEL** / The Guermantes Way